Interactive Cases in

ORGANIZATIONAL BEHAVIOR

Second Edition

Dennis J. Moberg
Santa Clara University

with

David F. Caldwell
Santa Clara University

To Kathleen, Carl, Christiaan, and Annalise

To Helen

ISBN: 0-673-99372-8

96 97 98 9 8 7 6 5 4 3 2

PREFACE

Our goal in writing *Interactive Cases in Organizational Behavior* was to produce an enjoyable way to master the tactical choices involved in putting organizational behavior principles into practice. By tactical choices we mean the discrete, minute-by-minute decisions managers must make in evolving situations every day. These choices include whom to talk to, what to talk about, and how to communicate expectations and create environments. This is the nitty-gritty of implementation and application that is often left out of the classroom.

Organizational behavior research has not addressed all possible tactical choices. Consequently, the Interactive Case approach presented here is much more useful as a discussion vehicle than as a definitive model for implementing principles. We have thoroughly classroom-tested all the Interactive Cases with undergraduates, MBAs, and executives, and they are presently being used in the executive development programs of several firms. While the cases are fictitious, all are based on real organizations. Some reflect our consulting experiences and others are derived from interviews with informed insiders. In all instances, the names of characters have been changed.

Interactive Cases in Organizational Behavior is intended to serve as a companion to standard textbooks and readers. As a supplement, it is suitable for undergraduate and graduate introductory courses in organizational behavior and management. As explained in the Introduction, the cases can be completed with paper and pencil or on a computer, depending on available resources.

We knew our concept for teaching decision-making skills was new when we began approaching publishers, but with perseverance we found a publisher equal to the challenge. Unlike most editors who inherit projects from their predecessors, Melissa Rosati of HarperCollins has been enthusiastic and actively helpful in working with us. Thanks too go to the very talented people who helped us with this project, including Lyman Porter (University of California-Irvine), Peter Frost (University of British Columbia), Rick Steers (University of Oregon), Skip Szilagyi (University of Houston), and Gary Johns (Concordia University).

Finally, we would like to offer special thanks to Shelby McIntyre of Santa Clara University's Marketing Department, who single-handedly taught the first author everything he needed to know to write the program that makes the Interactive Cases work on the computer.

Dennis J. Moberg
David F. Caldwell
Santa Clara, California

CONTENTS

Introduction

One goal of an organizational behavior or management course is to help you understand why people do what they do in organizations. This means studying theories from sociology and psychology that explain human behavior in organizations. For many students, the biggest difficulty in studying these subjects is not in mastering these theories but in seeing how they can really be used at work.

This book takes a different approach from that in most textbooks. Typically, texts summarize the major theories and research to explain the different ways the subject has been studied. Instead of providing a survey of all the important theories which might be related to a topic, we wanted to write a book that would help you learn to apply a few theories very well. We particularly wanted to help you explore the specific tactics one might use. By tactics we mean things as specific as when you raise issues, what you say to your boss, or how you present an assignment to a subordinate. *Interactive Cases in Organizational Behavior* may not be like other textbooks you have used. It will present less material for you to read and remember, but it will require you to use this material to a greater extent than other textbooks.

Organization of the Book

Interactive Cases in Organizational Behavior contains twelve modules, each covering a different topic in organizational behavior and management. Each module begins with a Module Reading that explains a series of concepts and an Interactive Case that gives you the opportunity to apply these concepts to a realistic case problem. Since the Interactive Case draws on the principles presented in the Module Reading, you should complete the reading before starting the Interactive Case unless your instructor recommends otherwise.

Module Readings. If you are using another textbook with *Interactive Cases in Organizational Behavior*, you may find that some of the material in the readings overlaps with what is in your text. However, please do not conclude that the readings simply duplicate what is in your other text. In all instances, the Module Reading will present material not in your text.

Interactive Cases. A major part of each module is the Interactive Case. Each case places you in the role of a manager who is facing a problem situation. After reviewing the initial information, you must decide how to proceed. Your options range all the way from doing nothing, to collecting more information, to taking decisive action. After making your decision, you see the case unfold. If you choose to ask for more information, you get it. If you take an action, you see its consequences. Once you see the results of your first decision, you are asked to make another decision. This process of making decisions, observing their results, and making more decisions continues as you work your way through the entire problem.

Interactive Cases are not like other cases you may have used. First, they require you to develop both a solution to the problem and a procedure for implementing it. Second, they unfold over time. Instead of simply making a recommendation, you have to make a series of decisions to solve the problem. As in real life, once you make a decision or take an action, the situation changes. Third, Interactive Cases give you feedback about the decisions you make. You see what outcomes your actions produce and how well your actions fit the theories described in the Module Reading. Unlike real-life situations, however, if your actions are not appropriate to the situation, you can reconsider your decisions.

Using Interactive Cases

There are two fundamentally different ways to complete the Interactive Cases. You can complete them on a computer or in a paper-and-pencil format. Both the computerized and non-computerized versions contain the same Interactive Cases and are completed in the same general way. Your instructor will tell you of the approved format.

Using Your Book to Complete the Interactive Cases. All you need to complete the Interactive Cases is your book and a pen or pencil. Unless your instructor has told you otherwise, complete the Module Reading before beginning the case. As you progress through the case, try to incorporate the principles from the reading into your decision making.

Begin by removing the Flow Diagram from the book. You will use this sheet to record your decisions, and you may be asked to turn in the completed Flow Diagram to your instructor. Next, read the description of the case situation. This material assigns you a role in a fictitious organization, describes the problem you face, and introduces you to some people with whom you may have to deal in the case. At the end of this material you are asked to choose from among several alternative actions.

Each alternative is followed by a statement directing you to a different page in the book. For example, following alternative A might be the statement saying GO TO 325, and following alternative B GO TO 449. These numbers and letters refer to decision points distributed randomly throughout the appendix of decision points.

After you make your choice, write the decision point number that you are referred to on your Flow Diagram. In the example above, if you decided alternative A was the best, you would write 325 in the rectangle labeled "1st Decision." If you felt alternative B was better, you would write 449 in the first rectangle.

Once you do that, turn to the appendix at the end of the book. There you will see the results of the action you have taken and will have to decide what you will do next. Again, make your choice, write the decision point number and letter in the second rectangle on your Flow Diagram, turn to that part of the appendix, and see the results of that decision. You continue to work your way through the case by making decisions, recording your movements on your Flow Diagram, and getting new information until you successfully solve the problem. You will know you are finished with the case when you are told the problem is solved; you will usually not fill all the rectangles on your Flow Diagram.

Occasionally, the decision you make will lead to bad outcomes. For example, you might take an action to solve one problem that creates another, worse problem. When this happens, you have can reconsider your decision. When your decision is incorrect, you get information about why it was not the best option. Then you are instructed to circle your present decision point on your Flow Diagram and return to your previous decision point. Once back to that decision point, you will choose another alternative, mark the decision on your form, and turn to the appropriate page. Only by keeping an accurate record of all your decisions on your Flow Diagram can you move back and forth through the case.

You should not be troubled if you make a few errors as you move through the case. Applying organizational behavior theories to a situation is not always easy, and not every action you take will be explained by the Module Reading. Above all, it is important to keep in mind that experts have honest disagreements over how organizational behavior principles are best applied. That means that your instructor may (and probably will) differ with us over which alternative is best in some situations. Therefore, as you progress through the case, if you find yourself unconvinced that an "incorrect" decision is really wrong, make a note of that and bring it up with your instructor.

Using a Computer to Complete the Interactive Cases. Completing Interactive cases on a computer is easy. The program gives you instructions as you go along. Using a computer to complete the cases will allow you to receive a summary of your decisions, give you feedback, and create a permanent record of your decisions. Your instructor will tell you how to call up the cases on the system that is being used on your campus.

As with the textbook version of the case, you begin by reading the case situation at the end of each reading in the book. It is important that you do this *before* you sit down at the computer, since some facts are presented in this material will not be repeated on the initial computer screen. Once you have finished reading the situation, you are ready to go.

Everything you need to operate the program is in the instructions the computer provides, but you may want to look over the following summary of commands. Basically, you work the program by typing letters associated with different commands in the program. There is no need to press the return (enter) key after these command letters; the program does that for you. There are three groups of commands that you will use in the computer version of Interactive Cases. The first group deals with reading the information provided at each decision point and making your choices. These commands are listed on the bottom of each screen to remind you what is available. They are as follows:

Command	Description
(N)ext screen	If more than one screen of information is available at any decision point, you will need to type N (or n) to move to the next screen.
(P)revious screen	Sometimes you will want to return to an earlier screen at a given decision point to review the information there. All you need to do is type P (or p).
(R)eady to choose	On occasion, you may find yourself ready to make a choice when you are not on the screen that lists the alternatives. Simply type R (or r), and you will be shown your alternatives and asked to choose one.
Choosing an action	When the line at the bottom of a screen asks you which alternative action you want, type the letter associated with that alternative (A through I).
(Q)uit	Regardless of what screen you are on, you can terminate the case and quit by typing Q (or q).

Completing Interactive Cases on a computer is really quite easy. The commands are clearly spelled out at the bottom of each screen where they apply. Some of our students have raised a few questions while completing the cases on the computer that we would like to answer for you.

1. What do I do if I have to leave a case before I finish it? If you have to leave a case before you get to the end, you can do so by typing Q for (Q)uit. In this case, you will lose your history file and will have to start over with the case when you reenter it. Thus, before you sit down at the computer, it is wise to budget at least 45 minutes for the case. That way you will not have to exit the case and start over later.

2. What happens if I do two or more cases at the same sitting? There is one thing you should know if you plan to complete two or more cases back to back. If you want to print out your history file, you must do so after completing each case. As soon as you begin another case, your history file for all previous cases you have worked on is destroyed.

3. If I don't use the program to print my history file, how do I print it? Your instructor can provide you with this information. This is important, for sometimes a computer laboratory printer is down when you want to print, or you may not have time to wait for it to print your job.

Summary

Interactive Cases in Organizational Behavior offers a fun way to learn about organizational behavior. Whether you complete the cases in your book or on the computer, you can make a great many decisions and get feedback from all of them. Using your book to work on the cases requires some careful bookkeeping with your Flow Diagram. With the computer version, the bookkeeping is done for you, but you need to master several rather straightforward commands.

As eager as you may be to get going in any of the Interactive Cases, remember to complete the Module Reading before you begin (unless directed otherwise). If you are using the computer, be sure to read the beginning of each case before you go to the computer.

All these instructions may strike you as somewhat forbidding. However, our students have found that by their second case the rules have receded into the background, and they really have fun with the cases.

MODULE 1

Motivation

MODULE READING

Beth Wilson and Joan MacKay are both clerks in the men's clothing section of a large department store. Beth is consistently rated as the highest performing clerk in the department, with sales 35 percent above average over the past two years. She is always friendly to customers and is ready to help with taking inventory or stocking tables whenever an extra pair of hands is needed. Joan's performance is just the opposite. Her sales are well below those of the other clerks, and she avoids doing extra work whenever she can. Her behavior in dealing with customers and co-workers is generally poor.

This situation is similar to those most managers face. Almost every work group has some employees who are performing at very high levels and some who are not. Often the difference is motivation. We know the unmotivated not just by their low performance, but by other things as well. Some work at levels far below their potential; others put forth effort only when someone is watching them. Still others seem motivated enough, but they just seem to get it wrong no matter what they are asked to do.

This reading describes a method that a manager might use for motivating people to peak performance. It details a step-by-step approach to converting low-performing, indifferent employees into those who work at or close to their potential.

Rules of Thumb About Motivating People at Work

There is nothing particularly mysterious about why some people perform up to his or her potential and some do not. No one can perform up to his or her potential without working hard. Poorly managed workers waste a lot of hard work. People work hard because they choose to. They make that choice for one essential reason: working hard is more personally rewarding to them than not working hard.

People Can't Perform at Peak Levels Unless They Work Hard. All of us have known people who could do great things effortlessly. However, no one performs well without a significant investment of personal energy. It may not show at the instant of accomplishment, but peak accomplishment requires effort.

Poorly Managed Workers Waste a Lot of Hard Work. Some people fail to perform well even though they put out a lot of effort. When this happens, it is usually the manager's responsibility. Either the manager has not given the person the opportunity to perform or he or she has not communicated the assignment clearly enough. Employees cannot be expected to perform well if they are not given a chance. By saddling them with inadequate resources, by allowing them insufficient time to master the task, or by giving them tasks that are neither stimulating nor challenging, managers do not offer employees the opportunity to excel. Similarly, people have to be given a clear picture of just what is expected of them. Otherwise, wasted effort is virtually guaranteed. If a manager asks someone to do something and gives unclear directions, it is almost assured that no amount of hard work will result in peak performance.

In a similar vein, workers who do not have good skills and abilities cannot perform at a peak level no matter how hard they try. In this case, a manager must provide sufficient training to allow the person to take on the job. Sometimes this may take the form of providing general training. Other times, it may be based on providing the employee with specific feedback and advice about techniques that can improve performance.

People Work Hard Because They Choose To. Hard workers are hard workers because they have decided to be hard workers. For them the hard work alternative is much more appealing than the "take it easy," "appear to be hard working while actually coasting," and "don't even try" options. This is important to remember because it undercuts the notion that there are good workers and bad workers and underlines the notion that any worker can work hard if he or she so chooses.

Employees Choose to Work Hard When Hard Work Is More Personally Rewarding Than Not Working Hard. If an employee works overtime and weekends to complete an assignment, that person most likely values completion more highly than other activities. That doesn't mean work is the first priority in the person's life or the person is a workaholic. It simply means that the person's evaluation of all the things that are likely to result from his or her efforts is more positive than the assessment of all the other options. In short, people to expend effort because doing so has more positive consequences than not doing so.

These straightforward principles of motivation enable us to zero in on the two most important parts of motivating: persuading workers to choose to work hard, and helping workers get the most from their efforts.

Persuading Employees to Choose to Work Hard

Getting workers to decide to put out effort is not the easiest sell in the world. Many people come to work with personal experiences that are often at odds with the decision to work hard. More over, organizations sometimes make it difficult to persuade employees that working hard is worthwhile. How can a manager convince a worker, then, that working hard is an attractive option?

Step 1--Develop a "Can Do" Attitude. Most people have sufficient self-confidence to try to perform well. If that is the case, the selling job will be a lot easier. Self-confident people are more willing to expend effort than those individuals who are not self-confident.

Unfortunately, many people lack the confidence to attempt to do any better than they are doing. They have come to believe that high levels of performance are not within their grasp. Sometimes, this is caused by a recent performance setback that they can't explain. Other times it comes from being told over and over again that they are not capable. Whatever the cause, it is difficult to motivate such people until they develop the belief that they can perform at peak levels.

Dealing with workers who lack a "can do" attitude can be very frustrating, and motivating those who gave up striving to perform well years ago can be a real uphill battle.

There are a number of actions that a manager can take to develop a "can do" attitude. Among them are the following:

(1) Gradually build up the worker's self-esteem by taking every opportunity to boost the person's confidence. This means giving positive feedback as well as negative.

(2) Set up a definite trial period in which the manager agrees to tolerate low performance if there is hard evidence of effort. This is best coupled with regular and direct performance feedback given in a personal, supportive way.

(3) Deal actively with disappointment. This often means interpreting failures as indicators of progress. Examples of this are statements like: "You can't learn unless you make mistakes"; "You are just having growing pains"; or "I've never known anyone who got it perfect the first time."

Not all individuals need such encouragement; however, it will be particularly valuable for those individuals with low self-confidence.

Step 2--Convince Workers That Peak Performance Will Be Rewarded. As we have indicated, peak performers choose to be peak performers. A manager can influence this choice only if it can be shown to people that performance will be rewarded handsomely. There are really two parts to this. First, it is necessary to demonstrate that peak performance does count. Second, a manager must ensure that the rewards given for high performers are the rewards people really want.

People are seldom motivated to high levels of performance unless high performers are rewarded better than those who are not peak performers. This is not nearly as easy as it sounds. Often an organization's reward policies conflict with a manager's desire to single out peak performers and come down on those who are not pulling their weight.

A manager has two options when the formal system of rewarding people results in allocations that are not consistent with performance standards: fight for greater rewards for high performers, or attempt to find creative ways to compensate outstanding people. Fighting for greater rewards is a useful but often temporary solution since bureaucratic interpretations of reward policies usually win out over time. A more realistic answer is for the manager to look for imaginative ways to reward valued performers. Specifically, consider the sorts of things most managers have to offer their people. A partial list of some of these rewards includes the following:

(1) interesting assignments, challenging tasks,

(2) favorable interpretation of the rules, exceptions from annoying regulations,

(3) opportunity to work unsupervised,

(4) praise, recognition, awards, symbols of accomplishment,

(5) access to top managers, access to outsiders.

Thus, it is important that the manager reviews how he or she reacts to high performers and to those falling short of this mark. Clearly, it is not motivating to treat everyone the same. Managers can best increase motivation by singling out and rewarding their best workers.

What a manager must also ensure is that he or she is rewarding peak performers in ways that they value. This requires sensitivity to the rewards people in the group value most highly. Some employees are responsive only to monetary rewards, while others are motivated by symbols. Some are attuned to things about the work place, and others are more geared to fringe benefits. To have a maximum effect, rewards should be tailored to the unique needs of each person. The important point to keep in mind is that something will be a "reward" to an individual *only* if it is something he or she really desires.

The best way to find out about just what rewards are motivating to a person is simply by asking him or her. A manager can ask during a counseling session about career advancement possibilities, during a chat about job likes and dislikes, or during an informal discussion on what things the individual would do if he or she were in charge. Managers can also discover the sort of rewards people prefer through trial and error and observation. A disadvantage of this approach is that it often takes longer and can be expensive.

Step 3--Be Fair in Rewarding and Punishing People. If subordinates think that their manager is being unfair, it will be very difficult to motivate them with positive rewards. By exercising good judgment and following several simple rules, a manager can avoid being seen as unfair. Among these rules are the following:

(1) living up to promises that are made,

(2) not making exceptions to reward principles, that is, avoiding playing favorites or giving special exceptions unless they are truly exceptional,

(3) explaining exceptions that are made, making sure everyone else who knows about it understands the logic for these decisions,

(4) giving everyone an equal chance to be successful.

In general, a manager wants to avoid situations where subordinates feel they have been treated unjustly. Sometimes, this is impossible. Most organizations occasionally create injustices unintentionally and unavoidably. When this is the case, to continue to motivate people, a manager should try to defend the logic behind the reward/punishment decision in question. This is sometimes extraordinarily difficult. Some people simply can not be persuaded that the rewards they (and others) have received are fair.

Helping Workers Get the Most From Their Efforts

As we saw earlier, not everyone who works hard performs at peak levels. Some employees fall short of peak performance even though they are putting out maximum effort. When this is the case, the manager should try to discover why this is happening. There are two common causes: impediments to good performance and lack of clarity. To address these problems, effective managers often take the following actions.

Step 1--Make Certain That There Are No Impediments to Peak Performance. When employees are putting out effort but are not performing well, this is often due to performance obstacles outside of the employees' control. Common among these impediments are poor equipment, inadequate budgetary resources, and poor training.

There are also some situations in which no matter how hard a worker tries, nothing seems to happen in the way of performance. For an otherwise highly motivated worker, this is very frustrating. Managers often do not learn about the presence of performance impediments until subordinates begin expressing signs of frustration. Some of the typical signs include:

11

(1) aggressiveness--worker deals with others in a combative fashion,

(2) displacement--worker shows anger in dealing with inanimate objects,

(3) fixation--worker repeats unsuccessful actions,

(4) daydreaming--worker is inattentive,

(5) pessimism--worker is unrealistically negative,

(6) resignation--worker seems to have given up.

Performance impediments should be removed as soon as possible. Workers whose performance is blocked for a long time are quite difficult to motivate.

Step 2--Make Clear What You Expect From Your People. All too often workers have an insufficient understanding of just what they are supposed to be doing. Obviously, this can result in people performing poorly even though they are highly motivated. In order to avoid this situation, a manager must be careful that subordinates are getting clear and direct information about (a) what is expected of them in terms of objectives, schedules, etc., and (b) how they are expected to accomplish them (procedures, guidelines, etc.). Not infrequently, people get mixed or unclear signals, and a manager must be ready to clarify expectations and clear up misunderstandings that arise about specific job requirements.

Individuals whose performance is faltering are especially in need of direction. The most effective vehicle for clarifying expectations with poor performers is the action plan. This is a written statement that summarizes precisely what is expected from problem performers in the future. To have a maximum impact, action plans should have three important characteristics:

(1) They should be as specific and concrete as possible (general admonitions to "do the best you can" are less successful than specific ones.

(2) They should deal first and foremost with performance, not just effort.

(3) They should be developed in conjunction with the problem employee and not imposed unilaterally by the manager.

Summary

Applying these guidelines can sometimes be difficult. The most important observation a manager can make is whether the worker is putting out sufficient effort. If he or she is, then the manager needs to do those things to elicit more effort. A manager can do this by removing performance obstacles and by making performance expectations more clear. If the employee is not expending adequate effort, then different actions are required. The best way to motivate people not presently putting out peak effort is by developing a "can do" attitude, by convincing the worker that peak performance will be rewarded, and by being fair in reward decisions. These points are summarized in Figure 1.

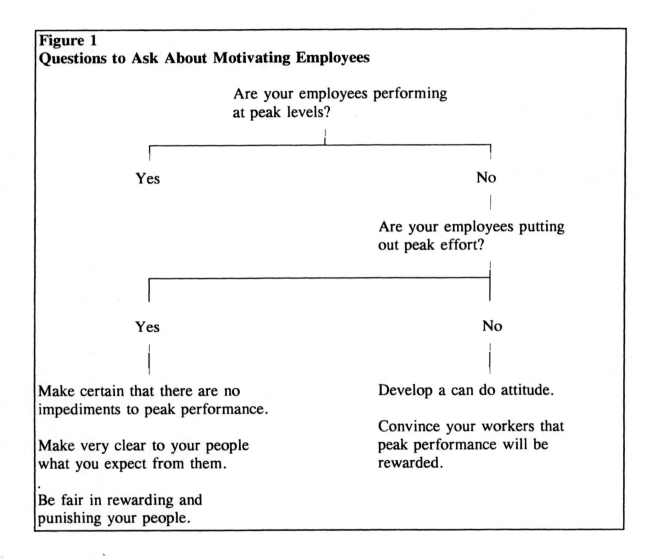

Figure 1
Questions to Ask About Motivating Employees

Are your employees performing at peak levels?

Yes

No

Are your employees putting out peak effort?

Yes

No

Make certain that there are no impediments to peak performance.

Make very clear to your people what you expect from them.

Be fair in rewarding and punishing your people.

Develop a can do attitude.

Convince your workers that peak performance will be rewarded.

References

Adams, J. S. 1963. Toward an understanding of inequity. *Journal of Applied Psychology* 67: 422-436.

Alderfer, C. 1972. *Existence, relatedness, and growth.* New York: Free Press.

Deci, E. 1975. *Intrinsic motivation*. New York: Plenum Press.

Hackman, J. R., & Porter, L. W. 1968. Expectancy theory predictions of work effectiveness. *Organizational Behavior and Human Performance* 3: 417-426.

Locke, E. A., & Latham, G. P. 1990. *A theory of goal setting and task performance*. Englewood Cliffs, NJ: Prentice Hall.

Luthans, F., & Kreitner, R. 1985. *Organizational behavior modification and beyond*. Glenview, IL: Scott, Foresman and Company.

Maslow, A. H. 1970. *Motivation and personality*. New York: Harper & Row.

Mitchell, T. R. 1983. Expectancy-value models in organizational psychology. In N. Feather (Ed.) *Expectancy, incentive, and action*. Hilldale, NJ: Erlbaum.

Porter, L. W., & Lawler, E. E., III. 1968. *Managerial attitudes and performance*. Homewood, IL: Irwin-Dorsey.

Steers, R., & Porter, L. W. (Eds.) 1989. *Motivation and work behavior*. New York: McGraw-Hill Book Company.

Vroom, V. H. 1964. *Work and motivation*. New York: John Wiley & Sons.

Course:_____   Name:_____

Instructor:_____   **Date**:_____

Flow Diagram for Motivation Interactive Case

Detach this page from your book before you begin the Interactive Case. As you make each decision, write the decision point number following the GO TO statement in the appropriate rectangle before you turn to that page. If you are referred to a previous decision point, circle the decision point number you last wrote and proceed to the first uncircled rectangle above that one in your flow diagram. Do not erase the numbers once you have written them. You will not necessarily fill all the rectangles.

Start	6th Decision	12th Decision
1st Decision	7th Decision	13th Decision
2nd Decision	8th Decision	14th Decision
3rd Decision	9th Decision	15th Decision
4th Decision	10th Decision	16th Decision
5th Decision	11th Decision	17th Decision

over

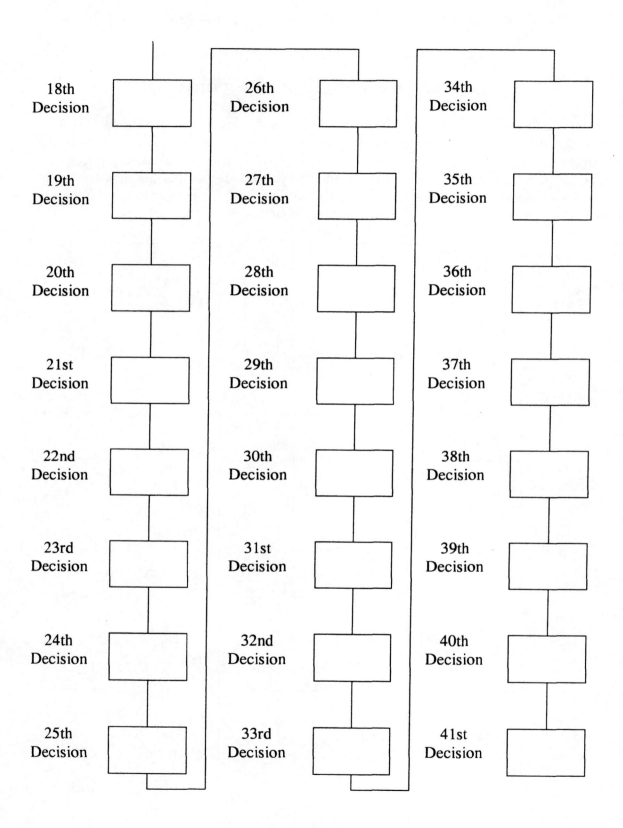

18th
Decision

19th
Decision

20th
Decision

21st
Decision

22nd
Decision

23rd
Decision

24th
Decision

25th
Decision

26th
Decision

27th
Decision

28th
Decision

29th
Decision

30th
Decision

31st
Decision

32nd
Decision

33rd
Decision

34th
Decision

35th
Decision

36th
Decision

37th
Decision

38th
Decision

39th
Decision

40th
Decision

41st
Decision

INTERACTIVE CASE

You are the regional sales manager of the obstetrics division of Omega Pharmaceutical Corporation, a medium-size firm specializing in obstetric, gynecologic, and pediatric prescription drugs. You have 12 sales representatives who report to you. Each of them is responsible for a different region in the Middle Atlantic states; that is, they operate independently of one another. Sales reps call on physicians "detailing" the advantages of the firm's product line and use their personal influence to encourage them to prescribe the company's products. In addition, reps are responsible for calling on pharmaceutical wholesalers to encourage them to stock the company's products so there will be adequate supplies when retail druggists place their orders. Experience 2pageshows that if wholesaler inventories drop below 50 days in a territory, retailer stock-outs will occur in the region. As a result, retailers will be unable to fill prescriptions with Omega's product and will substitute a competitor's product.

In reviewing the recent quarterly sales volume figures on page 18, note that five of your reps are not performing up to standard. Your boss also took notice of these five in your quarterly review with him. As he said, "You have six of the finest salespeople we have in the country. You also have the five worst. Next quarter, why don't you light a fire underneath them?"

Sales representatives are paid a straight salary plus a commission tied directly to their sales volume. The salary constitutes half of an average rep's earnings, so most reps are especially attentive to their volume figures. Promotions to sales management are infrequent, but such decisions are based on sales performance.

Turnover among reps at Omega is common. Last year 18.3 percent of Omega's reps throughout the U.S. left the firm. Presently, this is considered an acceptable turnover level. Candidates hired as reps usually have college degrees in the biological sciences and receive thorough training on the technical features of the company's total product line and on sales techniques before making their first sales call.

Several important developments have occurred in recent months. Nationwide, Omega's sales have been strong, but long-range forecasts indicate a gradual decline in the rate of growth in the obstetric line. The reason is the downturn in the birthrate coupled with the movement toward "natural childbirth." More important to your region are the economic conditions. The "softness" of the economy has forced pharmaceutical wholesalers to cut back on their inventories. Reps have had to redouble their efforts at persuading wholesalers to stock the company's products. One other development is a change in the territorial boundaries in your region. This was done to accommodate the arrival of a new rep, Lisa Dolan, to your group. Territorial boundaries are determined to allow each rep to complete a sales goal of 400 units per quarter. Factors like the birthrate, population density, and the concentration of wholesale outlets all go into the determination of territories. At the end of each quarter, you receive a computer printout that describes your reps' quarterly sales figures like the one below.

Quarterly Sales Report

Sales Rep.	This Quarter Sales Volume	This Quarter Volume Rank	Last Quarter Volume Rank	This Qtr. Last Yr. Volume Rank	Standard Vol./Birth-rate in Region	This Quarter	
						% M.D.s Con-tacted	Days Wholesaler Supply
M. Roth	550	1	2	1	8.71	100	61
R. Smith	545	2	1	2	8.53	100	63
S. Brown	520	3	3	-	10.92	91	51
M. Sanchez	515	4	5	5	9.01	97	53
A. Bishop	510	5	4	4	8.47	89	73
S. Chapel	500	6	9	8	9.13	100	57
L. Andrews	420	7	8	10	7.88	79	60
L. Dolan	360	8	-	-	6.71	100	50
J. Crosby	330	9	6	6	13.39	61	55
J. Clemmons	320	10	7	7	8.18	73	47
W. Thomas	310	11	11	9	6.62	77	38
W. Spaulding	280	12	12	11	9.34	70	42
Standard	400					90	50

You decide to try to motivate your five lowest performing reps in descending order starting with Lisa Dolan. Lisa is a new rep who just joined Omega five months ago. She completed her B.S. in biology from State University and was very impressive in her interviews (you personally hired her). In school, she succeeded at everything she tried. She was elected senior class vice president, had a minor in marketing, and carried a fine grade point average. She worked her way through school selling hyper-allergenic cosmetics through contacts supplied to her from dermatologists (her husband is in medical school specializing in dermatology). This background gave her excellent advantages over other new sales reps. Before she began work, she completed the company three-week sales training program.

How would you open your conversation with her?

A. Ask her how well she thought she had done during the last quarter. (GO TO 113)

B. Ask her if there is anything that has happened in her job that she was unprepared for. (GO TO 182)

C. Point out the importance of building up wholesale inventory levels in her region. (GO TO 223)

D. Offer to help her in any way you can to build up her sales. (GO TO 116)

E. Ask her if she is satisfied with her present levels of sales and wholesale inventory levels. (GO TO 129)

MODULE 2

Job Design

MODULE READING

In the last forty years, management thinking about the design of work has undergone a major change. Previously, the guiding force in thinking about job design was a movement called scientific management. With its origins dating back to the 18th century, scientific management prescribed job designs based on a maximum degree of specialization and efficiency. This translated into jobs that were as simple and repetitive as possible, scientifically derived procedures imposed on job holders, and little employee participation in job decisions. Scientific management principles did much to capitalize on the growth of industrialization in the last 150 years, but beginning at the end of World War II, concerns emerged that jobs were so routine and boring that they alienated employees from their jobs and created an uninvolved and dissatisfied work force.

Many of the early critics of the scientific management approach to job design were ignored until it became clear that employees in repetitive jobs acted out their dissatisfaction. High absenteeism, high turnover, and poor product quality alerted managers to the fact that the scientific management approach to job design let a lot to be desired. In response, the quality of worklife (QWL) approach replace scientific management as the accepted approach to job design.

The quality of worklife movement assumes that motivating jobs result in gains not only for the employees, but also for the organization in terms of savings in absenteeism, turnover, and poor product quality. This assumption is very compelling, but actually these savings are likely to be significant only in cases where labor market conditions strongly favor the employee. Organizations staffed by employees with few other employment options do not react negatively to un-motivating jobs. In other words, designing jobs that are motivating may be feasible only when absenteeism, turnover, and product quality constitute real business problems. Otherwise, designing jobs according to scientific management offers payoffs in terms of efficiency and predictability.

Qualities of a Motivating Job

Scientific management holds that jobs are motivating only to the extent that worker performance is directly related to financial rewards. The assumption is that workers are motivated only by money and can be bribed to occupy boring jobs. On the other hand, a great deal of research has been dedicated to finding out the characteristics of

21

jobs that are motivating in and of themselves. For the most part, this research has revealed that intrinsically motivating jobs have five attributes: skill variety, task identity, task significance, autonomy, and feedback. There are standard questionnaires that can be used to assess the motivating potential of jobs along these dimensions. The most famous is the Job Diagnostic Survey developed by J. Richard Hackman and Gregory R. Oldam.

Skill Variety. Motivating jobs permit employees to perform a wide range of operations in their work and make use of a number of their abilities. Such jobs allow individuals to work on many different tasks and can use many different pieces of equipment. More over, there is typically a flexible set of procedures associated with these jobs.

Task Identity. Task identity refers to the extent to which employees do a whole piece of work so they can clearly identify with the results of their efforts. In a classic case of building more task identity into jobs, assemblers of pumps for washing machines who had previously assembled only part of each pump were allowed to assemble the entire pump and complete an inspection as well. These enlarged jobs gave the assemblers a much more complete piece of work that was easier to identify with.

Task Significance. Jobs that are intrinsically motivating also have a substantial impact on the lives and work of other people. Teachers, health care providers, and airline pilots derive much of their satisfaction from the fact that their work has such impact. However, it is possible to redesign jobs in such a way that they take on greater task significance. For example, those responsible for putting together the "yellow pages" in telephone books can perceive more task significance if they are held responsible for an entire section of the book rather than an unrelated group of customers.

Autonomy. Some jobs lack motivational value because they allow employees little discretion. Autonomy is the extent to which workers have a major role in scheduling their work, selecting the equipment they use, and deciding on procedures they will follow. Autonomy implies freedom from arbitrary supervision and control. It creates largely self-managed jobs.

Feedback. Intrinsic motivation requires that employees receive information that reveals how well they are performing. Some jobs have such feedback built into them. Consider the job of waitperson or gardener. Employees in such jobs can easily discern how well they are doing. Other jobs lack built-in feedback; for example, peace-time soldiers and warehouse workers.

22

Job Redesign Strategies

When jobs lack these motivational characteristics, and this results in absenteeism, turnover, and poor product quality, managers can enact certain job redesign strategies as a means of solving these problems. These strategies include combining tasks, forming natural work units, vertically loading jobs, opening feedback channels, and establishing client relationships.

Combining Tasks. One way to increase the motivational potential of jobs is to include more tasks in each job. Classical approaches to job design create jobs that are deficient in terms of skill variety and task identity. Accordingly, if jobs have been designed for maximum specialization, they may not be adequately motivating. Two specific ways that tasks can be combined include job rotation and job enlargement. Job rotation involves moving employees between jobs that require similar skills so that the employees do many different things. Job enlargement means taking specialized jobs and redesigning them to include more tasks that require different skills. If properly implemented, both job rotation and job enlargement increase skill variety and task identity.

Forming Natural Work Units. Natural work units are composed of tasks arranged into meaningful groups. For instance, tasks might be grouped by customer, geography, or type of business. This strategy can be used to create enlarged jobs. For example, in one state prison, clerks performed incredibly monotonous jobs-- completing forms and performing routine data entry. Managers decided to enlarge these jobs, and they looked for ways of creating jobs that reflected natural, psychologically meaningful work units. They discovered that by assigning clerks to inmates in each prison cell block, the clerks were able to identify more with the work that they did. In fact, the clever enlargement of jobs to reflect natural work units increased not only skill variety and task identity, but also task significance.

Vertically Loading Jobs. So far the redesign strategies we have described involve including more tasks into jobs as a way of making them more motivating. Vertical job loading is a departure from this general approach. Instead of adding more tasks to jobs, vertical job loading means delegating to job holders the responsibility that was once reserved for managers. Alternatively known as job enrichment, this strategy involves making employees more responsible for their own self-management. They are free to establish the policies that regulate their work. Most of the decisions that deal with their jobs are left to them. This delegation of authority is coupled with increased accountability. They are still responsible for the results of their work. The essential feature of vertically loading jobs is that employees will be more motivated because their jobs have more autonomy.

Opening Feedback Channels. Not all jobs allow employees to get timely, accurate feedback about the results of their labors. Making up for this lack of knowledge can be accomplished by changes in information systems, but it can also be effected by changes in job design. For example, forest rangers typically work in an information vacuum about the ecological condition of the range they oversee. Requiring that they gather and analyze ecological information gives them the opportunity to monitor the results of their efforts.

Establishing Client Relationships. Many industrial workers today have limited access to the ultimate users of the goods and services they provide. Client contact stretches the skills of most manufacturing workers. The skills one uses in production often leave one unprepared to deal effectively with the users of one's labors. Moreover, designing jobs so that workers have client contact involves significant increases in autonomy. Consider, for example, the impact of allowing auto assembly people to work for two months in the service facilities of local car dealerships. Wouldn't that provide assembly workers with the skill variety, task identity, and feedback to motivate them?

Creating Autonomous Work Groups. To this point, we have dealt with job redesign strategies that purport to make the jobs of individual workers more intrinsically motivating. Job redesign can also assume a work-group focus. Here an entire work group is targeted for job redesign -- generally to combine the effects of job enlargement, job enrichment, and feedback for an entire group of workers. Potentially, this involves an increase in all the critical motivating attributes. For example, groups of coal miners have been formed such that their work is managed by the group itself, This includes considerable rotation of assignments (thus increasing skill variety and task identity) and responsibility for results (thus increasing task significance, autonomy, and feedback). Table 1 summarizes all of these redesign strategies.

Enabling Conditions

Implementing a job redesign strategy cannot be effective if an organization is unprepared for it. Whether their jobs are enlarged or enriched, employees subjected to job redesign will not respond favorably if the organization's climate is not conducive to job redesign. More over, some redesign strategies conflict with certain organizational climates, making them impractical to implement. Implementing job redesign is facilitated if an organization has a reward system that values skill acquisition as well as performance outcomes, offers its supervisors training on how to manage employees with redesigned jobs, and has a participative climate.

Reward Systems that Facilitate the Implementation of Job Redesign. Job redesign requires employees to develop entirely new ways of approaching their work. Accordingly, employees must have incentives for acquiring new skills. For example, if airline reservations clerks are to have their jobs enriched, they should be given rewards for acquiring the skills and abilities necessary to exercise the increased discretion their new jobs require. Job redesign also requires a reward system that is performance-based. Job redesign often runs into difficulties when it is implemented in organizations which reward seniority.

Table 1
Job Redesign Strategies that Address Motivational Deficiencies

A deficiency in:	Can be corrected by a redesign in the form of:
skill variety	combining tasks (job rotation and job enlargement) establishing client relationships creating autonomous work groups
task identity	combining tasks (job rotation and job enlargement) forming natural work units creating autonomous work groups
task significance	forming natural work units creating autonomous work groups
autonomy	vertically loading jobs (job enrichment) establishing client relationships creating autonomous work groups
feedback	opening feedback channels establishing client relationships creating autonomous work groups

---

Reward systems that facilitate the implementation of job redesign also allow a considerable degree of employee participation. Organizations that give employees a voice in the determination of acceptable performance levels provide an excellent climate for job redesign.

Supervisory Training Necessary for the Implementation of Job Redesign. Job redesign constitutes a significant departure from traditional superior-subordinate relationships in organizations. As such, those who supervise employees with redesigned jobs must be retrained to contend with these differences. They must learn to be more participative and to delegate certain decisions that are typical supervisory prerogatives to their subordinates. As part of this necessary retraining, an effort should be made to compensate for the supervisors' loss of influence. Perhaps supervisory jobs can be enriched as well.

Structural rearrangements are often necessary to reinforce the necessity for supervisors to adopt a more participative approach with their subordinates. For example, supervisors are often given a larger number of employees to supervise when employees have their jobs redesigned.

Organizational Climates that Facilitate the Implementation of Job Redesign. Not only must supervisors be more participative in order to support the redesign of their subordinates' jobs, but the entire organization must be participative as well. Decision-making authority should ideally be decentralized rather than centralized. The authors of this book were involved in a job redesign project with a company in which the climate of the company allowed little employee participation in decision-making. This helped make the implementation of the redesign effort a monumental failure. Clearly, not every organization is prepared to allow workers a significant voice in the affairs of the organization, so it is unwise to force redesign on such organizations even though other conditions may warrant it.

What About Workers Who Do Not Want Redesigned Jobs?

Not all employees respond favorably to job redesign even under the best circumstances. Some workers would rather have convenient jobs than jobs that are challenging and intrinsically motivating. Others are in it completely for the money, and if they are offered redesigned jobs will demand that their pay reflect the additional responsibilities. Clearly, job redesign is not for every worker.

There is an index that distinguishes between those will respond favorably to job redesign and those who will not. The index is called growth need strength. Basically, this is the degree to which a person desires complex, challenging work. Workers with high growth need strength thrive on opportunity and responsibility, so they respond very well to having their jobs redesigned. Those with low growth need strength prefer jobs that offer them security, good working conditions, and satisfactory pay. Such individuals are poor candidates for job redesign.

While workers with low growth need strength do not respond favorably to redesigned jobs, there are QWL changes that they do welcome. Among these are flexitime, job sharing and compressed work weeks.

Flexitime. Flexitime makes work much more convenient by helping workers make an easier transition between the demands of work and the demands of their private lives. Under flexitime, workers are required to work only during a core period during the middle of the working day. They can decide when to begin work and when they want to leave. The employees who like flexitime have a lifestyle that makes convenience important to them. Accordingly, levels of absenteeism and turnover may improve after the introduction of flexitime. Certain jobs are not possible to put under a flexitime schedule, however. If work is done in a coordinated group or it client contact is involved, flexitime is generally infeasible.

Job Sharing. Job sharing also makes work more convenient. With job sharing, two or more people share a single job. It is ideal for employees who cannot hold down a full-time job because of advanced age, lifestyle, or family demands. One commercial photo laboratory we know allows two retired men to share the job of delivery person. Job sharing is a recent development, and thus all of its implications are unclear. However, if the popularity of job sharing grows, it could radically change the work place.

Compressed Work Week. Another QWL intervention that makes work more convenient is the compressed work week. Instead of the typical five-day week, workers complete all the necessary hours in a more concentrated time period, usually four days. Because of the increased stress and physical demands created by the additional hours of work each day, this technique is not for everyone. Typically, though, younger and more vigorous employees find this type of arrangement very convenient.

Problems Created by Job Redesign

When job redesign was first proposed, a number of management experts saw it as part of a movement that would ultimately revolutionize work. This has not occurred. Like many other management developments, job redesign is a technique which makes sense in some circumstances but not in others. As we have seen, not all employees want more intrinsically motivating jobs. In addition, QWL requires an approach to management that not every manager is accustomed to and not every organization is prepared for.

Like most organizational changes, job redesigns often create problems elsewhere in the organization. Common among these are workflow disruptions as higher and lower levels of productivity emerge. Redesigns often lead to the appearance of a lack of orderliness and structure. Employees in redesigned jobs often appear disorganized and their methods erratic. Both of these problems require careful management. Workflow problems can be evened out effectively if employees are involved in decision making. In addition, the undisciplined behavior that follows redesign efforts should not stimulate severe or directive supervisory practices. Rather, patience is called for. The apparent chaos in the aftermath of a job redesign is generally replaced by a more predictable and manageable situation without management intervention.

Summary

Job redesign promises improvement in organizations plagued by absenteeism, turnover, and quality problems. Employees high in growth need strength respond positively to changes in the motivating potential of their jobs. This can be accomplished through such redesigns as combining tasks, forming natural work units, vertically loading jobs, opening feedback channels, establishing client relationships, and creating autonomous work groups. Individuals low in growth need strength require different QWL interventions including flexitime, compressed work weeks, and job sharing.

References

Aldag, R. J. and Arthur P. Brief. 1979. *Task design and employee motivation*. Glenview, IL: Scott, Foresman and Company.

Fried, Y., & Ferris, G. R. 1987. The validity of the job characteristics model: A review and meta-analysis. *Personnel Psychology* 40: 287-322.

Graen, G. B., Scandura, T. A., & Graen, M. R. 1986. A field test of the moderating effects of growth need strength on productivity. *Journal of Applied Psychology* 71: 484-491.

Griffin, R. W. 1982. *Task design: An integrative approach*. Glenview, IL: Scott, Foresman and Company.

Hackman, J. R. & Oldham, G. R. 1976. Motivation through the design of work: Test of a theory. *Organizational Behavior and Human Performance* 16: 250-279.

Hackman, J. R. & Oldham, G. R. 1980. *Work redesign*. Reading, MA: Addison-Wesley.

Hackman, J. R. & Lawler, E. E., III. 1975. Employee reactions to job characteristics. *Journal of Applied Psychology Monograph* 55: 159-170.

Herzberg, F. 1968. One more time: How do you motivate employees? *Harvard Business Review* 46, 2: 53-62.

Loher, B. T., Noe, R. A., Moeller, N. L. & Fitzgerald, M. P. 1985. A meta-analysis of the relation of job characteristics to job satisfaction. *Journal of Applied Psychology* 70: 280-289.

Pierce, J. L. & Dunham, R. B. 1976. Task design: A literature review. *Academy of Management Review* 1: 83-97.

Pierce, J. L., Dunham, R. B. & Blackburn, R. S. 1979. Social system structure, job design, and growth-need strength. *Academy of Management Journal* 22: 223-240.

Turner, A. N. & Lawrence, P. R. 1965. *Industrial jobs and the worker*. Cambridge, MA: Harvard University Press.

Flow Diagram for Job Design Interactive Case

Detach this page from your book before you begin the Interactive Case. As you make each decision, write the decision point number following the GO TO statement in the appropriate rectangle before you turn to that page. If you are referred to a previous decision point, circle the decision point number you last wrote and proceed to the first uncircled rectangle above that one in your flow diagram. Do not erase the numbers once you have written them. You will not necessarily fill all the rectangles.

Start		6th Decision		12th Decision	
1st Decision		7th Decision		13th Decision	
2nd Decision		8th Decision		14th Decision	
3rd Decision		9th Decision		15th Decision	
4th Decision		10th Decision		16th Decision	
5th Decision		11th Decision		17th Decision	

over

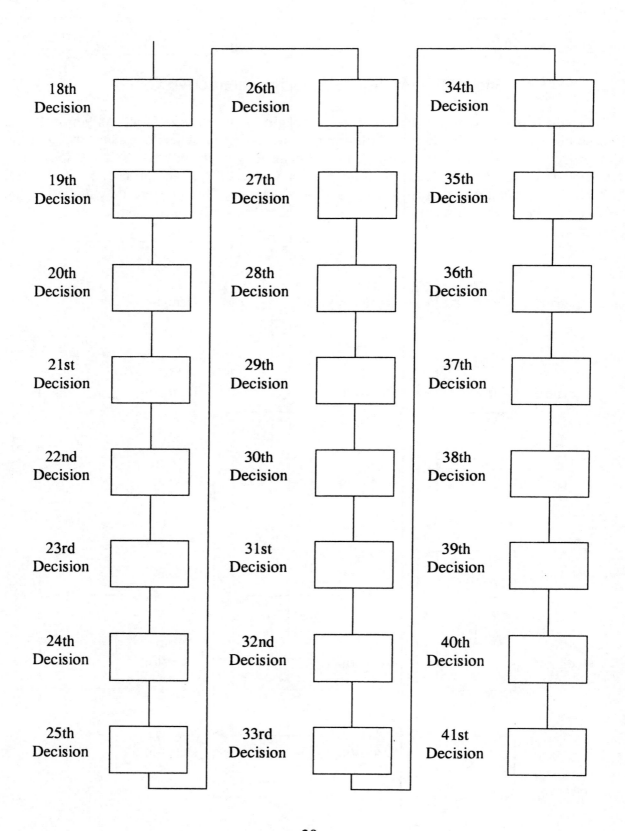

18th Decision

19th Decision

20th Decision

21st Decision

22nd Decision

23rd Decision

24th Decision

25th Decision

26th Decision

27th Decision

28th Decision

29th Decision

30th Decision

31st Decision

32nd Decision

33rd Decision

34th Decision

35th Decision

36th Decision

37th Decision

38th Decision

39th Decision

40th Decision

41st Decision

INTERACTIVE CASE

You are the Director of Quality of Worklife Programs for Angie Taylor Fashions, Inc., a firm that manufactures and markets designer blue jeans. The firm manufactures products at four different plants located in Texas and Arizona. You were hired because the vice-president of operations decided three months ago to design and implement quality of worklife programs wherever they are needed in the firm. You have spent the last three months familiarizing yourself with the company and getting to know key people.

Your first decision is to identify the plant that is most suitable to a quality of worklife intervention. This is an important decision. Not all of the plants seem suitable to QWL. For your own credibility, you want to be certain that your first efforts produce positive results. In addition, you will have to spend about eighteen months at the plant you choose for implementation, and you do not want to have an unsatisfactory experience. Since none of the plants is unionized, this is really not a consideration.

In discussions with a number of the firm's officials, you have learned that each of the company's four plants differs along three potentially important dimensions: the present level of turnover and absenteeism among its operators, whether there is a scarce or ample supply of experienced operators in the local labor market, and the extent to which the plant is either centralized or decentralized.

Which plant is the best candidate for a QWL intervention?

A. Astoria Plant - high turnover and absenteeism, ample supply of experienced operators in the local labor market, decentralized authority at the plant. (GO TO 136)

B. Eagle Point Plant - high turnover and absenteeism, scarce supply of experienced operators in the local labor market, decentralized authority at the plant. (GO TO 103)

C. La Casita Plant - low turnover and absenteeism, scarce supply of experienced operators in the local labor market, decentralized authority at the plant. (GO TO 149)

D. San Lorenzo Plant - high turnover and absenteeism, scarce supply of experienced operators in the local labor market, centralized authority at the plant. (GO TO 152)

MODULE 3

Socializing the New Employee

MODULE READING

Companies spend literally thousands of dollars for each new employee they recruit, train, and indoctrinate. Yet many new recruits, too many, leave their firms before they have become worthwhile investments. Also, some of those who stay on feel needlessly passive, isolated, and rejected during their first few months of employment. The cause of these unfortunate situations often is an ill conceived, poorly implemented orientation process. The challenge for managers is how to best socialize new people into the organization so that they can become effective employees.

It is easy for an experienced manager to forget the stresses of being a new employee. In a number of weeks or months, one is expected to be transformed from being a total outsider into an effective contributor to the organization. For the new employee, this often means new work skills, new friends, new values, and new behavior patterns. This can be intimidating, and many new employees have some difficulties in making these adjustments.

Research by Daniel Feldman suggests that new employees pass through three predictable stages as part of the process of moving from newcomer to veteran. Stage 1 is Getting in. This involves the entire recruitment process culminating with the end of the first day of work. Stage 2 is Breaking in, the period required to become a technically able contributor and a socially accepted team member. Stage 3 is Settling in, the final, and more tranquil period in which newcomers "feel" like team members but continue to suffer some "growing pains." These "pains" include problems with people outside their immediate work group and problems adapting their work life with the non-work responsibilities they have. The development of a successful new-employee orientation program involves tailoring the program to each of these socialization stages. Each stage creates different problems for the newcomer and each requires its own management action to contend with these problems.

Stage 1--Getting In

Orientation begins with the recruitment process. Recruiting practices set the stage for the entire orientation process. Every impression the recruit gets about the firm from applying for a job to interviewing for it affects the orientation process. If a candidate for a clerical position is told that he will have his own computer terminal when he is hired, then this establishes an expectation that, if not met, can negatively affect even the best orientation effort.

33

Realistic Job Previews. Experts agree that job candidates should be given realistic previews of their future positions. Overly positive or negative previews lead to unrealistic expectations that increase the likelihood of early turnover. Typically the new recruit is seeking accurate information about a number of factors in the job. Some of the important ones are the following:

(1) exactly what will be expected in terms of effort and commitment (e.g., Are 50-hour weeks common? If so, under what conditions?),

(2) what to expect from fellow team members when it comes to meetings and other occasions for group behavior (e.g., What do I have to do to prove myself to be a contributing member?),

(3) the promotional/transfer possibilities in the organization (e.g., Will I be given a chance to transfer if I don't work out in this job?),

(4) who are the other people that have a rightful demand on their time and resources (e.g., Can people from accounting tell me that I have to get a report to them?),

(5) the common supervisory posture used in their part of the organization (e.g., Will my supervisor allow me a voice in the future goals of the department?).

It is actually difficult to get all this information across. Often many people are involved in the recruiting process, and occasionally the applicant receives conflicting impressions about the job. Employees involved in the interviewing process often need be reminded how important it is to paint an accurate picture of the job the candidate is seeking.

The New Employee's First Day. Several things happen on the first day that are critical to the success of the orientation effort. First, someone has to be the initial contact person who sets the tone for the entire day. For example, consider the first-day recruiting program that was developed in one division of Texas Instruments. The initiate is told that he/she:

(1) has an excellent chance for success,

(2) should take initiative in communication,

(3) ought to disregard hall talk/rumors,

(4) must take initiative in getting to know her/his supervisor.

This is more than a series of platitudes. New employees are quite impressionable on the first day, and if they take this advice, they will be saved from much of the frustration that could otherwise follow.

The second important activity on that first day is introductions. New people should have the chance to meet as many of their co-workers as possible. It is often better if they have an opportunity for an informal visit with each one.

The Initial Assignment. Research indicates that the first assignment does much to influence whether or not the new employee stays in the organization or leaves. A number of characteristics seem to distinguish those initial assignments which lead to new employees' long-term success. First, the task assigned should be technically challenging. It should give the new person the feeling that the abilities for which he/she was hired are being used. Second, the task should not involve the person in work conflicts or political problems. New people are seldom well prepared to face these sorts of challenges. Finally, if possible, new recruits should be assigned tasks that place them in work groups that get along well and have good morale.

Stage 2--Breaking In

Stage 2 is a truly critical period. During this time, new employees sufficiently master the technical features of their jobs so that by the end of this stage, they are making a positive contribution. More over, this is the time when new people gain acceptance among their peers, finding a role to fill within their immediate work group. The amount of time required for this stage depends on the nature of the job. Figure 1 shows the length of Stage 2 for a number of different jobs.

The Assignment of a Mentor. New employees who successfully negotiate Stage 2 often have mentors. A mentor is simply an experienced person who looks after and advises the new worker. Because mentors are so helpful, some organizations formally appoint someone to handle this assignment. Commonly the new person's supervisor acts in this capacity. However, some organizations appoint one of the new person's co-workers to be in charge of breaking him in. At a few companies, new employees are assigned an individual who is on the same level as the person's supervisor.

If a mentor is assigned, that person should be chosen carefully. Mentors should be both technically able and socially skilled. They should know the new employee's job intimately, be familiar with the new person's work group, and be given sufficient time and other resources to do the mentoring. Most important, the mentor should be a good model for the new person.

The Technical Adjustment. New employees rarely enter a position with all the knowledge and skills necessary for making an immediate contribution. Often they are given training, which may range in form from highly formalized programs to extremely informal on-the-job training. Regardless of the type or quality of the training, new people still need to adjust to the technical demands the job places on them. They have to master procedures and other bureaucratic requirements. They may have to reckon with tools and equipment that they have not used before. And they have to learn the logic and rationale behind various organizational practices.

Figure 1
The Length of Time Certain Employees Spend in Stage 2

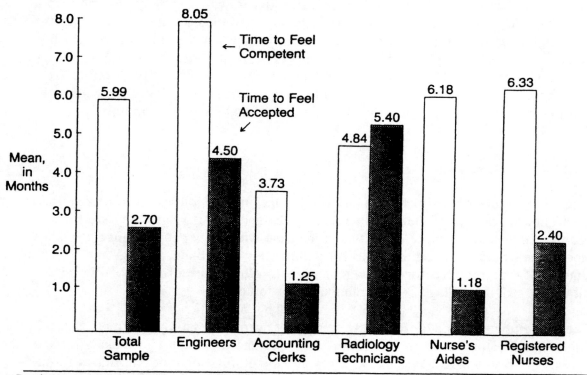

Mentors can be very helpful assisting new employees with this transition. They can define performance standards and help the initiate develop an appropriate sense of priorities. They can offer feedback and encouragement. Perhaps most importantly, a mentor can serve as an interpreter in making sense of otherwise confusing signals and messages.

While mentors can be extremely helpful to new employees, they should avoid being too directive, or the new person will not develop a sense of identification with his or her job. In this sense, mentors should not insist on too much conformity with organizational procedures or interfere with the newcomer's creation of an individual approach to the job. Within limits, the new employee should be permitted to develop his or her own task priorities.

The Social Adjustment. In the beginning, the relationship between a new employee and the immediate work group can be very tenuous. While new recruits generally want acceptance, groups tend to be wary of new members. New employees want to be accepted because their group offers them (a) a source of information about performance standards, (b) a defense against oppressive forces, (c) a source of emotional support, and (d) a storehouse of solutions to job-related problems. In spite of this eagerness, new people are often viewed as a potential threat to their group's comfortable social equilibrium. Groups have unwritten rules that new people don't initially know, and even after they do, it takes a while for them to prove themselves willing to live according to these rules. Some groups even haze new people, subjecting them to ego-deflating experiences as a means of testing their willingness to become a group member.

As a result of these two conflicting perspectives, earning acceptance as a functioning member of the organization can be as difficult as the job itself. One sales representative with a consumer goods firm told us that he felt alone and unattached from his co-workers and clients, and an employee with the phone company told us she found the need to travel to her parents' home to get support from family and friends about her problems with new co-workers.

New employees have a great deal to learn before they are accepted. They must learn to relax in the presence of their co-workers. They must establish a role for themselves in the group. They have to figure out what is expected of them as a group member, and how to behave in social interactions.

Clearly the mentor can play a vital role in all this. Not only can a mentor give the recruit information and advice about group members in advance and feedback along the way, but the mentor can also intervene on the novice's behalf. For example, some mentors ask group members to suspend hazing and coax co-workers into being more cooperative. Mentors also need to be conscious about the importance of first impressions. For example, new people who are introduced as "brilliant," or "the best we have hired in ages" may find themselves excluded from the group or severely tested for reasons that are beyond their control.

At the completion of Stage 2, new employees no longer feel new. They seldom feel self-conscious about their technical skills, and they have earned acceptance onto their work team. Yet there is more ahead. Pressures outside their work group and with their adaptation to working life loom large as adjustment challenges.

Stage 3--Staying In

There is more to adapting to a new position than mastering the technical and social aspects of the job. Most jobs require some interaction with employees outside the immediate work group, and many jobs place demands on people's private lives that are difficult to accommodate. These are the issues that challenge new employees during Stage 3.

Becoming Effective Employees Outside One's Immediate Work Group. New employees have a lot to learn when it comes to dealing effectively with employees outside their immediate work group. Seasoned workers know the subterranean organization: the structure that establishes that some departments are more powerful than others and that certain key people are much more powerful than their position would suggest. These "political realities" are not at all discernable to novices, and even graduating from Stage 2 does not qualify employees for savvy of this sort.

It is difficult, even for an experienced employee, to spell out all the "informal" knowledge necessary to make the bureaucracy function to help one accomplish his or her job, but certainly the newly hired have to learn about the individual personalities that are behind the impersonal public forms of communications one has to deal with. Equally important are the historical events that mark the relationships one must work within. Finally, one must somehow assimilate the confidential realities that exist in every organization, i.e., the "juiciest" facts that no one is told unless and until one has truly "paid the dues."

Mentors are especially critical during this part of Stage 3, for most of the knowledge that needs to be passed on is not available in print. This knowledge may be the "wisdom" of the organization, and few things can substitute for learning it directly from an experienced mentor. Dramatic events need to be de-mystified. Seemingly insignificant nuances need to be elevated in importance. Bland facts need to be colored. There is actually no substitute for experience at this stage.

Balancing Work Demands With Demands on One's Private Life. An often ignored aspect of orientation is that employees typically have problems adjusting to the conditions surrounding their employment. Balancing home and work demands is a challenge to everyone, but it is especially so for certain type of employees. For example, single parents, people new in the area, people with special commuting problems, and people without a well-developed social support system, often face very real difficulties that remain hidden.

Mentors can help with these sorts of problems, but only if they are truly sensitive to the situation. Unfortunately, lifestyle differences between the mentor and the new employee may make this difficult. For example, single people may not understand the problems and needs of new parents. Similarly, employees who live close to their work are often ignorant of the plight of the commuter. Mentors need to be careful about giving their proteges advice. Instead, they may be more helpful by introducing them to people who have successfully coped with their special problem. In addition, a mentor may put the new employee in touch with the resources that are available in the company to help with these problems.

Conclusion

Once a manager knows the principles, effective orientation requires little more than planning and good communication. Yet its returns can be great. Effectively oriented employees are likely to begin quickly to make a contribution. They are also committed and loyal.

References

Allen, N. J., & Meyer, J. P. 1990. Organizational socialization tactics: A longitudinal analysis and links to newcomers' commitment and role orientation. *Academy of Management Journal* 33: 847-858.

Feldman, D. 1976. A practical program for employee socialization. *Organizational Dynamics* 5: 64-80.

Feldman, D. 1976. A contingency theory of socialization. *Administrative Science Quarterly* 21: 433-452.

Feldman, D. 1981. The multiple socialization of organization members. *Academy of Management Review* 6: 309-318.

Gomersall, E. R., & Myers, M. S. 1966. Breakthrough in on-the-job training. *Harvard Business Review* 44, 1: 62-72.

Kram, K. E. 1985. *Mentoring at work: Developmental relations in organizations*. Glenview, IL: Scott Foresman.

Meglino, B. M., DeNisi, A. S., Youngblood, S. A., & Williams, K. J. 1988. Effects of realistic job previews: A comparison using enhancement and a reduction preview. *Journal of Applied Psychology* 73: 259-266.

Miller, V. D., & Jablin, F. M. 1991. Information seeking during organizational entry: influences, tactics, and a model of the process. *Academy of Management Review,* 16: 92-120.

Van Maanen, J., & Schein, E. 1979. Toward a theory of organizational socialization. In B. Staw (Ed.). *Research in Organizational Behavior* 1. Greenwich, CT: JAI Press.

Wanous, J. P. 1981. *Organizational entry*. Reading, MA: Addison-Wesley.

Course:_____ **Name:**_____

Instructor:_____ **Date:**_____

Flow Diagram for New Employee Interactive Case

Detach this page from your book before you begin the Interactive Case. As you make each decision, write the decision point number following the GO TO statement in the appropriate rectangle before you turn to that page. If you are referred to a previous decision point, circle the decision point number you last wrote and proceed to the first uncircled rectangle above that one in your flow diagram. Do not erase the numbers once you have written them. You will not necessarily fill all the rectangles.

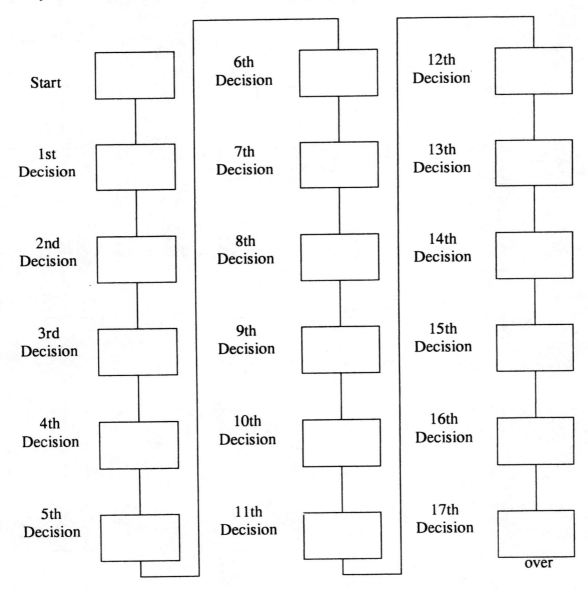

over

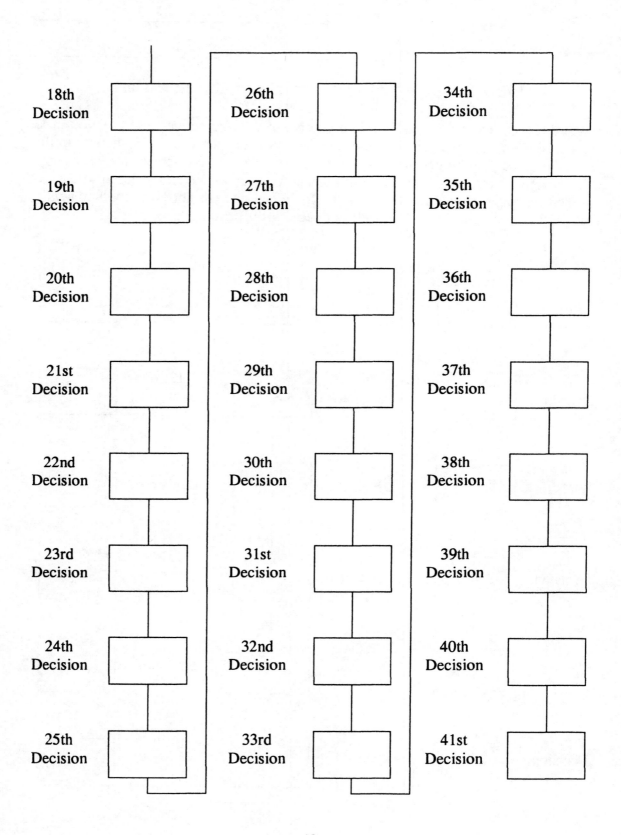

18th
Decision

19th
Decision

20th
Decision

21st
Decision

22nd
Decision

23rd
Decision

24th
Decision

25th
Decision

26th
Decision

27th
Decision

28th
Decision

29th
Decision

30th
Decision

31st
Decision

32nd
Decision

33rd
Decision

34th
Decision

35th
Decision

36th
Decision

37th
Decision

38th
Decision

39th
Decision

40th
Decision

41st
Decision

INTERACTIVE CASE

You are the Manager of the System Test Group of Venus Missile and Space Corporation, a large aerospace firm. You have 15 years of experience, six with Venus. You have nine subordinates (avg. age = 36) responsible for trouble-shooting missile system prototypes. You assign each of your subordinates a project assignment (duration 1-24 months), but you maintain direct supervision and control. They are not accountable to a project manager except through you. You are proud of the reputation for technical excellence your team has earned.

Bill Smythe has just joined your group. Fresh out of a major engineering school (a BSEE with high honors), Bill is a welcome addition to the team. He earned an A-average in college, was a member of the honor society, and was active in campus activities. He is older (26) and more mature than most new employees you hire. Bill is married with two school-aged children. He was a highly sought-after college recruit, receiving offers from virtually every company he interviewed with. During his plant visit, he impressed you as bright, eager to learn, and articulate. Venus gave Bill a very competitive salary offer, but he told you that it was not the highest he had received.

The Human Resources Department gave Bill a standard orientation to the company, and you have introduced him to the others in the group. He spent an hour with each of his new co-workers. You also instructed him to take initiative in contacting you whenever he runs into problems no matter how slight or trivial they seem.

You need to decide which of four possible assignments to give him. These four possibilities are described below. For each assignment, you note: (a) the likelihood that Bill can make a meaningful contribution to the team, and (b) the value to Bill's development if he is personally successful.

Assignment 1. Junior Control Engineer, *Dart* Project. Join a team of four members to test a ballistics control system for a *Dart* missile. Bob Blair is the project manager. The *Dart* missile is like other systems except that the new control system requires several standards never required before. Smythe's senior thesis dealt with ballistics control systems. Likelihood of Bill making a contribution to the team - Good. Value to Bill's development if he is personally successful - Fair.

Assignment 2. Junior Control Engineer, *Solaris* Project. Join a team of three members to test the propulsion control system for a *Solaris* booster. K. C. Wong heads the project. Wong is very enthusiastic about Bill joining the team (Wong graduated from the same engineering school as Bill). The *Solaris* project will require a unique control system that has never been implemented before. The project is presently behind schedule because of the novelty of its design. It would offer a fantastic learning opportunity for any junior engineer. Likelihood of Bill making a contribution to the team - Fair. Value to Bill's development if he is personally successful - Very Good.

Assignment 3. Junior Control Engineer, Systems Test Group. Act as your administrative assistant. Perform several studies regarding planning and scheduling in preparation for upcoming budget negotiations. While this assignment has only a modest technical component, it is a great way for Bill to learn the inner workings of your department. It also may allow him to find his own technical place in the group. Likelihood of Bill making a contribution to the team - Excellent. Value to Bill's development if he is personally successful - Marginal.

Assignment 4. Junior Control Engineer, Systems Test Group and member, *Micascope* Divisional Task Force. Join a task force of seven members conducting a manufacturing feasibility study of *Micascope*, a laser-refracting targeting system. The task force is chaired by the assistant to the divisional manager. The feasibility study proposed is controversial, with some task force members committed to manufacturing and some dead set against it. The division manager is said to favor manufacturing, but he has agreed to "let the chips fall where they may." While he hand-picked the members of the task force from other departments, he asked you to appoint the department member of your choice. Since all of your other people are busy with project work, Bill seems like a natural. Likelihood of Bill making a contribution to the team - Fair. Value to Bill's development if he is personally successful - Very Good.

At this point what would you do?

A. Ask Bill which assignment he would prefer. (GO TO 520)

B. Give him an assignment without asking for his preferences. (GO TO 478)

MODULE 4

The Problem Employee

MODULE READING

At one time or another all managers have to deal with the performance problem of one of their people. These are often the most aggravating challenges a manager must face. There are several reasons why this is so frustrating. First, correcting performance problems usually takes up a lot of time. Many supervisors find that the way they allocate their time among their subordinates follows the 80/20 rule: 80 percent of their time is spent supervising 20 percent of their people. Surely ineffective performance falls into this category. Second, handling problem employees is frustrating because the poor performance of one employee often affects the performance of others. Employees who are chronically tardy, for example, slow down co-workers who need their inputs. Third, problem employees often create political problems for a manager. The way the performance problem is dealt with is often quite visible no matter how privately the situation is handled. Typically the grapevine thrives on rumors about what was said and done. Such informal scrutiny is understandable, but it places the manager in a situation where he or she may be misquoted or second-guessed. This visibility is also a problem since upper-level management may attribute performance problems to poor supervision. In effect a manager can easily suffer politically from both below and above in the chain of command. Finally, problem individuals are exasperating because there are so many written and unwritten rules that govern what actions a manager can take. Fellow employees expect that the problem employee will be dealt with fairly and equitably. Top managers are concerned about any precedents that might be created. There are legal constraints that affect what the manager can and cannot do. Navigating through these various written and unwritten rules is indeed troublesome. It is small wonder that correcting performance problems is one of the least enjoyable aspects of most managers' jobs.

Yet, there are actions that can be taken. Some problem employees are turned around. Some managers develop a knack for avoiding the pitfalls of dealing with problem employees. What they do is not particularly mysterious. They usually follow a number of relatively simple principles.

Symptoms and Problem Causes

The way an effective manager deals with an employee with poor work habits may be likened to a physician's manner with a patient. Supervisors and doctors initially have little more to go on than a group of indicators or symptoms that something is wrong.

45

Physicians may see elevated temperature, a complaint of a headache, and nasal congestion. The symptoms a supervisor may observe include:

(1) low quantity of performance (e.g., deadlines missed, quotas not met, clients not served),

(2) low quality of performance (e.g., high rework rate, incorrect paperwork, computation errors, dissatisfied customers),

(3) poor attendance (e.g., tardiness, repeated absenteeism),

(4) unsatisfactory attitude (e.g., uncooperativeness, defensiveness, argumentativeness, resistance to change, disloyalty),

(5) disruptive behavior (e.g., illegal acts, insubordination, unwillingness to work overtime, dirty office politics, threats, sabotage).

Doctors are trained to diagnose organic problem causes from specific patterns of symptoms. Certain patterns of symptoms may be indicative of a bacterial infection, a broken bone, or heart disease. In medicine, the organic causes--not the symptoms--are the preferred target of treatment. Similarly, supervisors are best advised to first diagnose the cause or causes that account for the symptoms that are observed, and then focus the treatment on these causes. But just what are the things that cause performance problems? One research study (by Miner and Brewer) throws some light on the answer to that question. The researchers analyzed the causes of a large number of performance problems and developed a list of common causes of poor performance in the order of how frequently each cause was observed, including:

(1) company policy and management decisions (e.g., placement errors, management permissiveness or neglect, poor coordination mechanisms, unintended incentives on nonperformance),

(2) employee's motivation (e.g., poor work habits, low ambition, personal motives inappropriate to the job, low effort),

(3) emotional problems of the employee (e.g., mid-life crisis, emotional immaturity, inability to cope with job stress),

(4) problems the employee is having with his/her work group relationships (e.g., inability work with co-workers, misunderstanding of group norms, inability to deal with conflicting expectations of co-workers),

(5) difficulties in the physical work setting (e.g., excessive danger, overcrowding, isolation of work station, stressful commuting),

(6) inadequate technical skills (e.g., deficiency in job ability, defects in judgment, insufficient understanding of the job requirements),

(7) problem with the employee's personal relationships (e.g., family crises, lack of family support, divorce, death),

(8) adjustment problems due to being socialized to values inappropriate to the job (e.g., culture shock, inappropriate work values, inability to cope with contemporary life),

(9) employee's physical problems (e.g., deficiency in physical skill required by the job, physical illness or handicap, cleanliness standards of the individual).

Unfortunately, not as much is known about the relation between symptoms and causes in supervising as in medicine. While physicians have models that help them narrow down the possible organic causes of some set of symptoms, managers have yet to progress to that level of sophistication. Often supervisors have little more than logic to rely on. And in using logic, the manager should keep several things in mind:

(1) Problem causes aren't necessarily simple; they can involve more than one of the factors listed above.

(2) Different causes can result in the same symptom; a symptom of poor attendance may be due to a family problem, a motivational problem, etc.

(3) The same cause can result in different symptoms; an emotional problem may show itself in symptoms of low work quality, a poor work attitude, etc.

Even with these realities in mind, it is still possible for a manager to commit several logical errors when attempting to figure out what is causing an employee's failing performance. First, there is a tendency to act on unverified reports of symptoms. Often the first evidence of performance deficiency is not directly observed. A great deal of care must be taken in acting on second-hand reports. More than one supervisor has acted too quickly in treating a performance problem only to discover later that the first report of the problem was greatly exaggerated. Second, there is a tendency to ignore the distinction between acute symptoms and chronic symptoms. Acute symptoms are those that appear suddenly and without warning. Chronic symptoms are those that are gradually worsening. The difference between acute and chronic absenteeism is that the chronic symptom shows as a steady decline in attendance whereas the acute symptom appears as a more sudden drop in attendance. The usefulness of the acute-chronic distinction is that the appearance of acute symptoms generally follows a problem-causing event, (e.g., a family feud that has flared up). In contrast, the timing of a problem cause is much more difficult to identify with a chronic symptom. A third logical pitfall that managers occasionally fall into is the tendency to confuse reasons with problem causes. Reasons are excuses or justifications offered by poor performers themselves to explain their own behavior. Generally, reasons are self-serving, but that does not imply that they are incorrect; in some cases they may be. Fourth, there is a tendency to attribute poor performance symptoms to causes that are outside our sphere of influence. Occasionally managers fall into self-serving interpretations of what is causing an employee's problem performance. Thus, in inferring a problem cause, a manager may tend to ignore those causes that are really the responsibility of the manager, such as a failure to clearly communicate performance expectations. This may result in blaming the problem performer for something for which he or she is not responsible.

The Treatment of Problem Causes

In most circumstances it is generally better to treat problem causes than symptoms. Just as physicians treat symptoms only when they cannot determine the cause of an illness (or are faced with a cause that is not amenable to treatment), managers are also best advised to correct causes rather than symptoms.

The analogy of an iceberg is helpful in making this point. Symptoms are similar to the tip of the iceberg (see Figure 1). They indicate the presence of the problem (the entire iceberg) but are insufficient at defining its size and scope. Problem causes lurk under the surface, hidden from view. Treating symptoms is like sawing off the top of an iceberg at sea level. Those symptoms disappear, but the untreated causes show up in some other form--the iceberg buoys up to reveal other symptoms. Consequently, treating symptoms alone almost guarantees an ongoing battle of shearing off iceberg tips until the problem causes have dissipated naturally.

Consider this example. The supervisor of a group of 12 design engineers in a large aerospace firm noticed that the output of his people had declined since they were given a new missile system to work on. In addition, the length of time his employees were taking during morning and afternoon breaks was increasing steadily since the new assignment began. Perplexed, the supervisor called his staff together and asked for suggestions. When none were forthcoming, he asked everyone to restrict their breaks to the time allotted. While the time taken on breaks returned to acceptable levels, the output of the group deteriorated even more seriously than before. The supervisor had treated one symptom (the long breaks), but the problem cause remained untreated. In this case, the cause lay in the inability of his people to handle some of the technical problems in their designs. Each felt he or she alone was having problems. Their uneasiness about admitting this made them reluctant to tell the supervisor or bring it up in the meeting. They had been using the breaks to try to work out these problems with the help of their colleagues. So, by treating a symptom (long breaks), the supervisor was actually accentuating the problem cause.

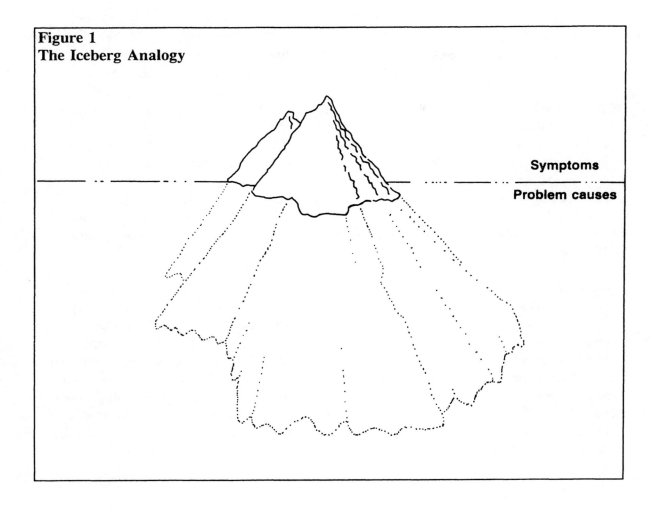

Figure 1
The Iceberg Analogy

Symptoms

Problem causes

Although treating problem causes is generally superior to treating symptoms, problem causes are certainly not easy to identify. In most all situations, it is vital to talk to the problem employee before feeling content with the diagnosis. There are several reasons for this. First, even though problem employees often give self-serving reasons for their deficient performance, if the problem cause lies in the personal life of the employee, there may be no other way to obtain this information. Sometimes merely talking to the employee may be sufficient to correct the problem cause. In many cases the cause of poor performance involves a misunderstanding of instructions or expectations which the manager can easily clear up.

Listening skills are particularly important in trying to identify the problem causes during a meeting with a problem performer. In particular, when the problem employee seems reluctant to disclose his or her views on the problem, a technique called active listening can be quite helpful. Briefly, active listening is based on the premise that people are much more prone to share private matters with their supervisor if they perceive that he or she is trustworthy; that is, they will not suffer punishment or be harshly judged for what they say.

49

The technique itself is relatively straightforward. When the employee makes a partially disclosing statement, the manager simply rephrases what the speaker has said. This allows the manager to test whether or not the employee's comments were heard accurately and makes it clear to the employee that he or she was actually listened to. Phrases such as "It sounds like you are saying ...," or "As I understand it, what you're saying is ...," can be used by the manager to test understandings. This may be coupled with an attempt to reflect the underlying feelings behind what the employee says. Phrases useful here include "I suppose that must have made you feel good ...," or "I guess that hurt a lot." Active listening is by no means a panacea. However, its use may help a manager uncover problems that employees are reluctant to reveal. Successful active listening requires understanding, empathy, and non-judgmental acceptance. Without these, it is doubtful that anyone can use the techniques most effectively.

Many managers are uncomfortable using this technique. Much of the reason for this, is a desire to avoid probing into personal or private aspects of an employee's life. Some managers avoid obtaining this kind of information because they believe it is not relevant to the job; others avoid obtaining it because they feel it would bias them. It is important to note that there is no research evidence that proves that supervisors who use active listening with problem employees do better than those who do not. Basically, it has to be considered a matter of preference. Users of active listening believe that active listening is a way to support a problem employee and that support at work is often just what the problem employee needs to turn his/her performance around. Moreover, users say that they have a legitimate interest in anything that causes performance problems at work.

The Treatment of Symptoms

Whether or not active listening is used, a manager is not always able to specifically identify what is causing a particular employee to perform poorly. This leaves no recourse but to treat the symptoms of the problem. The prognosis for this treatment is actually not as bleak as the iceberg analogy described earlier would lead us to believe. In many instances the treatment of symptoms motivates the employee to take responsibility for the problem.

Our most effective tool for treating symptoms is the action plan. An action plan is a document that outlines the problem employee's commitments to change the symptom or symptoms and the supervisor's commitments to help the problem employee in that effort. For action plans to be effective, they must have two attributes: they must be as specific as possible, and they must be arrived at in a collaborative fashion.

Research indicates that vague action plans such as "Do the best you can to improve" are much less effective than specific ones. Vague action plans lead the employee with poor work habits to test the manager. In addition, when vague action plans are used, it increases the chances that any further disciplinary decisions will come as a complete surprise to the problem employee. For an action plan to be specific, it should:

(1) identify as precisely as possible the dimensions of the symptoms. The problem employee should be given specific examples of what is considered symptomatic of poor performance.

(2) specify how reduction of the symptoms will be gauged. Measurable standards should be established if possible.

(3) articulate clearly what constitutes acceptable improvement and what does not.

(4) indicate exactly what will be done to support the problem employee's efforts to improve on these symptoms.

(5) describe what actions will be taken if there is improvement and if there is not.

A manager often can get clarity of this kind in a few words. A rather terse yet very clear action plan for a retail sales clerk is shown in Figure 2.

Figure 2
An Action Plan for a Retail Sales Clerk

The quality of Bill Jones' work has declined in the last three months. He has been responsible for 18 cash register errors in this period totalling $83.23. His sales area was rated unsatisfactory in cleanliness and orderliness in the independent audit during two of the last three months. Mr. Jones has agreed to be more careful in ringing up sales on the cash register and in maintaining a cleaner, more orderly work area. To satisfactorily improve, he is expected to make a maximum of three cash register errors totalling at most $25.00 during the month of June. He is also expected to be rated satisfactory or better on the June independent audit. In this respect, he should keep the floor around his work station free of boxes and debris and the shelves of merchandise neatly stacked and displayed. I will make weekly random inspections of his work area during June to give him specific feedback on cleanliness and orderliness. The June independent audit is scheduled for sometime during the last week in June. By June 30, if Mr. Jones does not meet both the expectations listed above, I will give him a written warning on his performance and have it placed in his personnel file.

A second attribute of effective action plans is that a manager should not impose a plan on the employee, but develop it with him or her. Research is clear that action plans developed by the supervisor unilaterally are usually not as effective as those developed jointly. For the plan to be motivating, the employee must feel that he/she has participated in its development. Imposed action plans often fail because the employee is not truly committed to their contents. Additionally, action plans developed without employee input often result in legalistic behavior in which the employee follows the letter of the plan but not the spirit. This undermines even the most specific action plan.

Putting together an action plan collaboratively need not result in a weak or permissive document. A manager can be as forceful as the situation merits while working out the plan with the employee. One useful test to see if the employee feels he or she has had some input is to ask if the employee thinks the final document is different than it would have been without the meeting.

In summary, a manager can treat symptoms effectively but only by developing an action plan. To be truly effective, action plans should be both specific and collaboratively reached.

Formal Discipline Systems

Most organizations have some sort of formal discipline system that might be used as a tool for managing an employee with poor work habits. Generally, formal discipline systems are termed "progressive" in the sense that they (a) link the severity of penalties to the severity of the employee's infractions and (b) specify a series of increasingly severe penalties for repetitions of relatively minor infractions. The rather mild infraction of tardiness might call for a written warning after the third infraction in one month, a one-day suspension for the fourth, a five-day suspension for the fifth, and discharge after the sixth. In contrast, drinking intoxicants on the job might require an immediate one-day suspension followed by discharge if repeated within a year.

If a formal discipline system is in effect, the manager should use it if the symptom is covered in the system. Otherwise he or she runs the risk of rendering the entire system ineffective. However, disciplinary procedures generally allow some flexibility, especially for less severe forms of nonperformance. Typically companies allow their supervisors to judge whether an instance of absenteeism should be excused or not.

In some organizations the formal discipline system is used only in cases where individuals are indeed chronic non-performers who exhibit a host of troublesome symptoms. In these situations, putting employees who display acute and rather mild symptoms on the same track to severe punishment may be highly demoralizing.

Legal Problems

There are a host of federal, state, and local statutes that apply to the case of a supervisor disciplining a problem employee. In general these laws cover three broad considerations: wrongful discharge, employment discrimination, and unfair labor practices. While detailing all of these statutes is clearly outside the scope of this chapter, several broad guidelines are listed below. In general, a manager should:

(1) document in writing all symptoms, meetings, and subsequent actions taken in the case of a problem employee,

(2) never refuse to talk with or counsel a problem employee about his/her unsatisfactory performance,

(3) act only on work-related problem causes and verifiable symptoms of poor performance,

(4) consult with professionals in personnel law before taking any action on protected-class employees,

(5) follow carefully formal discipline systems if in place,

(6) insure that the discipline action is work related,

(7) act consistently over time and persons,

(8) be certain that all actions and documents are in the spirit that the employee wants to improve.

The Steps to Improving Employee Work Habits

The following steps are offered to summarize this discussion. First, the problem should be stated clearly and specifically. As soon as a symptom of faulty work habits appears, it should be carefully verified. Facts should be obtained from appropriate sources in a way that does not invade anyone's privacy or convey the impression to others that the manager is "out to get" someone. Once gathered, the information and symptoms should be analyzed to identify probable problem causes.

Second, it is important to talk with the problem employee as soon as feasible. This meeting should be private and in a place free from interruptions. During this interview the supervisor should try to create a climate of problem solving and openness. The supervisor should give specific examples of the symptoms observed and be willing to discuss whether any supervisory actions have contributed to the problem.

Third, the manager should ask the employee for a solution and try to discover the cause of the problem employee's poor performance. If the employee is reluctant to discuss the cause, the supervisor should consider using active listening.

Fourth, the supervisor and employee should agree on an action plan that is formulated on symptoms and, if possible, problem causes. This plan should be specific and collaboratively reached. To be most useful, this plan should be written and specify:

(1) what the symptoms are,

(2) how changes in the symptoms will be measured in the future,

(3) what constitutes acceptable improvement,

(4) what the supervisor will do to support the employee's efforts to improve,

(5) the consequences if no satisfactory improvement is forthcoming.

Fifth, the manager should ensure that he or she has received a commitment from the employee to try and fulfill the action plan and should arrange for specific follow-up meetings.

References

Greenberg, J. 1990. Organizational justice: Yesterday, today, and tomorrow. *Journal of Management* 16: 399-432.

Kepner, C. H., & Tregoe, B. B. 1985. *The rational manager*. New York: McGraw-Hill.

Locke, E. A., & Latham, G. P. 1984. *Goal setting: A motivational technique that works*. Englewood Cliffs, NJ: Prentice-Hall.

Locke, E. A., Shaw, K. N., Saari, L. M., & Latham, G. P. 1981. Goal setting and task performance: 1969-1980. *Psychological Bulletin* 90: 125-152.

McAfee, B., & Poffenberger, W. 1982. *Productivity strategies: Enhancing job performance*. Englewood Cliffs, NJ: Prentice-Hall.

McGregor, D. 1957. Hot stove rules of discipline. In G. Strauss & L. Sayles (Eds.), *Personnel: The human problems of management*. Englewood Cliffs, NJ: Prentice-Hall.

Miner, J. B., & Brewer, J. F. 1976. The management of ineffective performance. In M. D. Dunnette (Ed.), *Handbook of Industrial and Organizational Psychology*. Chicago: Rand McNally.

Nash. M. 1985. Making people productive: What really works in raising managerial and employee performance. San Francisco: Jossey Bass.

Rogers, C. R., & Roethlisberger, F. J. 1952. Barriers and gateways to communication. *Harvard Business Review* 30: 46-52.

Sheppard, B. H., Lewicki, R. J., & Minton, J. 1992. *Organizational justice*. New York: Free Press.

Veiga, J. F. 1988. Face your problem subordinates now! *Academy of Management Executive* 2, 2: 145-152.

Flow Diagram for Problem Employee Interactive Case

Detach this page from your book before you begin the Interactive Case. As you make each decision, write the decision point number following the GO TO statement in the appropriate rectangle before you turn to that page. If you are referred to a previous decision point, circle the decision point number you last wrote and proceed to the first uncircled rectangle above that one in your flow diagram. Do not erase the numbers once you have written them. You will not necessarily fill all the rectangles.

Start		6th Decision		12th Decision	
1st Decision		7th Decision		13th Decision	
2nd Decision		8th Decision		14th Decision	
3rd Decision		9th Decision		15th Decision	
4th Decision		10th Decision		16th Decision	
5th Decision		11th Decision		17th Decision	

over

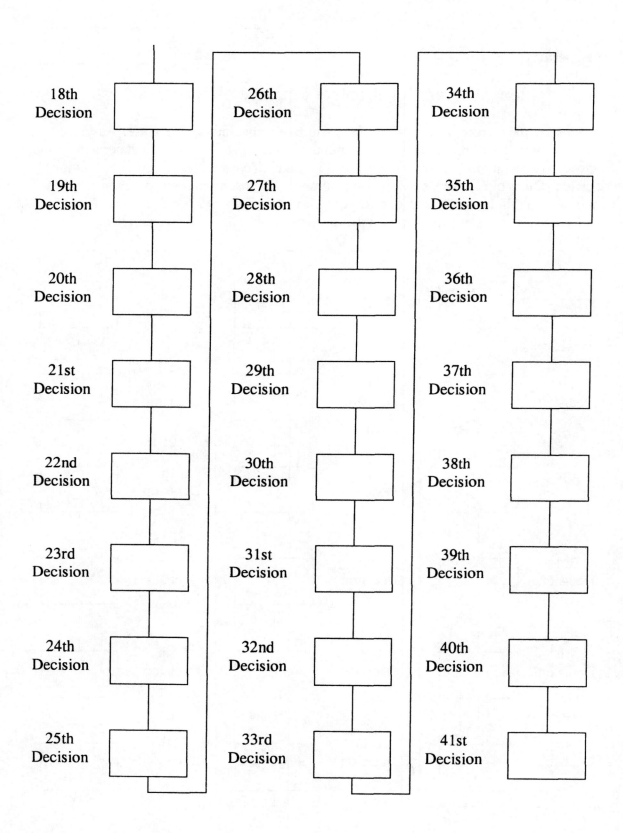

18th
Decision

19th
Decision

20th
Decision

21st
Decision

22nd
Decision

23rd
Decision

24th
Decision

25th
Decision

26th
Decision

27th
Decision

28th
Decision

29th
Decision

30th
Decision

31st
Decision

32nd
Decision

33rd
Decision

34th
Decision

35th
Decision

36th
Decision

37th
Decision

38th
Decision

39th
Decision

40th
Decision

41st
Decision

INTERACTIVE CASE

You are a first-line engineering supervisor. You have a team of 12 engineering aides and computer-assisted designers who draw up or codify diagrams based upon instructions from engineers. Your group is close-knit and has generally been productive.

Frank Wilson is one of your subordinates. He has been with you for three and one-half months and with the company for over three years. Frank has been well accepted by the rest of the group, and on occasion has been out-spoken in complaining about things that he thinks make it difficult for your group to complete its tasks. Frank is absent today (Monday). You know he has been absent quite a bit, but when you enter today's absence in your log, you are surprised to see that he has been absent three Mondays out of the last four.

Lately your group's productivity has been falling. The group is behind schedule, and you have had to use overtime to try to catch up. You know that this displeases your boss. You know that your boss wants you to do something quickly to boost productivity.

You suspect that part of the reason productivity is falling is excessive absenteeism. You are particularly concerned about Frank's absences and feel that you must take some action soon.

Which of the following actions would you take first?

A.   Talk to some of Frank's co-workers to see if they have any ideas about what might be causing Frank's absences. (GO TO 499)

B.   Check with Frank's previous supervisor to see what his past attendance record was like. (GO TO 594)

C.   Do nothing. Wait until Frank returns and then have a talk with him. (GO TO 618)

D.   Discuss the matter with your manager in order to get her advice in handling this matter. (GO TO 469)

E.   Call the Human Resources Department to see what disciplinary options are open to you. (GO TO 457)

F.   Call the Human Resources Department to see if there are other departments in the company that need people with Frank's qualifications so you can transfer him there. (GO TO 514)

MODULE 5

Communication

MODULE READING

Managers and supervisors spend nearly 80 percent of every day communicating. It is no small wonder that so many of the problems any manager faces are communication problems. Yet many of these problems are avoidable. It is not just a matter of trying harder or even being more "sensitive." One secret of more effective communication lies in understanding the differences between the types of relationships a manager must deal with and communicating accordingly. Managers must communicate upward, downward, and horizontally, and each of these directions requires a different set of techniques. It is the failure to act upon these differences that causes so many communication difficulties.

Figure 1 shows how frequently managers communicate upward, downward, and horizontally. Downward communication is most common, and upward and horizontal communication are less frequent. However, each horizontal and upward message is likely to be consequential. A failure to communicate with a manager's boss or a key peer can spell disaster.

A Fundamental Choice in Communicating in Any Direction

When a manager has a message to convey, the most fundamental decision is whether to communicate it orally or in written form. In general, some situations dictate communication in writing, some orally, and some both. Consider the general rules listed below.

Oral communication by itself is best when a manager:

(1) has to reprimand an employee,

(2) wants to communicate in confidence or "off the record",

(3) is settling a dispute between subordinates,

(4) is involved in a minor violation of a policy in order to solve a problem or get something done,

(5) wants to communicate something but does not want to establish a precedent.

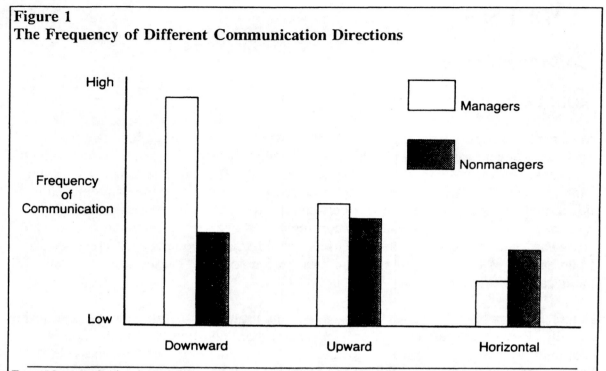

Figure 1
The Frequency of Different Communication Directions

From "Communication in Administrative Bureaucracies" by Samuel B. Bacharach and Michael Aiken in *Academy of Management Journal* 20, No. 3, 1977. Copyright © 1977 by the Academy of Management. Reprinted by permission of the Academy of Management and Samuel B. Bacharach.

Written communication by itself is best when a manager:

(1) wants to brief a large audience about non-urgent information,

(2) wants to get a reaction from someone who is hesitant to respond orally,

(3) wants to give someone information requiring future action.

Written communication followed by oral communication is best when a manager:

(1) wants to prepare someone for future group interaction (e.g., a meeting),

(2) wants to communicate with a majority, recognizing that the minority will require some oral communication.

Oral communication followed by written communication is best when a manager:

(1) wants to reinforce what has been communicated orally,

(2) wants to minimize the possibility of misunderstandings that sometimes arise when people "compare notes" about what has been orally said,

(3) wants to leave a clear trial of documentation should misunderstandings arise in the future.

It is also important to keep the receiver in mind when deciding whether to communicate orally or in writing. Some people are naturally listeners and others readers. Clearly, messages should be sent orally to listeners even though the situation would otherwise demand a written form.

When in doubt it is probably better to send a message orally than in writing. Talking to someone allows more immediate feedback than a written message. At the same time, a manager should not fall into the trap of believing that oral communication does not require careful planning. Listeners are challenged by the fact that the time difference between the rate of thought (400 to 500 words/min.) and the rate of speech (100 to 150 words/min.) is significant. In other words, it takes planning to assure that listeners exercise the patience to listen.

Good communication in any direction is sensitive to audience expectations. We will begin each of the following discussions of downward, horizontal, and upward communication with a discussion of the expectations of the audience of those communications.

Downward Communication

In downward communication, it is subordinate expectations that we need to be sensitive to. Subordinates rarely appreciate just how limited are the choices a manager can make. Typically they underestimate the narrow range of discretion defined by the constraints and demands on the manager. This often results in unrealistic expectations.

Realistic or not, subordinates have three types of expectations as to how a manager will handle situations. First, they expect the manager to be the definitive word on the formal policies and procedures governing their work and how these impact on how they do their jobs. For example, if two subordinates differ over how the vacation policy applies to their particular situation, they will turn to the manager for the correct interpretation. Second, they expect the manager to be the guarantor of justice in the workplace. Third, subordinates expect their manager to represent their interests in dealing with other groups and higher authorities.

Subordinate expectations are often behind much of the testing that every new supervisor experiences. Often subordinates will feel uneasy until they know how a new manager is going to handle certain situations. It is difficult to generalize about how a new manager should respond to these tests except to say that a manager should expect them, understand that they are efforts at uncertainty reduction not trickery, and be aware that the response to them may powerfully shape future expectations of subordinates.

These expectations are particularly important since the most frequent of all managerial communication is downward. The most common messages flowing in this direction are the following:

(1) job instructions,

(2) rationale for tasks in relation to the organization's goals,

(3) organizational policies and practices,

(4) help and encouragement,

(5) feedback about performance.

In this section, we will focus on three of these scenarios: giving instructions, providing counseling, and giving feedback.

Giving Assignments. When a manager gives an assignment to one of his or her employees, communication can be improved if the manager does certain things. These include:

(1) using language that the subordinate understands,

(2) being certain (with feedback) that the employee understands the logic and requirements of the assignment,

(3) being very direct about the ends that are expected,

(4) scheduling a time for reporting back the results of the assignment,

(5) trying, if possible, to ascertain whether the employee has the time and resources to complete the assignment,

(6) being open to the means the employee uses to meet the expected ends.

The most controversial point is the last one, but it is well-documented that employees feel most motivated by assignments in which they themselves can determine the method. In general, it is helpful if the manager asks subordinates if they have ideas about how to complete the assignment. Not only is this potentially motivating, but many times employees come up with far better methods for completing the assignment than the manager originally envisioned.

Providing Help and Encouragement. Managers counsel anytime they offer advice to an employee. Counseling, however, can be rather "touchy." Not everyone welcomes advice; even fewer appreciate advice that is poorly communicated. Accordingly, it is important to keep several principles in mind when a manager counsels an employee.

Many useful ideas about effective employee counseling can be drawn from the well-known psychologist Carl Rogers. He asserts that people communicate openly to the extent that they perceive their counterparts are trustworthy and authentic. When a person perceives another as incongruent (dishonest or unauthentic), he or she will "close down" and become dishonest and unauthentic. When counseling, a manager should try to be as open and truthful as possible. It is also helpful to try to respond to the totality of what is being communicated. This includes nonverbal as well as verbal messages, and the feelings behind messages as well as the messages themselves. Rogers suggests that counselors take the following steps:

(1) listen for the content of messages,

(2) listen for the feelings behind the messages,

(3) note all cues, verbal and nonverbal,

(4) reflect back to the other person, in the counselor's own words, what is being heard.

Should a manager communicate with an employee in a less than congruent way in a counseling situation, the employee will most likely detect that and the session will be seriously jeopardized. In addition, the nonverbal signals a manager sends in the session may convey unexpressed feelings that can disrupt the session.

These are some of the more important nonverbal cues a manager might watch for in communications with employees:

(1) the physical space between the manager and subordinate (close conveys intimacy, distance conveys perceived status differences),

(2) the orientation of body positions (face-to-face conveys competition, side-to-side conveys cooperation),

(3) the employee's posture (stiffness conveys formality, looseness conveys relaxation),

(4) facial expressions,

(5) gestures,

(6) eye contact.

Engaging employees in counseling can expose the manager to occasionally risky interpersonal situations. Once in a while employees will say (or otherwise communicate)
hurtful messages. These occur occasionally during counseling, and a manager should
be prepared for them. A good formula for responding to threatening comments is to
state, "When you X, it makes me feel Y, and I'd like to suggest Z." The alternative
of denying one's feelings is generally less effective since it is generally coupled with
nonverbal messages that contradict the verbal messages.

Giving Performance Feedback. Some managers approach feedback sessions with
employees with a strong point of view. These Tell-and-Sell managers typically provide very pointed performance feedback and then argue with any subordinate who
questions their appraisal. Not surprisingly, the result is seldom effective, but unfortunately, one continues to find many Tell-and-Sell managers in the workplace.

Tell-and-Listen is a much more appropriate stance for giving performance feedback.
Here the manager provides the evaluation but is more open to explanations, excuses,
or even revisions of the evaluation itself. A Tell-and-Listen philosophy is supported
by some very useful principles in providing performance feedback to employees.
These are summarized in Table 1. For example, supervisors should attempt to be
descriptive rather than evaluative, have a problem- rather than control-orientation, and
be as spontaneous as possible. Thus, employees who sense that they are being judged
or controlled or believe that the encounter is manipulative or set-up are not going to
receive the messages sent by a manager who wants to give meaningful feedback. In a
similar vein, messages that convey neutrality (I am indifferent to your problems),
superiority (you are not the person I am used to dealing with), or certainty (don't try
to explain or deny the charges, I have my mind made up) fail to communicate feedback effectively.

Horizontal Communication. Less frequent but potentially more important communications are those directed horizontally to peers and people who provide services. The
most common messages flowing in this direction are:

(1) coordination of activities,

(2) exercise of influence to acquire necessary resources and support,

(3) information about colleagues' work attitudes.

The most common problems in lateral communication are that (a) historically little information flows in this direction; (b) different units have entirely different ways of approaching organizational problems; and (c) different units often have conflicting stakes (i.e., the incentives do not always favor cooperation).

Table 1
Communicating Performance Feedback

Communication That Produces Defensiveness	General Principle	Communication That Produces Supportiveness
Evaluation	Messages that judge the subordinate increase defensiveness	Description
Control	Messages that accuse and control increase defensiveness	Problem Orientation
Strategy	Messages suggesting manipulation and hidden agendas increase defensiveness	Spontaneity
Neutrality	Messages conveying a lack of concern increase defensiveness	Empathy
Superiority	Messages that are condescending increase defensiveness	Equality
Certainty	Messages suggesting dogmatism increase defensiveness	Provisionalism

From "Defensive Communication" by Jack Gibb in *Journal of Communication*, 1961. Reprinted by permission of the International Communication Association.

The supervisors of other work groups also have definite expectations that every new supervisor should appreciate. Peers are potential competitors for resources and for their boss's attention. Accordingly, one expectation that experienced supervisors generally have of a new supervisor is that he or she will compete fairly. This rules out name-calling, currying favors with the boss in a devious way, and shifting blame. A second expectation that supervisors have of new peers is that they respect confidences. Peers have to believe that what is said "off the record" will not be related to others. Similarly, they expect that when they are quoted or their points of view represented, the new supervisor will do so accurately. Finally, other supervisors expect that the new supervisor will be no more permissive with their subordinates than they are. Permissive supervisors create tremendous pressures on their peers. For example, if a new supervisor is not as tough on tardiness as others are, it makes the experienced supervisors look unreasonable and overly strict.

Horizontal relationships are characterized by a power gap. When supervisors or managers turn to their peers for support and cooperation, they find themselves with less power and influence than they need. Authority differences exist between organizational levels, but when individuals at the same level communicate, they generally do so as equals. And when peers require cooperation from others, they must rely on the good faith of their colleagues.

In the absence of authority, managers have to rely on informal means of influence. Among these are:

(1) persuasion based on organizational logic, (i.e., what you think is in the best interest of the organization),

(2) the exercise of pressure,

(3) personal favors,

(4) persuasion based on the interests of one's counterpart.

Take the case of a supervisor who is trying to get a staff person from the human resources department to approve a merit raise larger than that allowed under existing policies for one of his key subordinates. The supervisor can argue convincingly that such a raise is in the best interests of the organization (persuasion based on organizational logic). She can exert pressure on the staff person that unless the raise is granted, the matter will be reported to an upper-level manager known to favor the policy exception (pressure). She can ask for the raise to be approved as a personal favor. Or she can search for "benefits" that approving the policy exception would give the human resources person. For example, if the person is known to be promoting a new training program, the supervisor can promise support for that program in return for a favorable decision (counterpart's interests).

In general, personal favors and benefit selling (informal means 3 and 4 above) are the most successful. The use of persuasion based on organizational logic and the use of pressure are frequently less effective. This implies that managers who try to exercise influence in horizontal communication should begin with an understanding of their counterpart's needs, wants, and points of view. It is simply good business to use good salesmanship in horizontal communication.

Upward Communication. For most managers, the most important person they must communicate with is their boss. The messages conveyed upward include:

(1) information on achievement, progress, and future plans,

(2) information about work problems that require assistance from higher up in the organization,

(3) ideas for improvement,

(4) information on subordinate attitudes about work issues.

A new supervisor's boss has important expectations. Probably the most important of these can be summed up in two words: "no surprises." Few things will upset a manager more than learning things from others that their subordinates should have told them earlier. Unfortunately, however, managers are not always precise in just what matters they want to be kept informed about. Consequently, a new supervisor will often find him- or herself in the position of having to guess about what should and should not be reported. Yet since the consequences violating the "no surprises" rule are so negative, it is often necessary to clarify just what things a boss wants to be kept informed of and what matters are unimportant to him or her.

A related expectation that bosses have is that a new supervisor respects their time. Virtually every manager experiences severe time pressures, and they expect that their subordinate supervisors (a) will not initiate contact unless it is really necessary, (b) will plan the encounter carefully to assure that it is efficient, and (c) will choose occasions in which the boss can devote the necessary attention to the subject at hand. Again, managers are not always clear about their preferences in these regards. Some bosses want all upward communication documented in writing, and some are more casual about it. Some want their subordinates to "get down to business" in an encounter without a lengthy exchange of pleasantries, while some seem to relish a "warm-up period." Finally, some managers are prepared to discuss any matter at any time, and others have daily rituals that make some times better than others. A new supervisor must be prepared to adapt to these individual differences.

Third, a boss expects support from those supervisors reporting to him or her. While this has many meanings, it typically implies doing nothing that will make a boss look bad. It also means accepting the boss's sense of priorities. This requires that the new supervisor have a good feel for the boss's problems and objectives. As we will discuss in a later section, this is one of the first things a new supervisor should attempt to find out.

One important fact that many subordinates fail to recognize is that their boss often experiences data overload. Most managers are exposed to much more data than they can possibly process and act upon. Data overload is often the reason bosses seem to be poor listeners, forget appointments, and seem distracted. Managing a boss who is experiencing data overload is difficult; however, there are some techniques that help in these situations. Individuals with such a boss should use their boss's time very selectively. They should plan every conversation with their boss, eliminating superfluous data and getting down to the bare essentials. One technique is to precede an encounter with the words, "I need five minutes of your time, during which I'd like to discuss topic X and after which I would like a decision on Y."

Conclusion

Most managerial problems are at some level communication problems. Effective managers solve these problems by being sensitive to the particular demands of the direction of the communication. It is not just a matter of being more clear. Giving assignments to subordinates demands a different approach from asking peers for help. Similarly, keeping bosses informed requires an approach much different from counseling a troubled employee.

References

Bacharach, S. B., & Aiken. M. 1977. Communication in administrative bureaucracies. *Academy of Management Journal* 18: 365-377.

Borman, E. 1992. *Interpersonal communication in the modern organization.* Englewood Cliffs, NJ: Prentice Hall, 1992.

Cummings, L. L., and D. P. Schwab. 1978. Designing appraisal systems for information yield. *California Management Review* 20: 18-25.

Fulk, J. & Boyd, B. 1991. Emerging theories of communication in organizations. *Journal of Management* 17: 407-446.

Harper, R. G., Wiens, A. N. & Matarzzo, J. D. 1978. *Nonverbal communication.* New York: Wiley.

Hawkins, B., & Preston, P. 1981. *Managerial communication.* Santa Monica, CA: Goodyear.

Kelley, R. 1985. *The gold collar worker.* Reading, MA: Addison-Wesley.

Kelley, R., & Caplan, J. 1993. How Bell Labs creates star performers. *Harvard Business Review* 78, 4: 128-139.

Kotter, J. 1985. *Power and influence in organizations.* New York: Free Press.

Level, D., Jr. 1972. Communication effectiveness: Method and situation. *Journal of Business Communication* 10: 19-25.

Luthans, F., & Larsen, J. K. 1986. How managers really communicate. *Human Relations* 39: 161-178.

Mintzberg, H. 1973. *The nature of managerial work*. New York: Harper & Row.

Rue, L., & Byars, L. 1980. *Communication in organizations*. Homewood, Ill.: Richard D. Irwin.

Simpson, R. 1959. Vertical and horizontal communication in formal organizations. *Administrative Science Quarterly* 4: 188-196.

Flow Diagram for Communication Interactive Case

Detach this page from your book before you begin the Interactive Case. As you make each decision, write the decision point number following the GO TO statement in the appropriate rectangle before you turn to that page. If you are referred to a previous decision point, circle the decision point number you last wrote and proceed to the first uncircled rectangle above that one in your flow diagram. Do not erase the numbers once you have written them. You will not necessarily fill all the rectangles.

Start		6th Decision		12th Decision	
1st Decision		7th Decision		13th Decision	
2nd Decision		8th Decision		14th Decision	
3rd Decision		9th Decision		15th Decision	
4th Decision		10th Decision		16th Decision	
5th Decision		11th Decision		17th Decision	

over

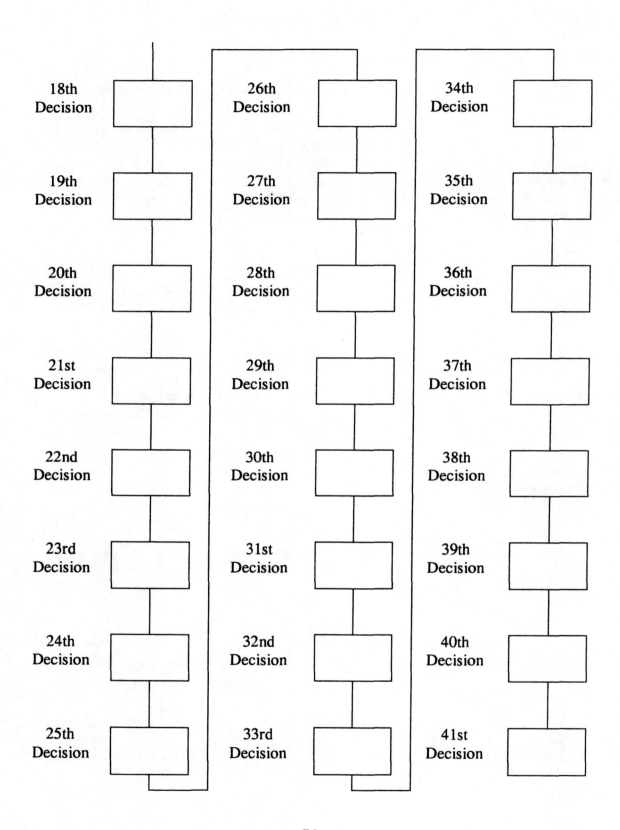

18th Decision

19th Decision

20th Decision

21st Decision

22nd Decision

23rd Decision

24th Decision

25th Decision

26th Decision

27th Decision

28th Decision

29th Decision

30th Decision

31st Decision

32nd Decision

33rd Decision

34th Decision

35th Decision

36th Decision

37th Decision

38th Decision

39th Decision

40th Decision

41st Decision

INTERACTIVE CASE

You work for Gamage-Nash, Inc., an eight-store chain of department stores located in Colorado. You are one of nine department managers at the store in the Academy Mall in Colorado Springs. You report to Marion Scott, the Softlines Division Manager at the store. An organization chart appears below.

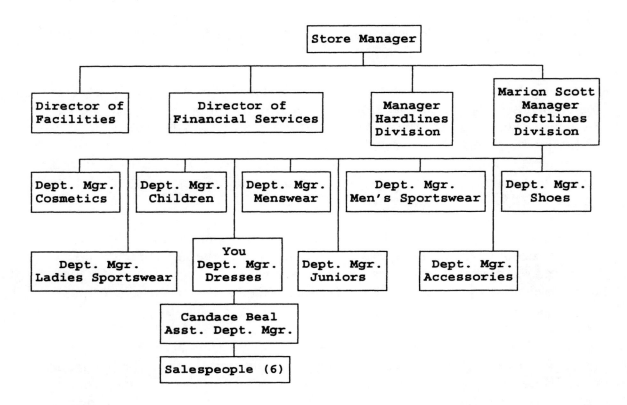

You carry four product lines in your department: coats and furs, contemporary dresses, traditionals and petites, and better dresses and suits. Accordingly, you interact frequently with the buyer for each of these lines, who is responsible for the merchandising of that line throughout Gamage-Nash. These buyers report along a completely different chain of command from the one shown above, and they divide their time among all eight stores.

In this case, you will have occasion to communicate with four different persons: Marion Scott, your boss and the Manager of Softlines; Candace Beal, your Assistant Department Manager; Becky Stark, one of your salespeople; and Jean Volk, the buyer for one of your lines, contemporary dresses. Each of these four individuals is described below.

Marion Scott (Manager of Softlines)--32, ten years experience. Has only been in this position for a year, and feels a bit overwhelmed. Is very well thought of by her boss and other company people, but has not yet found her self-confidence in this job. You like her very much, and it appears to be mutual, since you received a nice merit raise last year and a spot bonus two months ago. Not an avid reader, Marion dislikes paperwork. Unfortunately, she is so busy, so much on the go, that it is hard to tell if what you tell her really gets through. In fact, there have been a couple of instances when she has either forgotten what you told her or never even heard it. Sometimes you wonder what you could do to make yourself more credible so she would pay more attention to what you tell her.

Candace Beal (Assistant Manager, Dresses Department)--43, four years experience. You originally hired Candace as a salesperson. It was a bit of a risk since she was just getting over a divorce from a wealthy professional, and at that point did not have her feet on the ground. It was her first job in retailing, and for a while you had to do a lot of hand holding. However, she really took to it, and now she is eager to make retailing her career. Recently, you have decided to delegate more of your job to her to prepare her to be you replacement.

Becky Stark (Salesperson)--20, nine months experience. Becky is a delight. A modeling school graduate, Becky shows extremely good taste in the clothes she wears, and she dresses mannequins superbly. She works 20 hours a week for you. She is enrolled at a local college majoring in retailing. You plan to use her this summer and hope that she will join Gamage-Nash upon graduating.

Jean Volk (Buyer, Contemporary Dresses)--38, 10 years experience. Mostly, you have a good relationship with Jean, although there are tensions in working with any buyer. Buyers are responsible for acquiring the merchandise you sell, and there are often differences between the assortment you get from a buyer and the assortment you know will sell. For example, you have a good understanding of the modern dresses sold at other outlets on the Academy Mall, and customers often request particular styles and brands. Normally, Jean seriously considers your suggestions, but occasionally she does not and really misses the mark. Last fall, for example, you had to mark down one line because a specialty store on the mall offered the same item at nearly one-third the price. That miscalculation cost Jean considerably from a political standpoint. Rumor is that her immediate superior is monitoring her performance closely and that her job may be in jeopardy. Clearly, Jean now needs nothing to draw adverse attention to herself.

You have just completed your winter clearance sales to make room for the spring lines. One development that you want to take advantage of is because last winter was so mild, a furrier in the mall has recently gone out of business. This leaves a significant residual demand for your coats and furs section. To take advantage of this development, you want to increase the square footage of space allocated to this product group. This will require you to cut back on the space devoted to the better dresses and suits line, a move that buyer of that line will surely oppose.

Changes in the allotment of floor space are decisions made by your boss and her counterpart in the merchandising area (Divisional Merchandise Manager, Dresses and Cosmetics). For you to make this happen, you must persuade your boss that this reallocation makes sense. In communicating this message, what would you do?

A. Write her a thorough memo, specifying in some detail the basis of your thinking and the rationale of your proposal (GO TO 83).

B. Before her weekly staff meeting, tell her that you want to speak with her about a reallocation of square footage. Ask her when it would be convenient to get together (GO TO 61).

C. See her the first thing in the morning to discuss the matter (GO TO 89).

D. Ask Marion's secretary for advice on when would be a good time to discuss this matter (GO TO 19).

E. Since your boss is so busy, talk with the Divisional Merchandise Manager, Dresses and Cosmetics, informally to see if this issue--the change in square footage--is one that she might be concerned about. This would save you even having to bother your boss with this issue (GO TO 67).

MODULE 6

Managing Work Teams

MODULE READING

Most of us have very mixed feelings when we have to work on committees, task forces, and other teams. Sometimes they are a total waste of time; other times, incredibly effective. These conflicting experiences with groups are even reflected in recognizable sayings. We all know that "two heads are better than one." But we all have seen instances where "too many cooks spoil the broth."

These mixed feelings carry over into the decisions managers make about dealing with subordinates. At various times all managers have had teams that were highly productive. As well, most have been responsible for teams that found it difficult to accomplish even the simplest tasks. The purpose of this chapter is to lay out a set of actions a manager can take to improve the performance of a team of subordinates. We have little to say about the personalities of individual team members. Rather, we will consider the subordinates as a group. The actions we will describe are based on some very sound principles about work teams and begin with a diagnosis of the group in question.

Group Cohesiveness

The diagnosis begins with the manager attempting to gauge the cohesiveness of the group. Cohesiveness refers to how much group members like each other and how much they value their group membership. In highly cohesive groups there is an intangible sense of goodwill and team spirit. Some call it "esprit de corps." Members of these groups enjoy one another's company and consider the chance to work with their co-workers an important source of personal satisfaction. In less cohesive groups, this attraction is missing, and group members don't seem to value their membership on the team as highly. Instead of viewing other team members as friends or colleagues, they are seen as "people they have to work with." In extreme cases, individuals lack respect for their co-workers and may even be outwardly hostile toward them. Yet, overtly conflict-ridden groups are fairly rare; when we talk about groups with low cohesiveness, we generally mean those made up of persons who are outwardly indifferent rather than hostile toward one another.

Characteristics of Groups with High and Low Cohesiveness. Highly cohesive work groups have the following characteristics:

(1) Group members have a strong, positive regard for one another.

(2) Much of each employee's loyalty to the organization is due to group loyalty. A sense of team pride is apparent.

(3) There is very little apparent conflict on the team.

(4) Group members cooperate with each other voluntarily (the manager does not have to provide any special incentives to get team members to pull together).

(5) The way members of the group interact does not change much over time (the influence of informal leaders is quite stable).

A quite different set of characteristics is seen in work groups that have low levels of cohesiveness:

(1) Team members of the group feel either indifferently or negatively toward one another.

(2) Little of each employee's loyalty to the organization is the result of group loyalty (there is very little sense of team pride).

(3) The group has relatively high levels of conflict (even if this conflict is not openly expressed, members are likely to feel it).

(4) Cooperation between group members occurs only when the manager insists on it or when incentives require it.

(5) The way members interact varies greatly over time (informal relations shift; no one holds the respect of his fellows very long).

Is Cohesiveness Desirable? Not surprisingly, members of highly cohesive groups are happier at work and have higher morale than people in work groups with low cohesiveness. So if given the choice, employees would certainly prefer working in a cohesive work group. For the organization, though, the effects of cohesiveness are not as positive. As surprising as it might seem at this point, work groups with high cohesiveness perform no better on average than those with low levels of cohesiveness. It is true that people in cohesive groups are more cooperative, but they simply can't be counted upon to cooperate in ways that are truly beneficial to the organization.

This is not to say that cohesiveness has no effect on performance whatsoever. Actually it does, but its effect is primarily on the range of individual performance in a group, not the overall performance of the group itself. Individuals in highly cohesive groups are more likely to perform at about the same level, be it high or low, than are individuals in less cohesive groups. In contrast, people in groups with low cohesiveness perform at different levels; some perform much higher than their fellow group members and some much lower. There is one major reason for this. In a group where workers like and respect one another, they are much more likely to agree with one another about what constitutes a "fair day's work." This leads group members to strive for and enforce that agreed upon level of performance. In groups without these close social ties, members are less likely to talk about what each person "should be contributing," and even if they do, they are likely to disagree on what an acceptable level is.

In summary, cohesiveness is an attribute of a group. Some groups are highly cohesive and some are not. A group with high cohesiveness has strong ties between members, so much so that the group becomes an important source of work satisfaction for its members. Highly cohesive groups are virtually conflict-free; differences are settled informally through mutual adjustments. Most employees prefer to work in a highly cohesive work group. However, cohesiveness has a greater effect on the range of individual performance in a group than it does on the level of performance of the group as a whole.

Group Norms

Norms are the informal rules that develop and are enforced within a group about how group members should behave. In a sense, norms describe the "right" and "wrong" way for individuals to act as members of a group. An example of the types of norms groups develop include whether or not to talk about one's private life, whether or not to "tattle," whether or not to knock on office doors before one enters, and whether or not to "cheat" on expense accounts. Clearly not all norms a group develops are important to us as managers. The significant ones are those that have something to do with group performance.

Some groups develop norms that are consistent with how a manager wants workers to behave, and some do not. For example, if in a sales office the salespeople pressure each other for higher sales volume, this is a sign that group norms are aligned with performance. On the other hand, if the group has the norm that they should not excel for fear of making co-workers look bad, then this is a clear indication that norms are antagonistic to performance.

It is not hard to see the impact of norms on individuals in organizations. We have all been in work groups where it is "okay" to knock off work a little early or where group members expect one another to use sick leaves to take off "mental health" days. Similarly we have been members of work teams where people seem to be driven, where group members expect each other to put out maximum effort, and where team members help each other to perform well. The contrasts between these groups are due primarily to differences in group norms.

Characteristics of Groups with Norms Aligned with Performance and with Norms Antagonistic to Performance. Work groups with norms that are aligned with performance have the following characteristics:

(1) Group members informally enforce high standards of performance on one another (if one member is not performing satisfactorily, other group members will confront the poor performer and pressure him or her to improve).

(2) The best performing members of the group are given the most respect by their co-workers.

(3) When the group needs a spokesperson, it will choose the team's manager to represent its interests.

(4) Group effort and performance do not decline in the temporary absence of the manager.

When the norms of the work group are antagonistic to performance, groups have a different set of characteristics:

(1) Group members restrict performance by punishing or ridiculing workers who are top performers.

(2) The most respected members of the group are those who get away with low levels of individual performance or who are known by their rebelliousness or indifference to authority.

(3) The groups's manager is viewed as an outsider who does not represent the views of the work group.

(4) The group requires careful monitoring to insure that the methods and goals prescribed by the supervisor are followed.

Norms do not just form about things like how hard to work. At a fundamental level, norms represent *choices* group members make about how to perform. For example, in some manufacturing groups, a norm might develop that doing top quality work is the goal--no matter how long it takes or expensive it is. In other groups, the norm might be that meeting deadlines is critical. What this implies is that there is no one "right" set of norms in all circumstances. Whether a particular norm is aligned with performance or antagonistic to performance depends on the strategic goals managers have for the group. If a group has a norm to work as fast as possible, it will be aligned with performance if customers really value speed. On the other hand, if customers value quality above all else, a norm for speed may be antagonistic.

No one knows precisely how work group norms come into being. However, it is clear that managers usually have some impact over their development. Unclear, contradictory, or unfair management actions often set the stage for the development of antagonistic performance norms. Conversely, nothing contributes more to norms aligned with performance than effective managerial leadership.

Is Having Norms Aligned with Performance Desirable? In a word, yes. Groups with norms aligned with performance consistently outperform those with antagonistic norms. In such groups, the members themselves are committed to meeting organization goals and are even willing to help each another achieve these goals. When norms are not aligned with performance, members do not work as hard to achieve organization goals, nor are they prone to help each other do anything more than fool around. To summarize, groups all develop some set of informal standards of behavior to which group members are held. Violate them and group members risk exclusion from the group or worse. Norms heavily influence the performance of a work group. If a group has norms that are aligned with performance, then the group will perform well. In contrast, groups with norms that are at odds with performance typically do only well enough to get by.

Classifying Groups According to Norms and Cohesiveness

Earlier, we indicated that the first step in developing a more effective work groups is diagnosing its social attributes. Figure 1 shows how the two social dimensions of groups, cohesiveness and norms, combine.

Figure 1
The P-1 Model

		Low	High
Norms of the Group	Aligned with Performance	P-2	P-1
	Antagonistic with Performance	P-3	P-4

A P-1 group is one that is both cohesive and has norms aligned with performance. A P-2 is a noncohesive group with aligned norms, and so on. In this scheme, the numbers 1, 2, 3, 4, are more than just identifiers. As well they indicate the level of group performance that we would predict for any combination of norms and cohesiveness. The highest performing group is a P-1 group (high cohesiveness, aligned norms). This is followed by a group that has aligned norms but is not cohesive (P-2). A group with low cohesiveness and antagonistic norms (P-3) is third ranked in terms of predicted performance. And the group that we would expect to perform the worst is one that has antagonistic norms and is very cohesive.

If one thinks about it, this order of performance makes sense. The reason P-1s are predicted to be the best performers is not just that they have norms that support performance. This is also the case with P-2. P-1 has higher predicted performance because individuals in P-1 groups are socially bound to each other; they care what their colleagues think of them. This makes it much more likely that the group will effectively enforce its norms. P-2 and P-3 groups lack this kind of cohesiveness. Accordingly, the norms the group develops have less performance impact. Since group membership is not as important to members of these groups, it doesn't matter whether the group as a whole stands for performance or not. The same reasoning leads us to the conclusion that P-4 is the lowest performing group. As with P-1, P-4 groups are able to enforce its norms, and its norms in this case are antagonistic to performance.

To summarize the effect of cohesiveness and norms on work group performance:

> P-1 groups have the highest level of performance because the positive norms are shared among its members and the group does not tolerate poor performers.

> P-2 groups have the second highest level of performance. Although its norms are positive, the group is not very likely to enforce these norms. Many members of the group perform well, but there is a wide range of individual performance.

> P-3 groups have the third highest level of performance. The group is generally not supportive of good performance, but because cohesiveness is low, these norms are not very influential on individual group members.

> P-4 groups have the lowest level of performance. The norms of the group are antagonistic to high performance. Since the group is very attractive to its members, each member exerts little effort and restricts his performance to low levels.

Required Interaction Patterns (RIPs)

One other thing that is important to know in analyzing a group is its required interaction patterns, or RIPs for short. Basically, RIPs deal with the sort of inter- actions between team members required by the work assigned them. If the assign- ments allow each team member to work alone without any appreciable interaction with colleagues, then we would say that the group has simple RIPs. For example, if a manager supervises a team of tax accountants, that group would have a simple RIP because the people work alone; they interact with their peers only at infrequent staff meetings, training sessions, and technical briefings.

At the other end of the RIP scale, we have teams in which members have to interact frequently and in complicated ways in order to complete their work. Such groups have complex RIPs. Take the case of a team of three mechanics who modify stock automobiles for off-road racing. Interaction between them must be extensive, and a high level of cooperation is required.

There are four types of required interaction patterns from simple to complex. As we progress from simple RIPs to complicated ones, each level involves more extensive communication and coordination between team members in order to complete the task. The more complex the RIP, the more challenging the required relationship is for the team members. The four different levels of RIPs are described below.

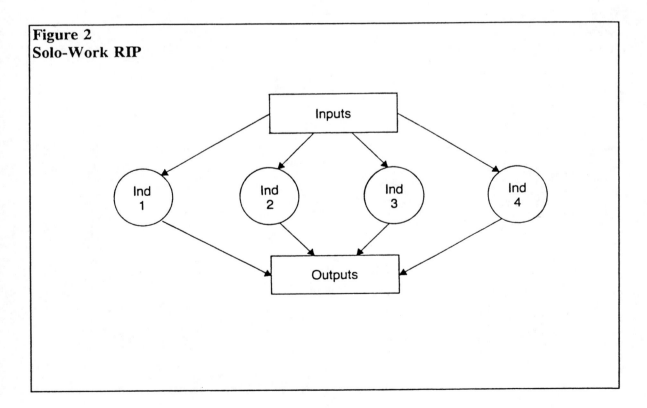

**Figure 2
Solo-Work RIP**

85

Solo-work. The simplest level of required interaction patterns is solo-work. Group members do not need to communicate or share anything with one another in order to complete their assignments. They are linked only by a common supervisor, a common set of resources, or common work inputs. Each member of the team works almost independently of the others. An example of a job that requires solo-work is a supermarket checker. Each checker works separately from the others, and the speed or quality of one worker does not directly affect the others. Other jobs that fall into this category are newspaper reporters, shoe salespeople, clinical psychologists, teachers, potters, telephone operators, and taxicab drivers. Figure 2 depicts solo-work as a RIP.

One-way Workflow. Groups with one-way workflow RIPs have to have more interaction and coordination. This RIP level exists when one worker's output becomes the "raw material" for the next worker. One example of this is an assembly line. The work follows a defined series of steps, passing from one worker to another, with each modifying or adding to the product of the last. This is a more complicated RIP than solo-work. Some communication is necessary especially between workers directly connected by the flow. If conflicts are not worked out, one worker's poor performance can have a negative effect on the next worker in line. Other jobs with a one-way workflow include workers in fast-food restaurants, steel workers, lumberjacks, cannery workers, and civil servants in motor vehicle registration activities. Figure 3 shows a one-way workflow RIP.

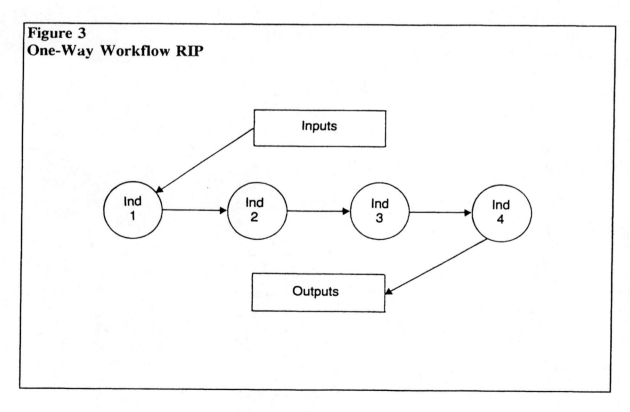

Figure 3
One-Way Workflow RIP

Two-way Workflow. When the flow of work in a group moves in two directions instead of just one, the RIP is best described as two-way workflow. Here the work may get passed back and forth between group members before it is completed. This is a more complex RIP than both solo-work and one-way workflow because the communication and coordination among workers has to be much more extensive than if the group can count on the workflow traveling in one direction or if it can be completed independently. An example of a work group that requires two-way RIP is a team of health care professionals in a neonatal ward. In such a group information needs to be sent back and forth between doctors, nurses, technicians, orderlies, etc. The information received by one member of the group needs to be conveyed to others and feedback is vital. Examples of other types of groups that are linked by a two-way workflow include: carpenters, highway construction workers, upholsterers, refinery workers, and commercial fishermen. Figure 4 represents two-way workflow.

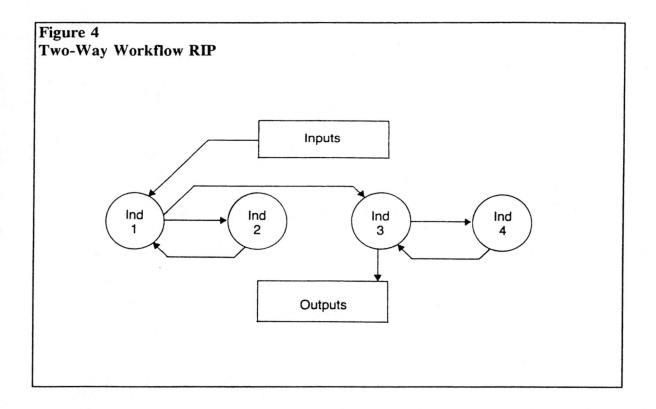

Figure 4
Two-Way Workflow RIP

Teamwork. The most complex required interaction pattern exists when an assignment cannot be divided into individual portions but must be completed by a face-toface group effort. An example of this might be found in a standing committee or in a task force. Here the workflow does not follow directional patterns, as in one-way workflow or two-way workflow, but grows out of an interaction of the entire group. Communication and coordination are extremely complicated, and any single team member can have a dramatic impact on team output. Teamwork RIP can be found in groups of professional athletes (of team sports), mortgage brokers (they make major decisions in committees), news film crews, surgical teams, disaster relief volunteers, and musicians in an orchestra. A diagram of teamwork RIP appears in Figure 5.

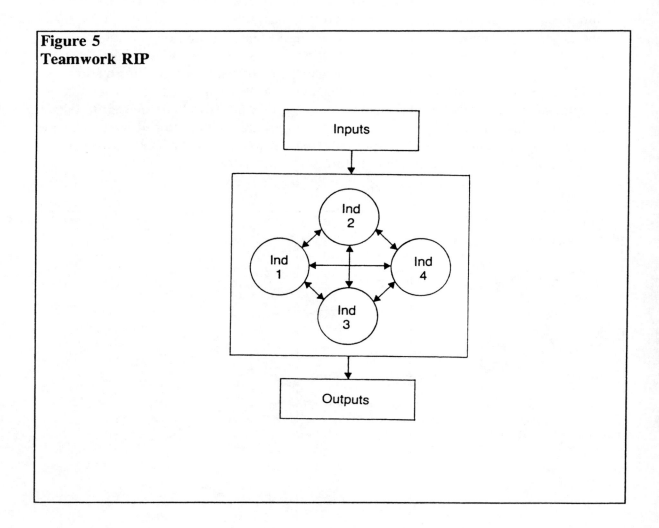

Figure 5
Teamwork RIP

Are More Complex Required Interaction Patterns Desirable? Would a manager want a group with complex RIPs or simple ones? For most of us, the answer is probably "simple." Certainly, groups with more complex RIPs are more difficult to supervise and more stressful for the members in them. But there are some advantages to having complex RIPs that are often ignored. First, people involved in complex RIP assignments are stimulated and challenged. Building more required interaction patterns into a job is remedy for boredom and work monotony. Even more important, organizations are able to tap much more of the potential of their work force if they have jobs with complex RIPs. Working independently, employees can produce only up to their individual limits, but an effectively managed, complex RIP team may experience synergy, a condition where the group output is greater than the sum of the individual contributions to it. Synergy is not possible when people are given solo-work assignments. It only occurs when there is complex RIP.

Synergy is not only restricted to a particular type of RIP, but also a particular type of work group. Not all groups are capable of synergy. Some groups consume much more than they produce when linked in complicated ways. Generally, synergy is only possible when the team is a P-1 or P-2 group. The reason should be clear. P-3 and P-4 groups use the additional interaction in a complex RIP setting to enforce their negative norms, to discourage each other from putting forth more effort. P-1 and P-2 groups, in contrast, thrive on complex required interaction patterns. As they interact more, they spur each other on to higher and higher levels of performance, and synergy is the result.

In a nutshell, we are saying that if a team is presently P-3 or P-4, a manager should try to structure assignments toward simple RIPs. With a P-1 or P-2 group, complex RIPs are ideal. Figure 6 summarizes these rules.

Figure 6
The P-1 Model with RIPs Shown

		Low	High
Norms of the Group	Aligned with Performance	P-2 Complicate RIPs. Increase cohesiveness.	P-1 Complicate RIPs.
	Antagonistic with Performance	P-3 Simplify RIPs. Align norms with performance.	P-4 Simplify RIPs. Decrease cohesiveness.

Improving Group Performance

Once a manager has concluded whether his or her group is P-1, P-2, P-3, or P-4 and identified the nature of the group's workflow, it is possible to develop a plan for increasing the probability that it will perform better.

Depending upon the diagnosis made, there are a number of things a manager can do to boost performance. We call these things action levers. They are simply the actions a manager can take to get leverage on performance. There are five action levers a manager can use to improve the performance of a team:

(1) increase cohesiveness,

(2) decrease cohesiveness,

(3) align norms with performance,

(4) simplify RIPs,

(5) complicate RIPs.

Action Lever 1--Increase Cohesiveness. It makes sense to increase cohesiveness when a group is in a P-2 condition (i.e., low cohesiveness, norms aligned to performance). If the manager is successful, the group will become a P-1 group, and we would expect a P-1 group to outperform a P-2 group. Below are some specific ways to increase cohesiveness.

Assign tasks according to the preferences of group members. Try to give everyone the task that he or she most likes to do. If this is not possible, distribute the most desirable work in a way that enables everyone to be able to do it. Spread the less desirable work equitably as well. The reason is clear; a major source of conflict in a group is a feeling that some group members are better off than others. By distributing tasks according to preferences, one can remove this source of jealousy and envy.

Emphasize what the members of the team have in common. Take every opportunity to point out common backgrounds, ways of thinking about things, or concerns about shared problems. Also, discourage subgroups based on similarities not shared by all team members. For example, if the team begins to divide into subgroups based on educational background, the manager should make sure these subgroups do not promote in-group/out-group thinking.

Give the team the experience of shared success. Few things bring a group together better than a success experience. Shared success can lower the barriers that would otherwise keep individuals from being friends. Shared success allows celebrations that create a real sense of fellowship. Basically there are two ways a manager can give the group the experience of shared success. One is by looking for ways to acknowledge or celebrate occasions when the team is successful. Another is to orchestrate the situation so a success is almost guaranteed. For example, when facing an assignment that will take a long time to complete, clever managers identify early interim milestones that are easy to attain so that the "automatic" success that results can be celebrated with great fanfare.

Identify a common threat or enemy that cannot be escaped without the group cooperating and pulling together. It has long been known that common threats can unify a group. Using this principle, though, can be risky. If the manager identifies someone or something as a common enemy that proves not to be so, his or her credibility will be seriously and perhaps irreparably damaged. Similarly, if a manager identifies someone inside the organization as a common enemy (e.g., a toughminded top manager, a competing division, or a service department that is difficult to work with), this tactic can easily backfire. How then can one successfully use a common threat? Generally, it is usually best for the manager to select a threat outside the organization. In addition, the threat selected should constitute a real threat and one that can be shown to be neutralized by cooperative effort. For example, the director of a family planning agency was plagued with a work force that was constantly bickering and squabbling. In order to create more cohesiveness, she announced that a community group was actively lobbying for a reduction in funding for the agency and that only by pulling together to mount a campaign on behalf of the agency could they be sure that their budget would not be seriously cut. This appeal worked, and for a while the internal disputes subsided.

Action Lever 2--Decrease Cohesiveness. If the team is in a P-4 condition, then decreasing cohesiveness makes sense. P-4 groups have negative performance norms and high levels of cohesiveness. This combination is likely to lead to low levels of performance and a lot of gray hair for the manager. Since it is very difficult to move a group directly from P-4 to P-1 by changing norms, decreasing cohesiveness is often the only answer. It is generally better to have a group divided when its values are contrary to performance than it is to have a group unified against the manager. This may seem to be a negative course of action. It is, but it is often a necessary first step to break up a group that is in a P-4 state. Once the breakup is complete, other, more positive actions can be taken. Until the group is moved out of P-4, though, positive actions rarely work.

Assign tasks in a divisive way. P-4 groups can be moved to P-3 by giving team members assignments that turn group members on one another. For example, if one member likes to do a particular task, a manager may move that person into a position where he cannot perform that task. Similarly, a manager might give the most desired tasks to workers who have the lowest status in the group.

Emphasize the differences between team members. A manager can also divide a group by constantly pointing out the differences between individuals and subgroups.

91

Single out individuals when the group has been successful. Instead of rewarding and praising the group, the manager might pick out one or two individuals and give them all the praise. Not surprisingly, this is likely to create conflict in the team.

Create subgroups and make them compete. A manager can decrease cohesiveness by using competition. If a manager finds ways to set up contests between individuals or subgroups, the unity within the group is likely to be reduced.

These techniques may seem unnecessarily cruel and disruptive. Clearly a manager should not use them without careful consideration; however, left on their own, P-4 groups are likely to be cruel and disruptive to the organization itself.

Action Lever 3--Align Norms with Performance. A third action lever that a manager can use to get more performance from a group is to align norms with performance. Aligning norms is a time-consuming process. Norms develop slowly, and a great deal of patience is required unless the manager is starting with a brand new group. This action lever is for groups in a P-3 position. It is not advisable for P-4s since norms are not easily changed unless cohesiveness is low.

Use incentive plans based on performance. There is probably no better way to align norms with performance than to make performance worthwhile for the entire group. Anything that can make good performance positively consequential and poor performance negatively consequential does the trick. Some managers use performance bonuses, awards, or symbols, but the incentives likely to work best are those that are valuable to the group. In addition, incentives have the best effect when they are group incentives, i.e., things that are awarded to the entire group for group achievement. Examples include a free dinner for making a monthly production quota, a traveling trophy for the best quality record, and a ring for each member of a Super Bowl team.

Give a compelling pep talk. Some managers can also align norms with performance by giving a really effective speech on the mission and meaning of the group task. Not every manager can do this well, but if done well, it can be very effective.

Be a model of high performance. Nothing undermines the development of aligned norms more than a manager whose own behavior is in conflict with the performance norms he or she espouses. Accordingly, it is important for the manager to be sensitive to the sort of messages his or her actions are sending out. It seems obvious that if a manager wants to convince people to work long hours, the manager should not go home early.

Identify a common threat or enemy that cannot be escaped without the group working up to high performance standards. Earlier we discussed identifying common threats as a way to increase group cohesiveness. With some fine tuning, this tactic also helps align norms with performance. The modification is that the threat has to be relevant to performance, i.e., if the group performs well, the threat will subside or the enemy will be defeated. Again, the manager has to be very careful to use a common threat that is actually a credible threat. In addition, if the manager uses an enemy, it should be someone or something outside the company.

A construction foreman used this action lever effectively when faced with a new interpretation of codes used by building inspectors. Apparently this change was brought about because builders had not supported the mayor in a recent election. The foreman called his workers together and pointed out to them that they would (unjustly) be subjected to standards far in excess of what was reasonable. He further challenged them to rise to the occasion in order to blunt the weapon of a dishonest city government. The tactic worked, and the inspectors soon abandoned their tough practices with no apparent damage to the foreman's firm.

Action Lever 4--Simplify Required Interaction Patterns. In our initial discussion of RIPs, we asserted that given a combination of norms and cohesiveness, some RIPs are better than others. Namely, for P-1 and P-2 groups the more complex the RIPs the better (teamwork is best followed by two-way workflow, one-way workflow, and solo-work). For P-3 and P-4 groups the situation is just reversed: the simpler the RIP the better (solo-work is best followed by one-way workflow, two-way workflow, and teamwork).

While under certain circumstances some RIPs are better than others, the interaction patterns required in a team may not be changeable. For example, the manager of a radio station would be hard-pressed to change the two-way RIP of his or her employees to one-way, solo-work, or teamwork. The interaction pattern is virtually fixed. Yet this is not always the case. Sometimes a manager can change the required interaction patterns that link people. For example, by simply requiring that a greater number of problems are brought up, discussed, and solved during staff meetings, a manager is increasing the level of RIP in the group. Similarly, by allocating the work such that there is more feedback between team members who would otherwise pass work on in a one-directional manner, the RIP level is increased. Situations sometimes allow the simplification of RIPs. Managers can disallow talking or isolate individual workers. They can position themselves in feedback loops so all information about performance comes from them rather than others. Meetings can be eliminated. Even when it appears that the RIP is fixed, there are generally certain small things that can done to simplify them or make them more complicated. Action Lever 4 deals with simplifying RIPs. As such, it is appropriate if a manager has a P-3 or a P-4 group.

Keep the face-to-face interaction between employees at a bare minimum. This means scheduling meetings infrequently, using little employee participation or group problem solving in decision making, and restricting informal contact between co-workers. Simplifying RIPs can also be accomplished by separating employees so that face-to-face encounters are difficult. Group members can be architecturally separated, allowed to interact only through forms or computer terminals, or restricted by a no-talking rule. Of course, we are not proposing that all P-3 and P-4 groups are placed in a sort of solitary confinement until they shape up and adopt the proper norms. We are only saying that groups in these conditions do not use complex interactions for the good of the organization, so there is often little to be gained by encouraging such complicated encounters.

Divide the work so that individual employees work alone and do not need to coordinate their efforts with their co-workers. While not always possible, some jobs lend themselves to this sort of division. Team teaching should be discouraged, telephone line-workers should not be assigned in pairs (unless safety requires it), shift workers should not have to use the same tools as workers on earlier or later shifts, and chefs should be given total responsibility for one food item (salad chef, sauce chef, pastry chef, etc.). By assigning overlapping sales territories for industrial salespeople, requiring carpenters to share one pneumatic nail gun, or allowing two teamsters to travel together on a coast-to-coast run, a manager is not simplifying the RIP.

Break down group performance measures into individual components. Make sure that each and every individual in the group has his or her own performance index separate and distinct from everyone else's. This enables team members to work on their own performance independent of their co-workers, and it gives the illusion of independence even where there is a more complex RIP.

Eliminate feedback from one worker to another or funnel it through one channel. Feedback is a major RIP factor. The more feedback one receives from one's fellows, the more complex the RIP. The larger the number of co-workers sending feedback to any one worker, the more complex the RIP. A supervisor of a group of artisans working on the restoration of a historical building learned the hard way about the importance of feedback in simplifying RIP. Three of his people were constantly bickering about how to texture the walls of an 18th- century mansion. Each would criticize the work of the others in spite of the fact that they each worked on separate rooms. Combined with the poor work norms these artisans had, the unrequested and unnecessary collegial feedback virtually paralyzed the job until the supervisor intervened and disallowed it.

Action Lever 5--Complicate Required Interaction Patterns. Complicating RIPs makes sense when a team is in a P-1 or P-2 condition. Here the potential for synergy (whole is greater than the sum of the parts) is at its peak. More interaction generally results in higher performance. While the RIP may not be infinitely variable, some complication is probably possible. Consider the following actions.

Encourage face-to-face interaction between team members. Just as a manager may want to eliminate personal encounters to simplify RIPs, he or she will want to encourage them to complicate RIPs. Meetings should be frequent. Problems should be solved as a team and decision making should be participative whenever possible. Barriers to interaction should be eliminated. Technologies should be used that enhance rather than eliminate personal contact. Settings should be created that encourage social contact during work breaks and after hours. Cafeterias and lounges ought to be attractive and set up with an eye to facilitate conversation and interaction.

Divide the work among subgroups rather than individuals. Avoid giving individuals assignments. Instead, a manager might try to team people up if only in twos and even better in threes or fours. Such divisions build more RIPs into the work and have the potential for higher levels of performance.

Calculate performance figures based only on group data. If a manager considers the performance of the group rather than of individuals, then the manager is, in effect, increasing the complexity of their RIPs. Each worker has to think about the group as a whole and must better gauge his own work in the context of the others'. While this might depress individual initiative in the short run, it may better harness this energy on behalf of the entire group.

Set up multiple feedback channels and encourage workers to help each other by giving suggestions, through peer training, and even with peer performance appraisals. In a P-1 or a P-2 group, feedback is generally correct, i.e., workers manage each other the same way the manager does. As such, a manager may want to encourage peer feedback of all kinds.

The list of actions represents many different alternatives for improving a group's performance. Managers must "fit" their actions to the situation of the group. Figure 7 summarizes these actions.

An Example. In order to demonstrate how this approach can be used in a real situation, put yourself in the following situation. You are the manager of six software engineers who create programs for missile defense systems. Initially, one senior software engineer works out a flow diagram and is then joined by a junior engineer who with him completes the initial programming. The completed initial program then is assigned to another senior engineer who tests and debugs the program. A fourth engineer then evaluates the program against system requirements. This involves cycling back to the original group for further modification if needed. Due to the complexity of the programs and system requirements, cycling of this sort is quite common.

The group is composed of highly mobile young engineers. It has experienced high turnover in recent months as competing firms have lured group members away from your firm with promises of lucrative contracts and plush working conditions. As such,

Figure 7
P-1 Model with Action Levers for Each Quadrant

		Low	High
Norms of the Group	Aligned with Performance	P-2 Complex RIP is best.	P-1 Complex RIP is best.
	Antagonistic with Performance	P-3 Simple RIP is best.	P-4 Simple RIP is best.

the group seems to have developed the view that your firm is but a stepping stone to better jobs. This translates into several attitudes that are of great concern to you. First, group members often prefer to be assigned programs that have commercial applications so they can build their "resumes." The problem is that few programs your group is assigned have commercial applicability. Second, group members cooperate with one another only when it does not conflict with their efforts to secure desirable assignments for themselves.

How would you approach this situation? The first step is to diagnose the norms and cohesiveness of your team and to determine what sort of RIP is presently being used.

Norms of Your Group. There are several things that indicate that your team has norms that are not aligned with performance. First, the attitude that your company is only a stepping stone in their careers is a sign that your people do not identify with the firm or care about performance unless there is something in it for them. Second, the members of your team only cooperate with you and with one another when they are given certain types of assignments. This is certainly not indicative of a group that enforces high performance standards on one another. Conclusion--norms are not aligned with performance.

Level of Cohesiveness in Your Group. As you may recall, cohesiveness refers to the level of interpersonal harmony in the group. On this score, your team cannot be rated very highly. With turnover being as high as it is, it would be very rare to have high cohesiveness. In addition, the fact that group members compete with one another for programs with commercial applicability further supports the conclusion that the group has low cohesiveness. Conclusion--low cohesiveness.

Required Interaction Patterns in Your Group. Evidence suggests that your team uses a two-way workflow RIP. Each program begins with the work of a senior engineer. It is then passed through the hands of a number of other engineers, each of whom adds to it. The important point is that there is considerable cycling and feed-back. This is typical of a two-way workflow RIP. Conclusion--two-way workflow RIP.

You have a P-3 group with a two-way workflow. If we put this diagnosis into our P-1 model, we get a look at what this means in terms of our action levers. As you can see from Figure 8, there are two strategies for getting leverage on the performance of your group. You can simplify the RIP to one-way workflow or solo-work. And you can try to align the norms of the group with performance.

To be precise about how you might deal with this group, take the action lever of simplifying the RIP of the group. The following are some of the specific actions that would increase performance:

(1) Assign the entire sequence of activities that go into each program to one software engineer. If this is infeasible, have all co-worker feedback flow through you.

(2) Minimize group meetings, committees, and task forces.

(3) Define performance standards for each engineer separate and independent of the accomplishments of the team.

If this was your group, it would also make sense to work on aligning norms with performance:

(1) Since programs with commercial applicability are so desirable, distribute them on the basis of who is the best performer. Think about other ways to make high performance consequential to your people.

(2) Give a compelling pep talk on the value of the group's work to our national defense. Perhaps bring in military strategists for a briefing on the importance of the missile systems your team is working on to our policy of deterrence.

(3) Personally model the sort of high effort/high performance you expect of your people.

(4) Point out how the development of the missile systems your team is working on is a vital response to the threat of nuclear annihilation, military dominance by our country's enemies, or the efforts of another aerospace firm to win future contracts. Emphasize the importance of high performance as a means of responding to these threats.

Figure 8
The Results of Our Diagnosis

		Low	High
Norms of the Group	Aligned with Performance	P-2 Complicate RIPs. Increase cohesiveness.	P-1 Complicate RIPs.
	Antagonistic with Performance	P-3 Simplify RIPs. Align norms with performance.	P-4 Simplify RIPs. Decrease cohesiveness.

Conclusion

For many managers, this is an entirely new way of thinking about work groups, but we think it is a valuable one. It begins with a careful diagnosis of the social circumstances in the work group, and it ends with a list of action items that are likely to lead to higher levels of group performance.

References

Bettenhausen, K. L., & Murnigham, J. K. 1991. The development of an intragroup norm and the effects of interpersonal and structural challenges. *Administrative Science Quarterly* 36: 20-35.

Feldman, D. C. 1984. The development and enforcement of group norms. *Academy of Management Review* 4: 47-53.

Hackman, J. R. Group influences on individuals. 1991. In M. D. Dunnette (Ed.), *Handbook of Industrial and Organizational Psychology*. Palo Alto, CA: Consulting Psychologists.

Herold, D. M. 1979. The effectiveness of work groups. In S. Kerr (Ed.), *Organizational Behavior*. Columbus, OH: Grid.

Janis, I. L. 1982. *Groupthink*. Boston: Houghton Mifflin.

Lott, A. J., & Lott, B. E. 1965. Group cohesiveness as interpersonal attraction. *Psychological Bulletin* 64: 259-309.

Mitchell, T. R., Rothman, M., & Liden, R. C. 1985. Effects of normative information on task performance. *Journal of Applied Psychology* 70: 48-55.

Porter, L. W., Lawler, E. E., III, & Hackman, J. R. 1975. *Behavior in organizations*. New York: McGraw-Hill.

Seashore, S. 1954. *Group cohesiveness in the industrial work group*. Ann Arbor, MI: Institute for Social Research, University of Michigan.

Shaw, M. E. 1981. *Group dynamics: The dynamics of small group behavior*. New York: McGraw Hill.

Slocum J., & Sims, H. 1980. A typology for integrating technology, organization design and job design. *Human Relations* 33: 193-212.

Course:_____   Name:_____

Instructor:_____   Date:_____

Flow Diagram for Work Teams Interactive Case

Detach this page from your book before you begin the Interactive Case. As you make each decision, write the decision point number following the GO TO statement in the appropriate rectangle before you turn to that page. If you are referred to a previous decision point, circle the decision point number you last wrote and proceed to the first uncircled rectangle above that one in your flow diagram. Do not erase the numbers once you have written them. You will not necessarily fill all the rectangles.

Start		6th Decision		12th Decision	
1st Decision		7th Decision		13th Decision	
2nd Decision		8th Decision		14th Decision	
3rd Decision		9th Decision		15th Decision	
4th Decision		10th Decision		16th Decision	
5th Decision		11th Decision		17th Decision	

over

101

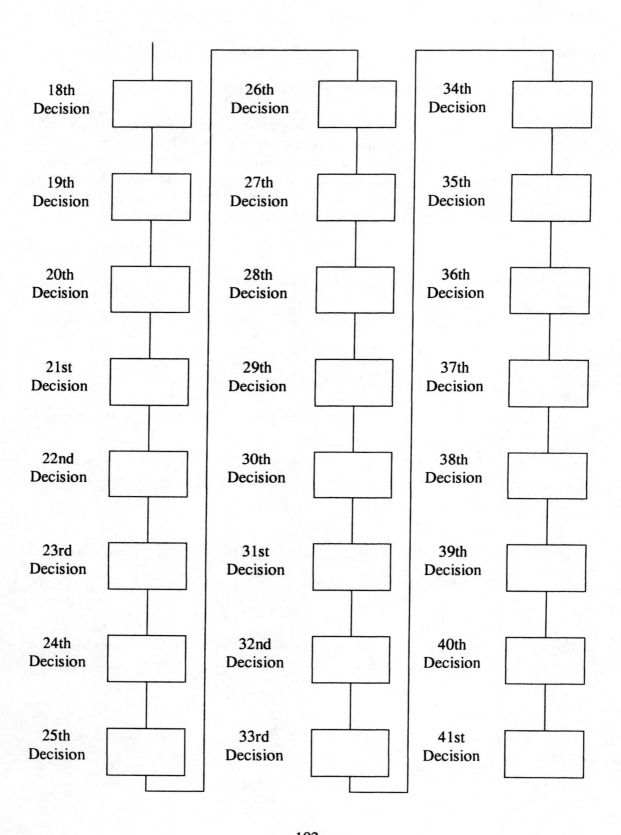

18th
Decision

19th
Decision

20th
Decision

21st
Decision

22nd
Decision

23rd
Decision

24th
Decision

25th
Decision

26th
Decision

27th
Decision

28th
Decision

29th
Decision

30th
Decision

31st
Decision

32nd
Decision

33rd
Decision

34th
Decision

35th
Decision

36th
Decision

37th
Decision

38th
Decision

39th
Decision

40th
Decision

41st
Decision

INTERACTIVE CASE

You are the new Director of Human Resources of a medium-sized sheet metal fabricating firm. You were hired to replace Doc Stevens, an experienced person who was very popular with your new work group. Stevens had the reputation of being very progressive. However, his ideas and proposals were consistently opposed by senior management on the grounds that they were ill-suited to the special problems of the company. Doc's vision for the human resources function involved *leading* the rest of the company to more human and humane employer-employee relations. Senior management, on the other hand, viewed human resources as a function that should *follow* and *serve* the needs of the rest of the organization. You were hired because you were thought to have a more practical perspective on the nature of the Human Resources function at the company. An organization chart appears below.

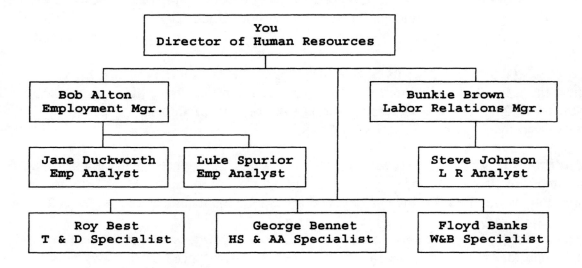

The eight human resource specialists who report to you are described below.

Bob Alton (Employment Manager) - 34, 5 years experience. Very popular with the members of the department. Excellent performance reviews but was passed over for your job because he advocated policies that were far too progressive for the rather conservative, manufacturing-dominated group of top executives.

Jane Duckworth (Employment Analyst) - 29, 3 years experience. Former executive assistant to the factory superintendent. Applied for and was granted a significant promotion under a job posting system. Known to be very loyal to Bob Alton and very progressive in her opinions about the role of human resources vis-a-vis manufacturing. You have heard unsubstantiated rumors that she was sexually harassed by her former boss. You have been told that the matter was handled internally with an apology and a transfer to her present job. From what you know, it was serious enough to have resulted in litigation.

Luke Spurior (Employment Analyst) - 27, 3 years experience. Supported Alton's promotion to your position since he thought that it would allow him to move up into Alton's position. Competent and promotable. A college classmate of George Bennet's.

Roy Best (Training and Development Specialist) - 41, 4 years experience. Very effective trainer of blue collar operators, but he has had difficulty getting an executive development program approved by top management. Very active in his professional association and thought to be actively pursuing other employment opportunities.

George Bennet (Health, Safety, and Affirmative Action Specialist) - 26, 5 years experience. Part-time law student. Competent but often the bearer of bad news to the organization regarding its noncompliance with the law. Good friend of Luke Spurior's.

Floyd Banks (Wage and Benefits Specialist) - 57, 21 years experience. Good performer, but a low key individual. Content in his position ("a lifer") but miffed by his less-than-average merit pay increase given in spite of your predecessor's recommendation to the Executive Salary Committee.

Bunkie Brown (Labor Relations Manager) - 41, 7 years experience. Gad-fly and friend of a number of people in modest places throughout the organization. His ability to get his job done is due more to his contacts and allies than his technical ability.

Steve Johnson (Labor Relations Analyst) - 28, 1 year experience. An individual brought into the organization six months before you. Experienced for his age but still tentative.

You have three immediate objectives to accomplish that call for differing levels of cooperation among your new staff. Since your team must work on these assignments on top of their regular work, you estimate that each assignment will take one month to complete. You base this estimate on some very solid historical data. You are confident that you have three one-month assignments to schedule over the next five months (i.e., two months slack).

Assignment 1 -- Preparation for Labor Negotiations. In five months your department begins negotiations with the Sheetmetal Workers Union for the first time in two years. Since the contract will affect each department member's specialty, you will solicit everyone's input. Bunkie Brown will draw up a list of probable union demands and send them to other department members for an assessment of economic and administrative impact. You will then aggregate these assessments into an integrated impact report that will serve to determine the company's negotiating strategy.

Assignment 2 -- Development of an Integrated Human Resources Policy. Top management has asked you to conduct an assessment of existing departmental policies and procedures. It is due in five months. Preparing this document will involve intensive meetings of all department members.

Assignment 3 -- Creation of an Annual Staffing Plan. In five months the staffing plan for the next fiscal year is due. This is a serial process beginning with Roy Best who estimates promotions and transfers. It then goes to Bob Alton's group (Alton, Duckworth, and Spurior) who calculate new staffing needs. From there it travels to George Bennet who justifies these figures into the affirmative action plan. Finally, Floyd Banks transposes these estimates into a budget form.

In considering the department as a whole, several things disturb you about the informal relationships on the team. First, Alton is the informal leader. Although he is very popular, you are concerned that he may subvert your efforts to bring the department into line with the thinking of top management. Second, the group is very close knit. They stick up and watch out for one another, and they evidently derive much of their job satisfaction from working with one another. Third, influenced largely by Doc Stevens, the group has adopted and enforces very professional work norms. Every member of the department is an active member of their respective professional associations. Moreover, department members have historically offered many proposals for changes that are professionally appropriate but unrealistic.

It is now the beginning of the first month. What would you do?

A. Give your team Assignment 1 now (GO TO 381).

B. Give your team Assignment 2 now (GO TO 387).

C. Give your team Assignment 3 now (GO TO 316).

D. Hold off on an assignment for a month to try to change the dynamics of the group (GO TO 431).

MODULE 7

Managing a Task Force

MODULE READING

Task forces are simply groups of people who are put together to tackle problems that require diverse talent for decision making and/or implementation. Several things make task forces tricky to manage. First, since they are composed of people with different backgrounds and affiliations, task forces are often conflict-ridden. Second, task forces are highly visible. They are typically composed of well-known and respected employees, and they are generally given significant assignments. This visibility creates special problems for the task force manager because the stakes are so great and because task force members are frequently subjected to attempts from colleagues not on the task force to influence them. Third, task forces are most often required to complete their assignments under very strict time demands. Yet its members have other work responsibilities, so the time pressures they experience are often enormous. Finally, task forces require the use of techniques of group decision making that some if not all of its members are unfamiliar with.

In this module reading, we lay out guidelines for use in managing a task force. We specify some of the things managers should do in refining their charter. We detail the number and type of people to include on a task force. We offer several suggestions about how to manage the all-important first task force meeting. And we acquaint you with some group decision-making techniques that you may not be familiar with.

Refining the Task Force Charter

The most common reasons task forces are created are to look into problems and suggest solutions, to implement changes, and to coordinate cross-departmental issues. Sometimes a task force is given a charter that includes all three of these assignments. For example, a task force may be asked to make recommendations about a problem, work on the implementation of its decision, and work through the coordination details.

Whatever the scope of the charter managers are given, they should try to get as specific a set of directions as possible. Unfortunately, there is a real tendency to leave certain parts of the initial assignment vague, and more than one task force has failed because of this. Managers should take initiative in clarifying the following:

   (1) the expected output of the task force in terms of deliverables and milestones,

(2) the authority of the group in terms of its access to information, its budget, and its independence in considering options without approval and in terms of requiring bosses to free task force members from other assignments,

(3) their boss's desire for involvement in the task force (as a final decision maker, as an evaluator at certain milestones, or as a reviewer of every task force decision),

(4) any other decision or commitment that has been made that affects the task force (promises made by those in authority, customs regarding task forces in the organization, commitments made to include certain individuals on the task force).

Selection of Task Force Members

A great deal of research has gone into the question of the proper size for a task force. Generally this indicates the superiority of odd-sized groups over even ones, with five as an optimal number and seven as second best. Groups much larger than that suffer from little participation and social loafing.

The choice as to who to include on a task force is an important one. As we have indicated, task forces are generally staffed with employees with a lot of visibility. This is the way it should be. Individually, task force members should possess the following attributes:

(1) organizational credibility,

(2) sufficient experience to be able to represent their constituency,

(3) an intrinsic interest in the task force issue,

(4) able to devote sufficient time and attention to the task force.

Collectively, it is also important to look for certain combinations. First, it is best to avoid groups that have personality conflicts. Building a task force with no work-related conflict is almost impossible, but combinations should be avoided that have conflicts of a personal nature. Second, managers should compose the task force so that there is a balance between the various constituencies that they want represented. The credibility of the entire task force usually hinges on the extent to which it represents groups that have a legitimate interest in its outcome. Third, managers should seek combinations of task force members that represent a balance between task-oriented members and people-oriented members. Task forces need task-oriented members to keep them focused on the job at hand and to give them a sense of urgency and direction. People-oriented members offer support and concern for such necessary social functions as reinforcement, encouragement, and humor.

The All-Important First Meeting

The first task force meeting is the most important. In the way they manage this meeting, managers set a tone that continues throughout the entire process. Therefore, it is important to plan this first meeting carefully. Above all, they should avoid paralyzing controversy. By that we mean any conflict that will polarize the committee prematurely. If managers suspect that there is a difference between task force members, they should check these out by talking with prospective members before the first meeting. They should be prepared to exclude members who refuse to work with other members because of personality conflicts or who are unwilling to negotiate key points.

After having thoroughly checked out members for their sensitivities, managers now must get their task force members together for the first time. As we have said, this meeting is critical to the success of the total effort, and good managers are careful to make no mistakes. Since the task force members may not know each other very well, it is important to do something to get members acquainted. There are two parts to this. First, managers should create an agenda that will help members get to know each other, and second, they should introduce members at the first meeting in the best way possible. According to George Huber, there are three ways to design an agenda to help people get to know one another:

(1) Send members of the task force biographical sketches of their fellow task force members.

(2) Schedule an early break to facilitate socialization.

(3) Before the first meeting, schedule a coffee hour or meal.

Whatever the agenda, members will have to be introduced at the first meeting. The two options are either to let members introduce themselves or to have the task force leader introduce them. Generally it is preferable for the manager to do the introductions. The reason is that some members are more likely to be modest than others, and sometimes dominant members take advantage of the floor to try to establish themselves. By doing the introductions, the manager starts everyone out on an even footing.

Once task force members know each other, the manager should tell them their charter. Here it is critical that managers give them as complete a picture as possible. Even if certain elements of the charter are controversial, they should withhold nothing.

This done, managers should then try to shape norms that the task force should follow. Norms are simply standards of behavior that the group accepts and enforces upon one another. Managers can help shape these norms in the first meeting by getting members to agree that they are needed for the group to be successful. Effective task forces have norms that regulate three areas of behavior: attendance, conflict, and representation. Accordingly, managers should get the task force to agree on the importance of each member's attendance at every meeting and on the importance of being on time. They also should try to get task force members to agree that work-related conflicts are a natural part of what will happen during meetings and that they are actually desirable. Many task forces fail because conflicts are smoothed over or avoided altogether. Finally, they should try to deal with the issue of representation in a direct and forthright way. Task forces are teamed by individuals drawn from different parts of the organization in order to represent certain skills and points of view. This creates a dual allegiance. Task force members are unsure whether they should be loyal to the task force or loyal to their constituency. This problem is compounded if task force members are subjected to pressures from their host departments during the process. Therefore, it is often helpful to get members to agree to keep their deliberations confidential. This minimizes pressures from the outside and allows members to develop some loyalty to the task force itself.

Guidelines for Managing Task Force Meetings

Most task forces require several meetings to complete their assignment. At each meeting, the task force leader should be prepared to manage the process with three things in mind: helping the group stay on track, assuring equitable participation, and using consensus as a way of settling differences.

Helping the Group Stay on Track. No one is more important than the task force leader in keeping the group pointed toward its objectives. While this involves bringing discussions that wander off the subject back to the issue at hand, the best time to intervene is at the beginning and end of each meeting. Consider the following four guidelines offered by George Huber:

(1) At the beginning of each meeting, review the progress that has been made to date and define the task of the meeting.

(2) At the beginning of each meeting, or as early as possible, get a report from each member with a preassigned task.

(3) At the end of each meeting, summarize what was accomplished, where this puts the task force on its schedule, and what the group's task will be at the next meeting.

(4) At the end of each meeting, make public and clear which members have which assignments to complete by the next meeting. Ask these members to publicly acknowledge their assignments.

If followed, these guidelines establish a very purposive, businesslike climate for the task force, where the focus is on objectives and where each meeting is seen as another step forward.

Assuring Equitable Participation. While one never has equal participation at every meeting, it is important that those who have a contribution to make do so and that the discussion is not dominated by a minority. All of us have been to meetings where one or two people do all the talking, and it is tough to get a word in edgewise. Managers don't want that to happen in a task force that they are responsible for, so they need to guide the process.

Although it is tempting to confront a domineering member, the best approach is to invoke the standard of fairness. If Bill is talking too much, a manager should simply say, "Bill, I think all of us understand your points, but in all fairness, I think we want to give others the chance to be heard." If this fails, try it again. If they are still unable to wrestle the floor from him, speak with him after the meeting and again use the word "fair" as the basis for an appeal to his sensitivities.

Overly quiet or reserved members need guidance to increase their participation. They could say something like, "Bob, we haven't heard your thinking on this matter." However, forcing people to participate like this may cause them to withdraw even further. Accordingly, it is better to say something like, "I hope that before this discussion ends, we hear from everyone who has a contribution to make."

Using Consensus to Settle Differences. It is inevitable that differences of opinion will arise on the task force. On these occasions, managers have several options. Some task forces settle differences through voting, allowing the majority or plurality to prevail. However, voting is actually a rather ineffective way of resolving differences on a task force, and it typically creates a minority that is uncommitted to the resolution. Using the consensus method is superior. A consensus decision is reached when:

(1) no member is opposed to the resolution,

(2) all members can live with the resolution,

(3) all members understand and appreciate the logic behind the resolution reached.

Notice that this is not the same as unanimity. It is not a resolution all members agree upon, only one they do not disagree with or can live with. As part of the consensus-finding process, it is crucial that managers make sure that everyone understands and accepts the logic behind the resolution of differences. That way, if anyone outside the task force asks, the logic behind the resolution can be correctly represented.

Task Force Decision-Making Techniques

There are four decision-making techniques that can be used in a task force. It pays to be familiar with all of them.

Ordinary Group Discussion. The most frequently used decision-making technique is a familiar one--an ordinary group discussion led by the manager that results in a consensus decision. The main advantage of this approach is its familiarity. Task force members have no doubt participated in groups of this sort, so they don't have to learn new behaviors. The disadvantage of ordinary group discussions, though, is that they are often quite open to biases. For one, they seldom result in the exhaustive search for alternatives. In addition, they tend to be dominated by the most powerful sub-group. Finally, they are often subject to premature solutions followed by bolstering.

Managers who use the ordinary group discussion method should utilize the following guidelines:

(1) Begin with an examination of the assumptions that bear on the decision to be made. For example, if you are implementing a change, ask whether the change has to be implemented all at once or whether it can be implemented in parts.

(2) Simplify complex decision problems. For example, some problems are entirely too complex to be handled all at once but can be divided into parts.

(3) Discuss the positive features of alternatives before you discuss the negatives. There is a tendency for negative attributes to be more salient than they should be.

(4) Separate the search for alternatives from their evaluation. First, articulate all the alternatives you can. After you are content that you have a complete list, evaluate them.

Use of Subgroups. A second decision technique is to divide the problem into parts and assign them to subgroups. This technique works well in very complex problems divisible into independent parts. When subgroups are used, however, it does create potential coordination problems that the task force leader is ultimately responsible for. Managers can either provide the coordination themselves, perhaps by attending all subgroup meetings and keeping them focused in complementary directions, or they can use complete task force meetings as the coordination vehicle.

Brainstorming. When managers believe the final decision relies heavily on the quality of the alternatives considered, they should consider using brainstorming. Here the task force is given a problem and is asked to develop alternative solutions. It is not used for choosing among alternatives, only for developing alternatives. The rules of brainstorming are as follows:

(1) Criticism is ruled out; judgment or evaluation of ideas must be withheld until a later time.

(2) Freewheeling is welcomed; the wilder or more radical the idea, the better.

(3) Quantity of ideas is wanted; the more alternative topics the better.

(4) Combination and improvement are desirable; task force members should suggest how the ideas of others can be turned into new ideas.

Managers who use this method must take an active role in enforcing these rules. In particular, they should stop any task force member who makes evaluative comments.

Nominal Group Technique. The Nominal Group Technique (N.G.T.) is helpful in both alternative generation and evaluation. It is useful in any complex decision-making situation where the quality of the output depends on the development of many unique alternatives and their consensual evaluation. The best way to describe the technique is as a series of steps:

(1) Team members work alone and in silence, writing down all the alternatives they can think of.

(2) Members share their ideas using a round-robin procedure during which members are encouraged to add items to their list of topic ideas.

(3) Participants discuss each recorded idea in order to clarify its meaning and intent and to provide initial evaluation.

(4) Task force members use rank-voting to indicate their feelings concerning the importance of the ideas. Group output is then determined by summing the ranked votes.

(5) Members discuss the results of the initial voting and take a final vote.

Each of these group decision-making techniques has its own strengths, and each suffers from unique problems. Table 1 summarizes these techniques.

Table 1
Comparison of Task Force Decision Techniques

Criteria	Ordinary	Subgroup	Brainstorming	N.G.T.
Number of ideas	Low	Low	Moderate	High
Quality of ideas	Low	Low	Moderate	High
Social Pressures	High	Moderate	Low	Moderate
Cost	Moderate	Low	Low	Low
Task Orientation	Low	Moderate	High	High
Potential for Conflict	High	Moderate	Low	Moderate
Feelings of Accomplishment	Varies	Varies	Low	Moderate
Commitment to Decision	High	High	Not Applicable	Moderate
Development of a "We" Feeling	High	High	High	Moderate

Politics of Task Forces

Managers need to be sensitive to the political aspects of managing a task force. Above all, it is important to appreciate that whenever a task force is established, it is a formal recognition that there is a problem with which the formal organization cannot cope. As such, there is almost always opposition to the formation of a task force, and this often means pockets of opposition to what the task force is trying to accomplish. Cautious task force managers realize this and try to identify the parties that oppose them so that they may be alert to sabotage efforts. A second political reality is that the task force is a springboard to individual politicking. As we said earlier, task forces are very visible, and they are often magnets to those who seek career gains from membership. It is wise to be careful to exclude those who want their involvement on the task force to be a springboard to their own career advancement.

Finally, it is important to note that members may be subjected to a great deal of outside influence during the entire process. They may be pressured by their bosses to take one position or another. Or they may be subjected to other interest groups with some interest they want represented. On occasion this results in members saying and doing things that are at cross-purposes with the task force itself. In any case, be very careful. As a manager of a task force, you don't want to alienate a task force member if that member's political activities are not "in the way."

References

Delbecq, A. L., Van de Ven, A. H., & Gustafson, D. H. 1975. *Group techniques for program planning.* Glenview, IL: Scott, Foresman and Company.

Filey, A. 1970. Committee management: Guidelines from social science research. *California Management Review* 13: 13-21.

Gallupe, R. B., Bastianutti, L. M. & Cooper, W. H. 1991. Unblocking brainstorms. *Journal of Applied Psychology* 76: 137-142.

Hogarth, R. 1980. *Judgment and choice.* New York: John Wiley & Sons.

Huber, G. P. 1980. *Managerial decision making.* Glenview, IL: Scott, Foresman and Company.

Janis, I. L., & Mann, L. 1977. *Decision making.* New York: Free Press.

Murninghan, K. 1981. Group decision making: What strategy to use? *Management Review* 70: 55-61.

Stumpf, S. A., Zand, D. E., & Freedman, R. D. 1979. Designing groups for judgmental decisions. *Academy of Management Review* 4: 589-600.

Ulshak. F. L., Nathanson, L. & Gillan, P. B. 1981. *Small group problem solving: An aid to organizational effectiveness.* Reading, MA: Addison-Wesley.

Flow Diagram for Task Force Interactive Case

Detach this page from your book before you begin the Interactive Case. As you make each decision, write the decision point number following the GO TO statement in the appropriate rectangle before you turn to that page. If you are referred to a previous decision point, circle the decision point number you last wrote and proceed to the first uncircled rectangle above that one in your flow diagram. Do not erase the numbers once you have written them. You will not necessarily fill all the rectangles.

Start		6th Decision		12th Decision	
1st Decision		7th Decision		13th Decision	
2nd Decision		8th Decision		14th Decision	
3rd Decision		9th Decision		15th Decision	
4th Decision		10th Decision		16th Decision	
5th Decision		11th Decision		17th Decision	over

117

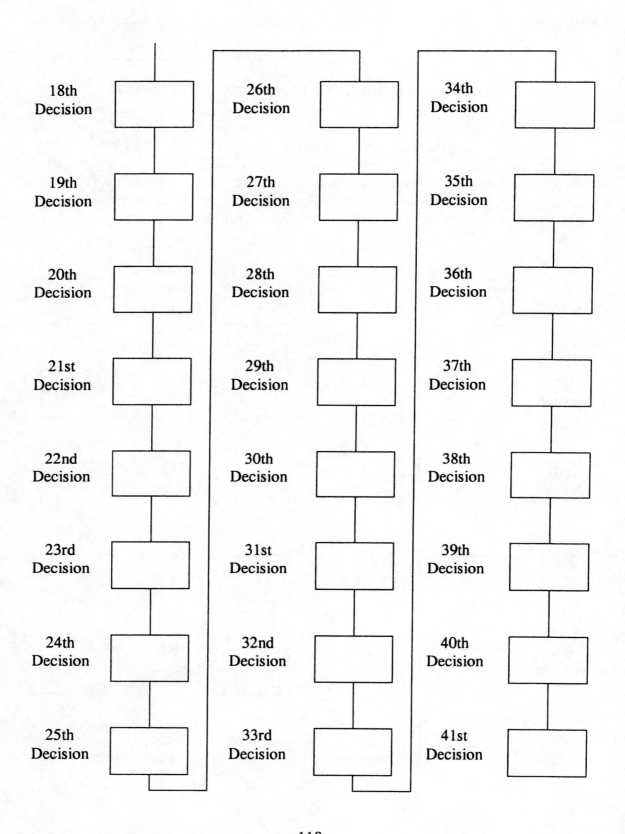

18th Decision

19th Decision

20th Decision

21st Decision

22nd Decision

23rd Decision

24th Decision

25th Decision

26th Decision

27th Decision

28th Decision

29th Decision

30th Decision

31st Decision

32nd Decision

33rd Decision

34th Decision

35th Decision

36th Decision

37th Decision

38th Decision

39th Decision

40th Decision

41st Decision

INTERACTIVE CASE

You are the Assistant to the Publisher of the *Madison Register*, a daily newspaper in a growing southwestern city. Presently the Register enjoys a circulation of 150,000 subscribers and runs advertisements from over 3,500 businesses. An organization chart appears below.

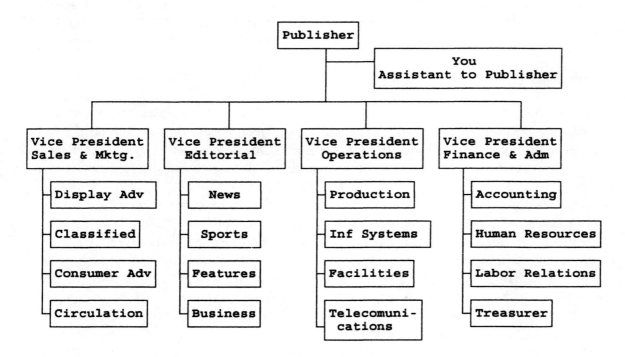

Each season you have the responsibility of mobilizing a task force that decides on the topic and works out the coordination details for the special seasonal edition. This is an important assignment. Eighteen months ago, your newspaper won a Pulitzer Prize for its special edition on the artificial heart. Last season the special edition topic was drugs and minor league baseball. While it was critically acclaimed, it had less effect on circulation and advertising revenues than your boss had hoped. Thus, you suspect that your boss will ask you to frame a topic this season that has more "bottom-line potential."

By tradition you have drawn your task force from among the Register's 16 directors (those managers who report to the vice presidents). The size of the task force has varied from four to 11, but your boss has always insisted that you include two representatives from the Editorial Department (by far the most influential group in the Register).

You enter the walnut-paneled office of your boss (the Publisher) to receive your final instructions. He is a gentle man, more humble than his credentials attest. He is the "dean" of the press in the Southwest, and has pulled the Register out of oblivion to real stature within the region. He directs you to an overstuffed chair in front of a coffee table on which 11 of the nation's greatest newspapers are fanned out before you. He clears his throat and begins, "I want our next seasonal issue to be special, very special. Since our Pulitzer, I think our people in Editorial have become a bit complacent and self-important. Our last special issue was amateurish from an editorial viewpoint, and I really think we should chart some new territory. Above all,"

You lean forward, anticipating that he will then give you your charter.

"I want this issue to sell newspapers. Mark [Vice President of Sales and Marketing] has been working real hard, but the results have been disappointing. We need something really dynamite to break the market open. Our competition is vulnerable right now [last week one of their most popular columnists defected to the Register].

"One more thing. You know all the problems we had last summer with Operations? [The layout of the last special edition required the use of three color photographic prints on interior pages that the pressmen had a great deal of difficulty with.] Well, let's keep them better informed. After all the problems with the last special [edition], I promised Tony [Vice President of Operations] that he will get all the background pieces 36 hours in advance of press time. I know that puts you in a bind, but a promise is a promise, and frankly, that line from Editorial that anything more than 12 hours is an affront to their professionalism is so much !#%*..." He goes on to recite a story you have heard before about his experiences as a cub reporter with a Milwaukee paper.

Your meeting comes to a close with the following surprise:

"So you don't question my sincerity in wanting you to do something really extraordinary, I intend to put my money where my mouth is. There is no need to broadcast this outside of the task force, but I have told Finance to free up a line budget of $28,000 for this edition [this is extraordinary; it is fully 50 percent more than he gave you for the previous special issue]. So, you see, I want a top-flight effort, and I don't want to hear from Operations or anyone else that there are any problems with coordination."

He then asks you if you have any questions. How would you respond?

A. "No. Do you have any other instructions?" (GO TO 315)

B. "What involvement do you personally want on this project?" (GO TO 451)

120

C. "Do you want me to continue the practice of having two representatives from the Editorial Department on the task force?" (GO TO 326)

MODULE 8

Leadership

MODULE READING

The subject of leadership has long intrigued historians and social scientists. Volumes have been written, scholarly conferences held, and biographies devoted in an effort to solve the mystery of what makes ordinary people effective leaders. Unfortunately, all this work has not resulted in one grand theory of executive leadership. Instead, it has resulted in several theories and important findings, some rather simple and some extraordinarily complicated, some overly abstract and some quite usable.

In this chapter, we detail a model of leadership that is one of the most practical and straightforward of all those available today. It suggests the types of behaviors effective leaders frequently display and indicates the circumstances under which the various types of behaviors are most appropriate.

A Brief Summary of Leadership Research

Simply defined, leadership is the ability to get things done through other people. Most people who have studied leadership have taken one of the following approaches: the trait approach, the leadership style approach, or the situational approach.

The Trait Approach. One group of researchers has tried to discover what common traits good leaders have. One example of this is the discovery that those candidates elected President of the United States have been physically taller than their opponents with few exceptions. Some of the personal traits that have been linked to successful leaders include supervisory ability, need for occupational achievement, intelligence, decisiveness, self-assurance, and assertiveness. As interesting as these results are, they may not be of much help to someone preparing to assume a leadership role. This is because these traits may be very difficult to develop if they are not already part of the individual's personality.

The Leadership Style Approach. Other researchers have been much more interested in what leaders do than in what traits they have. Beginning in the 1940s, studies were devoted to finding out what leaders do to get results from their groups. These early studies identified two major leadership styles: a task-oriented leadership style and a people-oriented leadership style. Some of the specific leader behaviors that fall into these two categories are described in Table 1.

123

Table 1
Task-Oriented and People-Oriented Leader Behaviors

The task-oriented leader | The people-oriented leader

The task-oriented leader

Lets work unit members know what is expected of them.
Encourages the use of uniform procedures.
Tries out his/her ideas in the work unit.
Makes his/her attitudes clear to the work unit.
Decides what should be done and how it should be done.
Assigns work unit members to particular tasks.
Makes sure that his/her part in the work unit is understood by the work unit members.
Schedules the work to be done.
Maintains definite standards of performance.
Asks that work unit members follow standard rules and regulations.

The people-oriented leader

Is friendly and approachable.
Does little things to make it pleasant to be a member of the work unit.
Puts suggestions made by the work unit into operation.
Treats all work unit members as his/her equals.
Gives advance notice of change.
Does not keep to himself/herself.
Looks out for the personal welfare of work unit members.
Is willing to make changes.
Explains his/her actions.
Consults the work unit before acting.

Adapted with permission of The Free Press, a division of Macmillan, Inc., from *Stogdill's Handbook of Leadership*, revised edition, by Bernard M. Bass. Copyright © 1974, 1981 by The Free Press.

Some experts note that these two categories are not mutually exclusive. It is indeed possible to be both task-oriented and people-oriented, and it is possible to be neither.

In the 1950s one other dimension of leader behaviors was identified and researched: participative versus directive. Participative leaders are prone to an extensive degree of delegation. When faced with problems or decisions, they tend to turn to their subordinates for information or suggestions, and they are more likely to push decision-making authority downward in the organization. Directive leaders, in contrast, reserve decision authority to themselves. Rather than consulting their people when problems arise, they tend to solve most problems themselves and then announce these decisions to their subordinates.

Once these sets of leader behaviors had been identified, researchers then attempted to discover whether any of these actions were related to successful group performance. In general, none of these behaviors (or styles) proved to be effective in all situations.

Leaders with a task-oriented style were effective in some situations but not in others. Similarly, a participative approach served some managers well as a leadership style, but it did not work as well for managers in different situations. These findings gave birth to the situational approach to leadership.

The Situational Approach to Leadership. During the 1960s, scholars turned their attention to the situational elements that made some leadership styles more effective than others. Thus far this has proved to be the most productive approach to the study of leadership. It has resulted in a number of theories that have been subsequently tested by practitioners for their applicability.

While several different situational approaches exist, few are more useful and practical as the path-goal theory of leadership proposed by Robert House and others.

The Path-Goal Theory of Leadership

The path-goal model differs from other situational leadership theories in one important respect--it is consistent with the expectancy theory of motivation that is discussed in most management texts and is described in Module 1 of this book. Expectancy theory proposes that individuals will perform well if they expect that their effort will result in rewards and if they value the rewards that are linked with their effort. In effect, expectancy theory proposes that high effort is the path and high performance is the goal. The role of leadership, then, is to clarify the path and make the goal rewarding. Task-oriented and directive leaders are most capable of clarifying the goal, and people-oriented leaders are most capable of making the goal rewarding.

Uncertain Tasks. When subordinates are performing uncertain tasks, their motivational problem is that they are not sure how to act to insure that high performance will result. They make lack experience on the job or the job may have ambiguous standards of performance. Motivationally, they need direction, and that is precisely the type of leadership that results in the highest level of performance and satisfaction-- task-oriented, directive leadership.

For example, a group of temporary workers performing highly complex accounting tasks for a firm facing an Internal Revenue Service audit. As temporary workers, they are inexperienced with all the procedures of the firm and the impending IRS audit makes most of what they do consequential. In this situation, a task-oriented, directive leadership approach would work best. These workers need a great deal of clarification regarding the path to the goal of high performance. They would not benefit from a people-oriented or participative approach.

Certain Tasks. Subordinates performing certain tasks would find a directive approach redundant. They are already very clear about the path to the goal of high performance. However, certain tasks have another motivational deficiency. They are often insufficiently satisfying to motivate high performance. Consider the case of fast-food restaurant employees. Once they have mastered how to make french fries and take customer orders, they must continue to perform such tasks over and over again with their wages providing the only satisfaction. Research has consistently shown that people-oriented leadership provides a secondary source of satisfaction for employees. Accordingly, when tasks are certain, people-oriented leadership makes the goal (high performance) more rewarding than it would otherwise be.

Individual Differences. The path-goal model also specifies the most effective leader behavior according to individual personalities of subordinates. The two most important personality dimensions are self-confidence and locus of control.

Self-confidence. Some employees are high in self-confidence and others are low. Employees high in self-confidence believe they have clear paths to the goal of high performance. As such, they do not respond favorably to directive, task-oriented leadership. Yet, people-oriented leadership is not the answer. Their self-confidence makes a people-oriented style superfluous; they do not need to feel accepted since they accept themselves. Instead, self-confident employees want to have an impact. In effect, they value opportunities to participate in the leadership of the enterprise. Accordingly, a participative leadership style is favored. Employees with low self-confidence require just the opposite leadership style. Their low self-confidence makes them unsure of the paths to high performance, and they respond best to a task-oriented, directive approach.

Locus of control. People can be classified according to their beliefs about the fundamental causes of what happens to them. Those with an external locus of control feel that events around them are caused by others or by fate. Employees with an internal locus of control belief that they do much to control their own destiny. Their belief is that much of what happens to them is due to their own actions.

Employees with an external locus of control think there are paths to the goals of high performance but they do not think they control them. They are typically open to advice and direction from others who they think know the correct paths and are best led by those with a directive, task-oriented style.

Internal locus of control employees are more confident about the paths that lead to high performance. In addition, they believe that they themselves have insights as to how best to accomplish goals. As such, they respond most positively to a participative leadership style.

The prescriptions of the path-goal model are summarized in Table 2. In general, the model suggests that leaders should modify their leadership approach according to the personalities of their subordinates and the uncertainty in their subordinates' work.

Table 2	
Path-Goal Leadership Prescriptions	
If Condition Includes:	Then Leadership Should Be:
Uncertain tasks	Directive; task-Oriented
Certain tasks	People-oriented
Subordinates who are self-confident	Participative
Subordinates who lack self-confidence	Directive; Task-oriented
Subordinates with an internal locus of control	Participative
Subordinates with an external locus of control	Directive; Task-oriented

Substitutes for Leadership

Table 3 summarizes the organizational conditions that Steven Kerr and John Jermier identified as substitutes for people-oriented or task-oriented leadership. Such factors as an intrinsically satisfying task or a cohesive work group can provide all the people-oriented leadership required of those in a certain task (the path-goal model suggests that those in certain tasks respond best to a people-oriented approach). If a leader conducted him/herself in a people-oriented way in these circumstances, it would have little effect; the substitutes neutralize the leader's actions and make them redundant.

There are also substitutes for a directive, task-oriented approach. Knowledgeable subordinates and tasks that have built-in feedback both substitute for this leadership approach. Even if tasks are uncertain, if these two conditions are present, no real leadership action may be necessary.

The significance of the substitutes model is that leaders may need to do nothing if the leadership required is provided by other elements of the situation. The substitutes neutralize any action the leader might take, and therefore no independent leadership behavior is necessary. Another implication is that leaders uncomfortable acting in a task-oriented or people-oriented manner may attempt to change the situation such that the required leadership is provided by the situation and not by them.

In the case of a subordinate with an external locus of control; the path-goal model tells us that the subordinate requires a task-oriented or directive style of leadership.

Table 3
Substitutes for Leadership

Characteristic	Tends to Neutralize	
	People-Oriented Leadership	Task-Oriented Leadership
Knowledgeable, experienced subordinates	X	
Subordinates with a high need for independence	X	X
"Professional" subordinates	X	X
Subordinates indifferent to organizational rewards	X	X
Subordinates doing routine work		X
Subordinates using standardized methods		X
Task has built in feedback		X
Task is intrinsically satisfying	X	
Organization is highly formalized		X
Organization has rigid rule		X
Work group is cohesive	X	X
Active and effective staff units		X
Rewards cannot be affected by supervisor	X	X
Large distance between supervisor and subordinate	X	X

Source: "Substitutes for Leadership: Their Meaning and Measurement" by S. Kerr & J. M. Jermier, *Organizational Behavior and Human Performance*, 1978, 22, 375-403.

The leader has the choice of either providing that type of leadership or assigning that person to a job with highly defined work standards or where active and effective staff support is available for the employee. Similarly, a leader can provide an employee in an uncertain job with people-oriented leadership or assign the employee to a cohesive work group or to a set of tasks that are intrinsically interesting. Once again, the organizational factors that substitute for leadership are delineated in Table 3.

Summary

Leadership is the ability to get things done through other people. Current approaches to the subject of leadership focus on a match between leader behavior and the situation. The path-goal model delineates what leader behavior fits certain types of subordinates and particular types of work. Under some circumstances, the leader may not have to do anything to provide the type of leadership required. The reason is that there are certain organizational conditions that function as substitutes for leadership.

References

Bass, B. M. 1981. *Stogdill's handbook of leadership: A survey of theory and research.* New York: Free Press.

House, R. J. A path-goal theory of leader effectiveness. *Administrative Science Quarterly* 16: 321-338.

House, R. J. & Desler, G. 1974. The path goal theory of leadership: Some post hoc and a priori tests. In J. G. Hunt & L. L. Larson (Eds). *Contingency approaches to leadership.* Carbondale, IL: Southern Illinois University.

House, R. J. & Mitchell, T. R. 1974. Path goal theory of leadership. *Journal of Contemporary Business* 5: 81-97.

Howell, J. P. & Dorfman, P. W. 1981. Substitutes for leadership: Test of a construct. *Academy of Management Journal* 24: 714-728.

Howell, J. P. & Dorfman, P. W. 1986. Leadership and substitutes for leadership among professional and nonprofessional workers. *Journal of Applied Behavioral Science* 22: 29-46.

Kerr, S. & Jermier, J. M. 1978. Substitutes for leadership: Their meaning and measurement. *Organizational Behavior and Human Performance* 22: 375-403.

Manz, C. C. 1986. Toward an expanded theory of self-influence processes in organizations. *Academy of Management Review* 11: 585-600.

Motowidlo, S. 1992. Leadership and leadership processes. In M. D. Dunnette (Ed.) *Handbook of Industrial/Organizational Psychology.* Palo Alto, CA: Consulting Psychologists Press.

Schriesheim, C. A. & von Glinow, M. A. 1977. The path-goal theory of leadership: A theoretical and empirical analysis. *Academy of Management Journal* 20: 398-405.

Schriesheim, J. & Schriesheim, C. A. 1981. A test of the path-goal theory of leadership and some suggested directions for future research. *Personnel Psychology* 33: 349-370.

Yukl, G. 1981. *Leadership in organizations*. Englewood Cliffs, NJ: Prentice-Hall.

Flow Diagram for Leadership Interactive Case

Detach this page from your book before you begin the Interactive Case. As you make each decision, write the decision point number following the GO TO statement in the appropriate rectangle before you turn to that page. If you are referred to a previous decision point, circle the decision point number you last wrote and proceed to the first uncircled rectangle above that one in your flow diagram. Do not erase the numbers once you have written them. You will not necessarily fill all the rectangles.

Start		6th Decision		12th Decision	
1st Decision		7th Decision		13th Decision	
2nd Decision		8th Decision		14th Decision	
3rd Decision		9th Decision		15th Decision	
4th Decision		10th Decision		16th Decision	
5th Decision		11th Decision		17th Decision	

over

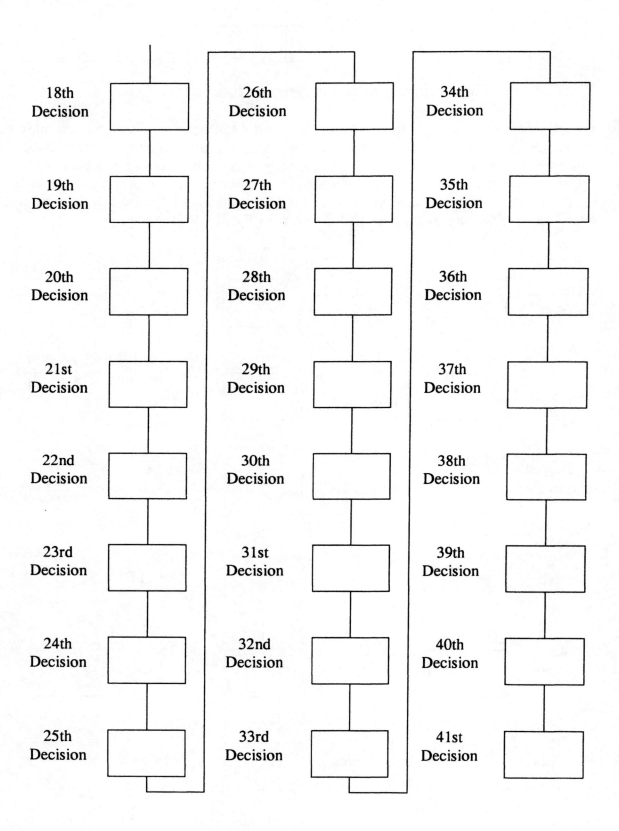

18th
Decision

19th
Decision

20th
Decision

21st
Decision

22nd
Decision

23rd
Decision

24th
Decision

25th
Decision

26th
Decision

27th
Decision

28th
Decision

29th
Decision

30th
Decision

31st
Decision

32nd
Decision

33rd
Decision

34th
Decision

35th
Decision

36th
Decision

37th
Decision

38th
Decision

39th
Decision

40th
Decision

41st
Decision

INTERACTIVE CASE

You are the Assistant Dean of the Graduate Business Programs of Morrisey University. MU is a large, private university located in an eastern city known for its concentration of high-technology businesses. There are 1,500 students enrolled in MU's three graduate business programs. The largest program is the part-time MBA program offering evening classes on campus. There is also an executive MBA program with classes on campus on Saturdays. The newest of the offerings is an off-campus MBA program for English-speaking students in France, Belgium, and The Netherlands.

You have a staff of nine full-time employees and twelve part-time student workers. The structure of your office is depicted in the following organizational chart.

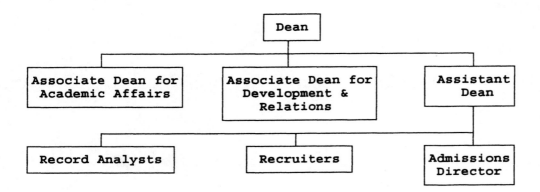

The record analysts perform two important functions. They maintain student records, and they oversee the applications documents that must be supplied by candidates for admission. The recruiters and admissions director visit colleges, companies, and admission forums, talking with students about the benefits of MU's programs.

It is a Monday morning, and one of your record analysts tells you that he has been having difficulty evaluating the transcripts from a number of the applicants for the program offered in Amsterdam. Even after consulting guidelines published by the school's accrediting agency, he has several questions about the equivalency of degrees earned at foreign universities to those in the United States. This is the third time issues like this have arisen among your record analysts. Their jobs are highly routinized and the uncertainties and ambiguities associated with the new European program have caused them a great deal of difficulty.

How would you respond to this general problem?

A. Call the record analysts together and ask them their advice as to how to proceed with the evaluation of transcripts (GO TO 88).

B. Research the issue yourself and develop guidelines and procedures that the record analysts can use to evaluate the transcripts (GO TO 39).

C. Ask the record analyst who brought you this issue to contact other schools that have European graduate programs and learn how they handle the issue. Express confidence in his ability to handle the situation himself (GO TO 47).

MODULE 9

Conflict

MODULE READING

One of the biggest challenges that a supervisor has to face is dealing with conflicts between employees. Although many of these disagreements are minor, some can be quite disruptive. If mishandled, these major ones can result in strained relations between people who have to work together to get the job done. Even the little disputes can snowball into serious feuds involving a host of people who were not even involved in the first place.

If a work group experiences conflict, a manager does not need to be overly concerned. Work conflicts are very common. One estimate is that supervisors spend almost one-fifth of their day dealing in some way with conflicts among their people. In spite of this, the evidence is that few managers feel they do a good job handling employee conflicts. This is unfortunate since there are some very helpful principles of bargaining and conflict resolution that have been successfully used to reduce some of the negative consequences of such conflicts. In the remainder of this chapter we will present and describe these principles.

Types of Work Conflicts

The list of issues over which employees can disagree is endless. One study dealt with the types of conflicts that lead employees to ask their supervisors for help. These are detailed in Table 1. Clearly some of these conflicts can be dealt with quite easily. Few supervisors would have trouble settling an argument over the way a policy should be interpreted. On the other hand, some of these conflicts are very difficult to handle. Accusations of discrimination, dishonesty, or breach of contract are very complicated indeed.

What Causes Work Conflicts?

Supervisors often blame work conflicts on the people involved. All of us have known people who are just disagreeable and argumentative. Yet it is better to think about the causes of conflict being difficult situations rather than difficult people. Some jobs and departments have high levels of conflict built into them. Even the most cooperative team player could not serve in these jobs and departments without experiencing conflicts with co-workers. This is important to keep in mind for two reasons. First, it is easier to change the work situation than the workers. A manager is usually given his or her employees and often has little authority to hire and fire unilaterally. Second, the manager is likely to be viewed as unfair if he or she labels certain employees as "problem people" just because they are in positions that open them up to conflicts with their fellow workers.

Table 1
Types of Conflicts Referred to Supervisors

Type of Conflict Between Employees	Frequency of Occurrence in Interviews	Percent
One employee complains about the job performance of another employee	41	25
Two workers disagree over a company policy	17	10
A worker complains that a co-worker has placed excessive demands upon him/her	12	7
One employee alleges discrimination	11	7
Disagreement between workers over pay	11	7
A worker accuses another of involvement in his/her duties	10	6
Result of an infringement on the property or rights of an employee	9	6
Disagreement concerning a breach of contract	9	6
One worker accusing the other of a dishonest act	9	6
Other types	32	20

From "Managers as Inquisitors" by Blair H. Sheppard in *Negotiating in Organizations*, edited by Max H. Bazerman and Roy J. Lewicki, p. 195. Copyright © 1983 by Sage Publications, Inc. Reprinted by permission of Sage Publications, Inc., and Blair H. Sheppard.

A number of things can make some jobs especially prone to co-worker conflict. Among them are the following.

Cause 1--Employees Must Deal with Co-workers Whose Duties Are Much Different from Their Own. Workers in jobs that require them to interact with a diversity of people have a more conflict-ridden experience. Compare, for instance, a high school French teacher and a high school custodian. Each day a French teacher must interact with two or three co-workers. In contrast, the custodian has to interact with a large array of different co-workers. What makes this diversity so potentially conflict ridden is that different jobs generally create different ways of looking at situations.

For the high school custodian, a science teacher creates one set of demands and expectations and a drama coach quite another. If employees are required to deal with a wide array of different individuals, then chances are the supervisor will have to contend with worker conflicts no matter how good the supervisor is or how good the employees are at staying out of trouble.

Cause 2--Subordinates Need to Share Limited Resources. Work conflicts are also caused by workers having to share such things as work space, funds, raw materials, tools, and equipment. Sharing of one kind or another is common to every organization, but when resources are particularly tight, the potential for co-worker conflict is greatly enhanced. This is the reason that there are often problems between people who work at the same work station on different shifts. It is also the reason that budget cutbacks often cause conflicts between co-workers. Co-worker conflicts are almost inevitable during financial adversity.

Cause 3--Subordinates Must Work with Other People in Complicated Ways. One of the most important causes of conflict is work interdependence. This refers to the situation where subordinates are required to work together in ways requiring complicated interactions or cooperation. Such complications arise when subordinates have to (a) rely on others for their inputs, (b) rely on others for feedback on how well they have done their work, or (c) interact with others face to face to complete their work. If the work of subordinates is interdependent, each has to rely on what the other does. Such mutual dependence is a chief factor in causing conflict between masons building the same brick wall, between a chemist and a lab assistant working on an experiment, and between a nurse and a surgeon in an operating room. Since the work between these individuals is highly intertwined or interdependent, it has a greater conflict potential.

Together, these three things--co-worker job diversity, shared resources, and complicated work relationships--create conflict between co-workers. In managing people who interact with a diversity of other people in complicated ways and under adverse circumstances, a manager is likely to have co-worker conflicts whether or not the employees are good at dealing with conflicts. So if a manager has subordinates in these types of jobs, the most effective way to reduce conflict may be to reduce the situational causes of the conflict. This is not always possible, of course, but it is worth looking at.

The Results of Work Conflicts for the Organization

While no supervisor enjoys working with people who are constantly bickering, arguing, and fighting, many experts believe that some conflict is healthy and that supervisors should not discourage conflict in all instances. In fact, mild conflicts like friendly competitions, good-natured rivalries, and minor differences of opinion can be quite positive. It is the serious conflicts that are the problem. The distinction is that serious conflicts involve two things that mild conflicts lack: blocking activities and unfair tactics. Blocking activities occur when one party keeps the other from getting all the information or resources he or she needs to do his work. Unfair tactics include labeling someone's work incorrectly, blaming others unjustly, or escalating differences to personal attacks.

Negative Results of Serious Work Conflicts. Serious conflicts can result in a host of negative things: loss of attention to work, feelings of frustration and stress, energy used in blocking opponents rather than working, poor communication, name calling, and other hurtful forms of ridicule. Besides being generally unpleasant for the parties involved, these results can be unpleasant for anyone who observes them, including uninvolved co-workers and, worst of all, clients and vendors.

Positive Results of Mild Work Conflicts. From time to time it may be wise for supervisors to stimulate arguments, surface disagreements, challenge authority, orchestrate occasions for competition, pick a fight to give emphasis to a problem, or create contests to reward victors. The following five commonly accepted principles below explain how mild conflict can help an organization:

(1) Individuals or groups in need of change require tension in order to change.

(2) Unexpressed conflicts allowed to persist for some time may have negative long-range effects on the person's ability to work with others.

(3) Competition, disagreements, and games (if free of blocking or unfair tactics) can stimulate higher performance without necessarily jeopardizing future goodwill.

(4) Insincere conformity does not allow needed information to be used in making decisions.

(5) Creating conflicts is sometimes the only way to get the attention of others in the organization.

In general, then, both too much and too little conflict can be bad for the organization. However, most managers spend much more of their time trying to reduce conflict than trying to stimulate it. One reason for this is that most managers have experienced the problems created by conflicts more than they have the problems caused by the absence of conflict.

The Results of Work Conflicts for the People Involved

It is also important to think about work conflicts from the viewpoint of employees. People generally sense the work conflicts they are involved in as win-lose situations, which means that they feel they cannot get what they want unless the other person gives in. However, not all conflicts result in winners and losers. Sometimes there are no winners, and less commonly there are multiple winners. The following are the different outcomes of conflict.

Win-Lose Results. Some work conflicts can be resolved in no other way than win-lose. Conflicts over facts, for instance, usually result in at best one winner. Similarly, when one indivisible prize is sought by both parties (a promotion, for example) any outcome other than win-lose is rare.

One very important reason managers dislike employee conflicts is that most conflicts initially appear to be win-lose situations, and this means that the manager has to (a) choose sides and (b) deal with losers' frustrations. Few managers relish choosing between subordinates and dealing with the disappointment of the losing side. For these reasons, some managers avoid even dealing with conflicts in the first place, and instead smooth them over or force the parties to work it out themselves. Some supervisors even punish those who bring them conflicts by making sure no one ever wins. There is another option, and it involves trying to convert win-lose situations into win-win outcomes.

Win-Win Results. Win-win means, of course, that both parties in a conflict feel that they got what they wanted. In other words, a way is found to allow both persons to achieve their desired goals. As we have said, win-win outcomes are elusive; few conflicts ever appear in a win-win way at first. An example may clarify this. Sam and Bill are both material handlers in a wholesale nursery. In June both apply to take their annual vacations in August, the peak harvesting month. Able to allow only one of his people to take his vacation at that time, Sam and Bill's supervisor has a problem. Choose one and the manager runs the risk of creating frustrations and perhaps losing the respect of other members of his team. Instead of choosing one or the other, a manager might begin by talking with both employees. In this case, after discussing the issue with both Sam and Bill, the manager discovered that while Sam wanted an August vacation for its own sake, Bill did not. Bill applied for August because that was the only time he could get reduced-fare flights to Phoenix to visit his parents. After making some inquiries with the company's internal travel officer, the supervisor learned that with company discounts, Bill could purchase tickets to Phoenix during November at the August equivalent. Given this careful work, the supervisor found out that the conflict could be resolved with both Sam and Bill winning. It is not possible to resolve all work conflicts in this way, but win-win results are certainly worth shooting for. Not only are both parties more satisfied, but also their settlement is more stable and their relationship better.

Lose-Lose Results. Conflicting subordinates can both lose as a result of a conflict. This occurs when settlements satisfy the total desires of neither party. For example, in the situation above the supervisor could have simply disallowed both August vacations on the grounds that if both could not take off in August, neither could. A similar lose-lose option in the example would have been if the manager had allowed both to take only half their vacation time in August.

As the name implies, lose-lose situations are not good for anyone, yet lose-lose results are not as uncommon as many people think. In order to avoid having to make potentially unpopular or incorrect choices, managers are occasionally tempted to smooth over a conflict situation or ask the parties to resolve the situation without help. In many of these cases, though, the result of these practices is a lose-lose outcome.

Managing Conflicts Between People

There are proven ways to manage work conflicts that have positive results both for employees and for the organization. However, much depends on the particular circumstances involved. For this reason, it is critical that the manager know both the people who work for him or her and the culture of the organization. This is vital for several reasons. First, knowing subordinates allows a manager to understand something about the history of the relationship between the parties. Conflicts are often the result of unresolved problems in the past or merely a form of some long-standing issue in the relationship. It is also important for the manager to know the people in order to tell whether individuals in the situation are speaking for themselves or representing others. Sometimes people speak for others in conflicts, either by fighting another person's battles or by joining the side of a popular co-worker.

It is also important that a manager appreciate how the culture of an organization affects expectations about conflict. Some organizations have cultures that suppress the expression of disagreement. Other organizational cultures are more uninhibited. Some companies have unwritten rules against going to higher authorities with unresolved conflicts and some do not. If a supervisor is not aware of these unwritten rules about conflict, it is easy to misjudge the importance of a particular conflict or to handle it in a fashion that others are not used to.

Step 1--Meeting with Each Employee Separately to Define the Conflict and Create the Proper Atmosphere. Once a manager knows that there is a conflict and has decided that it is serious enough to act on, the first step should be to find out how the conflicting parties see the issue. The best way to do this is to talk with the individuals separately and privately. During this meeting, the supervisor should keep several things in mind.

During the interview the manager should try to separate information and emotion. The initial interview is often emotionally charged. People sometimes say things that under other circumstances they would not say. Clearly, overheated situations like this require cool heads, and the supervisor must take the lead. First of all, it is important for the supervisor to be an attentive, non-judgmental listener. One technique is for the manager to respond to emotionally charged statements by restating them in a form that strips away the strong feelings. This both allows a ventilation of anger and makes it clear that the issue has an acceptable, nonemotional version. Second, it is important for the manager to appear initially neutral, to avoid taking sides. The conflicting parties will often try to coax the manager into making some sort of statement about how the situation will be resolved, but he or she should remain neutral. Third, the manager should begin to depersonalize the issue. Statements made against the personal character of one's "opponent" should immediately be ruled out of bounds.

During the interview the manager should try to change the way the parties are viewing the conflict. Research shows that if people view the conflict in certain ways, they will be more likely to find acceptable settlements. Table 2 details the perspectives that are favorable for settlement and those that are not.

Table 2
Views of Conflict That Make Resolution Easier and Harder

Resolution is *easier* if the person perceives the conflict this way	Resolution is *harder* if the person perceives the conflict this way
I appreciate the other person's point of view.	My viewpoint is the only correct and and valid one.
I know why the other person has taken his/her position.	I don't understand why the other person has taken his/her position
It's a problem between the two of us.	A lot of people are involved in this dispute.
The issue can be defined in simple, concrete terms.	The issue is complicated by symbols, words, and matters of principle.
I have hope that this conflict can be worked out.	I have little hope that this conflict can ever be resolved.
I don't represent anyone else in this dispute.	I represent a lot of people. I don't want to let them down.

The initial meeting is an ideal time to begin to work on these perspectives. If an employee expresses the opinion that losing is inevitable, the manager should immediately challenge that opinion. If a person believes that he will never have to work with a co-worker after the conflict is settled, again the manager should make it clear that they will be expected to work together in the future. Essentially, then, the manager should not just listen during this first meeting but should try to shape the way the issue is seen.

During the interview the manager should begin to distinguish between the demands of the parties and their interests. People in a conflict state their demands clearly and forcefully. By demands we mean what they say they really want, not what they wish they could get. Employees generally do not state the interests they have that underlie their demands. Research has shown that interests are much easier to reconcile than demands. Demands define one way to satisfy interests, but there are often other pathways to resolution.

Consider the case of two librarians arguing over whether a window should be open or closed. The demands were clear but not the interests of the parties. The head librarian overheard the argument and interviewed each of the individuals. She asked one party why she wanted the window open, and was told, "to get some fresh air." She asked the other why he wanted it closed and was told, "to avoid a draft." At that point, a solution was obvious--a window was opened in the next room.

Discovering interests is actually much more difficult than this example suggests. One reason is that people seldom respond honestly to "why" questions when they are involved in a conflict. Typically one has to probe more than once to find out all the interests that underlie a position, and unlike our example above, there is often more than one interest involved. Adding further to this difficulty is that interests are often organized into hierarchical trees with more basic interests underpinning the surface ones. So it is useful to go deeper than the interests first mentioned if these interests do not suggest a solution. In analyzing conflict situations it is helpful to look for complementary interests.

During the interview the manager should make it clear how he or she plans to deal with the conflict as the third party. This is the last thing to do during the initial interview. Basically there are three options depending on the amount of control the manager wants to maintain. Only one of these approaches is effective in most instances. Table 3 illustrates how these approaches vary.

One approach is called "arbitration." This is where the manager assumes the role of "judge" in the conflict. An example of this approach follows: The supervisor of a group of stock brokers was told by one of his subordinates that another broker had "stolen" one of her customers. The supervisor then went to the "thief" and asked if he knew that the customer was the other broker's.

When he answered positively, the supervisor told him never to do that again and asked the customer either to use the original broker or to take her business elsewhere. Arbitration is a fast, definitive process, and it is most effective when one of the conflicting parties has obviously violated a rule or policy. In most other situations, though, it is not very effective. Unless a manager is particularly good at finding win-win outcomes, he or she will probably not arrive at as good a settlement as the employees themselves might. More over, the parties to the conflict seldom are as committed to a settlement imposed upon them as one they have fashioned themselves. Consequently, some repetition of the conflict is very likely.

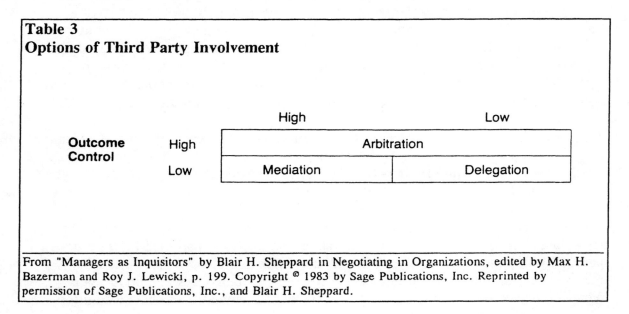

Table 3
Options of Third Party Involvement

		High	Low
Outcome Control	High	Arbitration	
	Low	Mediation	Delegation

From "Managers as Inquisitors" by Blair H. Sheppard in Negotiating in Organizations, edited by Max H. Bazerman and Roy J. Lewicki, p. 199. Copyright © 1983 by Sage Publications, Inc. Reprinted by permission of Sage Publications, Inc., and Blair H. Sheppard.

A second way of handling conflicts is called "delegation." Here the manager tells the two parties that they must solve the conflict themselves. Delegation is a popular approach among supervisors who would rather smooth over conflicts than deal with them. However, like arbitration, it is often not effective. Left on their own, conflicting parties are often unable to work through conflicts because they lack the skills, information, or impartiality to do so.

Generally the best approach for a manager to take in dealing with conflicts between people is "mediation." For this reason the rest of this chapter deals with the principles of mediation. When a supervisor mediates, he or she gives up some control over just what the agreement will be but exerts considerable influence over the resolution process. In effect, the supervisor guides the two parties to discover the solution to their problem. Although mediation is preferred by managers and subordinates alike, it is actually used less frequently than arbitration. For that reason, supervisors who declare their intention to mediate a conflict are sometimes not believed. More over, because most employees have little experience with mediation, they are often unsure how to respond to a supervisor who tries to guide the process without making a final decision.

Step 2--Getting the Parties Together for an Initial Meeting. Sometime very soon after the first separate meetings the manager should get the parties together. This first meeting will most likely be quite tense. At this point the parties are unsure what the final outcome will be, and they will probably not know what will be coming next. During this first meeting the manager should draw on one fundamental principle--keep communication open. This should be reinforced in everything done in the meeting starting with the location of the meeting. The meeting should be conducted in a "neutral" setting. The seating positions of the parties should symbolically convey the impression that the conflict is a problem the two parties have to solve. One way to accomplish this is for the manager to sit across from (not between) the two individuals and close to a chalkboard or easel. This will reinforce the notion that the session is devoted to solving the problem rather than conflict with one another.

It is useful for the manager to begin this meeting by asking each party to state their positions. Active listening, where the other party must repeat back his opponent's position, is often helpful at this point. As well, the manager must be ready to try to eliminate personal comments or aggressiveness.

Once the parties have stated their demands, the manager should try to see whether the parties are willing to talk to one another about the interests that underlie their demands. By this time the manager will probably have some sort of idea what these interests are from the separate meetings. However, if the parties talk about their interests, it may improve the chances of arriving at a mutually acceptable solution.

This process can be summarized as follows:

> (1) ask each employee to state the problem,
>
> (2) ask each employee to state the other's view of the problem,
>
> (3) ask each to confirm accuracy of the other's repetition.

Step 3--Asking Each to Suggest Solutions. Once positions have been laid out and understood, it is then possible to generate alternative solutions. Here it may be useful for the manager to use brainstorming. The rules of brainstorming are simple:

> (1) The object is quantity of ideas not quality.
>
> (2) Freewheeling is encouraged, the wilder the idea the better.
>
> (3) Piggybacking (building on the ideas of others) is welcomed.
>
> (4) Above all, no evaluation or judging of ideas is permitted.

During brainstorming, the manager should be mindful that the session will probably start slowly and may seem to end at several points as the parties struggle to come up with another idea. It is important that the manager continue through these apparently unproductive intervals. The best ideas often follow directly after quiet periods. While there are no accepted rules of thumb, if one is facing an important conflict, at least a half-hour should be invested in the brainstorming phase.

Step 4--Using Recesses Strategically. One of the most powerful tools a supervisor has in dealing with conflicts is the recess. Called at the proper time, the recess can mean the difference between a lasting settlement and one that is violated before the ink is dry. Recesses can do several things.

Recesses can be used to cool off emotionally charged episodes. Initial meetings between the parties can get quite heated, and a short recess can allow the parties to collect themselves. If a recess is called for this purpose, it is important that the manager make clear that this is the reason. In addition, the parties should be encouraged to spend this time alone considering whether they are doing everything they can to solve the problem.

Recesses can be called to conduct further private inquiries about interests. This essentially is "shuttle diplomacy." A manager can use the recess to explore interests or to test tentative settlements. Earlier we distinguished between interests and demands and indicated that supervisors should conduct separate meetings in order to explore interests before getting the parties together. We also stated that eliciting interests from the party to a conflict is very difficult; people are not used to talking directly about their needs. If a manager does not have a clear picture about the interests of the parties, a recess may be helpful before the brainstorming session is conducted. For example, after the parties have stated their demands at their first mediation session together, a manager could say, "Okay, I think we are now more clear about just what each of us wants. Let's take an hour to reflect on what we have just heard and to see if we can begin to come up with some viable solutions." During this hour the manager could then shuttle between the parties, further probing them for their interests and testing ideas about how the matter might be settled.

Recesses can be used to de-escalate the conflict. The threat of escalation is always present during joint meetings. Conflicts escalate when the parties become heavily committed to their viewpoints and argue relentlessly for their demands. Calling recesses allows the manager to break the cycle of strong statements and to refocus energy from the parties to the problem.

Step 5--Focusing on Objective Facts, Areas of Mutual Need, or Mutual Goals. Excellent win-win settlements sometimes are illuminated during brainstorming sessions or are otherwise proposed by one of the parties, but the manager must be prepared to develop win-win options if they do not come from the parties. Win-win alternatives come in many forms, but the most common are listed below:

Expanding the pie. Many work conflicts hinge on a shortage of such resources as time, money, space, or machines. When this is the case, win-win agreements can be devised by expanding the resources available. For example, if two product managers are arguing over which product is given priority in manufacturing, the vice president can expand production capacity through overtime to satisfy both parties. Similarly, a conflict due to the necessity of sharing a machine can be solved by buying duplicate equipment.

Expanding the pie seems an obvious solution to many work conflicts, yet there are occasions when the way to expand is not at all clear. For example, there were severe conflicts between teams of loading dock workers until it was discovered that the dock could be widened. Similarly, word processing specialists quarreled over not being able to get things done fast enough due to an overused printer until a flexible work schedule was introduced that enabled the company to spread the use of the printer over fourteen hours per regular working day.

Nonspecific compensation. The manager should also be watchful for options in which one party can offer the other compensation for "giving in" in some sort of unrelated "coin." For example, if two assistant football coaches believe that different players should be cut from the squad to get down to the legal team size, one could offer the other a "utility" player from his own group if that coach went along with the particular coach's preference. Or a chef could offer the headwaiter a prized recipe for agreeing to hire an unwanted relative as an assistant.

Table 4
Different Interests of Two Regional Managers

	Regional Manager 1	Regional Manager 2
High Priority	Minimize expense accounts	Provide incentives on developing new accounts
Moderate Priority	Reward top performers	Reward top performers
Low Priority	Reward servicing major customers	Minimize paperwork

---

Logrolling. In some conflict situations the interests of both parties can be ranked from the most important to the least important. In this case, one party might discover that by conceding his least important interest, the most important interest of his opponent would be served. Consider the case of two regional sales managers who disagreed over the form of a new incentive pay scheme for their salespeople. The interests the two had that underlay their demands fit the priorities in Table 4. When it was realized that if each regional manager gave in on his or her least important concern, the other's most important interest could be served, a new pay plan was quickly developed that satisfied both managers' most important interests.

Bridging. In bridging neither party gets what was originally asked for, but an option is invented that satisfies the most important interests of the parties involved. Take the example of two child-care workers who had been in constant disagreement over work methods until a new supervisor arrived. One worker wanted to allow the children to watch television while the other was dead-set against it as a matter of principle. When the new supervisor interviewed the two workers, he discovered that the workers had different but potentially complementary interests. The one who opposed television was most concerned about maximizing the exposure the children received to verbal rather than audiovisual stimulation and was suspicious about the quality of verbally oriented educational television. The one who wanted to use television was most concerned that the children be exposed to a multitude of media (records, films, television, etc.). Thus the new supervisor was able to help the two people settle their differences by having the person against television pre-screen programs the other suggested before allowing the children to see them. Notice that this solution was found because one party's strongest interest was content and the other's was form.

Structural solutions. Unfortunately, not all conflicts have win-win resolutions. Accordingly, it makes little sense to explore the situation endlessly until one is found. Before settling on a win-lose alternative, however, a manager should consider the feasibility of resolving the conflict in a structural way. Basically, structural options act on the causes of work conflicts: job diversity, resource sharing, and interdependent activities. If a win-win settlement does not seem possible, one of the structural options listed below may be suitable:

(1) Moving employees between jobs to develop an appreciation of each other's point of view (job rotation can be used to develop empathy for an opponent's position).

(2) Using rules to regularize resource sharing (when a valued resource must be shared, a rule could require that it be distributed according to seniority or turn-taking or some such thing).

(3) Separating the parties to the conflict and reducing the complexity of their required work interactions (some work conflicts can be settled by simply separating the parties from one another).

Step 6--Bring Both to Agreement of Specific Steps to Resolve Conflict. When win-win options are uncovered, the rest of the process is quite simple. All that needs to be done is to work out the implementation plan and agree on some sort of follow-through. When none of the alternatives are truly win-win, the process is a bit more tricky.

Using the criteria of quality and acceptability. One way to aid in implementation is for the manager to ensure that the final settlement is the best both technically and politically. A technically sound settlement may be doomed if it lacks the acceptance of the parties. And a popular settlement that lacks technical feasibility is equally poor.

Being alert to the importance of intangibles. As the parties talk about their favored solutions, it is important for the manager to be alert to unstated preferences for intangibles. Some important intangibles include appearing tough to co-workers, having the settlement implemented quietly or in a piece-by-piece fashion, and guaranteeing that the present settlement will not serve as a precedent in the future. Intangibles are often a stumbling block because the parties are reluctant to admit how important they really are. For that reason effective mediators are very careful not to require parties to justify their personal preferences. This is a particularly difficult thing for managers to avoid when they are acting as mediators. Unfortunately, many managers are in the habit of evaluating interests.

Using tentativeness as a tool. An important consideration that every mediator must master is that commitments should be considered flexible until the very end of any negotiations. Strong, seemingly irreversible statements by the parties should be respected as limiting, but not binding. Prior to the last step in the process, virtually everything is negotiable. Therefore, the manager should be very careful to respect firm statements but to view them as flexible. It is appropriate to write down (commit to permanence) only final agreements. Statements made prior to the final step should not be referred to except in the most general terms.

Making clear the responsibilities for follow-through. The final step in mediation is to let the parties know just who else will be responsible for the enforcement of the agreement. If a written statement is filed, it is appropriate to make clear that the document will be preserved as part of the record.

Conclusion

Work conflicts are a natural result of many forces in today's organizations. Although they are potentially quite disruptive, work conflicts are not universally negative. In fact, there are instances where a little more conflict increases effectiveness. This chapter focuses on a manager's responsibility to settle conflicts between subordinates. As in every problem situation, the first task is information gathering. Initially it is best to interview each of the conflicting parties to obtain data and begin to create a conducive climate for the negotiations. Following that, the manager should strive to keep communications between the parties open and to facilitate mutual problem solving. At the heart of the process is the search for the interests that underlie the demands of the parties in order to discover win-win options for the settlement.

References

Bazerman, M. H., & Neale, M. A. 1983. Heuristics in negotiation. In M. H. Bazerman & R. J. Lewicki (Eds.), *Negotiating in Organizations*. Beverly Hills, CA: Sage, 1983.

Filey, A. C. 1975. *Interpersonal Conflict Resolution*. Glenview, IL: Scott, Foresman and Company.

Fisher, R., & Brown, S. 1988. *Getting Together*. Boston: Houghton-Mifflin.

Fisher, R., & Ury, W. 1981. *Getting to Yes*. Boston: Houghton-Mifflin.

Lewicki, R. J., & Litterer, J. A. 1985. *Negotiation*. Homewood, IL: Irwin.

Mintzberg, H. 1975. The manager's job: Folklore and fact. *Harvard Business Review* 53: 49-61.

Pruitt, D. G. 1981. *Negotiation Behavior*. New York: Academic Press.

Pruitt, D. G. 1983. Achieving integrative agreements. In M. H. Bazerman & R. J. Lewicki (Eds.), *Negotiating in Organizations*. Beverly Hills, CA: Sage.

Robbins, S. P. 1978. Conflict management and conflict resolution are not synonymous terms. *California Management Review* 21: 67-75.

Savage, G. T., J. D. Blair, & R. L. Sorenson. 1989. Consider both relationships and substance when negotiating strategically. *Academy of Management Executive* 3: 37-48.

Shea, G. F. 1975. *Creative Negotiating*. Boston: CBI Publishing.

Sheppard. B. H. 1983. Managers as inquisitors. In M. H. Bazerman & R. J. Lewicki (Eds.), *Negotiating in Organizations*. Beverly Hills, CA: Sage.

Thomas, K. W., & L. R. Pondy. 1977. Toward an 'intent' model of conflict management among principal-parties. *Human Relations* 30: 1089-1102.

Thomas, K. W., & W. H. Schmidt. 1976. A survey of managerial interests with respect to conflict. *Academy of Management Journal* 19: 315-318.

Tushman, M. L. 1977. A political approach to organizations. *Academy of Management Review* 2: 206-216.

Walton, R. E. 1969. *Interpersonal Peacemaking*. Reading, MA: Addison-Wesley.

Flow Diagram for Managing Conflict Interactive Case

Detach this page from your book before you begin the Interactive Case. As you make each decision, write the decision point number following the GO TO statement in the appropriate rectangle before you turn to that page. If you are referred to a previous decision point, circle the decision point number you last wrote and proceed to the first uncircled rectangle above that one in your flow diagram. Do not erase the numbers once you have written them. You will not necessarily fill all the rectangles.

Start		6th Decision		12th Decision	
1st Decision		7th Decision		13th Decision	
2nd Decision		8th Decision		14th Decision	
3rd Decision		9th Decision		15th Decision	
4th Decision		10th Decision		16th Decision	
5th Decision		11th Decision		17th Decision	over

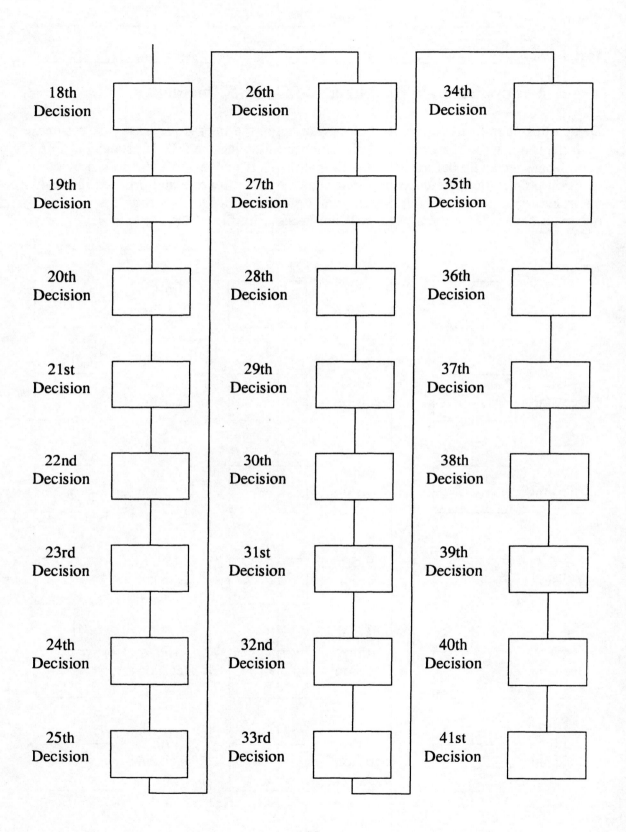

18th
Decision

19th
Decision

20th
Decision

21st
Decision

22nd
Decision

23rd
Decision

24th
Decision

25th
Decision

26th
Decision

27th
Decision

28th
Decision

29th
Decision

30th
Decision

31st
Decision

32nd
Decision

33rd
Decision

34th
Decision

35th
Decision

36th
Decision

37th
Decision

38th
Decision

39th
Decision

40th
Decision

41st
Decision

INTERACTIVE CASE

You are the general manager for a factory that produces brushes for a large health products firm. The plant is located in the southern part of the United States, is non-unionized, and has 109 full-time employees on its payroll. Your primary responsibility is to meet a weekly production quota supplied by the corporate headquarters. In two years as general manager, you met your quota 63 percent of the time. Although this is only average by corporate standards, it is quite good given the antiquated equipment you have to work with. Your boss understands these constraints, but little can be done because the brush market is considered a "loss-leader" in the corporate strategic plan. All in all, you are satisfied with your operation, and you enjoy the respect and admiration your employees have for you.

Today you have one pressing problem to solve. It deals with a work conflict between your internal auditor (Phyllis Smart) and one of your production supervisors (Virgil Stonehill). You decide to deal with this situation right away because it seems to have a direct and important impact on the effectiveness of the entire plant.

Phyllis Smart is the internal auditor of your plant. Her job is to break down weekly quota figures into discrete schedules and monitor progress against these standards. She is young and somewhat inexperienced, but you think she has made fine progress in her first 22 months with the organization. After completing her degree in industrial administration from a university, she was trained at headquarters before being assigned to your plant. She is an excellent analyst and a loyal subordinate.

Virgil Stonehill is the supervisor of your dental brush line. He supervises 18 people and has worked at the plant for 13 years. He worked his way up to his present position from machine operator to maintenance specialist to supervisor. Virgil is 53 years old and a retired Navy machinist.

Virgil is not one of your best supervisors. While he has a very good relationship with his crew, his line has had one of the worst quality records in the plant. Although this may be due in large part to the old equipment he has to use, you do not think that he is adequately quality-conscious. Three months ago a very serious quality problem occurred. Twenty thousand toothbrushes were produced that failed quality standards. This caused your plant to be rated the second lowest in performance within the corporation during that quarter. Following that incident, you conducted a full-scale investigation that discovered that Virgil had miscalculated the setup time necessary to meet weekly quotas. Although his line's machinery is old, he apparently did not account for these limitations and pressed his crew for a level of output that the machines could not bear. You learned of the conflict between Phyllis and Virgil through the following memo:

TO: You
FR: Phyllis Smart, Internal Auditor
RE: Production Reports

Mr. Virgil Stonehill has decided to obstruct my efforts to maximize the efficiency of the plant. I expressly informed him that he needed to submit his weekly production figures to me each Monday by noon. For the past two weeks he did not do so until Thursday morning. This caused serious problems in the procurement of dyes. This resulted in an overstock of clear brushes (now at 31 percent over the standard of 60 days). Please instruct Mr. Stonehill to comply with my information requirements.

What would you do now?

A. Call Phyllis into your office to clarify her memo. (GO TO 231)

B. Call Virgil in to get his side of the story. (GO TO 235)

C. Call both parties into your office to settle this issue face to face. (GO TO 145)

D. Instruct Virgil to get his information to Phyllis by noon Mondays. (GO TO 177)

E. Ask some other supervisors if they have difficulty complying with Phyllis' requirements to have their weekly figures in by Monday noon. (GO TO 252)

MODULE 10

Organizational Politics

MODULE READING

Organizational politics refers to attempts by individuals and groups to influence others by using methods that are not "officially" approved by the organization. Often, the term has a bad connotation. One reason is that individuals can use political techniques that are coercive or manipulative to pursue goals that are not in the best interest of the organization. Thus, many of us have very negative feelings toward the things we associate with politics: favoritism, selfish interests, and dirty tricks. Yet organizational politics in the broadest sense are not necessarily dirty or even unjust. They simply are a way to get things done outside the normal chain of command. In fact, managers cannot accomplish much without using politics. It is not only useful, it is essential. This does not excuse the excesses, of course, but it is important to consider organizational politics a tool as well as a problem.

The Power Gap

Playing politics is essential because managers are often not given enough authority to do their jobs. Consider the following examples. If a manager has an employee who is not performing and whose performance cannot be improved, can the manager fire the employee? Similarly, is the manager given full rein when he or she needs support from a staff person who is reluctant to help? How about policies that are put in force that are silly, even counterproductive? Can a manager really oppose them without jeopardizing his or her job? Most managers know that they do not have all the authority they would like to have. We call this difference between the power a manager needs to do a good job and the amount of authority he or she is given the power gap.

Power gaps differ from job to job, of course, but most managers know that they have a power gap in their work. It is one of the frustrating aspects of being a manager. Faced with a power gap, one successful remedy is to become political. This may not set well with some people, but it is a fact of organizational life.

We now examine some of the typical situations that require a manager to act politically. These situations fall into three groups: relations with superiors, relations with subordinates, and lateral relations.

Relations with Superiors. Most directives that come from people above a manager in the chain of command help rather than hurt getting the job done. Yet there are occasions when senior people make decisions that create real problems for the manager.

When this happens, it is difficult to know just what to do. Senior people are privy to information that those lower in the organization do not have, making it difficult to question decisions from above. At the same time, the individual manager is the expert when it comes to his or her own area of responsibility, so when decisions are made, an individual manager has a right to question whether the directive is suitable to the local problems of the group. Clearly a manager faces a significant power gap whenever he or she experiences conflicts with people above him or her in the hierarchy. To have any impact, it is sometimes necessary for the manager to exercise a considerable amount of informal influence.

Relations with Subordinates. Managers also experience a power gap in dealing with their own people. In certain circumstances, some subordinates may even have more power than their managers. Consider the following types of employees:

(1) experts in a particular part of the work,

(2) employees who are so popular with others that if they were disciplined, it would have serious repercussions,

(3) individuals who are almost impossible to replace,

(4) key people in the workflow.

Such individuals as these may be difficult to confront without some political maneuvering.

Lateral Relations. Most managers have a host of people in other work groups on whom they rely. Other groups provide them with the raw materials or support they need in order to perform well. If these other groups do not cooperate, managers cannot order them to do so. The manager may have no recourse but to use politics. Consider purchasing people, for example. If a manager needs a new piece of capital equipment, he or she will need their help even if there is a budget for it. Other managers in the department are also important. They can make the situation very difficult if relationships are poor.

Personal Power Resources

Power is the ability to influence others. Every position in an organization carries some power with it, but people can supplement this formal power with personal power resources. There are four types of personal power: information power, expert power, reward/punishment power, and relationship power.

Information power. Power accrues to those who have inside information about how the organization really works. Often there is more to understanding the organization than just the organization chart and policy manuals. Some policies are ignored; certain people are more or less influential than their position in the chart would suggest. Information about the following can be a source of power:

(1) the history of the organization,

(2) who the key people are,

(3) how certain people will react to particular situations,

(4) which policies are important and which are not,

(5) other employees' needs, interests, and ambitions,

(6) what a particular decision means for the future,

(7) the nature of the relationships among key people,

(8) the jargon of the organization,

(9) what the critical tasks and departments are,

(10) how committed others are to various positions on an issue.

Not surprisingly, information power is often related to seniority. The longer one has been with an organization, the more he or she knows about it. However, people do not get information power by just being around for a long time. It is cultivated by asking questions, by watching carefully as events unfold, and by testing ideas in order to learn more.

Managers with information power can reduce their power gap tremendously. If a manager knows his or her boss's background, friends, and ambitions, it gives an edge in upwards relations. Similarly, if a manager knows that a staff person he or she has to work with is not thought highly of and will soon be transferred, it enables action to be taken accordingly. In short, information power allows making the best use of the other personal power resources the manager possesses.

Expert power. A second source of personal power comes from expertise. If a manager has knowledge or skills that are both critical to the work and difficult to replace, then he or she can parlay that expertise into influence. All of us have seen many situations where people thought to be experts can persuade others.

One does not necessarily have to be an expert in order to have expert power. It is what other people think the individual knows or can do that really matters. Expert power is helpful in reducing the power gap. A boss is much more apt to defer to a subordinate who is seen as knowledgeable. Subordinates respect their manager more if they think he or she is technically able. And expert power is probably the most commonly used resource in lateral relationships.

Reward/punishment power. The ability to reward and punish is another power resource. All managers have some influence over merit pay and promotional decisions but often neglect the other ways they can reward others. For example, managers reward others every time they:

(1) give interesting or "visible" assignments,

(2) provide recognition in front of one's peers,

(3) excuse someone from an undesired requirement,

(4) write a congratulatory letter,

(5) introduce someone to a high official,

(6) interpret a policy so that it favors an individual.

Similarly, managers do not generally recognize all the ways they can punish others. For example, managers punish when they:

(1) ignore someone's call for help,

(2) supervise too closely,

(3) give unpopular assignments,

(4) allow someone to make a mistake they know about in advance,

(5) call attention to someone's failures,

(6) criticize someone's work.

Just as managers sometimes forget the various ways they reward or punish subordinates, they seldom think about the ways they do so in lateral or upward relations. Think, for example, how a manager might reward or punish the boss. Think also about what sorts of rewards or punishments might be used in dealing with others at the same level.

Most managers underestimate their abilities to reward and punish people other than their direct subordinates; however, there are often opportunities to do so. Take the case of a staff person with whom a manager has to work. Assume that the manager is not getting the sort of service from that person that is necessary. From an authority standpoint the manager has little recourse; the staff person does not report to him or her. It is easy to conclude that the manager is powerless in this situation, but if you consider what resources the manager has and what problems and needs the staff person has, it can open up possibilities. The staff member may be experiencing a lack of visibility, and the manager could help him or her meet certain key people in the organization. The staff person may be having difficulties obtaining some software, and the manager could lend him some. The staff member may be having a problem getting the budget he or she needs, and the manager could lobby for his or her case or support the staff person's efforts with discretely placed testimonials. A manager can reward people (or punish them) even when he or she does not have authority over them. It simply requires a careful analysis of needs and resources.

Relationship power. No personal power resource is better known than relationship power. We often hear of "old boy networks" or the saying, "It's not so much what you know as who you know." Such comments reflect an important political reality. It is easier (and more rewarding) to work with people who are liked, respected, and admired than those who are not liked or known. Additionally, most managers find that work conflicts are much easier to work through with friends than within the context of formal relationships.

Who a manager knows, and more importantly who he or she can work with harmoniously is important. Many successful managers could not get anything done if they did not have co-workers, bosses, and subordinates with whom they had solid relationships.

There are two dimensions to relationship power. One is goal compatibility and the other is interpersonal trust. Goal compatibility refers to the mutuality of interests and objectives. For example, two co-workers may develop a relationship based on their mutual interest in seeing a particular product succeed or in a shared vision for the organization. Interpersonal trust grows out of a relationship such that each party comes to count on the other even when the other may have incentives not to help or assist. For example, if a manager risks not completing an assignment to help a friend in need, then that is a demonstration of interpersonal trust. Similarly, a manager demonstrates trust when he or she "saves" a colleague from making a mistake, even when that mistake would make the manager look good personally.

The Use of Personal Power Resources

How does a manager influence someone over whom he or she has no authority? There are several means to choose between, some with a high likelihood of success and some with a low likelihood of success. We will start with those uses of political tactics that are seldom effective.

Ineffective Political Tactics. Certain political tactics have a relatively low likelihood of success. They either create ill feelings in their wake, thus promising at best short-term gains. Or, they are likely to fail to result in successful influence even in the short run.

Tactic 1--the use of powerless persuasion. Probably the most common influence attempt is the persuasive appeal. It may be directed upward to one's boss to get him or her to change priorities. It may be focused laterally at peers to build support for a pet project. And it may be targeted downward to attempt to elicit a higher commitment to objectives.

Persuasion is so common because it is a familiar tool of authority. Most authoritative communication is of a persuasive nature. The difference in using persuasion as a political tool is that there are not the sanctions attached to it that there are with authority. When your boss "persuades" you that a task needs to be completed by a certain date, there is the implied message that if you do so, you will gain approval and with it other rewards. In contrast, political persuasion has no such implicit sanction.

It is this lack of sanctioning with powerless political persuasion that accounts for its ineffectiveness. Unless a manager can mobilize power in support of the persuasive appeal, it will fall on deaf ears.

Tactic 2--the use of powerless pressure. The frequency with which pressure is used as a political tactic varies from organization to organization, but in most cases, it is relatively rare. The reason is that the use of threats and pressure seldom yields good long-term results.

The use of pressure generally results in bad feelings. No one likes to be pressured into doing things, and even if there is short-term compliance, there will likely be hard feelings that will have to be dealt with at some point. Moreover, the use of pressure is often seen as a sign of weakness rather than a sign of strength. People who use pressure frequently often take on the undesirable reputation of being insecure and unstable.

Powerless pressure even fails to result in short-term results. Without being able to back up a threat with some sort of power, it will often be ignored, and the manager will suffer all the negative aftereffects with no gains whatsoever.

To summarize, pressure is generally not a very effective method of political influence. It promises at best positive, short-term results. Even these are in jeopardy if the individual does not use other power resources to back up the threat.

160

Tactic 3--the use of manipulation. Of all the forms of political influence none arouses more concern and derision than manipulation. Basically manipulation involves concealing the attempt to influence. This takes two forms: the manipulation of situations and information.

The object of situational manipulation is to create the conditions that influence the target to some predetermined point of view. For example, a situational manipulator could orchestrate a staff meeting such that the people who agree with him are given more time to argue their case. Or a situation could be created that penalizes those who oppose a particular position.

The use of information to manipulate others is unfortunately quite common. Information can be distorted, released at the proper time, or withheld indefinitely as a means of manipulation. Similarly, manipulators can disguise themselves as impartial advisors but actually give slanted advice.

Manipulation suffers from one very important flaw--it is deceitful. If discovered, the manipulator becomes an outcast trusted by no one, his or her credibility forever lost. Candidly, there are probably many more attempts at manipulation than are ever discovered. The risks of discovery are high, though, and many people choose not to engage in manipulation because it is seen as sleazy.

Tactic 4--the use of escalation. Escalation is taking an issue to a higher authority for resolution. There are several reasons that it is generally ineffective. First, escalation is generally seen as a sign of failure. One does not typically escalate unless all other political tactics have been used. Second, one can never be sure of the outcome when one escalates. Even assurances stated before the fact don't guarantee the outcome. Third, escalation is organizational high drama. Other people soon discover what has happened, and the escalator seldom emerges with an unblemished reputation. Finally, escalation smacks of a despicable childhood behavior--tattling.

Effective Political Tactics. There are many tactics that hold much more promise. In general, they involve the intelligent use of personal power.

Tactic 1--the powerful use of persuasion. As we have seen, powerless persuasion is ineffective. If a manager persuades from a relatively strong power base, he or she holds much more potential to influence others. Some of the ways that persuasion can be strengthened with personal power include:

(1) Framing the appeal as appropriate within some compelling version of organizational realities. Assume that a manager is trying to convince an office manager that he or she needs more word processing support. The manager could frame the appeal in terms of a rumor that the office is currently under scrutiny by

senior management. This use of information power can add to the likelihood of success.

(2) Framing the appeal to take advantage of the manager's relative expertise. Expert power can increase the effectiveness of the appeal unless others who are equally expert, oppose the manager.

(3) Framing the appeal to the target's needs, interests, and problems rather than to the manager's. This essentially adds a personal reward or punishment element to the manager's request. By doing this, the manager is attaching a direct and attractive benefit to compliance.

(4) Framing the appeal as an investment in an ongoing relationship. Relationships carry with them the norm of reciprocity. People do favors for their colleagues either to compensate them for past favors received or in the anticipation of future favors in return.

Powerful persuasion is by no means the answer to every political situation. It requires that the target listens to what the manager has to say and respects the power put behind the appeal.

Tactic 2--the powerful use of pressure. Although pressure seldom reaps positive, long-term results, one should never exercise pressure without the support of an adequate personal power base. Otherwise the attempt at pressure will be seen as an idle threat. Some of the ways that one can strengthen pressure include the following:

(1) Framing the threat as appropriate within some compelling vision of organizational realities. For example, the manager could warn that he or she has inside information that certain bad things will happen if the target person does not comply.

(2) Framing the threat to take advantage of one's own relative expertise. Assume that a manager is knowledgeable about the market conditions relative to a new product, and wants to exert pressure against its release. In this case the manager could begin with a demonstration of his or her expertise and proceed to give an assessment of the reasons that the release will result in failure.

(3) Framing the threat to the target's needs, interests, and problems rather than one's own. This makes the threat more personally vital. For example, if a manager wants to stop a careless employee who is financially dependent on overtime wages from continuing to use unsafe methods, the manager could threaten to withhold his overtime unless he complies. Similarly, if the target values a relationship that the manager has some control over, the manager

162

could frame the threat in terms of the actions that could be taken to undermine that relationship.

(4) Framing the threat as a personal assault. By demonstrating that the undesired behavior is jeopardizing a relationship, a manager adds clout to the threat if the relationship is valued by the target.

Tactic 3--the use of coalitions. Alliances, interest groups, and coalitions are important factors in the political reality of any organization. People get together to support or oppose things, and effective politicians realize that they must form alliances when issues require more power than they themselves possess.

Tactic 4--the use of alternative relationships. Most political situations arise because a manager is dependent on someone either above, below, or at the same organizational level. So far we have described the political methods of managing those dependencies. However, a manager can also deal with dependencies by avoiding them altogether. For example, assume that a manager is not getting adequate support from a centralized computer center. One way of dealing with this problem is purchasing a microcomputer for the office or subcontracting the service "on the outside."

Most managers can think of ways to use alternative relationships in lateral relations and relations with subordinates, but it is sometimes harder to conceive of how this tactic can be used with superiors. Actually, the use of alternative relationships is not uncommon with bosses. Many managers build relations with senior managers who are not directly above them in the chain of command. Known alternatively as sponsors or mentors, these senior people act as counselors, advisors, and protectors much in the same way as one's own manager otherwise would.

Having a sponsor poses special problems. First, the manager must realize that the bond between mentor and protege carries with it certain expectations. The person being mentored is expected to act upon advice given, support the mentor in dealing with his or her peers and superiors, and use the sponsor's time selectively. Second, care must be taken not to alienate either one's own manager or the sponsor. This can be tricky if one receives conflicting directions. Finally, the choice of a sponsor is a critical decision. More than one manager has erred by "hitching his wagon to a falling star."

The Timing of Advocacy

Conflicts abound in every organization. New policies, reorganizations, changes in strategic direction, and personnel decisions are seldom popular with everyone. Yet to be an effective politician, a manager must be careful about just when, if ever, to take sides. Clearly one of the most difficult and elusive challenges one faces in playing

163

politics is exercising good timing. Many of us have a serious tendency of acting impulsively and not being sufficiently patient. As we have seen, political tactics enacted without an adequate reservoir of personal power are doomed to failure, and that often means waiting until power has been mobilized before acting.

Timing Considerations Before Contentious Decisions Have Been Made. Issues of consequence tend to polarize organizations. During the debate on these issues, some people line up in favor of or in opposition to the alternatives under debate, and others remain uncommitted to any alternative. It is at just such times that a manager should be especially vigilant to who is on what side. Considering the power each person brings to the debate often allows a sensitive manager to predict what decision will be made.

It is critical to remember that debates create coalitions. Individuals who share a side are unified by those commitments, and each finds such support rewarding. Similarly, people on opposite sides often resent each other and find their opponents' positions punitive. This implies that one's position on issues of conflict has political consequences far broader than whether or not one was on the winning side.

Assume, for example, that a manager wants a particular product introduced. His or her view is shared by a number of people, but the boss is opposed. In this sort of situation, pushing hard for introduction may solidify the manager's relationship with those who share his or her view but only at the risk of alienating the boss.

Because the risks of alienating key people during such debates are so high, some individuals prefer to remain uncommitted even though they favor a particular position. The strength of any commitment is a function of how clearly, irrevocably, and publicly the declaration is made. Consequently, a manager can remain uncommitted by not making clear, public, and irrevocable statements on the issue. This gives the manager flexibility to make a stand at some later time when the situation and the risks are more clear. In summary, then, declaring support or opposition to an issue under discussion is politically risky. It may earn you friends whose future support may be helpful, but it may also earn you enemies that you neither want nor need. Accordingly, it is generally prudent to time the stands a manager makes during debates to minimize these risks. Remaining uncommitted often gives an opportunity to test alternative political stands and reduce the risks of making the wrong choices.

Timing Considerations After Unwanted Decisions Have Been Announced. The politics associated with a debate do not end when the decision is announced and formalized. Those who originally supported the chosen option are filled with energy to make it a success, but others seldom share the enthusiasm. Those who were early opponents are expected to "climb on board" and make the decision successful, but they typically need encouragement to do so. And those who did not feel that their

164

voice was heard during the debate are especially annoyed, requiring even higher levels of encouragement to support the final decision.

The most important thing for a manager to realize about this post-decision period is that the winning coalition is strengthened politically by having been victorious. Those originally uncommitted have swung to the winning side and can counter any opposition by declaring that the debate has ended.

A manager must move very cautiously in opposition to a decision that has weathered a debate, but he or she does have two options. The manager can quietly build power that can be drawn upon in an attempt to mobilize opposition to the decision. Or the manager can build a case supporting a modification of the original decision. We will discuss each of these tactics.

Tactic 1--build power. As we have discussed, the victors in any debate generally enjoy a considerable amount of power. However, there are three groups of employees who remain potential allies behind anyone who wants to attempt a reversal: those who originally opposed the decision; those who did not feel represented in the decision process; and those who are dismayed to discover that the decision did not result in what it promised. To mobilize opposition, these are the groups a manager could turn to.

A manager should be prepared to move very quietly in building power in opposition to a decision of this kind. Immediately after the decision is announced, the victorious coalition is commonly poised to deal sternly with opposition, and the substantial power they possess at this point makes it unwise to be branded as "uncooperative." An unobtrusive posture is certainly warranted.

Tactic 2--build a rational case for a modification. Few major decisions are ever totally reversed. Total reversals make the original decision illegitimate and are entirely too great a threat to the face of the original proponents. The best a manager can usually hope for is something that can appear to be a modification, even if it is essentially a reversal. To accomplish these reduced goals, it is critical to mobilize a rational argument that makes the modification superior to the original decision.

The three most common rational arguments in favor of modification are as follows:

(1) the conditions are different than those considered in the original decision,

(2) the decision as it stands conflicts with important organizational norms or practices in ways that were not originally foreseen,

(3) the implementation of the decision needs to be fine-tuned to local conditions.

Whichever of these arguments a manager chooses to use, it should be framed in such a way that the original advocates are excused for any oversight. In addition, a manager should avoid using arguments that were used in the initial debate.

Clearly, turning around an unwanted decision is one of the most challenging of all political problems. Like any political move, it requires personal power. However, it also puts a premium on quiet coalition building and persuasion skills. Timing is vital at each point, for the opponents of modification are both strong and initially resistant to opposition.

Summary

Organizational politics can provide a manager with some of his or her greatest challenges. Everyone experiences a power gap, and the only recourse is to supplement authority with power. This can be a slow process, but the normal methods of influence without power are ineffectual without it. In any event, some tactics have little to recommend them. And others have a great deal more potential. Debates over alternative policies and organizational directions are heated politically. During such debates, managers should be careful about making stands that will jeopardize their political standing. After decisions have been made, new challenges arise.

References

Allen, R. W., Madison, D. L., Porter, L. W., Renwick, P. A., & B. T. Mayes. 1979. Organizational politics: Tactics and characteristics of its actors. *California Management Review* 22: 77-83.

Brass, D. J. 1984. Being in the right place: A structural analysis of individual influence in an organization. *Administrative Science Quarterly* 29: 518-539.

Cavanagh, G. F., Moberg, D. J., & Velasquez, M. 1981. The ethics of organizational politics. *Academy of Management Review* 6: 363-374.

Gandz, J., & Murray, V. V. 1980. The experience of workplace politics. *Academy of Management Journal* 23: 237-251.

Kipnis, D. 1976. *The powerholders*. Chicago: University of Chicago Press.

Kipnis, D., Schmidt, S. M., & Wilkinson, I. 1980. Intraorganizational influence tactics: Explorations in getting one's way. *Journal of Applied Psychology* 65: 440-452.

Kotter, J. P. 1977. Power, dependence and effective management. *Harvard Business Review* 55: 125-136.

Kotter, J. P. 1985. *Power and influence*. New York: Free Press.

Pfeffer, J. 1981. *Power in Organizations*. New York: Pittman.

Pfeffer, J. 1992. *Managing with Power*. Boston: Harvard.

Porter, L. W., Allen, R., & Angle, H. L. 1981. The politics of upward influence. In L. L. Cummings & B. M. Staw (Eds.), *Research in Organizational Behavior*, Vol. 3. New York: JAI Press.

Yukl, G., & Falbe, C. M. 1990. Influence tactics and objectives in upward, downward, and lateral influence attempts, *Journal of Applied Psychology* 75: 132-140.

Course:_____   Name:_____

Instructor:_____   Date:_____

Flow Diagram for Politics Interactive Case

Detach this page from your book before you begin the Interactive Case. As you make each decision, write the decision point number following the GO TO statement in the appropriate rectangle before you turn to that page. If you are referred to a previous decision point, circle the decision point number you last wrote and proceed to the first uncircled rectangle above that one in your flow diagram. Do not erase the numbers once you have written them. You will not necessarily fill all the rectangles.

Start		6th Decision		12th Decision	
1st Decision		7th Decision		13th Decision	
2nd Decision		8th Decision		14th Decision	
3rd Decision		9th Decision		15th Decision	
4th Decision		10th Decision		16th Decision	
5th Decision		11th Decision		17th Decision	

over

169

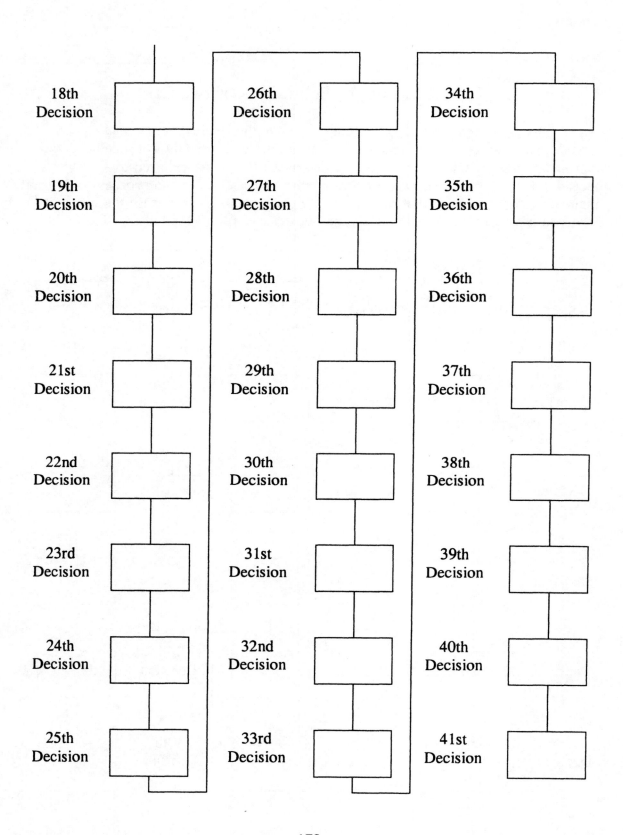

18th Decision

19th Decision

20th Decision

21st Decision

22nd Decision

23rd Decision

24th Decision

25th Decision

26th Decision

27th Decision

28th Decision

29th Decision

30th Decision

31st Decision

32nd Decision

33rd Decision

34th Decision

35th Decision

36th Decision

37th Decision

38th Decision

39th Decision

40th Decision

41st Decision

170

INTERACTIVE CASE

You are the Sales Manager of the Automation Systems Group of the Fluid Products Division of the Blake-Emerson Corporation, a Fortune 500 conglomerate. The Fluid Products Division manufactures and sells pumps, valves, cylinders, and compressors for industrial use. Emerson Billingsworth is the Director of the Fluid Products Division, and Bill Banquet, your boss, reports to him as Marketing Manager. An organization chart appears below.

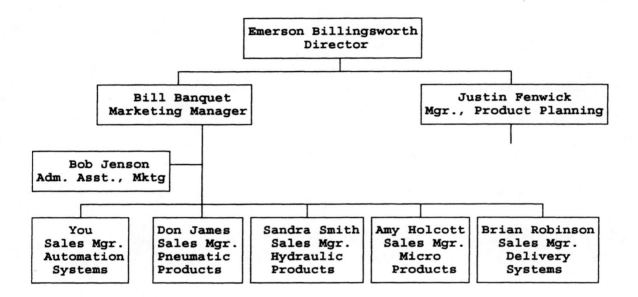

Banquet has five subordinates including you. Each of the others is responsible for a different product line: pneumatics, hydraulics, microproducts (miniature valves and cylinders), and delivery systems (pumps, tubing, storage vessels, etc.). Your product line is the most diverse, for you sell automation systems (i.e., integrated clusters of valves and cylinders used with tools in automated machinery). Such systems are used in packaging, customized fabrication, and robotics.

You have eight sales engineers reporting to you. Each is responsible for different sets of industrial applications, and each travels 50 percent of the time. They are a close-knit group, and your relationship with them is extraordinarily good considering that you have been with the corporation and in your position for only eight months. Your predecessor left the firm in what some describe as a messy situation arising from a difference of opinion with Bill Banquet's predecessor. Banquet himself has only been Marketing Manager for two months having formerly served as Sales Manager of the Delivery Systems Group.

Your relationship with Banquet seems fine, although he lacks the sense of humor on which you pride yourself. He is very bright and is clearly cautious about making waves until he has established himself in his position.

The performance of the Fluid Products Division has been very poor for the last 18 months. This has resulted in layoffs in most parts of the organization dealing with hydraulic and pneumatic products. The staff organization was surprisingly spared these cuts. In Product Planning, for example, no layoffs have yet occurred. Indeed, this department has had increasing influence due its central role in cost control during these hard times. This unit was known to be a favorite of top division management. Fortunately, your sales organization was relatively unscathed by the cuts. Only one sales engineer was laid off, and that was a year before you became Sales Manager. The reason your department has fared so well is that the demand for automation systems maintained acceptable levels throughout the downturn.

Two days ago a bombshell memo appeared in your morning mail. A copy appears below:

Memorandum

TO: Sales Managers, Fluid Products Division
FR: Emerson Billingsworth, Director
RE: New Policy

As you know, the economic performance of our division has suffered at the hands of the worst recession that has hit our industry in recent memory. A central factor that has contributed to our poor performance is our lack of control of inventory costs. At the recommendation of Justin Fenwick, and after careful consultation with several managers, I have decided to put in place a new policy. Add the following to your policy manual:

> "To facilitate production planning and to get inventory costs under control, all sales engineers must specify their monthly expected sales in all product categories. Any actual sales over the expected figure by 20 percent or more must be back-ordered if a stock-out is experienced. Any sales under the expected figure by 20 percent will require a negative adjustment against the unit's reported sales volume goals in direct proportion to the additional carrying costs that accrue."

I ask your cooperation in complying with this new policy. Mr. Fenwick's people have developed forms that should simplify reporting your monthly sales estimates. Those for next month should be submitted by the 15th to his office.

You are very concerned about the effects of this new policy on your group. Your product line is the most diverse among all those in the division, and sales are the most uneven. Thus, the new policy places extraordinary pressure on your subordinates to plan in the face of almost incalculable uncertainties. You know with certainty that if you enforce this policy, there will be many instances of overages and underages. This will surely discourage efforts to develop new accounts unless these new customers have product needs that are easy to estimate.

In general, how would you approach this situation?

A. Diplomatically oppose the new policy as it applies to your unique circumstances. Petition for an exemption. (GO TO 282)

B. Gather information about what this policy means to your peers, your boss, and the staff unit involved (Product Planning). (GO TO 379)

C. Instruct your subordinates what to do about his new policy. (GO TO 290)

MODULE 11

Managing Change

MODULE READING

No skill is any more vital to a manager than the ability to successfully implement change. The pace of change is accelerating in most organizations, and managers who do not possess change management skills will surely be left behind. There are basically three types of organizational changes: administrative changes, technical changes, and changes in the goods and services the organization produces. Administrative changes include reorganizations, personnel moves, and changes in policies and procedures. Technical changes emerge from advancements in what is known about how to do the work. This includes such current developments as the introduction of computers, the automation of the production facility, and the improvement of the techniques of dealing with clients. The introduction of new products and services also requires careful supervision. Some organizations face this type of change on almost a monthly basis.

In this module reading, we outline a number of principles that are extremely useful in implementing all of these types of organizational changes. We first describe the common reasons employees resist organizational changes. Resistance arises for many different reasons, and it is critical that managers respond carefully to the resisters according to the reasons for their resistance. Next we describe the most important single decision a manager has to make about implementing a change--whether it should be implemented through delegation or through a top-down process in which the manager makes most of the implementation decisions. Finally, we detail some of the specific steps that should be used in each of these types of implementation patterns.

Resistance to Change

Every experienced manager realizes that most organizational changes will be greeted by some resistance. However, too few managers plan systematically for resistance or respond to it effectively. Instead they tend to view resistance as a sign of misguided loyalty, selfishness, or failure on the part of the resisters to see the "big picture." This viewpoint can cause the manager serious problems. The reasons for resistance extend far beyond these factors, and the manager who does not devote careful thought to them is likely to be in serious trouble. The four most common reasons employees resist change are:

175

(1) a fear that the change will require them to lose things they value personally,

(2) a perceived threat to one's organizational vested interests,

(3) a misunderstanding of the implications of the change,

(4) an honest belief that the change does not make sense for the organization.

Fear of a Personal Loss. Most changes threaten some people personally. Technical changes like the automation of the assembly line, the introduction of a computerized information system, or the use of a new chemical in the production process may arouse real personal fears. Administrative changes and new product introductions have a similar impact.

The first question that many employees ask about a coming organizational change is probably, "Will the change eliminate my job?" Even if assurances are given, doubts and concerns will likely persist until late in the implementation process. Some employees have personal experience with job loss precipitated by an organizational change or have heard stories that keep the fears alive.

There is no easy way to contend with resistance motivated by a fear of a loss of position and income. People want a guarantee of their job security, but a manager cannot always do that with total honesty. Changes always involve some uncertainties; in some cases, a manager may not even be sure of the precise directions the change will take. This makes absolute guarantees difficult and may damage credibility if the manager must later terminate someone whose job is made obsolete by the change.

As a general rule, when honesty and giving guarantees conflict, a manager should opt for honesty. If possible, though, a carefully planned and worded statement may be provided that offers some assurance without going further than what possibly can be delivered. For example, a manager can offer to do everything in his or her power to protect jobs or can give guarantees conditional on employee cooperation with the change.

A related type of fear that employees experience when faced with a change is due to a disruption in the social equilibrium. Most employees settle into comfortable social situations at work. They adjust to what others expect of them and find stable roles within their immediate work groups. Many changes disrupt this social stability. They require employees to work with new people, they break up cohesive work groups, and they force employees to have to make entirely new social adjustments.

What makes social disequilibrium so difficult to deal with is that employees rarely see it as the cause of their discomfort. Most employees consider themselves self-reliant and may not be aware of the satisfaction they get from their immediate work group.

Cut off from their old social bonds at work, they may feel disoriented and may take out their frustrations on the change itself.

The best way to manage this cause of resistance is to plan for it. A manager can provide time and support for new co-workers to adjust, facilitate communication with previous contacts, and encourage new friendships to form.

Threat to Organizational Vested Interests. Employees may also resist changes that threaten the advantages their jobs offer them under the present system. Every position offers certain vested interests. A particular employee may not have to work especially hard, may be provided with an excess of resources, may be the beneficiary of certain favors, or may be in a position of considerable influence. Changes often threaten these benefits.

This type of resistance arises more frequently with administrative changes than technical or new product changes. Reorganizations and changes in administrative procedures almost always alter which jobs are most influential and may lead to a reallocation of privileges and benefits.

Again, this cause of resistance is best dealt with by careful planning. Those whose vested interests are threatened can be pinpointed, and their losses can potentially be lessened. In some cases a manager could even negotiate the particulars of new assignments to soften the blow of a change. For example, those who lose influence because of a change could be offered larger offices or more clerical support in order to "buy" their support for the change. Clearly such accommodations are not always feasible. In such cases, those adversely affected should be monitored carefully so they do not engage in disruptive political activity in an effort to sabotage the change.

Misunderstandings of the Implications of the Change. Employees also resist change when they do not understand how the change will impact them and the organization. Commonly this is due to a lack of trust in the initiators of change. To such employees the initiators lack the credibility to paint a believable picture either of the need for the change or of the organization after the change.

In many ways, this is the easiest cause of resistance to deal with. Two strategies are common. Individuals with credibility can be sold on the change individually and asked to speak out on behalf of the change effort. Alternatively, a manager can use scaled-down demonstrations to show precisely what form the change will take on a larger scale.

An Honest Belief That the Change Does Not Make Sense for the Organization. Loyal, honest employees often resist change for what are very good reasons from their perspective. Explanations about the need for or directions of the change simply do not persuade them that the change is in the organization's best interest. When con-

177

fronted with resistance of this sort, managers are often tempted to provide more information about the change and its intended effects. Interestingly, this sometimes does not work. Individuals opposing change because they do not believe it to be in the organization's interest often have their own information that is sometimes more credible than that offered.

A more effective way of dealing with this form of resistance is to include those who express reservations about the change in the planning of the change. Other factors (to be described in the next section) permitting, this is the best way of dealing with employees who have potentially helpful perspectives on the change. With such participation the change program may actually improve.

Implementation Patterns

Certain changes require that the specifics of the implementation plan be delegated to the people who will implement it, and other changes call for a top-down approach where the manager spells out the implementation plan. The conditions that are best for each appear in Table 1.

Factor	Favorable for Top-Down	Favorable for Delegation
Table 1 **Contingency Factors in Implementing Change**		
Time available for change	Change must be achieved immediately	No definite time limits for implementation
Degree to which the problem is	Crisis is recognized by everyone	Problem not generally recognized
Location of knowledge about the change	The manager is more knowledgeable than anyone	Knowledge is dispersed throughout the organization
Employee expectations	Employees expect authoritative change	Employees are used to being consulted
Power of manager	Great	Small

From *Managing Organizational Behavior* by Cyrus F. Gibson. Copyright © 1986 by Richard D. Irwin, Inc. Reprinted by permission of the author.

The time available for implementing the change is one factor that should be considered in choosing the implementation strategy. If time is limited, then it is better for the manager to implement the change rather than to involve subordinates directly in the implementation plan. The extent to which employees appreciate the need for change is a second factor. If the problem the change addresses is not widely sensed, then using delegation is the best approach. The location of the technical knowledge regarding the change is factor number three. If the manager is expert in the problem solution and the subordinates have little knowledge about the change, then a top-down implementation is called for. Alternatively, if subordinates have knowledge that may be necessary for the change to be successful, delegation is the preferred approach. The fourth contingency factor is the expectations employees have about being included in decisions. If employees have a history of being included in decision making, then it may be unwise to break with this practice when a change must be implemented. Lastly, a manager should be sensitive to his or her own power to implement the change without the involvement of others. Top-down implementation requires that the manager possess a great deal of power. If the manager does not have that power, then it is probably better to delegate the change effort.

When these five factors are all aligned, the preferred approach to change is clear. However, many situations are mixed. When mixed, a manager must use discretion. For example, if time is particularly pressing or if a manager totally lacks confidence in the technical abilities of subordinates to offer valuable technical inputs, then a top-down approach may be appropriate even though the manager lacks substantial power or suspects that the need for change is not widely appreciated.

Top-Down Implementation. A manager should attempt to follow four steps in a top-down implementation of a change:

(1)　detail the coming change and explain the reasons for it,

(2)　let employees ask questions, express opinions and concerns,

(3)　respond to employee questions and concerns,

(4)　get commitment and set up review.

There are certain principles that apply in each of these steps.

Step 1--detail the coming change and explain the reasons for it. When the decision is made to implement a change in a top-down fashion, substantial effort toward planning the change is necessary before the implementation process can begin. At the end of this planning period, the manager must address employees in a careful fashion. What is said (or not said) during this introduction can have a dramatic impact on the success of the change effort.

Several elements are usually included in effective announcements of the change. First, the manager should be very clear about the reasons for the change. This has two facets. It should be pointed out what is wrong with the present situation and what advantages will be offered by the new system. For example, if a new organization structure is being put into place, the manager should be ready to point out both how the present structure is causing problems and how the new structure promises the best solution to those problems. As obvious as this sounds, many managers do not do this. Often they have spent so much time planning the change that they do not realize their people are unaware of both the need for change and the advantages of the proposed approach. As a consequence, their employees react to their announcement with statements like, "If it ain't broke, don't fix it!" or, "I'm not convinced that the proposed change will deliver what is expected!"

As the manager makes the case for change, the following factors should be considered:

(a)   The most persuasive reasons for change include both external factors and internal factors. If possible, it should be pointed out how the change will improve internal operations and external relations (i.e., with customers, suppliers, or others outside the immediate work group).

(b)   Sometimes the best way to demonstrate the superiority of the new system is by using outsiders who are known experts in the new system. Some managers use outside consultants for this purpose. Others have outsiders experienced with the sort of change they are implementing come in and describe their positive experiences with the new system.

(c)   People tend to identify best with changes that are described in clear, understandable ways. Hence, it is advisable to avoid overly complex or detailed explanations of the new system. Too many technological innovations fail because a manager engages in unnecessarily technical descriptions of the change.

(d)   The use of banners, mottos, slogans, and acronyms often gives the change program both importance and meaning. Such symbols allow for a shorthand way of referring to the change and create a way of referring to the program more frequently. Repetition signals that the change is important. In addition, if the symbols are cleverly coined, it gives the program more visibility with others. For example, one change effort to selectively alter course load for professors was called CLAP (course load adjustment program). And the motto pinned on a safety program in a small community symphony was "See Sharp or Be Flat."

(e)   The explanation of the change will be most effective if it shapes expectations about when the positive results will be experienced. For example, if a manager is responsible for putting in a new telecommunications system, it is vital to let people know that they can expect the new system to have minor "bugs" for six months to a year.

Step 2--let employees ask questions, express opinions and concerns. Directly after the change is introduced, a manager must be prepared to address employee questions, opinions, and concerns. If the change was anticipated, one could expect many more questions than if it came as a surprise. In any event, it should be expected that questions will arise over the entire course of implementation. Hence a manager will want to keep channels of communication as open as possible. It is vital to recognize that as the change process unfolds, the manager will become more and more dependent on the efforts of those who have to accommodate the change. This implies that the manager can be much more directive and forceful early in the process, but will have to be more prepared for negotiation and accommodation later. This makes it especially important that expressions of resistance be encouraged early in the change process, when more response alternatives are available.

Step 3--respond to employee questions and concerns. As questions, opinions, and concerns arise, it is important for the manager to pay attention to the possible causes for resistance that underlie them. As we have mentioned, each cause for resistance requires a slightly different response pattern. Sometimes the manager's response will not be sufficient. In those cases one strategy is to ask others to testify about the change: what it involves and what it promises.

Although using others to support the change is sometimes required, it is not without risks. By not being available at critical times, a manager can inadvertently signal a lack of interest in the problems experienced by those who must shoulder the weight of the change.

Step 4--get commitment and set up review. One of the most powerful tools in eliciting commitment to a change is to implement it in phases. By implementing the change in stages, employees often find it easier to support the change. There are two reasons for this. First, phasing allows the involvement of those most committed to the change early and delays the commitments of those who are initially more reluctant. Second, it allows those initially less committed to observe directly what the change means before they have to put themselves irretrievably behind the effort.

Obviously phasing requires careful orchestration. It is important to select as the first phase that part of the total change program with the highest likelihood for success. Once the first phase is successfully completed, it is useful to celebrate the early successes and publicly acknowledge all those responsible for the success of the initial stages.

In expanding the change from its initial success, it is important for the manager to be sensitive to fine-tuning the implementation to local conditions and unexpected problems as they arise. Few changes are ever implemented completely according to the initial plan. Slight modifications are almost always necessary as factors that were not anticipated are discovered.

At the same time, successful top-down implementation requires the manager to be bold with those individuals who drag their feet as the final stages proceed. Effective managers continue to be sensitive to the various causes for resistance, but are not shy in their responses. They often use the argument that fairness requires at least trying the change and refuse to tolerate any resistance that jeopardizes the entire program. More over, they frequently use every occasion of voluntary turnover (top-down changes frequently result in people quitting or transferring) as an opportunity to bring in people more committed to the change.

Delegation Implementation. As we have described, using delegation to implement a change is warranted (a) when time is available, (b) when the problem the change addresses is not generally recognized, (c) when employees have valuable insights about the direction of the change, (d) when the manager lacks the power to implement the change alone, and (e) when employees have traditionally been included in change decisions in the past.

In spite of its clear advantages in certain situations, implementation by delegation is foreign to many managers and absolutely unknown in some organizations. For that reason it is important that the manager have a clear charter for managing the change process. Obtaining such a charter is often painstaking. Some bosses are reluctant to give the manager and particularly his or her group the discretion and authority that they need to work out all the implementation details. Often supervisors have proceeded with delegation with a vague "go ahead" from the boss only to discover that the group had made a series of decisions that the boss found unacceptable. Thus, even before beginning the delegation process, it is essential that the manager elicit a clear charter from the boss that indicates that delegating the implementation is acceptable and specifies the limits of the issue.

This is particularly true when the change has far-reaching implications. If the change is a minor one or in cases where delegation is commonplace, it is not necessary to clear intentions with the boss. However, if the change is major or the use of delegation is unique, then getting a clear charter is necessary.

With this charter in place, the following steps should be taken:

(1)   explain the need for delegation,

(2)   use delegation of the task to motivate,

(3)   explain the task and ask employee's view,

(4)   specify responsibility and authority,

(5)   confirm employee's understanding and set up review.

There are certain principles that apply in each of these steps.

Step 1--explain the need for delegation. Just as in top-down implementation, it is vital that the manager begin by offering the group a clear and complete description of the situation that creates the need for change. In doing so, it is important not to minimize the need for change. If the change is necessitated by a problem that jeopardizes the survival of the organization, employees are likely to be more motivated to change if they know that. Providing such information may be valuable even if the manager suspects that the group may not need to know. The reason for the complete openness about the need for change is that groups are seldom motivated to change without a real threat. The status quo is often too comfortable for a group to be motivated to change unless there is the necessary impetus. Moreover, it is very possible that the group will learn of all the elements that constitute the need for change as they progress, and it is better for them to hear it from the manager than to learn it themselves.

Step 2--use delegation of the task to motivate. Delegation can be a tremendous motivator and a source of frustration at the same time. It motivates best when:

(a)   employees trust the intentions of the delegator,

(b)   they are given sufficient time, information, and resources to work on the implementation plan,

(c)   they can see their plan put into action.

Delegation is frustrating when:

(a)   employees are suspicious about the intentions of the delegator,

(b)   they are given insufficient time, information, and resources to work on the implementation plan,

(c)   they are told they will have a voice in the implementation only to be told later their recommendations were unacceptable.

Accordingly, a manager should avoid sending mixed messages about intentions to delegate and make certain that sufficient time, information, and resources are

183

provided to the group. Finally, the manager must be prepared to pave the way for the group's decisions to be put into action. Most employees have had experience with counterfeit delegation that fails on one or more of these counts, so if a manager is to be successful, he or she must be prepared to meet these challenges directly and forthrightly.

Step 3--explain the task and ask the employee's view. When it is time to explain the task, it is generally helpful for the manager to develop a specific time line to give the group particular milestones. This makes the manager's expectations about performance very clear along the way to the group's ultimate product.

Many groups also need assistance with their group decision process. Here an effective manager should be prepared to intervene in order to assure that the conflict between the individuals of the group is at the correct level. In general a moderate degree of conflict is desirable, for it stimulates innovative solutions. It is not advisable for the group to be either too content with the first alternative it considers or too torn by disagreements about favored choices.

One technique in guiding the group's decision process is to require a consensus decision rule. Consensus is a decision tool in which the group agrees to seek those alternatives that everyone can at least "live with." Alternatively, it is a decision rule that requires every individual to understand and accept the logic behind the favored option. Not all employees are familiar with consensus, so often a manager must explain this decision rule to the group and be prepared to intervene when they have problems with it.

"Groupthink" is a related problem. Groupthink arises when the group is too ready to accept an alternative that is thought to be popular. Essentially its presence signals that there is insufficient conflict in the group's deliberations. When the group appears to be too quick to settle, effective managers often intervene. One useful technique is to appoint a devil's advocate (someone assigned the role of taking a contrary position) or to directly challenge the group's decision. This may ensure that delegation results in the best product.

Step 4--specify responsibility and authority. Few managers are entirely comfortable turning over decision-making authority to others. In delegating decision making, it is important that the manager understand his or her reservations and monitor the process closely, but at a distance, to assure that the group is staying on track. This will require the manager to be alert to a tendency to take back decision authority from the group.

One reason managers are so gun-shy about delegating a change to their people is that they suspect their boss will second-guess their group's decision. Much of this concern will be allayed if the supervisor has received a clear charter from his or her boss

184

before beginning the change effort. Even having done this, it is wise for the manager to provide the boss with ongoing reports as the group progresses with its deliberations. This not only serves to remind the boss of the original charter, but also tends to surface concerns which can be dealt with before exposing the group decision to a veto from someone high in the organization.

Step 5--confirm the employee's understanding and set up a review. After having explained expectations about both the process and outcomes of the group's activities during delegation, a manager can expect questions. Some of them may even be heated and emotionally laden. It is important to understand that when delegation is used, the approach to resistance to change is fundamentally different than it is when a change is implemented in a top-down fashion. While top-down implementation deals with resistance by understanding and responding to it as it unfolds, delegation strives to eliminate it by involving people directly in the implementation decisions.

Conclusion

Supervising change is one of a manager's most challenging assignments. Implementing change is a problem-filled endeavor. But with the principles we have outlined in this chapter, implementing change can potentially proceed smoothly and with less difficulty.

References

Beer, M. 1980. *Organizational change and development: A systems view.* Glenview, IL: Scott Foresman.

Cotton, J. L., Vollrath, D. A., Froggratt, K. L., Lengnich-Hall, M. L., & Jennings, K. R. 1988. Employee participation: Diverse forms and different outcomes. *Academy of Management Review* 13: 8-22.

Gibson, C. F. 1980. *Managing organizational behavior.* Homewood, IL.: Irwin, 1980.

Greiner, L. E. 1967. Patterns of organizational change. *Harvard Business Review* 45 (1967): 119-130.

Hedberg, B. L. T., Nystrom, P., & Starbuck, W. 1976. Camping on seesaws: Prescriptions for a self-designing organization. *Administrative Science Quarterly* 26: 66-80.

Kanter, R. M., Stein, B. & Jick, T. 1992. *The challenge of organizational change.* New York: Free Press.

Kotter, J. P., & Schlesinger, L. A. 1979. Choosing strategies for change. *Harvard Business Review* 57: 109-127.

Lawrence, P. R. 1954. How to deal with resistance to change. *Harvard Business Review* 30: 49-58.

Leavitt, H. J. 1965. Applied organizational change in industry. In J. G. March (Ed.), *Handbook of organizations.* Chicago: Rand McNally.

Lewin, K. 1952. Group decision and social change. In G. E. Swanson, T. M. Newcomb, and E. L. Hartley (Eds.), *Readings in social psychology*. New York: Holt, Rinehart & Winston.

Nadler, D. A. 1987. The effective management of organizational change. In J. W. Lorsch (Ed.), *Handbook of organizational behavior*. Englewood Cliffs, NJ: Prentice-Hall.

Zaltman, G., & Duncan, R. 1979. *Strategies for planned change*. New York: John Wiley & Sons.

Flow Diagram for Managing Change I Interactive Case

Detach this page from your book before you begin the Interactive Case. As you make each decision, write the decision point number following the GO TO statement in the appropriate rectangle before you turn to that page. If you are referred to a previous decision point, circle the decision point number you last wrote and proceed to the first uncircled rectangle above that one in your flow diagram. Do not erase the numbers once you have written them. You will not necessarily fill all the rectangles.

Start		6th Decision		12th Decision	
1st Decision		7th Decision		13th Decision	
2nd Decision		8th Decision		14th Decision	
3rd Decision		9th Decision		15th Decision	
4th Decision		10th Decision		16th Decision	
5th Decision		11th Decision		17th Decision	

over

187

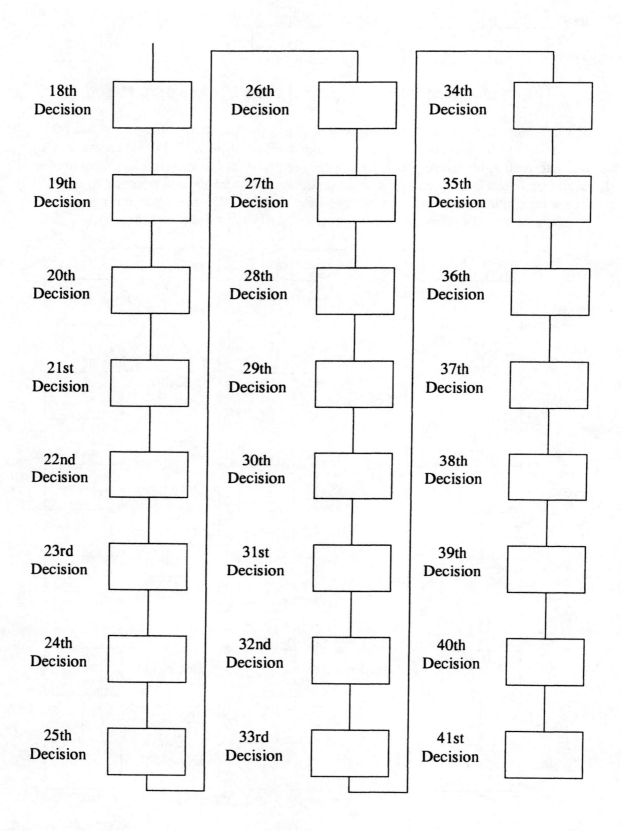

INTERACTIVE CASE 1

You are the newly appointed Head Librarian of the Lake County Library District (LCLD). An organization chart appears below:

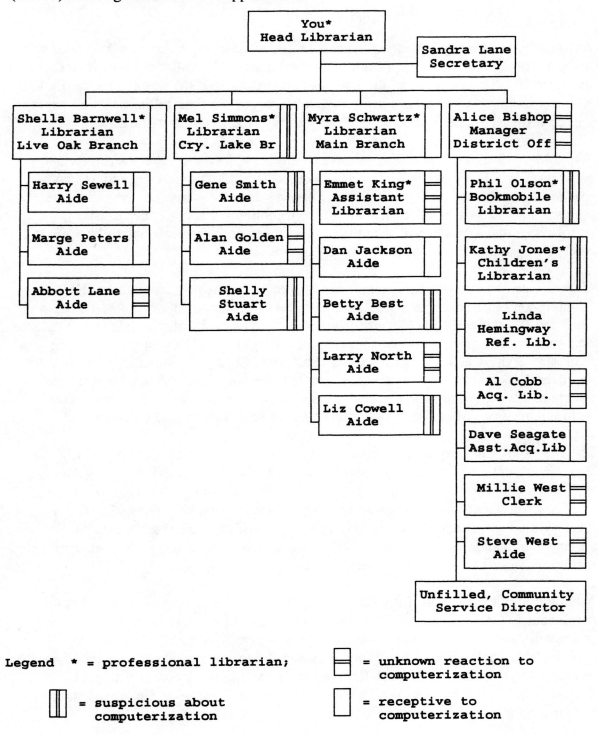

LCLD has three branches and employs 25 full-time people including ten professional librarians. The LCLD has a fine reputation for community service. This is due more than anything to your predecessor, Ms. Alma Brickhouse. Ms. B (as she is known throughout the county) prided herself that there were more library cards issued per capita in Lake County than in any other county in the state.

Assisted by her husband who served as Community Service Director and retired with her a month ago, Ms. B was a highly visible figure in the entire county. In speeches to community service groups, she consistently summarized the mission of the LCLD with the motto, "the county is served when we make the time to listen." This saying appeared on all LCLD stationary and on library cards given to patrons.

While Ms. B had a commanding presence (she is six feet tall), she was more than a caricature. She knew every person who worked for LCLD by name, and she commanded respect from most all of them. This was especially true for the older ones who she had hired and indoctrinated with her community service ideals. Ms. B's approach to management was traditional. She reserved most decisions to herself, and rarely delegated or involved others in policy making.

If there was any short-sightedness in her approach, it was professionalism. Her emphasis on local concerns alienated almost every professionally-oriented librarian she hired. At the end of her tenure, she left a staff more devoted to her as a matriarch than to the standards of modern librarianship. Tangible evidence of this emphasis was State University's action against LCLD. Last year, State U dropped LCLD from the approved list of library systems for its graduate interns. Other library systems use interns as an important source of inexpensive labor and as a force for improvement and revitalization. Ms. B held that interns are trouble-makers and problem-finders.

Ms. B's rather anti-professional posture had one other negative effect on LCLD. The state library commission recently put LCLD on probation. Accordingly, the district will only qualify for additional state grants if it "takes immediate action to restore a level of professionalism commensurate with a system of its size." One deficiency cited by the accrediting agency is "the level of use of computer technology in cataloging, circulation, maintenance of reference sources, and linkage with other information resource centers." Computers are not used at all at LCLD.

Your appointment as Head Librarian was testament to the county government's concern about LCLD's questionable accreditation record. You were selected over several other applicants because you had experience with computerized library systems. Your clearly stated charter from the county is to install and implement a computer system in one year. This is an extremely tight schedule for any library system like LCLD. In addition, the county has told you to expect no increases in the system's operations budget for the next few years.

190

Directly after your appointment, you had a chance to talk with each of your people. Each was aware of your charter. After your interviews, you noted three classes of openness toward computerization: one group openly receptive, one group uncommitted, and one group openly suspicious. The organization chart on page 189 shows how these three groups are distributed over the organization.

The suspicious group believe that computers (1) will be used as an excuse to "weed out unneeded personnel," (2) will require people to learn extensive programming skills they have neither the aptitude for nor the interest in, and (3) will dilute efforts at delivering personal service. These concerns are not entirely unfounded. First, LCLD is currently over-staffed. If it hires two interns per year at minimum wage, it could scale down two positions that presently call for professional librarians King's and Seagate's) to senior clerical positions. While your employees are covered by civil service protection, you are confident that the commission will rule on behalf of a change in job classification. Second, computers will require that all personnel become literate in *BIBLIOTEK*, the standard library software program by the end of the year. Third, the system *will* necessitate a temporary reduction in personal service to patrons. While this service reduction should only last a year, you will require the total cooperation of the staff so that nothing happens to tarnish the fine image of the LCLD in the county. You wonder what is the best way to implement this computer system.

Considering all these facts, would you?

A. Implement computerization as a top-down change. Prescribe the necessary directions yourself. (GO TO 558)

B. Implement the change by involving all employees in decisions about *how* to put the system in place. (GO TO 501)

C. Implement the change by involving all employees in decisions about *whether* or not LCLD should implement a computer system. (GO TO 531)

D. Implement the change by involving a select group of employees in decisions about how to put the system in place. (GO TO 455)

Flow Diagram for Managing Change II Interactive Case

Detach this page from your book before you begin the Interactive Case. As you make each decision, write the decision point number following the GO TO statement in the appropriate rectangle before you turn to that page. If you are referred to a previous decision point, circle the decision point number you last wrote and proceed to the first uncircled rectangle above that one in your flow diagram. Do not erase the numbers once you have written them. You will not necessarily fill all the rectangles.

Start		6th Decision		12th Decision	
1st Decision		7th Decision		13th Decision	
2nd Decision		8th Decision		14th Decision	
3rd Decision		9th Decision		15th Decision	
4th Decision		10th Decision		16th Decision	
5th Decision		11th Decision		17th Decision	

over

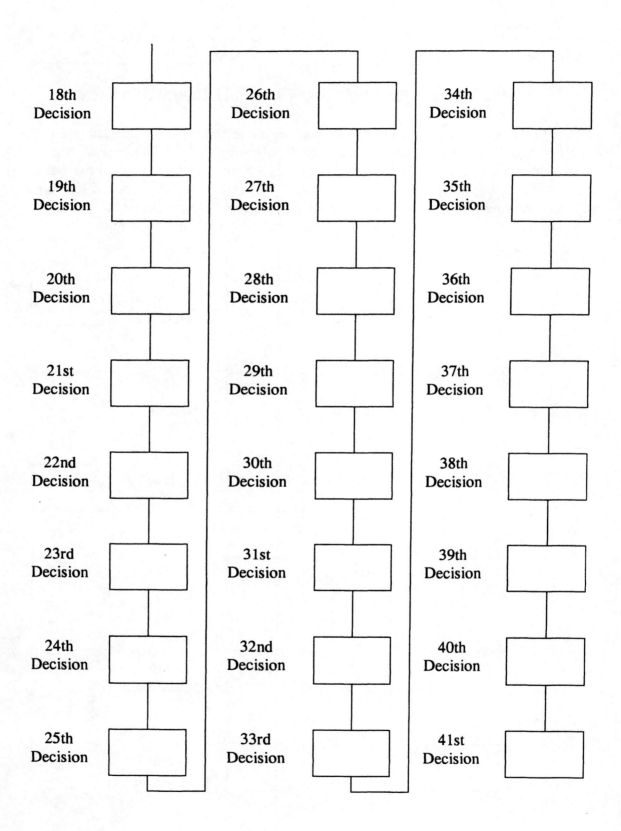

18th
Decision

19th
Decision

20th
Decision

21st
Decision

22nd
Decision

23rd
Decision

24th
Decision

25th
Decision

26th
Decision

27th
Decision

28th
Decision

29th
Decision

30th
Decision

31st
Decision

32nd
Decision

33rd
Decision

34th
Decision

35th
Decision

36th
Decision

37th
Decision

38th
Decision

39th
Decision

40th
Decision

41st
Decision

194

INTERACTIVE CASE 2

You are the Manufacturing Manager for Arion Systems, a company that produces and sells telecommunication equipment. Most of Arion's business comes from a few lines of relatively standard PBX systems. Arion competes in the PBX market primarily on price. This price advantage comes from efficiencies that you and your colleagues have introduced into the manufacturing process.

You have a team of three talented professionals working for you. In the one year you all have been together, production has improved substantially. It seems that your group has been able to pull together and solve most every problem that has come up. Your team members are:

Larry Beeson - Assembly Supervisor - Larry is responsible for 207 assemblers who are organized into assembly teams. He has been at Arion for two years and has 8 years of industry experience. He is a particularly competent manager who "runs a very tight ship."

Robin Broderick - Test Supervisor - Robin is responsible for 43 technicians who test incoming parts and competed systems. They also re-work defective systems and perform warranty repairs. Robin was promoted into this position from within the test group about 3 years ago.

Marilyn Wilson - Material Supervisor - Marilyn has been with Arion for one year. Previously she worked for a large aerospace firm. She is responsible for scheduling and procuring component parts. She supervises 5 scheduling specialists and 16 parts clerks.

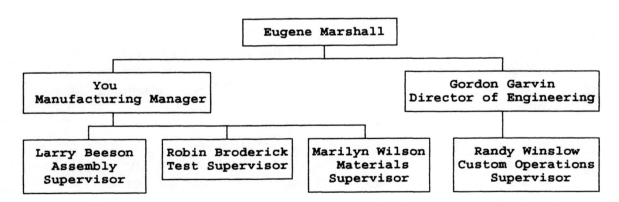

After a weekly staff meeting this morning, *Eugene Marshall*, Arion's President, cornered you to discuss something that was entirely new to you. It regarded custom production. Presently, only a small part of Arion's business comes from systems designed after the unique needs of a particular customer. This custom production is located in the Engineering Department. Each custom system is designed by the engineering staff and is built by small groups of technicians assigned to various engineering teams. In your conversation, Eugene tells you that he expects that custom work will become a larger and larger part of the business in the next five to ten years. More over, Eugene has decided that in order to enjoy more efficiency he wants to begin to incorporate the custom production into your department. Eugene further mentions that he has talked to some friends at another company who use "flexible assembly" to handle custom jobs. He described this as the development of assembly groups that have the manpower and equipment to do long production runs *and* custom items simultaneously. He ends the conversation by saying, "let's try that approach if it makes sense for us."

After this brief encounter, you return to your office and start thinking about what needs to be done. You don't know much about how custom production is done in the Engineering Department, but you do know that 18 technicians are involved in the process. Further, these technicians are assigned in groups of between 2-4 to various engineers. The technicians are highly skilled, and view themselves as "associate" engineers. The engineers and technicians work closely together on projects and often spend hours talking about the engineering problems involved in particular systems. The person responsible for the technicians is an engineer by the name of Randy Winslow. At the staff meeting this morning, it was announced that Winslow would be leaving in two weeks to visit the Birmingham England plant of Arion on a six-month trouble-shooting assignment. It is common knowledge that Winslow will probably be permanently assigned to the British affiliate of Arion, and that may have been a contributing factor in Eugene's decision to give you Winslow's unit.

As you begin to think about how to absorb custom production into your Department, you know you have many options. After some study, you identify three main alternatives:

> *The "Superteam" approach* - Under this plan the engineering technicians would develop their own independent assembly group with specially assigned test workers and scheduling people. This group would handle custom and short production run items.

> *The "Flexible Assembly" approach* - This option divides the technicians among your Assembly group (headed by Larry Beeson) so that each group would be capable of both standard and custom production. This is the approach that Eugene Marshall mentioned.

> *The "Contracting" approach* - This would assign the technicians to your Test group (headed by Robin Broderick). There they would handle all single item

orders. As some of these became market successes, they would be assigned to Assembly for longer production runs.

All of these approaches have advantages and disadvantages, and your team may even have other options worth considering. At this point, would you?

A. Schedule a meeting with Eugene to clarify the assignment he has given to you. (GO TO 593)

B. Decide yourself which of the above approaches you should choose as a method of bringing custom production into your group. (GO TO 566)

C. Call a meeting of the members of your group to consider which of the alternatives should be implemented. (GO TO 617)

MODULE 12

Management Ethics

MODULE READING

All managers face ethical challenges in their professional lives, some more frequently and some more vexing than others. These challenges often take the form of a dilemma between doing the right thing for a person or group and advancing the interests of the entire organization. For example, a manager might find it painful to eliminate a department for business reasons when it is staffed by very senior people who have no other equivalent employment options. Other challenges arise when managers are faced by the need to choose between two bad alternatives as in "damned if you do, damned if you don't" situations.

In this module reading, we will lay out certain ethical principles that managers find helpful in facing these moral challenges. At the end of this reading, we will tackle an issue many students raise while studying organizational behavior. Namely, we will examine what constitutes a *manipulative* as opposed to ethically acceptable application of organizational behavior principles.

The Emerging Field of Management Ethics

Management ethics is different from business ethics. Management ethics deals with the moral problems practicing managers face that may or may not be business related. For example, the problem of giving ethically justifiable performance appraisals is not a business issue per se. Rather, it falls under a broader umbrella of management ethics. In a similar vein, if a manager chooses to exclude an individual or group from an organizational directive that applies to everyone else, then that is a case for management ethics rather than business ethics.

In an ideal world, an important basis for judging the morality of management action would be the manager's employment contract. Such a document would specify the employing organization's performance expectations of the manager very precisely, and this would become the manager's responsibility as the condition of employment. In reality, employing organizations provide far less precision. Usually, a manager's responsibilities are poorly defined in order to hedge unknown future contingencies. The inability of employers to specify precise employment conditions is due to business uncertainties. In effect, employing organizations force their managers to "sign on" to an *incomplete* employment contract where both parties expect the conditions to flow with the circumstances. The employee shares the risks of uncertain business conditions with the employer. This inevitably involves trust. Organizational officials trust that managers will execute policies that cannot be forecast, and managers trust that officials will be "reasonable" in their unspecified future demands.

Although employment conditions are seldom specified with any precision, managers are bound by several features implicit in any employment contract. First, they are expected to place the interests of the organization above their own interests and the interests of other groups inside and outside the organization. For example, managers are bound by their employment contract to take the organization's position in a dispute with an employee, department, vendor or customer. Second, managers are expected to communicate as officials of the organization. They represent the organization, and what they say is taken as *the* official communication of the organization. Third, managers are expected to support (be obedient to) the directives of those who have authority over them. Fourth, managers are expected to be stewards of the organizational resources within their purview.

Promise-keeping is a strong norm for most people, so most managers fret over situations in which there appear to be good reasons to betray one's employing organization. Moreover, many managers have difficulty when their contractual duty involves advancing the interests of the entire organization when this is unpopular with people with whom they must work closely. Nevertheless, this is the stuff of management ethics: problems in living up to contractual obligations and problems in betraying them.

Three Standards for Ethical Action

Ethicists have developed three basic approaches to moral issues. Each approach uses different kinds of criteria to evaluate the ethics of action. They are:

(1) *Utilitarian approaches*. These judge behavior in terms of its effects on the welfare of everyone.

(2) *Approaches based on justice*. These focus on the fair distribution of benefits and burdens imposed by an action or policy and on the processes designed to reach just distributions.

(3) *Approaches based on rights and duties*. These emphasize the personal entitlements of individuals and the duties of others to respect them.

Each approach has a long, venerable history. Utilitarianism is a direct descendent of Adam Smith's *On the Nature and Causes of the Wealth of Nations* (1776). It was precisely formulated by Jeremy Bentham and John Stuart Mill in the Eighteenth Century. Approaches based on justice were first spelled out as early as the Fifth Century, B.C. by Aristotle and Plato and have been more recently developed by John Rawls.

Notions of rights and duties were first developed in the Seventeenth Century by Thomas Hobbes, John Locke, and Immanuel Kant. Each of these ethical traditions is currently undergoing further analysis and refinement.

Notice how these three approaches compare and contrast with one another. Utilitarian approaches focus on the *ends* or consequences of action. Utilitarianism is concerned with the well-being of *all persons*. Justice concentrates on *both means and ends* and is most concerned with the welfare of *under-represented minorities*. Rights and duties approaches focus on *the individual*. Moreover, rights and duties focus entirely on the *means* of action. Together, then, these three approaches are symmetrical. They are concerned alternatively with ends, means and ends, and ends alone. They hold as the relevant "level of analysis" alternatively all of humanity, under-represented minorities, and the individual.

Utilitarian Criteria for Ethical Decisions. Utilitarianism judges actions, plans, and policies by their consequences. Moral acts are those that produce the greatest good for the greatest number. This means that managers need to estimate the impact that alternative actions will have on all affected parties and to select the one that optimizes the satisfactions of all those parties. Two types of acts are unethical under utilitarianism: those that result in outcomes that fall short of the greatest good for the greatest number and those that represent inefficient means to accomplish such ends.

The line of thinking called for by utilitarianism is not foreign to managers. Managers conventionally evaluate decisions alternatives according to their likely impact on some sort of performance measure like profit margin, unit volume, or market share. Utilitarianism replaces these economic performance measures with a broader, more abstract criterion: the greatest good for the greatest number. Clearly, there are instances where utilitarianism and economic performance measures support the same alternative. However, that is not automatic. Accordingly, a debate has raged over the past 35 years over the social responsibilities organizations have beyond maximizing their economic returns.

Being a conscientious utilitarian involves a significant cognitive burden. Estimating and aggregating the individual satisfactions of everyone affected by a decision is often daunting. In addition, people's satisfactions are not always stable over time. For example, utilitarians should be careful not to choose alternatives that promise immediate satisfaction when other alternatives offer far more welfare in the long-run. So, a conscientious utilitarian must consider the interests of everyone affected, now and in the longer term, and somehow aggregate all these individual assessments into one measure that will allow comparison between alternatives.

Consider the case of the new manager of a poor performing group who needs to decide between making major changes in the first few days of her tenure or deferring action until she can learn more about the group and the organization. If these are her only two options, she needs to identify all the parties that will be affected by her choice. The organization is an important party, but she must also consider the effects on the members of the group, her immediate predecessor, her boss, and others in the organization. Once she has identified these parties she needs to estimate the effects of each alternative on each party, both short-run and long-run. Then she needs to select the alternative that serves the greatest good for the greatest number. How would you decide in this instance?

Rights and Duties Criteria for Ethical Decisions. Approaches to ethics based on *rights* assert that human beings have certain moral entitlements that should be respected in all decisions. These entitlements or rights guarantee an individual's most fundamental personal rights (life, freedom, health, privacy, and property, for example). These have been spelled out in such documents as the U.S. Bill of Rights and the United Nations Declaration of Human Rights. They also provide the moral basis for many of our laws.

Rights create commensurate *duties* to respect other's rights. If I have the right to free speech, you have the duty to do nothing to impede my expressions. Most duties take the form of "not interfering." There are certain special duties called "positive duties" that require action as opposed to restraining action. For example, one might argue that people have a positive duty to give aid and assistance to someone who is injured and clearly in need of the kind of help others can provide. Such a duty is positive in the sense that it requires action instead of restraint.

There is considerable debate regarding what rights employees are entitled to in the work world. Some are reluctant to prescribe even the most basic employee rights, while people on the other extreme believe that employee's rights are even more inclusive than those due people in society.

One formulation that falls somewhere in the middle of these extremes is as follows:

(1) *The Right of Free Consent.* Employees have a right to be treated only as they knowingly and freely consent to be treated. In particular, a person in a position of greater power over another individual should not exercise that power by deceiving the individual or by taking advantage of the individual's trust, ignorance, gullibility, or fear.

(2) *The Right of Privacy.* Employees have the right to do whatever they choose to do outside working hours and to control information about their private life. In particular, the individual has the right not to be secretly observed, and not to have his or her confidential conversations betrayed or his or her belongings searched.

(3) *The Right to Freedom of Conscience*. Employees have the right to refrain from carrying out any order that violates the commonly accepted moral or religious norms to which they adhere.

(4) *The Right of Free Speech*. Employees have the right to criticize conscientiously and truthfully the ethics or legality of the actions of others so long as the criticism does not violate the rights of other individuals.

(5) *The Right of Due Process*. Employees have the right to a fair and impartial hearing when they believe that their rights are being violated.

(6) *The Right to a Healthy Workplace*. Employees have the right to be protected from harmful or potentially harmful conditions in the workplace.

Rights criteria are much easier to apply that those of utilitarianism. One simply rules unethical any act that violates an individual's rights. Absent is the concern with the welfare of "the greatest good for the greatest number"; instead, actions are rejected when they victimize only one.

Several years ago, a famous high technology company used drug-sniffing dogs to search for illegal drugs suspected to be in one of the company's Southern California sales offices. The site was company-owned, so there was no obvious invasion of the employees' private property, but some people questioned whether personal effects kept in company desks were protected under the right to privacy. What do you think? Is this ethical or unethical?

Justice Criteria for Ethical Decisions. Justice requires that managers be guided by fairness, equity, and impartiality. Just outcomes are conditions characterized by an equitable distribution of the benefits and burdens of working together. Just processes are those that are impartial and even-handed. Several "canons" of justice are particularly relevant to management ethics.

(1) *Equal Treatment*. The basic rule for distributive justice is that individuals who are similar to one another in terms of relevant, job-related qualities should be treated similarly, and individuals who differ from one another in these relevant ways should be treated differently and in proportion to the differences between them. This canon is the basis of contentions that certain pay scales, for example, are "fair" or "unfair."

(2) *Consistent Administration of Rules*. Justice requires that rules be administered fairly and impartially. Rules, job descriptions, and the like should be clearly written and communicated. Acts committed in ignorance, under duress, or involuntarily should be excused. This canon governs "procedural justice."

(3) *Restitution*. Justice also provides guidelines regarding the responsibility for injustice. A person who commits an injustice upon another should be held responsible for the costs of the victim's suffering.

As general guides, justice criteria can be difficult to apply. There is the problem of defining the criteria upon which differential treatment is to be based, the problem of ascertaining the facts surrounding a particular episode in question, and the complex problem of establishing responsibility when injustices are committed. Despite these difficulties, one cannot ignore notions of justice in considering the ethics that arise from any specific situation.

Managers face justice issues whenever they are asked to interpret or apply a policy or rule. Few managers are unmoved by a good excuse or situation beyond an employee's control, but such exceptions create precedents that allow others to claim similar exemptions. How do you feel about the policies in this course? Are they fair?

The Unethical and Manipulative Use of Organizational Behavior

Students of organizational behavior often find themselves vaguely troubled by what they are learning. On the one hand, they are grateful for the personal insights and principles that they can incorporate into their own organizational behavior. On the other, they realize that some of what they are learning could be used "on them" without their knowledge. This argument is that organizational behavior is a form of social engineering, and most people are uncomfortable being the unknowing object of such a technology. The operative word here is "unknowing," because most of us fear being manipulated. In this section, we try to figure out just what manipulation is, and on what grounds it is morally objectionable. Then, we outline a series of guidelines that enable us to apply the principles in this book in an ethical, non-manipulative fashion.

Manipulation as a Special Case of Influence. First, let's try to understand what constitutes manipulation. Manipulation is a special case of influence. It is more tricky than influence, but the object is the same as any influence attempt--to elicit compliance from someone else. Influence is found in any group of interdependent persons. We influence each other to adjust to one another.

Most of us do not object to attempts by others to influence us unless, of course, it is done in a disrespectful way. For example, most object to being coerced or forced to comply. Similarly, if we find out that some degree of deceit was used in someone's influence of us, we generally perceive ourselves to have been used. This perception is commonly accompanied by feelings of anger toward the user and shame at falling for the user's plan. While some attempts at such influence are so successful they are never detected, those that are typically result in hard feelings. On these grounds alone, one might question whether attempts at manipulation are ethical on utilitarian grounds, i.e., the risks of negative outcomes outweigh the promise of successful compliance. This is a very good question, for not only do people react negatively to being manipulated, but as we will see, manipulation flourishes only under very particular circumstances, meaning that it is fraught with potential manipulator miscalculation.

Is Manipulation Simply Influence with a "Hidden Agenda?" Some people believe that what distinguishes manipulation from other forms of influence is that manipulation requires a hidden agenda. This means that the manipulator has a plan for the party manipulated that is hidden from that party. Another way of putting this is to say that the object of influence is not known to the person subjected to the influence. Actually, hidden agendas are not restricted to manipulative influence. A great deal of non-manipulative influence occurs with a hidden agenda. The confusion here is often due to an inability to distinguish truth-telling from candor.

Truth-telling is an important norm in civilized countries. Those who make misstatements for deceptive purposes are not models of morality. Lying and deceit are not virtues. Yet, there is another side to truth-telling that is much more morally cloudy-- candor, or telling the *whole* truth. If you ask whether others have a right to expect you to say only what you know to be truthful, most would say, "yes." But ask if people have a right to expect you to tell them everything you think or feel on a given issue, and most would say, "no." Most people believe that some thoughts should be private, even from those closest to us. So, a moral standard requiring total candor in all circumstances is absurd. We all harbor certain thoughts that are no one else's business, and we have no duty to reveal these thoughts to others.

Does this same standard of privacy apply to situations in which we have plans or hopes for others' behavior? Most of us would say yes. There are occasions in which we have private plans that if made public would surely be thwarted. Let's say that a manager must decide which among three able subordinates will receive the only promotion that manager is entitled to give. It would seem unreasonable to expect that as soon as she has made that decision, she would be ethically bound to make it public. In other words, there is likely to be a time period in which the manager knows that two of the three will soon be unhappy and one of the three will soon be pleased. In the meantime, most of us would grant this manager the freedom to interact with the three in full knowledge of the final result unless, of course, she used this knowledge irresponsibly. A lack of candor alone is not manipulative. We are under no obligation to tell others secrets if those plans would not flourish in public. We may choose to be candid about our plans, but we under no moral obligation to do so under ordinary circumstances.

Most applications of organizational behavior principles are not done in an atmosphere of total candor. A manager preparing to give a subordinate a performance review may review the content in the module on communication to be more effective during this interview. The subordinate is likely not to know that the manager is making a concerted effort to be descriptive rather than judgmental during the interview. And, as we have seen, the manager is under no ethical observation to reveal his or her "hidden agenda."

But does this application of organizational behavior constitute manipulation? It may, but if it is, it is not due to the presence of the manager's hidden agenda. Under most circumstances, we are morally justified in keeping plans to ourselves regarding the influence of others.

The Ethical Objection to Manipulation. It is not the presence of a hidden agenda that makes manipulation unethical. The moral objection to manipulation lies in its violation of the right of free consent discussed on page 202.

Using notions of rights and duties, most ethicists argue that manipulation is *prima facie* unethical. This means that they believe that manipulation is unethical under normal circumstances, but it may be ethical in extraordinary ones. The basis for this general indictment is a principle developed by Immanual Kant known as "the categorical imperative." This principle holds that we are all morally duty-bound to treat people as ends and never as means only. It reinforces the need to treat humans as free, autonomous persons. Manipulation clearly violates the categorical imperative, for it transforms individuals into means or instruments that serve the ends of the manipulator. It is totally contrary to the notion of individual autonomy; indeed it cheats people of their liberty. Manipulation involves an undignified treatment of persons, and thus it is unethical.

Some people claim that manipulation is harmless since it is infrequently detected. This is a particularly weak claim, for there is no reason to excuse an immoral but undetected act over a detected one. A more compelling claim is that manipulation might be good for the person manipulated. Indeed, one could imagine situations in which manipulation advances the interests of the person manipulated. Years ago, Hollywood celebrities were manipulated into settings in which they were surprised with apparently satisfying "This is Your Life" retrospectives. More germane are cases in which persons manipulate those they care about for the cared-for's benefit. While these may be among those that justify manipulation, there is the moral concern of *paternalism*. Ethicists generally frown on cases in which people trick or fool people for their own benefit. Such a practice robs the party tricked of the autonomy that dignified treatment requires.

If neither paternalism nor ignorance alone justify manipulation, what does? For one, manipulation is easier to justify if the manipulated person is not materially harmed beyond their loss of autonomy. Practical jokes, playful trickery, and orchestrated surprise celebrations, although manipulative in the strict sense of the word, are usually so harmless that few would object to them on moral grounds. Indeed, one might argue that such rituals enliven social life. A second factor in determining whether a manipulation is ethically justified involves overwhelming consequences. For example, when the Iraqi military was manipulated into believing that the UN attack would be from the south during the 1991 Iraqi war, that resulted in a tactical advantage that ultimately saved lives and ended an immoral Iraqi occupation of Kuwait. Similarly, when an act of manipulation results in the advancement of justice or the improvement of the human condition, it may be justified.

Precisely What Constitutes a Manipulative Use of Organizational Behavior.
Manipulation occurs whenever a manipulator acts toward a target to produce an effect on that target on the basis of knowledge the manipulator has about the target that the target lacks about him/herself. Therefore, manipulation requires that:

(1)   knowledge exists about a target that the target does not have about him/herself, i.e., the knowledge is not *common-sensical*,

(2)   this knowledge allows the possessor to elicit an effect on the target with certainty, i.e., the knowledge is an *effective* instrument of social influence,

(3)   the manipulator is motivated to produce the effect on the target, i.e., the effect *is important enough* to motivate the manipulator to influence the target in this fashion,

(4)   the manipulator has reason to believe that manipulation is a less costly means to producing the effect on the target than a non-manipulative form of influence, i.e., the manipulator considers manipulation *superior to other influence options*.

Manipulation is not the automatic outcome of someone applying a knowledge of organizational behavior. Such knowledge may be known by the target, the knowledge possessed may not capable of reliably eliciting the desired outcomes, the effects produced may be unimportant to the person with the knowledge of organizational behavior, and other non-manipulative forms of influence may be more attractive. So it makes no sense to label all applications of organizational behavior manipulative per se.

Indeed, an examination of points one through four above indicates that successful manipulative applications of organizational behavior are probably rare. First, a large number of people have been exposed to the field. Most graduates of business schools can be expected to have a working knowledge of the field, and this disqualifies many from being naive targets of manipulative influence attempts. Second, the findings of organizational behavior research are probabilistic rather than deterministic. That is, one can never be totally certain of an outcome from a particular application of organizational behavior principles. Third, there are many situations in which no organizational behavior principle applies. For example, precious little is known about how workforce diversity alters fundamental principles. And finally, manipulation is rarely the only attractive means of influencing someone. A "direct" approach may suffice in all but extreme circumstances. In short, the issue of manipulation with the use of organizational behavior arouse more concern than its practice warrants.

The Ethical Application of Organizational Behavior

What can a conscientious person do to insure that his or her use of the principles in this book is ethical? Clearly, possessing the knowledge you now have puts you in a position of considerable influence when it comes to organizational behavior. You may steer clear of a manipulative use of these principles, but there are always moral questions that arise when one person has knowledge that others may lack.

In society, people who possess special technical knowledge are generally expected to use and apply this knowledge responsibly. Indeed, we hold physicians, architects, and lawyers to high ethical standards in part because the superior knowledge invites the potential for abuse. An examination of these standards may help lead us to some insights about the ethical application of organizational behavior.

In general, professionals are held to three ethical standards regarding their interaction with clients: diligence, disinterestedness, and disclosure. Diligence implies that professionals should make certain that they are correct in their technical decisions and that they should assiduously maintain their own skill and knowledge level. Disinterestedness refers to the norm that professionals should always hold their client's welfare above their own. And disclosure means that professionals should keep their clients sufficiently informed so that they (the clients) can make informed decisions about their welfare.

It is useful to take these three standards as benchmarks for the ethical application of organizational behavior. The diligence norm requires that those who apply principles of organizational behavior base their understanding on an accurate knowledge of the discipline. Continuing to apply the same principles over the years without checking to see if they have been amended by subsequent research is unprofessional and questionable from an ethical standpoint. Disinterestedness is an equally important norm, for principles can be used to advance the interests of the applier at the expense of the target of application. Such a practice is morally suspect. Finally, disclosure implies that while full candor is unnecessary, those we subject to applications of organizational behavior should be informed of everything we know from this field that they might benefit in knowing. For example, if we are attempting to create dissatisfaction with the status quo as a means to begin an organizational change process, and someone asks us why we are criticizing present practice, we should respond honestly.

Summary

Principles of organizational behavior are certainly not morally neutral. It is not a form of social engineering that should be used indiscriminately. Management ethics requires attention to utilitarianism, justice, and rights and duties as moral benchmarks. In addition, manipulation *is* a moral concern, and we certainly should avoid practicing it. However, we are probably best to set aside the concern that we are subject to frequent manipulation in the workplace at the hands of those who are clever appliers of organizational behavior. Indeed, a knowledge of the principles discussed in this book are probably the best inoculation against the sick and unethical use of organizational behavior.

A Different Kind of Interactive Case

The interactive case that follows is very different from the other cases in this book. In previous cases, you have received feedback about the *effectiveness* of your action by being told what happened in the case. Because management ethics is not a social science, there is no guarantee (or even likelihood) that "doing the right thing" always results in the best outcome. We wish it were that way, but it is not. Accordingly, in the interactive case that follows, we will simply tell you what ethical principles are consistent with your choices. Hopefully, that will lead to some introspection on your part. It is certainly not our intent to dictate a specific ethical behavior in each case. Ethics scholars differ in their conclusions except the one that says that a conscientious use of ethical principles results in far less guilt and shame than a cavalier indifference to such principles.

References

Bok, S. 1978 *Lying: Moral choice in public and private life*. New York: Pantheon Books.

Bok, S. 1982. *Secrecy*. New York: Pantheon Books.

Cavanagh, G. F., Moberg, D. J., & Velasquez, M. 1981. The ethics of organizational politics. *Academy of Management Review* 6: 363-374.

Haring, B. 1975. *Ethics of manipulation*. New York: Seabury Press.

Keeley, M. 1988. *A Social-Contract Theory of Organizations*. Notre Dame, IN: University of Notre Dame Press.

Moberg, D. J. forthcoming. An ethical analysis of hierarchic relations in organizations. *Business Ethics Quarterly*.

Moberg, D. J., & Meyer, M. 1990. A deontological analysis of peer relations in organizations. *Journal of*

Business Ethics 9: 863-877.

Rudinow, J. 1978. Manipulation. *Ethics* 88: 338-347.

Waters, J. A., Bird, F., & Chant, P. D. 1986. Everyday moral issues experienced by managers. *Journal of Business Ethics* 5: 373-384.

Wilson, J. R. S. 1978. In one another's power. *Ethics* 88: 299-315.

Flow Diagram for Management Ethics Interactive Case

Detach this page from your book before you begin the Interactive Case. As you make each decision, write the decision point number following the GO TO statement in the appropriate rectangle before you turn to that page. If you are referred to a previous decision point, circle the decision point number you last wrote and proceed to the first uncircled rectangle above that one in your flow diagram. Do not erase the numbers once you have written them. You will not necessarily fill all the rectangles.

Start		6th Decision		12th Decision	
1st Decision		7th Decision		13th Decision	
2nd Decision		8th Decision		14th Decision	
3rd Decision		9th Decision		15th Decision	
4th Decision		10th Decision		16th Decision	
5th Decision		11th Decision		17th Decision	

over

211

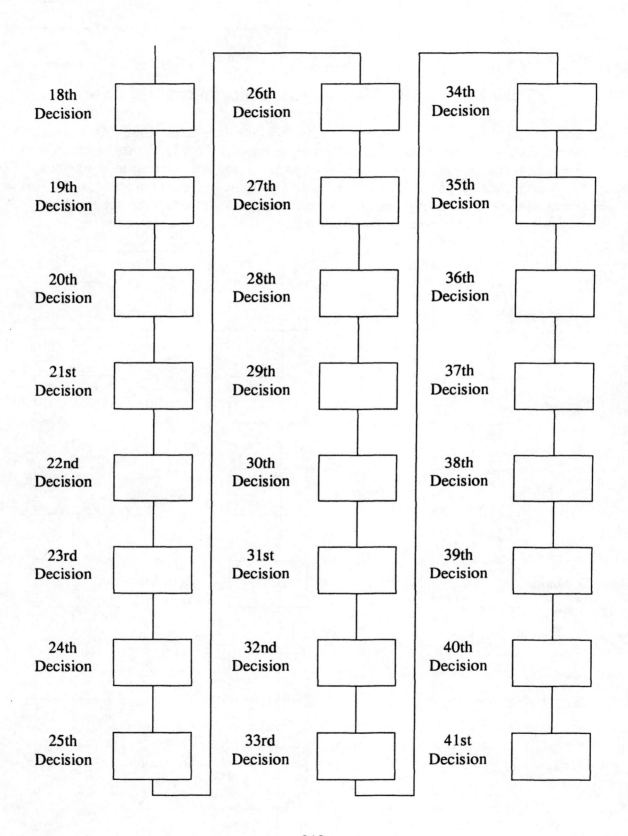

18th
Decision

19th
Decision

20th
Decision

21st
Decision

22nd
Decision

23rd
Decision

24th
Decision

25th
Decision

26th
Decision

27th
Decision

28th
Decision

29th
Decision

30th
Decision

31st
Decision

32nd
Decision

33rd
Decision

34th
Decision

35th
Decision

36th
Decision

37th
Decision

38th
Decision

39th
Decision

40th
Decision

41st
Decision

INTERACTIVE CASE

You are the General Manager of Navajo Semiconductor, a division of a large electronics firm. You are responsible for all operations at this division site. It is Tuesday morning, the phone rings, and it is Joy Sorenson, the Director of Quality Assurance. Sorenson is one of the thirteen directors who report directly to you.

"I just heard from Ed Summit in the state lab. Thank goodness he called me rather than putting it in writing, but he's a old friend of mine. Remember that we thought it was a good idea to have our well tested? Well, the results indicate a level of Benzoate-Toluene-Hydrochloride (BTH) of 50 parts/billion."

At this point, your mind is working a million miles an hour. BTH is used in one of the cleaning operations in manufacturing, and it is a chemical that doesn't exist in nature, so it must have come from a leak or a spill.

Sorenson continued, "As soon as I found out, I called the local EPA and the State Department of Water Quality to get a read on what standards are in place that govern BTH and ground water. Although I didn't tell them we had a problem, they weren't particularly interested."

"Not interested?" you respond.

"No, they've had their budgets seriously cut, and they're working what they call higher priority issues. It seems that there isn't a firm standard on BTH yet because the stuff is so new. Ed Summit confirmed that. He told me that there had been little research on the health effects of BTH except in very high (1,000 parts/billion) levels. Even then, the only studies showed that it produced cancer in mice but not in rats and that no human studies had been conducted. Funny thing is that the fluorine in most drinking water systems neutralizes the poisons in BTH, so if it leaches from our well into the aquifer, it will not have any effect on municipal water quality."

"Trouble is, we've been using the well for our drinking water. My first reaction was to ask employees not to drink the water in the plant, but then we'll have to tell them why. If we do, it will take five minutes before reporters will be at our doorstep wanting to know when we started poisoning the community."

"As I see it, we have roughly seven different actions we could take right now [A - G below and on page 214]. What do you think we should do?"

A. Consult with the legal staff (GO TO 93).

B. Arrange to have a second test done at the well (GO TO 32).

C. Seek to discover if the problem is caused by a continuing leak or an old spill (GO TO 9).

D. Retain a consultant to investigate the problem and provide a recommendation (GO TO 45).

E. Shut off all drinking fountains and instruct employees not to drink the water. Tell them a test had detected some impurities but be vague about precisely what has been found at this time (GO TO 18).

F. Shut off all drinking fountains and tell the employees exactly everything you know at this point. Tell them you are conducting more tests (GO TO 69).

G. Shut off all drinking fountains, tell employees exactly everything you know at this point, inform all affected outside agencies (EPA, Department of Water Quality), and announce the situation through a press release (GO TO 99).

Appendix of Decision Points

Decision Point 1

She responds, "I don't know. I can't just cut back on my hours. That would mean having to move out of the dorm and back home. I hate to say this, but the last time I asked for your help in a situation like this, things didn't work out at all." (Four months ago you went to much trouble rescheduling the hours your people worked during the Christmas rush to adapt to Becky's need to prepare for exams.) Her comment really disappoints and hurts you.

What would you say now?

A.   "Becky, you are not being fair. Do you know how tricky it was to juggle schedules last Christmas?" (GO TO 27)

B.   "I'm surprised and disappointed to hear you say that my rescheduling didn't help. Maybe if you told me more about your situation, we could find a solution." (GO TO 16)

C.   "Just because it didn't work out before doesn't mean that it can't work out this time. Do you have any suggestions we might put to use?" (GO TO 85)

Decision Point 2

You console her by telling her how much pressure the dean is under to keep his budget under control. She coolly thanks you for your understanding but seems annoyed by your rather paternalistic comment.

Your response was not the best one. Remember that your Director of Admissions is a professional with an internal locus of control as you re-evaluate your last decision. Circle the #2 you just wrote in your flow diagram, and move to the last uncircled step in your flow diagram.

Decision Point 3

Your final ethical challenge began with a visit from one of your best procurement specialists, Janice McCall. Procurement is a vital function at Navajo Semiconductor, as it is with most companies in the industry. The reason is that certain electronic components are controlled by a small number of suppliers who virtually dictate cost and availability. Procurement people are therefore "at the mercy" of their vendors, an arrangement quite different from other corporate enterprises.

216

Two months ago while sharing lunch in the company cafeteria, Janice complained that one of her vendors was harassing her. Since this was a rather off-handed remark, you mistakenly didn't think much about it, but yesterday, Janice gave you an ultimatum based on the same incident. It seems that the salesman at a major supplier has been sexually harassing Janice for several months and at the last private meeting between the two he touched her against her will. After relating the situation, Janice told you that she refuses to deal with that supplier in the future.

What makes this situation so complicated is that there is only one other procurement specialist at Navajo--Elizabeth Morton, a young and inexperienced professional who has always given you the impression of being overly concerned about making a good impression with you. There is another procurement position authorized, but it has been vacant for some time and the only acceptable male candidate for the job is not as qualified as the two other female candidates. The demands of your job do not permit you to take on the troublesome vendor yourself.

What would you do about this situation?

A.   Hire the male candidate and assign the troublesome vendor to him (GO TO 77).

B.   Assign the troublesome vendor to Elizabeth Morton--the other procurement specialist (GO TO 40).

C.   Personally contact the troublesome vendor representative and confront him about his sexual harassment. Let him know that you are unwilling to continue the business relationship if his objectionable behavior continues (GO TO 21).

D.   Meet with the manager of the troublesome representative and report the instance of sexual harassment. Indicate that you will have to discontinue business with the vendor unless the situation is rectified (GO TO 72).

E.   Offer Janice McCall the option of counseling to deal more effectively with the vendor (GO TO 44).

F.   Refer the problem to your boss who you know has a personal relationship with people in the vendor organization with the idea that he can probably de-escalate this situation with his personal influence (GO TO 48).

G.   Discontinue business with the vendor in question (GO TO 12).

Decision Point 4

You decided to give your boss a 20-minute briefing during which you would lay out the issue in some detail, outline the options, and make a recommendation for approval.

This was not a good plan. Your boss is experiencing data overload. In interacting with her, you should be guided by the KISS principle (Keep It Simple Stupid!).

Re-evaluate your last decision. Circle the #4 you just wrote in your flow diagram. Then move to the last uncircled step in your flow diagram.

Decision Point 5

You decide to look into the basis for their suggestion. Working with the testing agency and the accreditation agency, you develop a fair and equitable way of dealing with applicants from this country. Your leadership is this situation worked out well since you were dealing with a cohesive work group and accordingly had no need to supply either directive or supportive leadership.

It is now August and the peak season for your record analysts. Unfortunately, one of your people resigned, and you had to hire someone without conducting the typically exhaustive search you usually do. Two weeks after you hire this person, he comes to your office and tells you he is worried and depressed about his ability to handle the start of the new academic year. How would you react to his concern?

A. Express your heart-felt concern that you would not have hired him if you did not think he could handle the demands of his job (GO TO 76).

B. Ask him specifically what he is concerned about so you can give him detailed instructions in areas he is uncomfortable with (GO TO 25).

C. Be firm in asserting that he should put his feelings aside and concentrate on the year ahead (GO TO 31).

Decision Point 6

Twice you were offered a list of alternatives that would seem to have given you a better chance for plugging the leak at Navajo Semiconductor. Most of them violated certain rights of one kind or another (e.g., private investigation) or they were questionable from the standpoint of justice (e.g., transferring employees with relatives in competing firms). You stayed away from these options apparently because the benefits to the company were not sufficiently strong to justify your violating these ethical tenets.

Would your actions have been different if over 90% of your personal net worth was in Navajo stock? Would it have any moral significance if, because of the leaks, the company could not pursue an electronic devise that would reduce the likelihood of Sudden Infant Death Syndrome (SIDS)? What we are doing here is changing the case obviously, but it may be useful for you to consider if there are circumstances within which you would temper your conclusions about more effective but invasive options.

GO TO 3 for your next ethical challenge.

Decision Point 7

She thanks you for your offer and promises to think about it. Three days later you contact her again. She tells you she has discussed the matter with others and that a replacement of the summer assortment is out of the question. Apparently you were not forthright enough in making it more attractive for her to comply with your request.

Re-evaluate your last decision. Circle the #7 you just wrote in your flow diagram. Then move to the last uncircled step in your flow diagram.

Decision Point 8

You call all of the record analysts together, tell them of the problem and ask for suggestions on how the situation might be improved. They recommend that you give the assignment to the student workers. This is unacceptable, since you do not think it is prudent to allow students to work on the files of other students. You point that out, but they insist that if you don't like the way they do it, perhaps you should give it to someone else to do.

One reason your approach did not work well is that your record analysts are dealing with tasks that have clear procedures for completing the task. With very certain tasks, the path-goal theory recommends that leaders make follower jobs more satisfying. With that in mind, re-evaluate your last decision. Circle the #8 you just wrote in your flow diagram, and move to the last uncircled step in your flow diagram.

Decision Point 9

You ask Joy to investigate whether the contamination was caused by an old spill or an existing leak. She discovers that there is no ongoing leakage problem so it is likely that the problem occurred three years ago when an employee who no longer works for the company dropped three drums of the substance off of a loading dock by mistake.

Would you take any other action?

A.   No (GO TO 55).

B.   Yes. Arrange to have the well tested periodically to order to monitor BTH levels (GO TO 86).

C.   Yes. Retain a consultant to investigate the problem and provide a recommendation (GO TO 45).

D.   Yes. Shut off all drinking fountains and instruct employees not to drink the water. Tell them a test had detected some impurities but be vague about precisely what has been found at this time (GO TO 18).

E.   Yes. Shut off all drinking fountains and tell the employees exactly everything you know at this point. Tell them you are conducting more tests (GO TO 69).

F.   Yes. Shut off all drinking fountains, tell employees exactly everything you know at this point, inform all affected outside agencies (EPA, Department of Water Quality), and announce the situation through a press release (GO TO 99).

Decision Point 10

You attempt to discredit the arguments of the marketing research people. This has little effect. Jean's report is an impressive document, and your argument falls on deaf ears.

Re-evaluate your last decision. Circle the #10 you just wrote in your flow diagram. Then move to the last uncircled step in your flow diagram.

Decision Point 11

You ask her what she is going to do now. She tells you she will not press the matter at this point but may quietly lobby for the change she wants at a later time. Your approach in dealing with the Director of Admission was a good one. As a professional, she required neither directive nor supportive leadership. Your approach was neither.

A week later, one of your student workers approaches you with an interesting proposition. He has noticed that many MBA students are using the copy machine located across the street in the student union building. He suggests that if a machine is put on the ground floor of the business school building, the revenues from the machine might be used for some sort of business student social function.

This student worker is perhaps the most conscientious worker you have. He is a vice-president in the MBA student association, he carries a 3.7/4.0 grade point average, and he is also a part-time employee of a large computer firm. How would you respond to his comments?

A. Ask him what he thinks the next step should be (GO TO 95).

B. Offer advice as to how he might proceed with his suggestion (GO TO 43).

C. Give him encouragement that his idea is excellent, and that you will investigate its merits (GO TO 79).

Decision Point 12

You decide to discontinue business with the vendor in question. You discover that other vendors cannot meet the specifications you require, so you are now in the position of either seriously jeopardizing the well-being of the company or continuing to do business with this vendor. You take the matter to your boss who tells you that it is strategically imperative that you acquire units from this vendor. Now what?

A. Hire the male candidate and assign the troublesome vendor to him (GO TO 77).

B. Assign the troublesome vendor to Elizabeth Morton--the other procurement specialist (GO TO 40).

C. Personally contact the troublesome vendor representative and confront him about his sexual harassment. Let him know that you are unwilling to continue the business relationship if his objectionable behavior continues (GO TO 21).

D. Meet with the manager of the troublesome representative and report the instance of sexual harassment. Indicate that you will have to discontinue business with the vendor unless the situation is rectified (GO TO 72).

E. Tell Janice McCall that it is her job to deal with the vendor in question and if she is unwilling to do so, you will have to take disciplinary action (GO TO 15).

F. Refer the problem to your boss who you know has a personal relationship with people in the vendor organization with the idea that he can probably de-escalate this situation with his personal influence (GO TO 48).

Decision Point 13

She tells you that replacing the merchandise will come to the attention of her boss and may cause her problems. In addition, it would involve a great amount of paperwork that she personally does not have the time or the resources to do.

What would your say now?

A. Offer to help her with the paperwork and agree to talk with your boss about getting the message to her boss that she is being extremely helpful and alert to local conditions (GO TO 97).

B. Remind her that her boss is likely to be more pleased with volume figures than with the consistency of product across the entire chain. Translate your expected volume for a fashion-versus-quality assortment into volume figures to reinforce your point. Offer to help her with the additional paperwork (GO TO 38).

C. Be sympathetic but offer no help. After all, the mistake was hers (GO TO 65).

Decision Point 14

You are able to give Marnie a number of suggestions. Namely, you suggest that she arrange to set up a recruiting booth at an annual professional conference for engineers and to ask the dean to help her gain entry with local firms. Both suggestions bear fruit, and Marnie's numbers improve.

The reason your leadership worked in this instance is that Marnie apparently has an external locus of control. She did not see any options other than the ones she had tried and considered failures. In situations like this, directive leadership works best and that is exactly the kind of leadership you provided.

Four days later, you attend a meeting on campus on the implementation of a new university-wide computer information system. In attendance is one of your subordinates, the Director of Admissions. As you walk out of the meeting, she tells you that the dean has rejected her plans for a new recruiting brochure. You were aware that she was going to speak to the dean about an idea to design a brochure that would be potentially more effective but at an additional cost. She seems disappointed by the dean's decision, but she is a very professional person with more than eighteen years of experience.

How would you respond to her disappointment?

A. Give her suggestions as to how to proceed from this point (GO TO 54).

B. Console her. Let her know how much pressure the dean is under to keep his budget under control (GO TO 2).

C. Ask her what she is going to do now (GO TO 11).

D. Listen to her but say nothing (GO TO 84).

Decision Point 15

You tell Janice McCall that it is her job to deal with the vendor in question and if she is unwilling to do so, you will have to take disciplinary action. She reacts to your comments by resigning and filing a nuisance law suit.

Fundamentally, this part of the case pits principles of justice against those that represent the best interests of the firm (utilitarianism). You decided to deal with this tough moral issue by giving considerable weight to the interests of the organization.

There is really no answer to this dilemma that would be authorized by all ethics experts. It is controversial; indeed it is difficult to say whether justice has weight over the interests of the firm in this circumstance. Feminists may contend that the historical practice of ignoring instances of sexual harassment gives additional strength to the moral argument on behalf of injustice. As in all parts of this case, the answer is your answer. The feedback you have received in this case is intended to give you food for thought and to stimulate you to further develop your ethical thinking, not to reflect any correct answers but to be more carefully thought-through. Congratulations on completing the Management Ethics Interactive Case.

Decision Point 16

Becky bolts a bit at your reaction, "Oh, I'm sorry, it's not that I didn't appreciate your help, believe me. It's just that I'm having a heckuva time balancing school and work, and it seems that rescheduling is not the answer. I need more time to study, but I need the money too." Her voice is quivering.

You discuss the matter further and hit on a satisfactory arrangement. You will reduce her hours slightly during the school year and compensate by increasing her hours dramatically during her spring and summer breaks.

Later that afternoon your boss tells you that there is a crisis with the Easter Sale scheduled this weekend. It seems that advertisements have already appeared offering a particular outfit that lists for $89.95 for $79.95. The problem is that the buyer of that line (petites and traditionals) just revealed that the supplier is facing labor problems and is unable to ship the product. This means that someone must assess the stock on hand and assemble a range of sizes and styles that is a comparable value at the sale price. If a list of merchandise is completed by tomorrow at 3:00 p.m., you can look it over, calculate the revised margins, and have the salespeople begin to mark down the sale items. You know the selection will be tricky, for you do not want any item marked down more than 30%. The last time you faced this situation two years ago, you knocked around a lot before you discovered how to do it. At last, you asked the financial people to give you a readout on the relevant product lines according to price. This enabled you to put together the assortment quickly (in about seven hours). You have a very busy schedule for tomorrow, so you decide to delegate this job to your assistant, Candace Beal.

How would you begin to communicate this assignment to her?

A.   "I need you to do something for me that is vitally important. It will take 7 or 8 hours, but you'll have to start right away. It will take a minute or two to describe, but I want to make sure you have the time. Do you?" (GO TO 22)

224

B.   "I hate to ask you to do this, but would you mind arranging for an equivalent range of sizes and style for the Easter Sale. You see, the vendor for this sale is unable to deliver, so we must make do with our present assortment." (GO TO 87)

C.   "Candace, drop everything you are doing and get the financial people to give you a readout on all the lines in petites and traditionals. Our vendor for the Easter special can't deliver, so we must do with our present assortment. Once you have the printout, decide which outfits are equivalent. Then give me the list for review, and if it's okay I'll get the clerks to start marking the price tags." (GO TO 81)

Decision Point 17

You invite the student workers to give you suggestions on how they would like to deal with this situation. They tell you that it would help if you could rearrange their schedules to accommodate some problems they are having with their school work. You do so even though it involves juggling the schedules of some of your full-time people.

Although things seem to improve for a while, three weeks later you begin to hear some of the same complaints that brought the problem to your attention in the first place. The problem you face with this group of student employees is that the students are indifferent toward the rewards that you have to offer them. Keep that in mind as you re-evaluate your last decision. Circle the #17 you just wrote in your flow diagram, and move to the last uncircled step in your flow diagram.

Decision Point 18

You shut off all drinking fountains and instruct employees not to drink the water. Further, you tell them that a test had detected some impurities but you are intentionally vague about precisely what has been found. A week later, one of your female employees who is expecting a baby asks you what the contaminant in the water is. Would you tell her?

A.   Yes (GO TO 80).

B.   No (GO TO 74).

Decision Point 19

Marion's secretary tells you that she is most receptive in the morning. Therefore, you decide to meet with her then. Precisely how would you approach her on this subject?

A. Plan for a 5-minute briefing during which you will lay out an abbreviated description of the issue, outline at most three options, and make a recommendation for approval (GO TO 53).

B. Plan for a 20-minute briefing during which you will lay out the issue in some detail, outline the options, and make a recommendation for approval (GO TO 4).

C. Plan for a 30-minute meeting, but let your boss control how it unfolds (GO TO 70).

Decision Point 20

You ask the record analysts involved if there is some way that you can help them complete their assignments more accurately. They tell you that the present database of student records cannot give them an array of final grade point averages from the highest to the lowest. This necessitates the creation of an array by hand, and that is both time-consuming and error-prone. You were not aware of this problem, so you ask one of your part-time student workers to create a program using the database software to generate the necessary array. Students never complain about their honors status again.

Calculating an array of grade point averages is a task with clear procedures. Accordingly, supportive leadership was required. Your action provided this support and stimulated helpful improvements.

Two weeks later, you hear some disturbing facts about a situation you have been watching for some time. During evenings when the MBA classes are being conducted on campus, you employ two part-time student workers to "cover" the information booth in the office. This task involves answering student questions about adding and dropping courses, program policies and rules, and graduation requirements. When questions come up that they cannot answer, they are instructed to take the student's name and phone number for a follow-up phone call. In general, the job is rather routine.

You have heard several complaints from faculty members and students alike that these students view their jobs more as an opportunity to make friends and "fool around" than to help students with their questions. You have talked to the student workers before about the importance of helping students and maintaining a professional decorum. You concluded that these students probably did not need the job nor were they particularly motivated by any of the other rewards that you could promise them. When you confront them again, they are embarrassed and contrite, but they respond no differently than they did last time. What would you do?

A. Dismiss the students from their jobs and replace them with student workers who place more value on the rewards you have control over (GO TO 28).

B. Be directive with the students making clear how important it is for them to maintain a professional decorum (GO TO 68).

C. Ask the student workers if there is some way that you can help them complete their assignments more effectively (GO TO 62).

D. Invite the student workers to give you suggestions on how they would like to deal with this situation (GO TO 17).

Decision Point 21

You contact the troublesome vendor representative and confront him about his sexual harassment. You inform him that you are unwilling to continue the business relationship if his objectionable behavior continues. He absolutely denies the facts given you by Janice McCall. You decide to go back to Janice, and she confirms your gut feelings that the man is lying.

You ask your administrative assistant to evaluate how important this representative is to your total business. He assures you that without the supplies provided by this vendor at the present price levels, the profitability of Navajo Semiconductor will suffer dramatically. Now what?

A. Hire the male candidate and assign the troublesome vendor to him (GO TO 77).

B. Assign the troublesome vendor to Elizabeth Morton--the other procurement specialist (GO TO 40).

C. Meet with the manager of the troublesome representative and report the instance of sexual harassment. Indicate that you will have to discontinue business with the vendor unless the situation is rectified (GO TO 72).

D. Offer Janice McCall the option of counseling to deal more effectively with the vendor (GO TO 44).

E. Refer the problem to your boss who you know has a personal relationship with people in the vendor organization with the idea that he can probably de-escalate this situation with his personal influence (GO TO 48).

F. Discontinue business with the vendor in question (GO TO 12).

Decision Point 22

You now need to communicate this assignment. You decide to open your statement to Candace with the following lines: "Our vendor for the Easter Sale can't provide the product. So, we need to supply the sale from our existing merchandise. It's real important that you create a comparable assortment to serve as our sale items from our existing stock..."

What would you say next?

A. "The only constraint you have is to avoid marking down any item more than 30%. Get back to me tomorrow by 5 pm to let me know what assortment you have chosen. Do you have any questions?" (GO TO 56)

B. "This is a difficult problem, but I think if you work hard, you can solve it. Ask the financial people to give you a readout on all the lines involved. This will be your guide in deciding what items to mark down. Stay away from products that involve a markdown of more than 30%. I need the list by 5 p.m. tomorrow." (GO TO 81)

C. "I'll need the list by 5 p.m. tomorrow so I can get the salespeople started on the markdowns. Keep items out of your assortment that exceed a markdown of 30%. When I had to do this last autumn, I began by asking the financial people to give me a readout on all the lines involved. This was my guide in deciding what items to mark down. You may want to do this job the same way, but it's really up to you." (GO TO 24)

Decision Point 23

Your pattern of responses is common in this episode. First try something that might work but is less invasive, and if that doesn't work, try something with a much higher promise of a positive outcome but that is objectionable as a rights violation.

One thing to think about here is whether you think there is much of a moral difference between your first decision to talk to people and your decision to use a private investigator who would have probably invaded their privacy. If you do, how is your action qualitatively different from a student who only resorts to cheating after he has tried to study for an exam? If you are open to this parallel, consider that it is rather egotistical for us to reason that if an action we took didn't work, that it was a poor action. It might have been the right action but a poor execution. So, before poor outcomes lead you to under-estimate the moral problems with subsequent actions, ask yourself whether one attempt at doing "the right thing" is enough.

GO TO 3 for your final ethical challenge.

Decision Point 24

Candace decides not to use the readout method, and this really delays her completion of the assignment. However, the method she did use enabled her to discover a mistake in pricing that, once corrected, saved the company $6,000. The delay cost you $40 in overtime, so on net, Candace did very well.

The Monday following the Easter Sale, a load of summer dresses arrives from the warehouse. You and Candace do an initial inspection and look over the manifests. Both of you conclude that the assortment represents a level of fashion that is far too avant-garde for your clientele. It appears that Jean Volk (the buyer for dresses) really screwed up. You decide to confront Jean with your observations and try to get her to send you a different assortment.

How would you address this issue with Jean?

A. Send Jean a memorandum detailing your concerns. Send a carbon copy to her boss (GO TO 30).

B. Meet with Jean to discuss the matter (GO TO 46).

Decision Point 25

The new employee tells you his concerns, and you direct him as to what the policies and procedures are. This seems to satisfy him for the time being, but he returns to your office shortly before the beginning of the school year with the same concern. You again give him direction, and he seems satisfied that he is prepared. Directive leadership is called for in situations where subordinates have low self-confidence.

The students return to campus, and your new record analyst performs very well. He is prepared, and he seems to have gained confidence from the experience. Congratulations! You have successfully completed the Leadership Interactive Case.

Decision Point 26

You hire a private investigator to look into the matter. The investigator runs a background credit check to see if any of your salespeople has financial problems. She next follows several suspected employees after work to identify their associates, and conducts a thorough background check on a number of high-probability employees.

After one month, the investigator tells you that he has no definitive information on any employee except one who was found to have a step-sister working for a competing firm. Further, the investigator recommends a sting operation in which several employees would be placed in a position of selling company secrets to see if they would.

Before considering your next move, reflect on the result of the action you have taken. Investigations were conducted that some may find a morally objectionable invasion of privacy. True, the stakes were high for the company, and perhaps this justifies such action, but consider two things. First, your moral responsibility for any violation that might be said to occur cannot be delegated to a private investigator. As your agent, he or she acted with your moral authority. Second, this investigation "worked out" well in that no one ever discovered that you had ordered it. Some investigations are discovered, and when they are, employees often feel a tremendous sense of betrayal that their employer did that to them. Thus, a moral use of private investigators to search for leaks of company secrets should be measured against potential employee rights violations and the potential negative effects when private investigations become not all that private.

Now that you've considered the matter thoroughly, what would you do?

A.   Authorize the sting investigation (GO TO 35).

B.   Arrange to have an individual meeting with each member of the sales force in which you will talk broadly about the security problem, listen carefully to responses, and urge them to maintain very strict standards of secrecy (GO TO 36).

C.   Require that each employee take a polygraph (lie detector test) regarding their involvement with competing firms [In this jurisdiction, the use of lie detectors for this purpose is legal.](GO TO 41).

D. Talk first with those people who are in a better position to divulge corporate secrets to competitors. Tell them they are under suspicion and that any leak traced back to them will be dealt with as a severe violation of company policy (GO TO 90).

E. Talk privately with each employee and tell them that you will pay a large monetary "bonus" for information leading to the identification of any sales employee who is releasing company secrets in an unauthorized way (GO TO 82).

F. Call the entire sales staff together and inform them of the importance of corporate security. Let them know that if information on new products gets out prematurely, it could mean a serious decline in the health of the company and may result in the loss of jobs (GO TO 96).

G. Transfer those salespeople who are related to individuals in competing firms to other positions where security is not as critical (GO TO 64).

Decision Point 27

Becky apologizes, but your rejoinder has a chilling effect on the rest of the conversation. Your meeting ends with no resolution. Two days later you arrive at work to discover a note from Becky on your desk. It reads:

> "I got my Statistics test back, and it was a D-. I've talked to my Dad, and he's given me a loan so I won't have to work any more. I'd like to work for you this summer, but I can't give you hours until then. I hope you understand."

You call her, but she has her mind made up. You have lost a valued employee needlessly. Counseling an employee can be a difficult interpersonal situation. Maintaining a counselling relationship requires that you avoid getting into an argument with the employee even if the employee says things that are not completely accurate or fair.

Re-evaluate your last decision. Circle the #27 you just wrote in your flow diagram. Then move to the last uncircled step in your flow diagram.

Decision Point 28

You dismiss the problem student workers and replace them with others who really need the money the job offers. The problem disappears.

This may strike you as a rather harsh leadership action. It is. However, the principle is that leader actions have little or no influence when employees are indifferent to the rewards offered by the organization. If disruptive behavior occurs, leaders have little choice other than to find rewards that are motivating. You were not given any options, other than the one you chose, that involved the discovery of such rewards.

Six weeks later, Marnie Chase, one of your two recruiters, comes into your office and tells you that the recruiting for next year is not going well. Marnie is responsible for recruiting students from local businesses for the evening MBA program and for the executive MBA program. At the beginning of the year, she was given a quota of applicants based largely on historical standards. Yet, the high-tech sector of the economy is depressed this year, and that means that firms are not very supportive of recruiters who visit and try to talk students into taking advantage of company tuition-reimbursement policies. This has meant that Marnie has been frustrated in her attempts to visit local firms to recruit students. Accordingly, her numbers are way down, and she is upset. In her words, "How can Morrisey expect me to bring them students when the whole industry is depressed? I've done everything I know to get more students to apply, believe me. It's really out of my control!"

How would you respond to Marnie?

A. Tell her the situation will probably improve soon and that she shouldn't be too concerned. Emphasize the positive accomplishments she has made in the past as a means of buoying her sagging ego (GO TO 71).

B. Call others involved in recruiting into the discussion with Marnie, and facilitate a group problem-solving session (GO TO 57).

C. Offer suggestions as to how she might recruit students under the conditions she has described (GO TO 14).

Decision Point 29

A second issue that crosses your desk that appears to have ethical implications regards a security problem. It is critical to keep information secure about new products being developed by Navajo Semiconductor. If such information falls into the hands of competing firms, it could seriously jeopardize the firm's competitive position. Recently, you were contacted by a headquarter's senior vice president who indicated that a leak of new product information from your divisional sales staff had been detected. Apparently, a "sting operation" had been conducted by headquarters where your entire sales force was given trivial disinformation about the company's future new products. The senior vice president learned that this information got out to one competitor.

This is particularly important since the sales staff is about to be briefed on a development that, if it got out, would cost the company a very significant amount of development money. The sales force *must* be briefed on this development. Otherwise, they will not be able to develop tactical sales plans that are critical to the new product's ultimate success.

This has been a problem you have had before. Some of your company's competitors are very ruthless, so you are uncertain whether your sales people have been part of a conspiracy or been unsuspecting dupes in a campaign of industrial espionage. One fact that has always troubled you is that one of your salespeople is married to an engineer in a competing company, and two others are more distantly related to officials of competing firms.

In the past when this issue has arisen, you have worked directly with Mark Felix, your vice president of sales, in addressing the issue. This time, however, the headquarter's people tell you that he too is a suspect.

What would you do?

A. Arrange to have an individual meeting with each member of the sales force in which you will talk broadly about the security problem, listen carefully to responses, and urge them to maintain very strict standards of secrecy (GO TO 36).

B. Require that each employee take a polygraph (lie detector test) regarding their involvement with competing firms [In this jurisdiction, the use of lie detectors for this purpose is legal.](GO TO 41).

C. Talk first with those people who are in a better position to divulge corporate secrets to competitors. Tell them they are under suspicion and that any leak traced back to them will be dealt with as a severe violation of company policy (GO TO 90).

D. Hire a private investigator to look into the matter (GO TO 26).

E. Talk privately with each employee and tell them that you will pay a large monetary "bonus" for information leading to the identification of any sales employee who is releasing company secrets in an unauthorized way (GO TO 82).

F. Call the entire sales staff together and inform them of the importance of corporate security. Let them know that if information on new products gets out prematurely, it could mean a serious decline in the health of the company and may result in the loss of jobs (GO TO 96).

G. Transfer those salespeople who are related to individuals in competing firms to other positions where security is not as critical (GO TO 64).

Decision Point 30

This pressure tactic fails miserably. Jean is very resentful of your intervention with her boss. She is not motivated to develop a new assortment. By the end of the year, your sales in the dress line are at an all-time low.

By sending a copy of your memo to Jean's boss, she may have felt you were trying to pressure her. Pressure oftentimes backfires by strengthening the other party's commitment to his or her original position. Pressure tends to be effective only after other influence techniques have been tried. Re-evaluate your last decision. Circle the #30 you just wrote in your flow diagram. Then move to the last uncircled step in your flow diagram.

Decision Point 31

You are firm in asserting that he should put his feelings aside and concentrate on the year ahead. The worker reacts neutrally and goes back to work. The next day he quits, citing insensitive leadership. You may have missed the point that this new employee had poor self-confidence.

Re-evaluate your last decision. Circle the #31 you just wrote in your flow diagram, and move to the last uncircled step in your flow diagram.

Decision Point 32

You ask Joy to have another test done on the well. Eight weeks later the results show a reading of 47 ppb compared to 50 ppb on the first test. This tells you that the BTH levels were probably caused by an old spill.

What would you do now?

A. Nothing (GO TO 55).

B. Arrange to have the well tested periodically to order to monitor BTH levels (GO TO 86).

C.   Retain a consultant to investigate the problem and provide a recommendation (GO TO 45).

D.   Shut off all drinking fountains and instruct employees not to drink the water. Tell them a test had detected some impurities but be vague about precisely what has been found at this time (GO TO 18).

E.   Shut off all drinking fountains and tell the employees exactly everything you know at this point. Tell them you are conducting more tests (GO TO 69).

F.   Shut off all drinking fountains, tell employees exactly everything you know at this point, inform all affected outside agencies (EPA, Department of Water Quality), and announce the situation through a press release (GO TO 99).

Decision Point 33

She responds, "Yes, I have a tutor, but she is no help either." She is growing increasingly frustrated with your conversation.

How would you react to this?

A.   "Why don't you wait until you get your exam back before you worry. Who knows, maybe you did fine." (GO TO 59)

B.   "Are you telling me that you want to cut back on your hours?" (GO TO 42)

C.   "I'm sure you'll work it out. Things will get better, you'll see. You're a smart person." (GO TO 73)

D.   "Sounds like a frustrating situation. Can you think of anything I might do to help?" (GO TO 1)

Decision Point 34

You advise the group on how it should proceed from this point. The group does not accept your recommendations but instead goes its own way. In fact, your advice caused the group to go out of its way to avoid following it. Accordingly, since one of your suggestions was valid, the group fails to get the results it hoped for. Moreover, they blame you for their failure.

The point that you may have missed is that you are dealing with a very cohesive group that has all the leadership activities contained within itself. In a very real sense, any leadership you try to create is superfluous.

Re-evaluate your last decision. Circle the #34 you just wrote in your flow diagram, and move to the last uncircled step in your flow diagram.

Decision Point 35

On the basis of your private investigation, you decide to authorize a sting investigation. Coming after your choice to use a private investigator, this decision indicates that you do not give much weight to privacy rights for employees. Realize that others may disagree with your position. It might be useful for you to consider just what rights employees have. Does an employer have the right to strip-search its employees? If employees go through a divorce or changes religious affiliation, should they be required to inform his or her employee? These are important questions for you because your responses to this episode indicate that you do not apparently think employee rights are an important moral concern.

GO TO 3 for your final ethical challenge.

Decision Point 36

You decide to arrange to have an individual meeting with each member of the sales force during which you talk broadly about the security problem, listen carefully to responses, and urge them to maintain very strict standards of secrecy. Nothing special comes up during these meetings, but you feel you have communicated that security is a high priority.

Two months after the meetings the sales force is again briefed on highly secret product information so they can do their necessary tactical planning. The very next week, information filters back to you that competing firms are already positioning their product against your firm's as yet, officially unannounced products. A leak has occurred again, and high officials at corporate headquarters are very disappointed in your actions.

At this point, it is possible to evaluate your actions from an ethical viewpoint. Specifically, utilitarian ethics holds that actions are unethical if they produce outcomes that are less effective than the outcomes of other alternatives. The question here is whether it is reasonable to expect that the option you chose might have worked, i.e., produced effective outcomes. It didn't work, but that is not the whole question. It appears that you excluded some options because they were more invasive but might have stopped the leaks.

What would you do now?

A. Require that each employee take a polygraph (lie detector test) regarding their involvement with competing firms [In this jurisdiction, the use of lie detectors for this purpose is legal.](GO TO 66).

B. Talk first with those people who are in a better position to divulge corporate secrets to competitors. Tell them they are under suspicion and that any leak traced back to them will be dealt with as a severe violation of company policy (GO TO 90).

C. Hire a private investigator to look into the matter (GO TO 23).

D. Talk privately with each employee and tell them that you will put a large monetary "bonus" for information leading to the identification of any sales employee who is releasing company secrets in an unauthorized way (GO TO 82).

E. Call the entire sales staff together and inform them of the importance of corporate security. Let them know that if information on new products gets out prematurely, it could mean a serious decline in the health of the company and may result in the loss of jobs (GO TO 96).

F. Transfer those salespeople who are related to individuals in competing firms to other positions where security is not as critical (GO TO 64).

G. Meet with people individually once again and try to motivate them to maintain better security practices (GO TO 6).

Decision Point 37

You change the procedures to reflect the possibility for errors by asking a second record analyst to check the work of the first. This results in a modest improvement in the error rate, but two new problems appear. First, conflicts develop between the workers and those checking their work. Second, several of your employees balk at being asked to perform the task since it is seen as very tedious. As you look back over what you did, you wish you had not changed the procedures.

One reason your approach did not work well is that your record analysts are dealing with tasks that have clear procedures for completing the task. With very certain tasks, the path-goal theory recommends that leaders make follower jobs more satisfying. With that in mind, re-evaluate your last decision. Circle the #37 you just wrote in your flow diagram, and move to the last uncircled step in your flow diagram.

Decision Point 38

Jean finally agrees to replace the assortment. You follow up by helping her with the paperwork and by feeding the grapevine via your boss to hers. The new line arrives and it is an excellent one. Your summer sales volume hits an all-time high. You made Jean more willing to change by showing how replacing the line would be in her interest as well as yours. You also made it easy for her to act by helping with the work.

Congratulations! You have just completed the Communication Interactive Case.

Decision Point 39

You look into the matter of the evaluation of international transcripts and develop a series of procedures that help your record analysts with the problem. All seems to go well with the new arrangement; the procedures handle all but the most unique contingencies which you are able to handle on a case-by-case basis.

Your leadership in this instance was effective because your record analysts were experiencing uncertain tasks. Under such circumstances, directive leadership is called for, and your action provided that.

Two weeks later a second issue emerges. All graduating students who are in the upper 15 percent of their class qualify for graduation with honors, a special distinction of considerable importance to students. To determine which students qualify for the honors award, your record analysts must go through the transcripts of graduating students and separate out those whose grade point average puts them in the upper 15 percent. The problem is that several graduating students complain to your office that they qualified for honors status, but did not receive that award. After looking through the procedures and questioning record analysts who worked on this assignment, it is clear that several mistakes were made. Whether oversights or miscalculations, you feel these mistakes are serious enough to require corrective action.

What would you do?

A. Change the procedures to reflect the possibility for errors. Ask a second record analyst to check the work of the first (GO TO 37).

B. Identify the analysts who worked on the assignment and call their attention to the problem and insist that it does not happen again (GO TO 98).

C. Call together all of the record analysts, tell them of the problem and ask for suggestions in how the situation might be improved (GO TO 8).

D. Ask the record analysts involved if there is some way that you can help them complete their assignment more accurately. For example, perhaps distractions that you have some control over are the problem (GO TO 20).

Decision Point 40

You assign the troublesome vendor to Elizabeth Morton--the other procurement specialist. This solution works exceptionally well. Indeed, you are very impressed that one procurement specialist could have such a different experience than another. Three months later, however, and Elizabeth too complains about the vendor representative. Apparently, this situation was not just the trumped up complaint of one salesperson but rather a genuine complaint of a sincerely troubled employee.

Re-evaluate your last decision. Circle the #40 you just wrote in your flow diagram. Then move to the first uncircled step above this one in your flow diagram.

Decision Point 41

You decided to require that each employee take a polygraph (lie detector test) regarding their involvement with competing firms. This is objected to by several sales representatives as an invasion of their privacy. The tests are conducted, and three sales representatives fail. One who failed had no relatives working for competitors. One had a nephew working for a competitor. And a third had never before admitted it, but she had a step-sister working for a competitor--a fact that may have never been revealed without the polygraph. In deciding what to do with these three individuals (fire, transfer, give a second chance, etc.), would you treat all three the same or differently?

A. The same (GO TO 51).

B. Differently (GO TO 58).

Decision Point 42

She responds, "I can't cut back on my hours. That would mean having to move out of the dorm and back home. I hate to say this, but the last time I asked for your help in a situation like this, things didn't work out at all." (Four months ago you went to much trouble rescheduling the hours your people worked during the Christmas rush to adapt to Becky's need to prepare for exams.) Her comment really disappoints and hurts you.

What would you say now?

 A.   "Becky, you are not being fair. Do you know how tricky it was to juggle schedules last Christmas?" (GO TO 27)

 B.   "I'm surprised and disappointed to hear you say that my rescheduling didn't help. Maybe if you told me more about your situation, we could find a solution." (GO TO 16)

 C.   "Just because it didn't work out before doesn't mean that it can't work out this time. Maybe you have some suggestions I might put to use?" (GO TO 85)

Decision Point 43

You advise him on how he might proceed with his suggestion. He does not seem to welcome your advice. Instead, he follows-through in his own way and ignores one critical piece of advice that you gave him--perhaps only because you offered it. As a result, the dean rejects his proposal, and your relationship with him becomes very cold.

A critical feature of this situation is that this student has an internal locus of control.

Re-evaluate your last decision. Circle the #43 you just wrote in your flow diagram, and move to the last uncircled step in your flow diagram.

Decision Point 44

You offer Janice McCall the option of counseling to deal more effectively with the vendor. She refuses telling you that she will resign if you force her to do business with him again. Now what would you do?

A. Hire the male candidate and assign the troublesome vendor to him (GO TO 77).

B. Assign the troublesome vendor to Elizabeth Morton--the other procurement specialist (GO TO 40).

C. Personally contact the troublesome vendor representative and confront him about his sexual harassment. Let him know that you are unwilling to continue the business relationship if his objectionable behavior continues (GO TO 21).

D. Meet with the manager of the troublesome representative and report the instance of sexual harassment. Indicate that you will have to discontinue business with the vendor unless the situation is rectified (GO TO 72).

E. Tell Janice McCall that it is her job to deal with the vendor in question and if she is unwilling to do so, you will have to take disciplinary action (GO TO 15).

F. Refer the problem to your boss who you know has a personal relationship with people in the vendor organization with the idea that he can probably de-escalate this situation with his personal influence (GO TO 48).

G. Discontinue business with the vendor in question (GO TO 12).

Decision Point 45

You decide to call Marcia Ball, a consultant in liquid waste management, to investigate the problem and provide a recommendation. Two months later, she gives you a report that concludes that it would be prohibitively expensive to clean up the spill.

What would you do now?

A. Nothing (GO TO 55).

B. Arrange to have the well tested periodically to order to monitor BTH levels (GO TO 86).

C. Shut off all drinking fountains and instruct employees not to drink the water. Tell them a test had detected some impurities but be vague about precisely what has been found at this time (GO TO 18).

D. Shut off all drinking fountains and tell the employees exactly everything you know at this point. Tell them you are conducting more tests (GO TO 69).

E. Shut off all drinking fountains, tell employees exactly everything you know at this point, inform all affected outside agencies (EPA, Department of Water Quality), and announce the situation through a press release (GO TO 99).

Decision Point 46

You ask Jean to come over to the mall. The two of you exchange pleasantries, and you get her a cup of coffee. She opens the issue by asking you how you like the summer line. You admit to her that you think it is entirely too daring and not well suited to your customer base. She tells you that the Manager of Marketing Research advised her to put more fashion into her line. How would you respond?

A. Present a logical argument that she should replace the line with another better suited to your customer pool (GO TO 75).

B. Tell her she must replace the line with one better suited to your customer pool. It she refuses, tell her your will hold her responsible for any volume decline (GO TO 49).

C. Ask her to give you more information about why she wants to build more fashion into her line (GO TO 63).

Decision Point 47

You ask the record analyst who brought you this issue to contact other schools that have European graduate programs and to learn how they handle the issue. He does so, but the findings are highly conflicting. Apparently, each school has its own way of dealing with this problem.

What would you do about this situation?

A. Call the record analysts together and ask them their advice as to how to proceed with the evaluation of transcripts (GO TO 88).

B. Research the issue yourself and develop guidelines and procedures that the record analysts can use to evaluate the transcripts (GO TO 39).

Decision Point 48

You refer the problem to your boss who you know has a personal relationship with people in the vendor organization with the idea that he can probably de-escalate this situation with his personal influence. This works out very, very well. Your boss speaks off the record with officials of the vendor organization, and the particular vendor representative is promoted and subsequently replaced with someone more professional.

The only significant negative development is that Janice McCall leaves the organization feeling betrayed that the vendor representative was apparently promoted for his misdeeds because of the actions of your boss.

Fundamentally, this part of the case pits principles of justice against those that represent the best interests of the firm (utilitarianism). You decided to deal with this tough moral issue the same way that other pragmatists do--through the exercise of quiet diplomacy, power politics, and the proverbial "old boy" network. This is not morally defective except that it allows an injustice to go unresolved. As in all parts of this case, the answer is your answer. The feedback you have received in this case is intended to give you food for thought and to stimulate you to further develop your ethical thinking, not to reflect any correct answers but to be more carefully thought-through. Congratulations on completing the Management Ethics Interactive Case.

Decision Point 49

She accepts that challenge and remains firm that you should stock the assortment she has assembled. Apparently your message had no effect.

Re-evaluate your last decision. Circle the #49 you just wrote in your flow diagram. Then move to the last uncircled step in your flow diagram.

Decision Point 50

You congratulate the group on how conscientious it has been, and then look into the matter. You conclude that the group's idea is a good one and you move ahead and implement it. When you announce your action, you expect some appreciation from the group members. Instead, they react rather indifferently to your announcement. You are tempted to ignore this strange reaction, but you ask one of the members why the group is so unappreciative.

She tells you that she doesn't think the group's reaction is peculiar. She tells you that at times you seem to be trying too hard to be a good leader. This set-back is not a particularly important one except to your ego. The point that you may have missed is that you are dealing with a very cohesive group that has all the leadership activities contained within itself. In a very real sense, any leadership you try to create is superfluous.

Re-evaluate your last decision. Circle the #50 you just wrote in your flow diagram, and move to the last uncircled step in your flow diagram.

Decision Point 51

Your polygraph results in the identification of three employees with three different associations with competitors. You indicate that you would treat them all the same. In doing so, you are being very consistent in your approach to the problem of leaks. Previously, you did not find significance in the nature of these associations, i.e., you forced everyone to submit to the test. Thus, your actions in this episode cannot be questioned on the basis of standards of distributive justice.

There remains, though, the fact that you employed a polygraph to detect the source of an employee security problem. Polygraphs are used in business, particularly in businesses that must handle information of vital national security importance. Is it justified in this case? Not a few would object, a matter that you probably considered carefully. But aside from the standard objection about violating people's rights, the fact that lie detectors create both false positives and false negatives raises justice concerns as well. How would you feel if you were unlucky enough to be detected a liar when you were telling the truth?

GO TO 3 for your final ethical challenge.

Decision Point 52

You decide to discontinue any action regarding the spill. Three years later in a test conducted by the EPA, no BTH contamination is detected.

Your actions seemed predicated on a utilitarian analysis. You apparently believed that the costs of remedying the situation (e.g., informing employees) was far greater than its benefits (the marginal value having people aware of a inconsequential contaminant).

Another moral perspective accords employees (and perhaps even fellow-users of the water in the aquifer) moral rights to uncontaminated water and to information about any contamination. As you reflect on this episode, you may want to consider if you would have continued to drink the water at the plant given the uncertainties surrounding BTH.

GO TO 29 for your next ethical challenge.

Decision Point 53

At the end of your briefing, Marion approves your increase of square footage for furs contingent on her discussing the matter with the Divisional Merchandise Manager, Dresses and Cosmetics. Four days later Marion calls you and gives you the go-ahead. You rearrange your section to increase the space for furs. By meeting face-to-face with Marion at a time when she was not distracted and by keeping your communication short and focused, you were able to command her complete attention.

The following Tuesday afternoon, Becky Stark approaches you obviously distraught. You ask her what the problem is, and she says:

"I'm in a terrible fix. I think I just flunked my Statistics midterm. I don't know, I just can't seem to get math. I've talked to the professor, but he's no help. I just don't know what to do."

What would you say?

A.   "Well, have you considered getting a tutor?" (GO TO 33)

B.   "Why don't you wait until you get your exam back before you worry about it. Who knows, maybe you did fine." (GO TO 59)

C.   "Are you telling me that you want to cut back on your hours?" (GO TO 42)

D.   "I'm sure you'll work it out. Things will get better, you'll see. You're a smart person." (GO TO 73)

E.   "Sounds like a frustrating situation. Can you think of anything I might do to help?" (GO TO 1)

Decision Point 54

You decide to give her suggestions as to how to proceed from this point. She bristles at your suggestions, in effect telling you to mind your own business.

One thing you apparently did not appreciate in choosing this action is that your Director of Admissions is a professional individual with an internal locus of control. As such she did not respond positively to your directive action.

Re-evaluate your last decision. Circle the #54 you just wrote in your flow diagram, and move to the last uncircled step in your flow diagram.

Decision Point 55

You decide to do nothing after you learn that it would be prohibitively expensive to clean up the spill. Three years pass, you have the well tested again, and there is no sign of contamination.

Your actions seemed predicated on a utilitarian analysis of the situation in that the costs of remedying the situation seemed far greater than its benefits. Another moral perspective accords employees (and perhaps even fellow-users of the water in the aquifer) moral rights to uncontaminated water and to information about any contamination. As you reflect on this episode, you may want to consider if you would have continued to drink the water at the plant given the uncertainties surrounding BTH.

GO TO 29 for your next ethical challenge.

Decision Point 56

Candace follows your instructions to the letter, but it takes her 11 hours instead of the seven hours you had estimated. Although your assignment was effective in terms of clarifying your expectations about results, it did not invite participation about means. By engaging Candace in a discussion of how she planned to proceed, you might have learned whether or not she had some good ideas. It also would have provided you an opportunity to introduce her to what you learned when you completed the assignment.

Re-evaluate your last decision. Circle the #56 you just wrote in your flow diagram. Then move to the last uncircled step in your flow diagram.

You call others involved in recruiting into the discussion with Marnie and facilitate a group problem-solving session. Several suggestions are made, but Marnie dismisses all of them as either impractical or something she has already tried. As the meeting ends, you grow convinced that Marnie has an external locus of control. This decision did not work out very well, since participative leadership works much better with people who have an internal locus of control.

Re-evaluate your last decision. Circle the #57 you just wrote in your flow diagram, and move to the last uncircled step in your flow diagram.

Your polygraph results in the identification of three employees with three different associations with competitors. You indicate that you would treat them differently. In doing so, you may be being inconsistent in your approach to the problem of leaks. Previously, you did not find significance in the nature of these associations, i.e., you forced everyone to submit to the test. But now, whether someone has associations with competitors is somehow important. You may have something in mind, but you probably want to think carefully about the pattern of actions you take in morally charged situation. Seeming morally inconsistent has caused more than one manager serious problems.

In addition, there remains the fact that you employed a polygraph to detect the source of an employee security problem. Polygraphs are used in business, particularly in businesses that must handle information of vital national security importance. Is it justified in this case? Not a few would object, a matter that you probably considered carefully. But aside from the standard objection about violating people's rights, the fact that lie detectors create both false positives and false negatives raises justice concerns as well. How would you feel if you were unlucky enough to be detected a liar when you were telling the truth?

GO TO 3 for your final ethical challenge.

Becky responds, "I don't have to wait. I know. If I passed the exam, it will be a miracle. Besides, I know in my heart that I am not getting it." At that point, she breaks down and sobs.

How would you react?

A. "Becky, things are not as bad as you think, you'll see. In the meantime, if you want me to rearrange your hours, let me know." (GO TO 42)

B. "Sounds like you are really frustrated. That's really understandable. You don't have to tell me right now, but if there is anything I can do to help you through this difficult time, please let me know." (GO TO 1)

C. "Becky, try to get hold of yourself. This situation is frustrating, but believe me, in a month or two, you'll look back on this time and laugh." (GO TO 78)

Decision Point 60

You decide to monitor the scientific literature for developments on BTH. Three years pass, and no research appears on the substance. You decide to have the well tested again, and there is no detectable contamination.

Your action is consistent with the practice of equating moral obligations with legal obligations. Perhaps it was the scientific uncertainties in this episode that led you use the law as your moral compass.

Another moral perspective accords employees (and perhaps even fellow-users of the water in the aquifer) moral rights to uncontaminated water and to information about any contamination. As you reflect on this episode, you may want to consider if you would have continued to drink the water at the plant given the uncertainties surrounding BTH.

GO TO 29 for your next ethical challenge.

Decision Point 61

The two of you agree on a time, and the meeting proceeds. Later at an agreed-upon time, you appear at her office. Her secretary tells you she is in conference and cannot be disturbed. You tell her you are expected, but she tells you she knows nothing of your scheduled meeting. Apparently your boss forgot the appointment. You caught her at a bad time when you tried to set up the appointment just before the staff meeting.

Re-evaluate your last decision. Circle the #61 you just wrote in your flow diagram. Then move to the last uncircled step in your flow diagram.

Decision Point 62

You ask the student workers if there is some way that you can help them complete their assignment more effectively. They tell you that it would help if you could rearrange their schedules to accommodate some problems they are having with their school work. You do so even though it involves juggling the schedules of some of your full-time people.

Although things seem to improve for a while, three weeks later you begin to hear some of the same complaints that brought the problem to your attention in the first place.

The problem you face with this group of student employees is that the students are indifferent toward the rewards that you have to offer them. Keep that in mind as you re-evaluate your last decision. Circle the #62 you just wrote in your flow diagram, and move to the last uncircled step in your flow diagram.

Decision Point 63

She says that her boss hasn't spoken to her about this, but that the marketing research people have been urging her to make her line more fashion conscious. She then shows you a 20-page report completed a year ago that indicates that in women's ready-to-wear, Gamage-Nash is seen as the outlet for upscale, fashion conscious consumers. Moreover, it shows that your store lags behind all but one other store (the outlet in Pueblo, Colorado) in the volume for fashion goods. You counter that there are two other retailers in the Academy Mall that deal with women's fashion goods. Your store, like the one in Pueblo, is THE high-quality store in the mall.

She seems unpersuaded by that logic. What would you say next?

A. Tell her that the new summer assortment is really all wrong for your store and insist that she replaces it (GO TO 91).

B. Remind her that her boss is likely to be more pleased with volume figures than with the consistency of product across the entire chain. Translate your expected volume for a fashion-versus-quality assortment into volume figures to reinforce your point (GO TO 94).

C. Discredit the arguments of the marketing research people by asserting that they are not sufficiently close to local conditions (GO TO 10).

D. Find out how difficult it would be for her to replace the merchandise that you have received with an assortment more tailored to your store's needs. Offer to help her with the additional effort required to make that happen (GO TO 13).

Decision Point 64

You transfer those salespeople who are related to individuals in competing firms to other positions where security is not as critical. Two months pass and no further leaks are detected. However, two of the three you transfer leave the organization claiming that they don't think they can live down the damage that has occurred to their "credibility." One of them joins the sales force of Navajo's fiercest competitor, and you suspect that that person may have been passing secrets in the past. The other goes on unemployment and moves out of the area.

How do you feel about how this all worked out? Most people who choose this action end up feeling somewhat confident that they made the right decision, and they bolster that conclusion by reasoning that the salesperson who left the firm was probably at best not very loyal and at worst a spy.

But let's think about the moral issues in this episode. First, there was a very serious set of negative outcomes that would have occurred unless you could take effective action to stop the leaks. Thus, the utilitarian criterion would argue for action. Trouble is, there is no specific action that would work in all circumstances. So, you had to balance the likely result for the company *against* any burdens that would have to be carried by the salespeople. Some actions involved considerable burdens like the use of a lie detector. Arguably, that would have constituted a violation of employee rights. Others, like the one you chose, involved requiring some to carry more burdens than others, i.e., you did not confront those people who did not have relatives working for competitors. Drawing on the standards of justice, one could ask whether it was fair to require these individuals to carry all of these burdens. After all, these employees didn't choose their relatives. Is it fair to make them suspects on these grounds? Your action minimized the number of people who were negatively effected, but is that enough to justify all the possible hardships like those endured by the person now on unemployment? This is a very difficult moral quandary.

GO TO 3 for your next ethical challenge.

250

Decision Point 65

She advises you that she will think about your request to replace the summer assortment. Three days later you contact her again, and she announces that she has discussed the matter with others and that a replacement is out of the question. Apparently you were not forthright enough in making it easier for her to comply with your request.

Re-evaluate your last decision. Circle the #65 you just wrote in your flow diagram. Then move to the last uncircled step in your flow diagram.

Decision Point 66

Your pattern of responses is common in this episode. First try something that might work but is less invasive, and if that doesn't work, try something that promises a positive outcome but that is objectionable as a rights violation.

One thing to think about here is whether you think there is much of a moral difference between your first decision to talk to people and your decision to force them to submit to a lie detector test. If you do, how is your action qualitatively different from a student who only resorts to cheating after he has tried to study for an exam? If you are open to this metaphor, consider that it is rather egotistical for us to reason that if an action we took didn't work, that it was a poor action. It might have been the right action but a poor execution. So, before poor outcomes lead you to under-estimate the moral problems with subsequent actions, ask yourself whether one attempt at doing "the right thing" is enough.

GO TO 3 for your final ethical challenge.

Decision Point 67

The Divisional Merchandise Manager "hits the ceiling" when you mention the change. She immediately phones your boss, who joins your meeting. After the meeting, your boss gives you a tongue-lashing the likes of which you have never gotten before.

As well meaning as your action was, it had serious consequences. You violated the most important rule of subordinate-boss relations--NO SURPRISES!

Re-evaluate your last decision. Circle the #67 you just wrote in your flow diagram. Then move to the last uncircled step in your flow diagram.

Decision Point 68

You are directive with the students and make it clear how important it is for them to maintain a professional decorum. They react much the same way as they have in the past. Two weeks pass, and you hear nothing more of the problem. Then a crisis develops. After an undergraduate student party, two of your student workers show up to work slightly intoxicated. Their rowdy behavior during their work shift disturbs several students who complain to the dean.

The problem you face with this group of student employees is that the students are indifferent toward the rewards that you have to offer them. Keep that in mind as you re-evaluate your last decision. Circle the #68 you just wrote in your flow diagram, and move to the last uncircled step in your flow diagram.

Decision Point 69

You shut off all drinking fountains and tell your employees everything you know about the contamination. The following day you receive a phone call from the local newspaper asking for further information. Realizing that you cannot withhold any information at this point, you tell them everything you know. The following morning the local newspaper runs a headline story on the spill that is very critical of the company. A week later, a female employee who is pregnant files a law suit against your company alleging that damage may have been done to her fetus. A month later at a meeting at corporate headquarters, a senior staff official in public relations tells you that the president of the company strongly disapproved of your handling of the situation. Apparently, the president feels that it would have been better for the company if you had kept your mouth shut about the spill.

At this point you may be wondering whether you did the right thing. Certainly it was impossible to know that one of your employees would file a law suit and that the president of the company would disagree with your actions. However, the news story was predictable as was the leak that preceded it. Perhaps if you had been more open with the press the news story would have been more positive.

Your decisions in this episode, however, appear to be based less on utilitarian ethics than on a moral concern about the rights of the parties involved. Specifically, your actions seem to be consistent with the reasoning that employees have a moral right to drinking water that is free of contaminants from the plant and a right to be informed of the facts of any previous contamination. What is interesting, though, is that you apparently did not extend that right to members of the community who are on wells potentially contaminated by the same spill. Maybe you did not think of that because of the facts regarding fluorine, or maybe you assumed that there were no other wells on that aquifer.

As you reflect back on this episode, try to think whether your decision would have been the same if you had known in advance about the negative consequences. That may give you some sense as to how strong employee rights are in your thinking.

GO TO 29 for your next ethical challenge.

Decision Point 70

You decided to let your boss dictate how the meeting unfolded. This proved to be a problem. Distracted and perturbed by your apparent lack of preparation, your boss fails to grasp the issues or trade-offs. Finally, at the end of the meeting, she does not give you a decision but tells you she will think about it and get back to you.

Two weeks later you ask her if she has decided, and she confesses that she doesn't remember what decision she had to make. You are right back where you started.

Re-evaluate your last decision. Circle the #70 you just wrote in your flow diagram. Then move to the last uncircled step in your flow diagram.

Decision Point 71

You tell her the situation will probably improve soon and that she shouldn't be too concerned. Further, you emphasize her positive accomplishments as a means of buoying her sagging ego. She thanks you for your support but tells you that conditions have changed and there is little she feels she can do any more to meet her quotas.

The problem with Marnie at this point is that she seems to have an external locus of control. You should take that into account in your next decision.

Re-evaluate your last decision. Circle the #71 you just wrote in your flow diagram, and move to the last uncircled step in your flow diagram.

Decision Point 72

You meet with the manager of the troublesome representative and report the instance of sexual harassment. You indicate that you will have to discontinue business with the vendor unless the situation is rectified. He tells you that there have never been any complaints about this individual and that he has no intention of reassigning anyone else to your account. He tells you that he thinks the matter probably was just blown out of proportion by a woman who was suffering from "PMS." This remark makes you confident that this vendor has an antiquated culture when it comes to women's issues.

How would you react to this?

A. Hire the male candidate and assign the troublesome vendor to him (GO TO 77).

B. Assign the troublesome vendor to Elizabeth Morton--the other procurement specialist (GO TO 40).

C. Personally contact the troublesome vendor representative and confront him about his sexual harassment. Let him know that you are unwilling to continue the business relationship if his objectionable behavior continues (GO TO 21).

D. Refer the problem to your boss who you know has a personal relationship with people in the vendor organization with the idea that he can probably de-escalate this situation with his personal influence (GO TO 48).

E. Discontinue business with the vendor in question (GO TO 12).

Decision Point 73

Becky seems a bit relieved by your reassurance. Two days later you arrive at work to find the following note on your desk.

> "I got my Statistics test back, and it was a D-. I've talked to my Dad, and he's given me a loan so I won't have to work any more. I'd like to work for you this summer, but I can't give you hours until then. I hope you understand."

You call her, but she has her mind made up. Becky needed more than simple reassurances. By providing her some counselling you may have been able to avoid losing a valued employee.

Re-evaluate your last decision. Circle the #73 you just wrote in your flow diagram. Then move to the last uncircled step in your flow diagram.

Decision Point 74

You decide not to tell the pregnant employee about the specific contamination involved. Instead, you attempt to reassure her that the health risks are minor, but she seeks out independent scientific advice. Two months later she sues the company for endangering the health of her fetus.

At this point you may be wondering whether you did the right thing. Certainly it was impossible to know that one of your employees would file a law suit. However, once you announced that there was a contamination, it is only logical to expect that some employees would have a genuine interest in the specifics.

Your decisions in this episode appear to be based on several competing ethical concerns. First, you seemed to be concerned that providing detailed information to employees or members of the community would result in negative consequences for the firm. At the same time, you did apparently think that your employees had a right to be informed that there was some contamination. This also could have been due to a need to explain the disconnecting of the fountains (a concern founded on utilitarian reasoning).

As you reflect further on this episode, it may be useful to consider if there were other considerations behind your decision not to tell people the whole truth besides the concern that it would be overly costly to the firm? If your thinking touched on the issue of withholding information because you wanted to protect people from themselves (they would needlessly worry), ask yourself how you would feel if others were making such decisions about information that might concern you.

GO TO 29 for your next ethical challenge.

Decision Point 75

Your logic is unpersuasive. She asserts that the marketing research data show that the assortment should reflect a higher level of fashion. What would you say now?

A. Say that if she does not replace the line with a suitable one, you will hold her responsible for any volume decline (GO TO 49).

B. Ask her to give you more information about why she wants to build more fashion into her lines (GO TO 63).

Decision Point 76

You express your heart-felt concern that you wouldn't have hired him if you didn't think he could handle the demands of his job. The worker reacts neutrally and goes back to work. The next day he quits, citing insensitive leadership. You may have missed the point that this new employee had poor self-confidence.

Re-evaluate your last decision. Circle the #76 you just wrote in your flow diagram, and move to the last uncircled step in your flow diagram.

Decision Point 77

You decide to hire the male procurement person with the idea that he could handle the vendor who was sexually harassing your female employee. This has the apparent moral advantage of helping the organization solve an important business problem. However, others would contend that any female candidate for the position was discriminated against unfairly. Indeed, this action may be illegal.

One important question raised by this episode is: should a firm be forced into discriminating unfairly because of competitive pressures? When posed this way it places two ethical criteria up against one another. One is what is best for the business, i.e., one measure of the utilitarian criterion, and the other is what is just, i.e., women can do the job just as well as men. Therefore, the principal moral issue in this part of the case dealt with justice versus the interests of the firm. There is really no answer to this dilemma that would be authorized by all ethics experts. It is controversial; indeed it is difficult to say whether justice has weight over the interests of the firm in this circumstance. Feminists may contend that the historical practice of ignoring instances of sexual harassment gives additional strength to the moral argument on behalf of injustice. As in all parts of this case, the answer is your answer. The feedback you have received in this case is intended to give you food for thought and to stimulate you to further develop your ethical thinking, not to reflect any correct answers but to be more carefully thought-through. Congratulations on completing the Management Ethics Interactive Case.

Becky looks at you angrily and storms off. Two days later upon arriving at work you see the following note on your desk.

> "I got my Statistics test back, and it was a D-. I've talked to my Dad, and he's given me a loan so I won't have to work any more. I'd like to work for you this summer, but I can't give you hours until then. I hope you understand."

You call her, but she has her mind made up. At this point, Becky needed more than simple reassurance. With some further counseling you may have been able to avoid losing a valued employee.

Re-evaluate your last decision. Circle the #78 you just wrote in your flow diagram. Then move to the last uncircled step in your flow diagram.

You encourage him by telling him that his idea is excellent and that you will investigate its merits. At first, he is pleased that you want to get involved in his idea. However, when you return to him with what you have found, he becomes very distant and never brings up the subject again.

A critical feature of this situation is that this student has an internal locus of control. Re-evaluate your last decision. Circle the #79 you just wrote in your flow diagram, and move to the last uncircled step in your flow diagram.

You decide to inform the pregnant employee who asked you about the specific contamination involved. You attempt to reassure her that the health risks are minor, but she seeks out independent scientific advice. Two months later she sues the company for endangering the health of her fetus.

At this point you may be wondering whether you did the right thing. Certainly it was impossible to know that one of your employees would file a law suit. However, once you announced that there was a contamination, it is only logical to expect that some employees would have a genuine interest in the specifics.

257

Your decisions in this episode appear to be based on several competing ethical concerns. First, you seemed to be concerned that providing detailed information to employees or members of the community would result in negative consequences for the firm. At the same time, you did apparently think that your employees had a right to be informed that there was some contamination. This also could have been due to a need to explain the disconnecting of the fountains (a concern founded on utilitarian reasoning). Finally, you conceded special treatment to an employee who you apparently considered to have a legitimate need to know about the impurity. If this was your reasoning, it is evidence of reliance on a standard of justice--deciding whether special treatment is justified.

As you reflect further on this episode, it may be useful to consider what gives a pregnant woman a stronger moral claim to information than others. Might there be a person in the community with a well on the same aquifer who has an equivalent moral claim? Similarly, were there other considerations behind your decision not to tell people the whole truth besides the concern that it would be overly costly to the firm? If your thinking touched on the issue of withholding information because you wanted to protect people from themselves (they would needlessly worry), ask yourself how you would feel if others were making such decisions about information that might concern you.

GO TO 29 for your next ethical challenge.

Decision Point 81

Candace follows your instructions to the letter, but it takes her 11 hours instead of the seven hours you had estimated. There were two problems with the way you gave the assignment. First, by telling her to "drop everything," you were insensitive to the fact that she may have had other pressing things to do. Second, by telling her precisely how to complete the assignment instead of leaving that up to her (within limits), you robbed her of some motivation. In giving assignments, it is far better to be directive on ends than means.

Re-evaluate your last decision. Circle the #81 you just wrote in your flow diagram. Then move to the last uncircled step in your flow diagram.

Decision Point 82

You decide to offer a bounty for employees to turn in their colleagues if they suspect them of releasing company secrets in an unauthorized way. This results in no progress being made to detect the cause of the leaks. Moreover, it creates a great deal of mutual suspiciousness in the sales force to the point of damaging the level of trust necessary for salespeople to cooperate with one another. In general, the use of bounties to elicit responses that involve employee-employee betrayal are difficult to justify except in extreme situations. For most people, it is far more acceptable for authorities to increase their surveillance than induce peers to betray one another.

There are other alternative actions that you could have taken that would have higher net payoffs (the utilitarian criterion). Re-evaluate your last decision. Circle the #82 you just wrote in your flow diagram. Then move to the first uncircled step above this one in your flow diagram.

Decision Point 83

You decided to write your boss a thorough memo. This was incorrect. Your boss suffers from a common malady--data overload. Your detailed report is likely to add to this overload, and you can count on her missing the forest for the trees. One rather crude way of classifying the communication styles of bosses is that some are readers and some are listeners. Marion is a listener (a poor one at that), and she dislikes paperwork. Therefore, think again about how to approach her orally and in an abbreviated way.

Re-evaluate your last decision. Circle the #83 you just wrote in your flow diagram. Then move to the last uncircled step in your flow diagram.

Decision Point 84

Your approach in dealing with the Director of Admissions was a good one. As a professional, she required neither directive nor supportive leadership. Your approach was neither.

A week later, one of your student workers approaches you with an interesting pro-position. He has noticed that many MBA students are using the copy machine located across the street in the student union building. He suggests that if a machine is put on the ground floor of the business school building, the revenues from the machine might be used for some sort of business student social function.

This student worker is perhaps the most conscientious worker you have. He is a vice-president in the MBA student association, he carries a 3.7/4.0 grade point average, and he is also a part-time employee of a large computer firm.

He has always impressed you by his determination and his resolve in the face of adversity. How would you respond to his comments?

A. Ask him what he thinks the next step should be (GO TO 95).

B. Offer advice as to how he might proceed with his suggestion (GO TO 43).

C. Give him encouragement that his idea is excellent and that you will investigate its merits (GO TO 79).

Decision Point 85

Becky notices that your body language (communicating disappointment and hurt) is incongruent with your words. Accordingly the discussion becomes strained and ends without resolution. Two days later, upon arriving at work, you find a note from Becky on your desk. It reads:

> "I got my Statistics test back, and it was a D-. I've talked to my Dad, and he's given me a loan so I won't have to work any more. I'd like to work for you this summer, but I can't give you hours until then. I hope you understand."

You call her, but she has her mind made up. You have lost a valued employee needlessly.

Counselling an employee can be a difficult interpersonal situation. Maintaining a counselling relationship requires that you avoid getting into an argument with the employee, even if the employee says things that are not completely accurate or fair. Re-evaluate your last decision. Circle the #85 you just wrote in your flow diagram. Then move to the last uncircled step in your flow diagram.

Decision Point 86

You decide to schedule additional tests to monitor the BTH levels in the water. In three months the levels go up surprisingly to 67 ppb. Now what?

A. Monitor the scientific literature on BTH but take no other action (GO TO 60).

B. Seek to discover if the problem is caused by a continuing leak or an old spill (GO TO 9).

C. Retain a consultant to investigate the problem and provide a recommendation (GO TO 45).

D. Since 67 ppb continues to be far below quantities associated with negative health effects, discontinue any action on the issue (GO TO 52).

E. Shut off all drinking fountains and instruct employees not to drink the water. Tell them a test had detected some impurities but be vague about precisely what has been found at this time (GO TO 18).

F. Shut off all drinking fountains and tell the employees exactly everything you know at this point. Tell them you are conducting more tests (GO TO 69).

G. Shut off all drinking fountains, tell employees exactly everything you know at this point, inform all affected outside agencies (EPA, Department of Water Quality), and announce the situation through a press release (GO TO 99).

Decision Point 87

The apologetic tone of your message emphasizes the negative features of the assignment. As such, Candace lacks motivation for the assignment and fails to meet your deadline. In communicating assignments, avoid phrases like "I hate to ask you to do this..." and "...would you mind...?"

Re-evaluate your last decision. Circle the #87 you just wrote in your flow diagram. Then move to the last uncircled step in your flow diagram.

Decision Point 88

You call the record analysts together and ask them their advice as to how to proceed with the evaluation of transcripts. At first, the discussion is slow to develop, but later it livens up. Several of the analysts offer suggestions that others find unacceptable for one reason or another. The meeting ends with no agreement and with a lot more frustration than before the meeting.

One thing you may not have recognized is that your record analysts are experiencing a great amount of uncertainty in trying to deal with this problem. The path-goal theory of leadership suggests that when a group is facing uncertainty, motivation will be highest when followers have clear direction. Take that into account when you re-evaluate your last decision. Circle the #88 you just wrote in your flow diagram, and move to the last uncircled step in your flow diagram.

Decision Point 89

Precisely how would you approach her on this subject?

A. Plan for a 5-minute briefing during which you will lay out an abbreviated description of the issue, outline at most three options, and make a recommendation for approval (GO TO 53).

B. Plan for a 20-minute briefing during which you will lay out the issue in some detail, outline the options, and make a recommendation for approval (GO TO 4).

C. Plan for a 30-minute meeting, but let your boss control how it unfolds (GO TO 70).

Decision Point 90

You decide to talk first with those people who are in a better position to divulge corporate secrets to competitors. You tell them they are under suspicion and that any leak traced back to them will be dealt with as a severe violation of company policy.

Most react very quietly to these conversations, but Mark Felix, the vice-president of sales tells you later that it had a very chilling effect on all of the sales people.

Two months pass and no further leaks are detected. However, two of the three with contacts with competitors leave the organization claiming that they don't think they can live down the damage that has occurred to their "credibility." One of them joins the sales force of Navajo's fiercest competitor, and you suspect that that person may have been passing secrets in the past. The other goes on unemployment and moves out of the area.

How do you feel about how this all worked out? Most people who choose this action end up feeling somewhat confident that they made the right decision, and they bolster that conclusion by reasoning that the salesperson who left the firm was probably at best not very loyal and at worst a spy.

But let's think about the moral issues in this episode. First, there was a very serious set of negative outcomes that would have occurred unless you could take effective action to stop the leaks. Thus, the utilitarian criterion would argue for action. Trouble is, there is no specific action that would work in all circumstances. So, you had to balance the likely result for the company *against* any burdens that would have to be carried by the salespeople.

262

Some actions involved considerable burdens like the use of a lie detector. Arguably, that would have constituted a violation of employee rights. Others, like the one you chose, involved requiring some to carry more burdens than others, i.e., you did not confront those people who did not have relatives working for competitors. Drawing on the standards of justice, one could ask whether it was fair to require these individuals to carry all of these burdens. After all, these employees didn't choose their relatives. Is it fair to make them suspects on these grounds? Your action minimized the number of people who were negatively effected, but is that enough to justify all the possible hardships like those endured by the person now on unemployment? This is a very difficult moral quandary.

GO TO 3 for your next ethical challenge.

Decision Point 91

Your assertiveness has no effect. Now what?

A. Remind her that her boss is likely to be more pleased with volume figures than with the consistency of product across the entire chain. Translate your expected volume for a fashion-versus-quality assortment into volume figures to reinforce your point (GO TO 94).

B. Discredit the arguments of the marketing research people by asserting that they are not sufficiently close to local conditions (GO TO 10).

C. Find out how difficult it would be for her to replace the merchandise that you have received with an assortment more tailored to your store's needs. Offer to help her with the additional effort required to make that happen (GO TO 13).

Decision Point 92

You decide to consult your group as to how you should respond. They are surprised by your request and offer little in the way of advice. You are tempted to just ignore this strange reaction, but you ask one of the members why they reacted so peculiarly to your request. She tells you that she doesn't think the group's reaction was peculiar. She tells you that at times you seem to be trying too hard to be a good leader.

This set-back is not a particularly important one except to your ego. The point that you may have missed is that you are dealing with a very cohesive group that has all the leadership activities contained within itself. In a very real sense, any leadership you try to create is superfluous.

Re-evaluate your last decision. Circle the #92 you just wrote in your flow diagram, and move to the last uncircled step in your flow diagram.

Decision Point 93

You decide to consult with the attorney on staff in the division. He tells you that the company is under no legal obligation to inform anyone of a substance in the well unless there is reason to believe that it is harmful. He further informs you that he doesn't think what you know would lead a reasonable man to the conclusion that it is harmful.

Now what would you do?

A.   Monitor the scientific literature on BTH but take no other action (GO TO 60).

B.   Arrange to have a second test done at the well (GO TO 32).

C.   Seek to discover if the problem is caused by a continuing leak or an old spill (GO TO 9).

D.   Retain a consultant to investigate the problem and provide a recommendation (GO TO 45).

E.   Shut off all drinking fountains and instruct employees not to drink the water. Tell them a test had detected some impurities but be vague about precisely what has been found at this time (GO TO 18).

F.   Shut off all drinking fountains and tell the employees exactly everything you know at this point. Tell them you are conducting more tests (GO TO 69).

G.   Shut off all drinking fountains, tell employees exactly everything you know at this point, inform all affected outside agencies (EPA, Department of Water Quality), and announce the situation through a press release (GO TO 99).

Decision Point 94

She seems persuaded by your arguments but tells you that replacing the merchandise will come to the attention of her boss and may cause her problems. In addition, it would involve a great amount of paperwork that she personally doesn't have the time or the resources to do.

What would you say?

A. Offer to help her with the paperwork and agree to talk with your boss about getting the message to her boss that she is being extremely helpful and alert to local conditions (GO TO 38).

B. Be sympathetic but offer no help. After all, the mistake was hers (GO TO 65).

C. Offer to help her with the paperwork (GO TO 7).

Decision Point 95

The student follows through by talking with a number of copier firms and finding out what maintenance is involved in coin-operated machines. He uses his influence with the student association to get them to sponsor the machine. This helps you because it means that tending the machine will not be an added responsibility of the people in your office.

Your leadership in this instance was effective because it was predicated on the principle that individuals with an internal locus of control require participative leadership. The student in question seems to have such a way of thinking as evidenced by his determination and resolve.

The next situation you face involves your record analysts. Three of them work together in maintaining student records. They are a very cohesive group; all of them are unmarried and in their twenties, and they seem to enjoy talking about the "singles scene" in the local area. Last year when you were conducting annual performance reviews, two of the three told you that they would quit their jobs if anything prevented them from working with their colleagues. While it has been tempting for you to view this three-person group as a destructive clique, you do not really think the group is a problem. All three are hard-workers; in fact, they urge high productivity on one another.

For the most part you have ignored this group until today. One of the members, John Daniels, approaches you with a problem. He shows you records of applicants from one foreign country that seem unreasonably favorable. Test scores of the applicants from this country are much higher than those submitted by applicants in the past. You look over the group's data and applaud the analysts' careful scrutiny. They suggest that all applicants from that country be refused admission for a year.

How would you respond to this suggestion?

265

A.   Look into the basis for their suggestion and assess it on a factual basis (GO TO 5).

B.   Consult them as to how you should respond (GO TO 92).

C.   Congratulate the group on how conscientious it has been, and then look into the matter (GO TO 50).

D.   Advise the group how to proceed from this point (GO TO 34).

Decision Point 96

You call the entire sales staff together and inform them of the importance of corporate security. You tell them that if information on new products gets out prematurely, it could mean a serious decline in the health of the company and may result in the loss of jobs. Nothing special comes up during these meetings, but you feel they have communicated that you hold security as a high priority.

Two months after the meetings the sales force is again briefed on highly secret product information so they can do their necessary tactical planning. The very next week, information filters back to you that competing firms are already positioning their product against your firm's as yet, officially unannounced products. A leak has occurred again, and high officials at corporate headquarters are very disappointed in your actions.

At this point, it is possible to evaluate your actions from an ethical viewpoint. Specifically, utilitarian ethics holds that actions are unethical if they produce outcomes that are less effective than the outcomes of other alternatives. The question here is whether it is reasonable to expect that the option you chose might have worked, i.e., produced effective outcomes. It didn't work, but that is not the whole question. It appears that you excluded some options because they were more invasive but might have stopped the leaks.

What would you do now?

A.   Require that each employee take a polygraph (lie detector test) regarding their involvement with competing firms [In this jurisdiction, the use of lie detectors for this purpose is legal.](GO TO 66).

B.   Talk first with those people who are in a better position to divulge corporate secrets to competitors. Tell them they are under suspicion and that any leak traced back to them will be dealt with as a severe violation of company policy (GO TO 90).

C.   Hire a private investigator to look into the matter (GO TO 23).

D.   Talk privately with each employee and tell them that you will put a large monetary "bonus" for information leading to the identification of any sales employee who is releasing company secrets in an unauthorized way (GO TO 82).

E.   Transfer those salespeople who are related to individuals in competing firms to other positions where security is not as critical (GO TO 64).

F.   Meet people individually and try to motivate them to keep better security (GO TO 6).

Decision Point 97

Jean finally agrees to replace the assortment. You follow up by helping her with the paperwork and by feeding the grapevine via your boss to hers. The new line arrives and it is an excellent one. Your summer sales volume hits an all-time high. You made Jean more willing to change by showing how replacing the line would be in her interest as well as yours. You also made it easy for her to act by helping with the work.

Congratulations! You have just completed the Communication Interactive Case.

Decision Point 98

You identify the analysts who worked on the assignment and call their attention to the problem and insist that it doesn't happen again. This results in considerable resentment on the part of most of your employees. They view the task as one of the most boring tasks they do and believe that your criticism indicates that you really do not appreciate them. Morale suffers, and absenteeism begins to become a bigger problem.

One reason your approach did not work well is that your record analysts are dealing with tasks that have clear procedures for completing the task. With very certain tasks, the path-goal theory recommends that leaders make follower jobs more satisfying.

With that in mind, re-evaluate your last decision. Circle the #98 you just wrote in your flow diagram, and move to the last uncircled step in your flow diagram.

Decision Point 99

You shut off all drinking fountains, tell employees exactly everything you know at this point, inform all affected outside agencies (EPA, Department of Water Quality), and announce the situation through a press release.

The following day you receive a phone call from the local newspaper asking for further information. Realizing that you cannot withhold any information at this point, you tell them everything you know. The following morning the local newspaper runs a headline story on the spill that is very critical of the company. A week later, a female employee who is pregnant files a law suit against your company alleging that damage may have been done to her fetus. A month later at a meeting at corporate headquarters, a senior staff official in public relations tells you that the president of the company strongly disapproved of your handling of the situation. Apparently, the president feels that it would have been better for the company if you had kept your mouth shut about the spill.

At this point you may be wondering whether you did the right thing. Certainly it was impossible to know that one of your employees would file a law suit and that the president of the company would disagree with your actions.

Your decisions in this episode, however, appear to be based less on utilitarian ethics than on a moral concern about the rights of the parties involved. Specifically, your actions seem to be consistent with the reasoning that individuals have a moral right to drinking water that is free of contaminants from the plant and a right to be informed of the facts of any previous contamination. You have extended this right even in situations where there is some uncertainty about the health effects of the contamination.

As you reflect back on this episode, try to think whether your decision would have been the same if you had known in advance about the negative consequences. That may give you some sense as to how strong individual rights are in your thinking.

GO TO 29 for your next ethical challenge.

John reacts with the following: "But that's not really fair. The redistricting plan is unfair, and you know it!"

At this point how would you respond?

A. Try to persuade John that the redistricting plan is fair. Be prepared to compare his performance with Susan Brown's (such comparisons are not improper since performance records are open within the company). (GO TO 236)

B. Tell John that you do not like his attitude, and that you cannot give his future employers a good recommendation unless he improves his performance next quarter. (GO TO 221)

C. Ask John what changes in redistricting that he would suggest to correct the inequity that he is experiencing. (GO TO 147)

D. Tell John you will be sorry to see him go, but you understand that if he still thinks the redistricting is inequitable after your last discussion with him, perhaps this is the best thing for him to do. (GO TO 211)

E. Ask John what things he likes about his present territory with the idea of trying to remind him of the positive things about his job instead of the negative things he seems to be emphasizing in his own mind. (GO TO 104)

Virgil says, "The beginning of each week is really hectic. My crew needs me then for setup help and troubleshooting. Those reports take me at least two hours to complete, and I don't have the time. Lately we've been having so much trouble with the "Weber" (an extrusion machine) that I have to help Ivan fine-tune it. You remember the defective brushes that came out of that 'baby' three months ago? If you want to risk another disaster like that, I'll be happy to get my reports in on time. But don't tell me to take two hours on a Monday and then come down on my case if we have quality problems!"

At that point you consider several options: (a) doing a major overhaul on the machine in question, (b) having someone else help Ivan with the Monday adjustments, and (c) encouraging Virgil to get a head start on the production reports. However, there are credible reasons that make each of these options unworkable.

You then turn to Phyllis for her statement. She says, "Well, the quotas we get from headquarters are weekly quotas. I've tried to get them to give us more advance time, but they won't do it. They know that smaller runs increase costs, but the savings in inventory costs outweigh these. It's a well-thought-out mathematical solution they give us, and it is correct. I had an elaborate briefing on the formula during my training."

At this point you try to find out why headquarters cannot give biweekly schedules for the brushes produced by Virgil's crew since it is a special case. Phyllis tells you that she has tried to convince headquarters of that with no success. Unfortunately, you do not consider your ability to convince headquarters any better than hers.

Secretly you are beginning to believe that there is no way to settle this matter without siding with one or the other. What would you do now?

A.   Ask Phyllis and Virgil to each prepare a memo documenting how their solutions are in the best interests of the organization. Announce that you will make a decision based upon what they produce. (GO TO 150)

B.   Ask the two parties to estimate the financial consequence of complying with Phyllis' position. Phyllis would estimate the financial impact of procurement and inventory problems likely to occur if Virgil continues to submit his reports late. Virgil would estimate the financial impact of quality problems likely to occur if he does his report Monday as she wants. These calculations will enable you to determine whose position would result in the lowest expected loss for the plant. (GO TO 193)

C.   Ask the parties to brainstorm other options with you. (GO TO 174)

D.   Tell Phyllis and Virgil that they should meet together without you and get back to you with a solution to their disagreement within three days. (GO TO 198)

Decision Point 102

You accompany Lisa on several calls and notice several errors that she is making. First, she is not particularly friendly to receptionists and other people who could get her in to see the doctor. Second, she is too quick to leave company literature without seeing the obstetrician personally. And third, she uses powerless and overly polite language in her detailing speeches.

You give her feedback on these observations and watch her practice techniques that you give her on subsequent calls. Confident that she has benefited from your counseling, you return to your other responsibilities. In a month, you contact her again and ask for a progress report. Since it is optimistic, you decide to wait for the next quarter results. They are excellent. Her sales volume has improved to 440 units and her inventory levels to 57 days!

You correctly deduced that Lisa had a problem with abilities and skills. To recapitulate, when you originally talked with Lisa, you learned that she believed that her efforts would lead to outcomes she valued. Thus, effort was not the problem. This left "Abilities and Skills" and "Understanding of the Job" as key factors. By accompanying her on her sales calls, you were able to discover that she lacked specific skills associated with making effective sales calls to obstetricians.

GO TO 234 to move on to your next motivational problem, John Crosby.

Decision Point 103

Your choice of the Eagle Point plant was correct. Since it faces scarce labor market conditions, each instance of an employee quitting is quite costly to the plant. Thus, its high rate of turnover and absenteeism translates into a very costly situation. Finally, the fact that the plant is decentralized provides an appropriate context for some type of QWL.

You arrive at the plant and spend your first few weeks studying the plant, meeting people, and explaining the values of QWL to the management group. The plant manager, whom you met two months ago, is pleased that you have selected his plant for an intervention. The plant employs 113 operators, 18 foremen and inspectors, 3 machine repair specialists, 4 people in shipping and receiving, and an office staff of 23.

The operators are organized functionally into cutters, sewers, and finishers. Cutters prepare denim blocks from patterns using power cutters. Sewers assemble these blocks into basic garments and complete top-stitching. Finishers attach labels, zippers, and the Angie Taylor logo. By convention, all the operators are paid on an individual piece-rate incentive scheme--that is, the more articles they complete the higher their wages. New operators draw an hourly wage for thirty days until they have mastered the necessary skills to qualify for the piece rate scheme.

The foremen, inspectors, repair specialists, and shipping and receiving people all work on an hourly basis, and the office staff is salaried.

You decide to begin your design effort by calling a general meeting of all employees and explaining the objectives and methods involved in QWL. At the end of this meeting you administer a questionnaire to all the operators and to members of

271

the office staff who are not managers. The questionnaire is the Job Diagnostic Survey (JDS), a standard instrument that assesses employee perceptions of the motivating characteristics of jobs and each individual's growth need strength. Based on the JDS, you are able to come to the following conclusions about the different groups in question:

Group	Low Perceived Job Characteristics	Growth Need Strength
Cutters	skill variety, task identity	moderate to high
Sewers	skill variety, autonomy, task significance	high
Finishers	skill variety, autonomy	moderate to high
Office Staff	none	low

These data persuade you to attempt three interventions, one for the cutters, another for the sewers and finishers (as a combined group), and a third for the office staff.

You decide to begin first with the cutters. Which type of QWL intervention makes the most sense for this group?

  A. Vertical loading. (GO TO 155)

  B. Opening feedback channels. (GO TO 158)

  C. Combining tasks. (GO TO 257)

  D. Forming natural work units. (GO TO 162)

  E. Flexitime. (GO TO 168)

  F. Concentrated work week. (GO TO 172)

Decision Point 104

This is an excellent motivational strategy, but not in this situation. Emphasizing the positive aspects of a job is an effective approach, but only as one part of a long-range motivational strategy. In this situation, you face a short-term, emergency situation. Persuasiveness of this sort is unlikely to be enough to create a set of perceptions which would result in better performance.

Re-evaluate your last decision. Circle the #104 you just wrote in your flow diagram. Then move back to the first uncircled number above this one in your flow diagram.

Decision Point 105

Jim says, "I really don't know. I'd miss some parts of the job like seeing some of the doctor friends I have now, and I'd really miss working with you. But I certainly don't need the job financially anymore. My dad left us a real nice inheritance, so I don't have to work to eat anymore."

How would you respond?

A.   Tell Jim that you will be sorry to see him go, but that you have to have 400 units per quarter from a sales rep in his region, and you cannot afford to keep him while he decides what to do. (GO TO 219)

B.   Ask Jim if he needs some time off to get himself together now that his personal crisis has passed. (GO TO 214)

C.   Indicate to Jim that you don't want to stand in his way if he doesn't want to work anymore, but that there may be some way that you could work something out with him. (GO TO 135)

D.   Tell Jim that you will be personally disappointed if he gives up on his job and that you wish he would reconsider. Remind him of what he would be giving up in terms of the nonfinancial rewards the job gives him. (GO TO 194)

Decision Point 106

Virgil responds, "Okay, I understand what you are getting at. Listen, if you side with Phyllis on this issue, my crew is really going to think that I have no influence whatever in this organization. I can't afford to lose their respect, believe me. There is nothing worse than a supervisor whose crew thinks he has 'lost control.'"

"Furthermore," he continues, "paperwork is a real pain in the neck for me. When I come in Monday morning, I want to get my hands dirty; I don't want to pansy around shuffling papers!" In effect, Virgil has just told you that he has two interests beside the risk of quality problems: (1) he wants to appear in control with his crew; and (2) he does not like doing paperwork on Mondays.

As your private meeting with Virgil ends, what would you say?

A. "While I agree with you that seeming in control is important to every manager, I don't accept your reasons for not doing paperwork on Mondays. Doing paperwork is part of your job, and if that's what your job is, you should do it. I don't think there is any room for personal preferences in these negotiations. When we get back together, I hope you will keep that in mind." (GO TO 256)

B. "This meeting has been really helpful, Virgil. When we get back together, let's focus on alternatives that reflect all your interests. For example, think about finding an alternative that will not result in your losing the respect of your crew." (GO TO 156)

Decision Point 107

John agrees to try harder if you promise to look into the fairness of his territory. You agree to get back to him at the end of the following quarter.

In the meantime, what would you do?

A. Get John to commit himself to calling on a specific number of M.D.s during the next quarter. (GO TO 132)

B. Tell John that you are very pleased that he has agreed to improve, and encourage him to do the best he can. (GO TO 157)

C. Negotiate a level of performance with John that you would consider an adequate sign John is doing all he can with the territory he has been given. (GO TO 161)

Decision Point 108

Your decision to provide some additional incentives for acquiring skills was correct. Otherwise, you may have experienced some reluctance to attend training since that would have involved some sacrifice in the cutters' opportunity to make money.

You announce the changes to the cutters, and they begin rotating between cutting machines and blank assignments. This change immediately reduces absenteeism, but several cutters resign. Apparently, their growth need strength was not sufficient enough for them to see the advantages of the new job arrangements. Both of the individuals who leave worked for the foreman who had expressed some reservations about job rotation, but six months later this foreman becomes converted when he notices that the cross-training of cutters allows him more flexibility in making assignments to make up for absent employees.

Your attention now turns to the sewers and finishers. Recall the questionnaire results for these two groups as follows:

Group	Low Perceived Job Characteristics	Growth Need Strength
Sewers	skill variety, autonomy, task significance	high
Finishers	skill variety, autonomy	moderate to high

You interview the members of these two groups and conclude that growth need strength is apparently quite high but that the groups are not particularly cohesive-- group members are much more interested in doing well as individuals than in working together as a group.

You know that one element of your QWL intervention should involve combining tasks because sewers and finishers believe their jobs are deficient in terms of skill variety. Is there any other QWL element that you should build into your QWL intervention?

A.   Vertical loading. (GO TO 114)

B.   Forming natural work units. (GO TO 196)

C.   Flexitime. (GO TO 201)

D.   Concentrated work week. (GO TO 207)

E.   No other element. (GO TO 212)

Decision Point 109

In analyzing this situation, you realized that there was no alternative for Buff but discharge. His performance had been low, he consistently violated a major company policy, and you had little likelihood of changing his behavior. After discharging Buff, a new set of problems develops for you. Buff's replacement seems to have a hard time making contact with doctors, and wholesalers' inventories drop to a lower level than Buff's. Two large wholesalers tell you that they were thinking about dropping your obstetric line because "Doctors just aren't prescribing it." Your colleagues in other districts mention that there is a rumor going around among doctors that Omega was "out to get" Buff and that you summarily fired him rather than let him resign. Since Buff continues to see his old Omega clients--because of the real estate deals-- you know these rumors won't die easily.

You were clearly justified in discharging Buff; however, you might like to select another way of doing so.

Re-evaluate your last decision. Circle the #109 you just wrote in your flow diagram. Then move back to the first uncircled number above this one in your flow diagram.

Decision Point 110

You ask to accompany Jim on a sales call. He agrees and the two of you leave early the next morning. Observing him, you conclude that Jim knows the products well and is effective in detailing them. One call to a pharmaceutical wholesaler results in a hefty order. Clearly Jim's motivational problem has nothing to do with his sales abilities or job understanding.

What would you do now?

A. Ask Jim how the death of his father has changed his outlook on his work. (GO TO 169)

B. Let him know you think his performance is really seriously low, and you would like to know exactly what he plans to do about it. (GO TO 208)

C. Find out whether he realizes that his sales are probably suffering from the low inventory levels being held by wholesalers in his territory. (GO TO 251)

D. Ask Jim if he needs some time off now that his personal crisis has passed. (GO TO 214)

E. Suggest that Jim may want to attend a sales seminar sponsored by the company next month. Coincidentally, it is being conducted in the city where Jim lives. (GO TO 204)

F. Ask Jim why he was only able to contact 73 percent of the doctors in his territory. (GO TO 260)

G. Do nothing. It is clear to you that Jim's performance problem is caused by a factor outside of your control. (GO TO 203)

Decision Point 111

Virgil is willing to work overtime for an amount of $2,000 a year. Thus, your net savings amounts to $2,157. However, since you did not try to gauge the flexibility of the parties' positions, you missed a chance to solve this problem without spending any money at all.

Re-evaluate your last decision. Circle the #111 you just wrote in your flow diagram. Then move to the last uncircled step in your flow diagram.

Decision Point 112

With the action plan complete, you now have to decide how to implement it without regular contact with Wilson Thomas.

What would you do?

A. Keep in touch with him by phone asking for weekly progress reports. (GO TO 232)

B. Schedule a return visit in one month in order to go with him on some sales calls again. (GO TO 230)

Decision Point 113

"I thought I would do much better. My husband and I were counting on me making 400 units so we could make our first house payment."

"I really don't know what it is. I visited every obstetrician's office in my territory at least once. I wasn't really prepared for how difficult it is to get to see doctors. It's tough even getting in the door. And when you do, the most you have is five minutes. And that's a very distracted five minutes, I'll tell you. As for my relations with wholesalers, I called on each one twice during the quarter. Even though their supply is only 50 days right now, that's up from 43 when I started."

You were not aware of this improvement in inventory levels, which is fairly substantial; therefore, you congratulate her on her improvement.

Given this information, how would you motivate Lisa?

A. Transfer her to a different territory within your district known to be an easier region for sales. (GO TO 118)

B. Tell her not to be discouraged since building a relationship with the doctors is often a time consuming process, and it may take a while to reach her 400-unit quota. (GO TO 218)

C. Ask to accompany her on several sales calls with obstetricians. (GO TO 102)

D. Ask her to attend a seminar on salesmanship offered by an industry association to develop her skills. (GO TO 264)

E. Ask her how much her house payment is, and then calculate what her sales volume would have to be for her to earn a satisfactory commission. (GO TO 170)

F. Indicate that unless her sales volume improves, you may be forced to take disciplinary action. (GO TO 239)

Decision Point 114

You chose vertical loading as a way of implementing QWL among the sewers and finishers. This was correct. The generally high growth need strength that the sewers and finishers demonstrated on their questionnaires indicates that a change in job characteristics would result in an improvement in absenteeism and turnover. In addition, both parts of this group perceive that their present jobs are deficient in skill variety and autonomy--that is, sewers and finishers desire job loading in these dimensions.

Redesigning the jobs of these groups by combining tasks seem easy enough. You could employ either job rotation or job enlargement for this purpose. However, vertical job loading gives you a slightly different challenge. You have to figure out a way to give them more latitude from their foremen--that is, more authority to do things the way they want. In addition, you should look for ways to expand their jobs to include more responsibility.

After discussions with managers above and below you in the chain of command and with a task force of representatives from each of these two groups, you conclude that there are several areas of vertical job loading that would, by their very nature, increase job scope as well. One is machine maintenance and minor repair. Presently, sewers and finishers work at either high-performance sewing machines, rivet machines, or staplers. Both the preventive and corrective maintenance of these machines are presently the responsibility of the three repair specialists employed by the plant. About 75 percent of their time is spent in significant repair and overhaul activities, so that when a routine maintenance or a slight adjustment is required, there is often a delay in response time. Such delays are a major cause of dissatisfaction among the sewers and finishers because it affects their ability to increase their productivity and thus their wages. Accordingly, one area of job expansion would be to teach sewers and finishers to perform routine maintenance and minor adjustments on their machines.

A second area of potential job expansion is procedural control. Two years ago the firm commissioned an industrial engineering consulting firm to investigate all operators' jobs and to develop a series of specific procedures outlining how each operation should be conducted. Currently, foremen of the sewers and finishers groups are enforcing these procedures even though certain operators claim that they were using more efficient, and equally quality-conscious procedures before the study was conducted. Thus, a second type of vertical loading would be to allow operators to use whatever procedures they choose--provided that quantity and quality standards are upheld.

In talking with the foremen and machine repair specialists, you encounter much more resistance from the former than the latter. The repair specialists seem eager to give up some of the more mundane aspects of their work, particularly when you explain to them that this change would constitute no threat to their jobs (the fact that several cutting machines with complicated maintenance have just been purchased makes this a very reasonable assurance). However, the foremen balk at allowing their subordinates the additional discretion about procedures. They argue that the reduced control will most certainly create bottlenecks in the workflow and that operators cannot be trusted to develop better procedures than "the experts."

You decide to speak with the plant manager about this matter, and you find him very open to the scheme you have developed. You estimate that if less supervisory vigilance were required, you could reduce the number of foremen by 20 percent. What would you propose to him about how to deal with the foremen?

A. Propose that the number of foremen governing the sewers and finishers be decreased in some humane way (through transfers or reassignments). Provide the remaining foremen with training in how to be more participative supervisors. (GO TO 268)

B. Maintain the present number of foremen, but provide them with training in how to be more participative supervisors. (GO TO 213)

C. Implement the changes in the jobs that involve additional machine maintenance, and then see if further changes are really necessary. (GO TO 217)

Decision Point 115

Jim says, "I just am not sure. I've told you my priorities have changed. I want to spend more time with my family. I know the amount of work necessary to make my quota, and that's about all I am prepared to do."

What would you say now?

A. Tell Jim it sounds like his job with Omega isn't important enough for him to work to keep it. (GO TO 105)

B. Indicate that unless he is willing to try for higher level of sales, you'll have to ask for his resignation. (GO TO 219)

Decision Point 116

She thanks you for your kind offer, but she admits to not being able to determine the problem. She seems very frustrated.

At this point what would you do?

A. Ask her if her frustration stems from the low amount on her commission check. (GO TO 129)

B. Indicate that her problem may be that she's not calling on pharmaceutical wholesalers. (GO TO 223)

C. Ask her if there is anything that has happened in her job that she was unprepared for. (GO TO 182)

Decision Point 117

You expressed a desire to mediate the conflict between Phyllis and Virgil but reserved the option of arbitration should initial negotiations end in a stalemate. The first part of your statement was fine; mediation is the preferred way of dealing with conflicts of this type. However, one does not want to announce one's intention to resort to arbitration before a mediation has begun. Doing so may harden the position of those who seem not to be benefiting from mediation. Saying nothing about arbitration does not preclude a manager from resorting to it to break a deadlock.

Re-evaluate your last decision. Circle the #117 you just wrote in your flow diagram. Then move to the last uncircled step in your flow diagram.

Decision Point 118

Lisa opposes the option of being transferred since it would separate her from her husband, who is in medical school. More over, this option is very unpopular with some of your other sales reps, notably John Crosby.

Your analysis of Lisa's motivational circumstances revealed several important pieces of information. First, it is clear that Lisa does believe that her efforts will produce positive results since she has a history of succeeding in nearly everything she has ever attempted. In addition, given the reward system she certainly must believe that her monetary outcomes are in direct proportion to her performance. Monetary outcomes are important to her because she is counting on her commission check to make her first house payment.

Given these factors, it is not surprising that Lisa's efforts are high (she called on 100 percent of M.D.s and each wholesaler twice). However, her performance particularly regarding her obstetrician calls is not up to expectations. In light of this assessment, think through what additional factors may account for her low performance.

Re-evaluate your last decision. Circle the #118 you just wrote in your flow diagram. Then move back to the first uncircled number above this one in your flow diagram.

Decision Point 119

You carefully review his performance record since you became his manager and detail what you've done to help him with his work. Then you ask him for a renewed commitment to do something about his "marginal" performance.

His response is markedly defensive. He blames anything and everything besides himself for his low performance. For example, he asserts that many obstetricians are more interested in the gifts and favors given to them by competing firms than the attributes of the products. He even claims that competing firms have targeted his territory as a place in which they are making most of their sales and advertising expenditures (this is impossible to verify). He then delivers a description of his sales approach that you've heard before:

"I have always believed strongly that a professional sales approach is not a pressure approach. I come on slow, building my credibility and expressing interest in the physician's individual problems with malpractice, uninformed patients, and unqualified hospital staffers. You can't be product-driven in this business; you have to be doctor-driven. What you might gain in the short run, you lose in the long haul."

While you don't disagree in principle, you are concerned that Thomas's soft-sell approach is too indirect for wholesalers. What now?

A.   Accompany him on a series of sales calls. (GO TO 154)

B.   Confront the differences between his stated approach and the sort of approach you know works well for some of your highest performing reps. (GO TO 247)

C.   Tell him that you think he is being defensive. (GO TO 160)

D.   Tell him that this is it--that you are at the end of your rope with him. Establish your willingness to help in any way you can, but either he comes up to standard next quarter or he's through with Omega. (GO TO 151)

E.   Tell him his sales approach may be correct, but he can't make it work unless he improves his effort. Ask him to explain why he only was able to contact 77 percent of the doctors in his region and why his inventory figures are so low. (GO TO 197)

F.   Assert that you don't disagree with his personal sales technique, but you think he needs to be hard-hitting when the occasion calls for it. Schedule him for a training program known to emphasize a contingency approach to selling. Warn him that this is his last chance. (GO TO 272)

G.   Check to see if his job is really important to him. (GO TO 242)

Your approach works well. The vice-president is satisfied with your explanation and with the reaction of the operators, who explain to him the superiority of their techniques to the procedures they previously followed. As he leaves, he tells you to "keep up the good work." The plant manager overhears this remark, and that solidifies his commitment to the new work design.

As the newness of the new arrangement begins to wear off and absenteeism and turnover figures level off in the groups, a problem begins to appear that jeopardizes the entire QWL system. The sewers begin to outperform the finishers. The economics of this situation is that if something is not done, you may have to lay off some sewers (there is insufficient demand for designer jeans for you to increase production). You look into the problem in some detail and realize that it is due to two factors. First, finishing machines are more sensitive than the machines used by the sewers. This means more routine repair and maintenance by the finishers than by the sewers. Second, the sewers were much more effective in improving upon prior procedures than with the finishers.

What would you do about this problem?

  A.   Lay off the proper number of sewers to decrease the workflow unevenness. (GO TO 233)

  B.   Call a meeting among the sewers and finishers to discuss the workflow unevenness. (GO TO 126)

  C.   Consult with the corporate industrial engineer about how to handle the situation. (GO TO 237)

  D.   Let the situation take care of itself. Since the sewers will soon run out of fabric (from the cutters), they will have to slow down. (GO TO 241)

Jim's performance during the next quarter continues to be poor. His commitment to do better was not sufficient as a motivator.

Re-evaluate your last decision. Circle the #121 you just wrote in your flow diagram. Then move back to the first uncircled number above this one in your flow diagram.

Decision Point 122

Jim Clemmons has worked for Omega for three and a half years, and never before has his performance been so low. You are unsure what is causing this situation. His performance figures are listed on page 18.

Your meeting with Jim takes place at his home while you are on a business trip. (This is common, as most reps work out of an office in their homes; more over, you have a friendly relationship with Jim). After a pleasant dinner, the two of you move into his office in a small bungalow behind the family residence. You ask him if he's seen the sales data. He responds: "Yes, I have, and I'm embarrassed by them. You may not know this, but my Dad passed away five months ago. He'd been ill for some time, but I guess I just let things slip. I guess I'll have to put all that behind me now and build up those figures." Out of courtesy, you spend some time talking about Jim's father. Clearly Jim took the loss of his father very hard.

What would you say after the conversation turns again to his performance?

  A.   Ask Jim how the death of his father has changed his outlook on his work. (GO TO 169)

  B.   Let him know you think his performance is really seriously low, and you would like to know exactly what he plans to do about it. (GO TO 208)

  C.   Find out whether he knows that his sales are probably suffering from the low inventory levels being held by wholesalers in his region. (GO TO 251)

  D.   Ask Jim if he needs some time off to get himself together now that his personal crisis has passed. (GO TO 214)

  E.   Suggest that Jim may want to attend a sales seminar sponsored by the company next month (By coincidence, it is being conducted in the city where Jim lives). (GO TO 204)

  F.   Ask to accompany Jim on a series of sales calls. (GO TO 110)

  G.   Ask Jim why he was only able to contact 73 percent of the doctors in his area. (GO TO 260)

  H.   Do nothing. It is clear that Jim's performance problem is caused by a factor or factors outside your control. (GO TO 203)

Decision Point 123

You secretary prepares a summary of the responsibility that each party has. You give copies to Virgil and Phyllis and keep a copy for your files. Doing this helps avoid any misunderstandings between the parties and reminds them that you will be monitoring their agreement.

The next week, Virgil's report is late but he provided Phyllis with the background information he promised. That is the last time Virgil's report is late. Three weeks later, Phyllis is invited to headquarters to meet with the staff about the toothbrush line problem. She returns very happy for two reasons. First, the headquarters staff decided to extend the planning cycle to two weeks for that line. And second, she had the opportunity to meet with several highly placed executives that she had not met before.

Congratulations! You have dealt effectively with a very touchy conflict between two of your subordinates.

Decision Point 124

Jim tells you that he will sell 425 units next quarter. However, halfway through the next quarter he phones to tell you that he won't be able to meet that goal. When you express disappointment, he tells you he has decided to resign. Establishing precise performance targets is usually an effective motivational technique. However, in this instance, it does not work. Jim is suffering from a great deal of inner conflict which you haven't dealt with.

Re-evaluate your last decision. Circle the #124 you just wrote in your flow diagram. Then move back to the first uncircled number above this one in your flow diagram.

Decision Point 125

She exclaims, "Very disappointed! My husband and I were counting on me making 400 units to make our first house payment."

How would you motivate Lisa?

A. Transfer her to a different territory within your district known to be an easier region for sales. (GO TO 118)

285

B. Tell her not to be discouraged since building credibility with obstetricians is often a time consuming process, and it may take a while to reach her 400-unit quota. (GO TO 218)

C. Ask to accompany her on several sales calls with obstetricians. (GO TO 102)

D. Ask her to attend a seminar on salesmanship offered by an industry association to hone her skills further. (GO TO 264)

E. Ask her how much her house payment is, and then calculate what her sales volume would have to be for her to earn a satisfactory commission. (GO TO 170)

F. Indicate that unless her sales volume improves, you may be forced to take disciplinary action. (GO TO 239)

Decision Point 126

The sewers seem upset by the prospect of a layoff especially since they are now making more money than ever before (thanks to their increased productivity). They quickly generate an alternative. Three of the operators are expecting babies, and they will shortly be resigning. This attrition will take care of the problem if the sewers simply reduce their production until that event transpires. This would, of course, reduce their individual wages in the short run in order to be assured of later earnings.

The finishers see no problem with this plan, so you approach the plant manager with the idea. He is so impressed with the plan that he talks to each of the pregnant sewers and tells them he will insure that they can rejoin the firm in comparable jobs if they choose to take medical leave instead of quitting. This act boosts the morale of the entire group of operators.

The situation with the cutters, sewers, and finishers stable, you next turn your attention to the Office Staff. This group is made up of clerical and secretarial personnel performing rather routine but important tasks such as bookkeeping, record keeping, word processing, and structured report preparation. Most of the assignments are relatively discreet--that is, little coordination among them is required. While the turnover of the group is not intolerably high, absenteeism is a problem. Most of the Office Staff members are either single parents or individuals in their late fifties and sixties. The Office Staff is managed by an office administrator, a recently hired graduate of State University with a degree in business management. Recall the results of the JDS for this group:

Group	Low Perceived Job Characteristics	Growth Need Strength
Office Staff	none	low

What type of QWL intervention would be appropriate for this group?

A.   Combining tasks. (GO TO 246)

B.   Flexitime. (GO TO 131)

C.   Concentrated work week. (GO TO 250)

D.   None. (GO TO 253)

Decision Point 127

It is clear to you that Buff's goodwill could be very valuable in helping his replacement establish good relations with the doctors and wholesalers in his territory. Also, it seems to you that Buff's primary concern is in not getting immediately cut off from company benefits. You make him a proposal that would have him work with the new representative for six weeks in exchange for a continuation of his employee benefits for six months. He makes a counter proposal, and you negotiate an agreement whereby he will make calls with the new representative for three weeks and be on call to help his replacement for another three weeks. In return, you will pay him two weeks salary and continue his benefits for six months. Both personnel and your supervisor agree to his plan, and you put it in operation.

This seems like an effective solution in that Buff's replacement is likely to benefit from the goodwill that clients accord Buff. In addition, you have removed a poor performing employee with a minimum of disruption to the rest of the group. The problem presented by Buff was a difficult one. Spaulding was performing poorly because he had great incentives on nonperformance. By identifying and verifying those incentives, you were able to use those circumstances to allow Buff to make a positive contribution at the same time that you terminated him. Making an agreement such as this one represents a difficult choice.

In the six months this case covers, you have faced a variety of motivational problems. By applying the motivation theory to each individual, you have been able to diagnose and make recommendations which lead to effective solutions.

Congratulations! You have successfully completed the Motivation Interactive Case.

Decision Point 128

Neither Virgil nor Phyllis says anything. You coax them further, but they still say nothing. What would you do now?

A.   Ask them to use brainstorming to get some more alternative settlements "on the floor." (GO TO 199)

B.   Tell them that if they cannot suggest alternatives, it will force you to make a decision siding with one or the other. (GO TO 189)

C.   Say, "Well, it seems that we have two alternatives on the floor. One, proposed by Virgil, is that Phyllis refashions production schedules to cut back on setup time. The other, proposed by Phyllis, is for Virgil to turn in his production reports to her office by Monday at noon. At this point I'd like to ask each of you what impediments you are experiencing to keep you from doing what the other wants. Let's start with you, Virgil. Why can't you get your reports in on time?" (GO TO 101)

Decision Point 129

She exclaims, "Very disappointed! My husband and I were counting on me making 400 units to make our first house payment." What would you say now?

A.   Indicate that physician calls are important but that it is equally important for her to build up wholesale inventory levels in her region. (GO TO 141)

B.   Offer to help her any way you can to build her sales volume. (GO TO 178)

Decision Point 130

When Buff arrives, you tell him that his plan to put off making a decision for six months is unacceptable. Also, you tell him that it appears to you that he has already decided to go with a real estate career and that under the circumstances, what he can provide Omega is not worth six months salary.

Buff responds by saying that he likes doing real estate deals and that he has been successful in them. He goes on to say that he is indeed thinking about forming a corporation and selling real estate full time, but he is not sure that he wants to give up the security--particularly such things as a steady paycheck and good insurance--which Omega can provide. As Buff continues to talk, it seems clearer to you. that his goal is to develop his own business but that he doesn't want to leave until he has arranged some details, such as replacing the company car and getting insurance.

What would you do now?

A. Discharge Buff and begin making plans for his replacement. (GO TO 109)

B. Try to negotiate a deal with Buff in which you would keep him on in a limited capacity. (GO TO 127)

Decision Point 131

You chose to implement flexitime for this group. The new office administrator is thrilled since she studied the concept in school. The office staff members quickly adapt to the plan and absenteeism plummets. Flexitime makes work much more convenient for both the single parents and the older members of the staff.

Congratulations! You have successfully completed the Job Design Interactive Case.

Decision Point 132

You and John agree that he should try to call on 90 percent of the obstetricians in his territory next quarter. You follow this up with a phone call half way through the next quarter to remind him of his commitment and to get feedback.

When the quarter is over, the record indicates that John called 90 percent of his physicians (exactly). However, his performance dropped from 330 to 315.
When you call him on this performance deficiency, John asserts: "I told you the territory divisions were inequitable. Look, I called on 90 percent of the obstetricians as we agreed, but I still produced only 315 units!" This places you in an impossible situation. By increasing his effort but not his performance, he calls the entire redistricting plan into question. However, it is likely that John's calls on M.D.s were not intended to develop sales. In general, it is not prudent to establish effort goals without associated performance goals.

Re-evaluate your last decision. Circle the #132 you just wrote in your flow diagram. Then move back to the first uncircled number above this one in your flow diagram.

Decision Point 133

"As a matter of fact, I've been giving it some thought. I view life very differently now. My priorities are my life first, my family second, and my job third. For example, I find myself more involved in my son's activities. He's been in soccer for eight years, but I never got involved. Now I'm an assistant coach. My wife's been trying to get involved in my work. She goes with me on most of the out-of-town calls I make, and as a nurse herself, she understands Omega's products. The biggest problem that I have is making calls on rural doctors. I don't like being away from home for more than two days, and that really makes certain physicians out of reach."

"If I resigned, I'd miss some parts of the job like seeing some of the doctors I know well, and I'd really miss working with you. But I certainly don't need the job anymore. My dad left us a real nice inheritance, so I don't have to work to eat anymore."

How would you respond?

A.   Tell him that you will be sorry to see him go, but that you have to have 400 units per quarter from a sales rep in his region, and you cannot afford to keep him while he decides what to do. (GO TO 219)

B.   Ask Jim if he needs some time to get himself together now that his personal crisis has passed. (GO TO 214)

C.   Indicate to Jim that you don't want to stand in his way if he doesn't want to work anymore, but you aren't sure there isn't some way that you could work something out with him. (GO TO 135)

D.   Tell him that you will be personally disappointed if he gives up on his job and that you wish he would reconsider. Remind him of what he would be giving up in terms of the nonfinancial rewards the job gives him. (GO TO 194)

Decision Point 134

She leaves your office, and you ask Virgil to come in. He enters, and after exchanging pleasantries, you open the discussion of his conflict with Phyllis and invite him to comment.

He responds: "I guess I am in the doghouse again, huh? Well, okay, I'll try harder to work with "Miss Smarty-pants.""

How would you respond?

A. "Yes you are in the doghouse. From what Phyllis tells me you have been pretty uncooperative." (GO TO 263)

B. "Let's soft-pedal the name-calling, Virgil. I want your side of the story. Here's a list of situations that Phyllis has prepared. How can you explain what you have been doing?" (GO TO 139)

C. "You're not in the doghouse, Virgil. You are a vital member of this organization. I'm trying to get to the bottom of what is going on between the two of you. Name-calling is not going to get us anywhere." (GO TO 240)

Decision Point 135

The two of you begin to talk about alternatives, and it appears that if you are in agreement, he and his wife might be willing to share the territory as "co-reps." This would enable Jim to be with his son for more time while covering for the rural portions of the territory. You and Jim invite Jim's wife, Kathy, into the bungalow, and she is enthusiastic about the plan to share Jim's job.

You follow up with a call to the Director of Employee Relations (at home) to be sure that this arrangement is possible. It is, and Jim's wife is scheduled for company training. This settled, you stress the necessity of making the standard 400 units per quarter. Both Jim and Kathy agree to coordinate their work to meet that figure. The next quarter's performance figures are better than your wildest dreams Jim and Kathy produce 525 units!
Your questioning revealed that Jim's motivational problem was the value he had for the outcomes offered by the job. Because of a personal tragedy, Jim began to question the rewards (financial and otherwise) that he was getting from his work. You determined that by problem solving with Jim, you could turn Jim's altered lifestyle into an advantage. Such successes are not always possible. However in circumstances such as this, exploring options with the employee may be useful.

Congratulations! GO TO 249 to begin to deal with your next motivational challenge, Wilson Thomas.

Decision Point 136

You chose to implement a QWL intervention at the Astoria plant. This plant has a record of high absenteeism and turnover, two signs that QWL may bring about improvements. However, there is an ample supply of labor in the Astoria labor market making it economically feasible to postpone a QWL intervention in favor of plants where market conditions are less favorable. Economic factors are not the only basis for making decisions that affect the quality of working life of employees. But when you have a number of different plants and a limited amount of resources to dedicate to QWL, then it makes sense to use them where they will have the most positive impact.

Re-evaluate your last decision. Circle the #136 you just wrote in your flow diagram. Then move to the last uncircled step in your flow diagram.

Decision Point 137

William Spaulding has been a difficult person for you to understand ever since you joined the company. His recent sales performance figures are on page 18.

"Buff," as he is called by his friends, has been with the company for eight years, and his performance has been nothing short of terrible for the last two years. What makes Spaulding's performance so hard to understand is that in so many ways, he appears a natural for this business. He has a fine educational background, is very personable, and possesses a marvelous, relaxed sense of humor. And then there is his golf. A former PGA professional, Buff is an avid golfer, a hobby he uses to entertain his clients on their days off. Buff is something of a "character" at the company. He always shows up at company functions in brightly colored golf clothes, tanned and well groomed. He asks questions articulately. What with his fashionable clothes and large home (on a golf course), you have often wondered how he maintains his lifestyle in the face of such low commissions. His persuasive, slick, sophisticated personality has bought him a great deal of time from you. In fact, you feel rather taken advantage of. He has promised improved performance on many occasions, but somehow he has never delivered. You are not proud that you have let him get away with such "subpar" performance.

How would you approach your conversation with him?

  A.   Ask around the company discreetly to find out more about Buff's reputation as a salesman and how he is able to maintain his life-style when his earnings are so low. (GO TO 206)

  B.   Tell him that if he does not turn his performance around, you are prepared to take disciplinary action like never before. (GO TO 267)

  C.   Ask to accompany him on several sales calls. (GO TO 175)

Decision Point 138

Wilson is reluctant to put his commitments down on paper. You press him for specifics, and after making a few, it becomes clear to him that you want something quite detailed; that is, you want him to submit a weekly schedule of planned activities on the Thursday following each week.

At that point he says: "You know, I felt you and I got to know each other this week. I began to develop an appreciation of your point of view, and I find myself respecting you more than I ever did. However, you're treating me like a five-year-old. I thought you were beginning to respect some of my sales practices, but what you're asking me to do is humiliating!"

How would you respond?

A. Review the positive feedback you have given him, and indicate that he has earned your respect on these aspects. Indicate that you don't intend humiliation, only building respect based on results. (GO TO 270)

B. Tell him that you would do the same for any employee who was not performing up to expectations. Tell him that he has to earn your respect. (GO TO 144)

C. Back off on your expectations a bit since you don't want to damage Wilson's self-respect. (GO TO 186)

Decision Point 139

You advise Virgil, "Let's soft-pedal the name-calling, Virgil. I want your side of the story. Here's a list of situations that Phyllis has prepared. How can you explain what you have been doing?"

It is good that you confronted him on his use of name-calling. However, you did not go far enough in assuring him that you intended to be open-minded in dealing with this issue. Specifically, Virgil opened his remarks by asking you if he were still in the doghouse, an apparent reference to his previous quality problem. Accordingly, you should have given him some assurance at that point that you intend to view this situation from a neutral posture.

Re-evaluate your last decision. Circle the #139 you just wrote in your flow diagram. Then move to the last uncircled step in your flow diagram.

Decision Point 140

When Buff arrives, you lay out the evidence of his violation of policy and tell him that he could either agree to end real estate dealings with his Omega clients and improve his performance or resign. He seems taken aback by your abruptness and for the first time in your memory is at a bit of a loss for words. As you press him, he becomes defensive, first denying that his real estate interests are in any way related to his Omega responsibilities, later almost bragging about how he has signed up most of the doctors in his area to one or another of his partnerships. The meeting ends with Buff announcing that he isn't going to give up his real estate practice and if it was an "issue" with you, you could have his resignation.

The outcomes of Buff's resignation are mixed. Although you have eliminated a poor performer and someone who was in direct violation of company policy, the timing and nature of his departure cause difficulties. First, you do not have anyone to replace Buff on such short notice and the district is not covered by two months. Second, you hear from reps in other districts that doctors are saying that Omega has really been unfair to Buff. You suspect that these stories are coming from Buff and the doctors in his real estate deals, but they are affecting Omega's reputation and the reps' morale, nonetheless.

Given Buff's violation of policy, requiring him to leave Omega is appropriate and, in fact, the right thing to do. However, you might have been able to get Buff out without so many negative consequences.

Re-evaluate your last decision with the idea of how you might terminate Buff in a less disruptive fashion. Circle the #140 you just wrote in your flow diagram. Then move back to the first uncircled number above this one in your flow diagram.

Decision Point 141

She responds as follows: "But I called on each wholesaler in my region twice during the quarter. And even though the average supply is only at 50 days right now, that's up from 43 when I started."

You were not aware of this improvement in inventory levels, which is fairly substantial; therefore, you congratulate her on her improvement. Given all this information, how would you motivate Lisa?

  A.   Transfer her to a different territory within your district known to be an easier region for sales. (GO TO 118)

B. Tell her not to be discouraged since building credibility with obstetricians is often a time consuming process, and it may take a while to reach her 400-unit quota. (GO TO 218)

C. Ask to accompany her on several sales calls with obstetricians. (GO TO 102)

D. Ask her to attend a seminar on salesmanship offered by an industry association to further hone her skills. (GO TO 264)

E. Ask her how much her house payment is, and then calculate what her sales volume would have to be for her to earn a satisfactory commission. (GO TO 170)

F. Indicate that unless her sales volume improves, you may be forced to take disciplinary action. (GO TO 239)

Decision Point 142

You decided to tell Phyllis to work out the problem she is having with Virgil herself. You encouraged this effort by telling her that her promotability may depend on her ability to handle this situation effectively alone. This is not an uncommon managerial approach to conflict resolution. Unfortunately, however, it is often not very effective.

The problem with this method is twofold. First, Virgil may not be as motivated as Phyllis to resolve the conflict. Thus, by delegating, you are stacking the deck in his favor. Second, delegating conflicts is appropriate only if the problem's importance justifies no manager involvement or if the issue provides an important development opportunity for the parties. In this situation, you simply do not know yet how important this issue is.

Re-evaluate your last decision. Circle the #142 you just wrote in your flow diagram. Then move to the last uncircled step in your flow diagram.

Decision Point 143

You spell out the issues for your supervisor and summarize the issues and risks as you see them. Your supervisor agrees with your analysis and says that he thinks that Buff has to go and that he will do whatever possible to back your decision. In short, your supervisor has said that he understands the situation and will support you in what you do--but he doesn't have much specific advice about how you should handle Buff and the potential problems his resignation might create. At this point what would you do?

   A.   Call Buff in and attempt to find out why he wants six months to make his plans about resigning. (GO TO 130)

   B.   Discharge Buff and begin making plans for his replacement. (GO TO 200)

Decision Point 144

Wilson's statement that you are treating him like a five-year-old is an attempt to salvage his self-respect. The past week has been hard on him, and now that you are insisting that he not only digest your criticism but also act on it, his ego has become very fragile. Had your statement been more balanced and personal, it would have provided him with more motivation for turning his behavior around.

Re-evaluate your last decision. Circle the #144 you just wrote in your flow diagram. Then move back to the first uncircled number above this one in your flow diagram.

Decision Point 145

You decided to call both Phyllis and Virgil into your office to settle this issue face to face. This is really premature. While confrontation meetings can be useful in conflict resolution, a manager should never schedule them before discovering where each party stands. In this instance you do not really know what Virgil's position is or how Phyllis will act in his presence. It is much more prudent to interview each party to the conflict individually before you arrange a confrontation meeting. This gives you a better idea of what to expect.

Re-evaluate your last decision. Circle the #145 you just wrote in your flow diagram. Then move to the last uncircled step in your flow diagram.

Decision Point 146

Jim is notably nervous in responding, "I'm disturbed that I've let you down, believe me. I don't want to disappoint you, but I'm not sure what to suggest. I'll try harder if you like, but I'm hesitant to promise much more than 400 units for the time being."

How would you respond?

A. Ask Jim if he needs some time off to get himself together now that his personal crisis has passed. (GO TO 214)

B. Probe whether he really wants to continue as an Omega sales rep. (GO TO 105)

C. Tell Jim that you do not consider 400 units good enough. Ask him why he cannot commit to do even better. (GO TO 115)

D. Do nothing. It is clear to you that Jim's performance problem is caused by a factor outside of your control. (GO TO 203)

Decision Point 147

This is not advisable. Any redistricting would simply create problems with other reps. In addition, a deviation from the scheme sanctioned by the company and endorsed by others in the industry requires more than one person's lack of satisfaction with it. Re-evaluate your last decision. Circle the #147 you just wrote in your flow diagram. Then move back to the first uncircled number above this one in your flow diagram.

Decision Point 148

Both Phyllis and Virgil leave the meeting in high spirits. Unfortunately, two weeks later, Phyllis and Virgil are back in your office complaining about each other once again. The final step in any mediation is to clarify and document the responsibilities for implementing the settlement.

Re-evaluate your last decision. Circle the #148 you just wrote in your flow diagram. Then move back to the last uncircled step in your flow diagram.

Decision Point 149

You chose to implement a QWL intervention at the La Casita plant. This plant has a record of low absenteeism and turnover. Therefore, a QWL intervention is not likely to improve the economics of the situation. Economic factors are not the only basis for making decisions that affect the quality of working life of employees. But when you have a number of different plants and a limited amount of resources to dedicate to QWL, then it makes sense to use them where they will have the most positive impact.

Re-evaluate your last decision. Circle the #149 you just wrote in your flow diagram. Then move to the last uncircled step in your flow diagram.

Decision Point 150

You chose to resolve this conflict by arbitration. This is a very common way of resolving conflicts between employees. Sometimes it is appropriate in situations like the one you are facing. If you cannot help the parties structure their own agreement, deciding it for them is always your option. However, it is a bit early in the process to abandon your efforts to mediate the conflict. There are still some simple things you might do to help Phyllis and Virgil solve the conflict themselves.

Re-evaluate your last decision. Circle the #150 you just wrote in your flow diagram. Then move back to the last uncircled step in your flow diagram.

Decision Point 151

He responds: "Well, if you have your mind made up that you're going to can me, then there's nothing I can do about it."

You assure him that your mind is not made up, but you are going to have to see significant improvements in his performance. He asks you what he has to do. You respond by negotiating a standard of performance (400 units, 95 percent of doctors contacted, and wholesale inventory level of 45 days). Halfway through the following quarter, Wilson phones you to tell you that he knows his inventory figures are not going to meet your agreed-to goal. He tells you that Omega's competitors are offering an attractive incentive plan to their reps and that he is finding it difficult to make progress.

How would you respond?

A.   Tell him that you don't consider competitors' perks an acceptable excuse. Let him know that you're expecting him to live up to the terms of your agreement. (GO TO 243)

B.   Accompany him on a series of sales calls. (GO TO 154)

C.   Schedule him for a training program that involves modern sales techniques. Warn him that this is his last chance. (GO TO 272)

D.   Check to see if his job is really important to him. (GO TO 242)

Decision Point 152

You chose to implement a QWL intervention at the San Lorenzo plant. Certainly the economic conditions favor this choice. There is scarcity in the local labor market, making the plant's high level of turnover an important problem. You begin the implementation, but immediately run into two problems. First, while the plant manager is initially open to the intervention, especially since he likes the visibility it gives him at corporate headquarters, he soon becomes pessimistic about what QWL will do to his power in the plant. Second, the employees at the San Lorenzo plant have never been consulted on work related matters before and are very reluctant to assume responsibility. After seven months of careful work, you conclude that the intervention is plagued by the attitudes of both those in senior management positions and those on the shop floor. Consequently, you decide to abandon the intervention.

The problem here is that the centralized authority at the plant interfered with the intervention. In general, QWL interventions are more successful in decentralized organizations than in centralized ones.

Re-evaluate your last decision. Circle the #152 you just wrote in your flow diagram. Then move to the last uncircled step in your flow diagram.

Decision Point 153

You decided to tell Phyllis that Virgil can be a problem, but that you want to hear his side of the story before taking action. As reasonable as your statement seems, it is actually premature. The problem is that Phyllis has engaged in behavior-labeling of a sort that, if not confronted on the spot, leads to an escalation of the conflict. Effective third parties confront such statements and make clear that labels like "obstructionist," "uncooperative," and "unprofessional" are not helpful but counterproductive to conflict resolution.

Re-evaluate your last decision. Circle the #153 you just wrote in your flow diagram. Then move back to the last uncircled step in your flow diagram.

Decision Point 154

You accompany Wilson on an entire week of his sales calls. Your observations are as follows: (1) Wilson does not budget his time well. He takes a large number of breaks, and he does not push himself during the day. (2) He has an excellent reputation with older obstetricians, but the younger ones are impatient with his slow, plodding approach. (3) He has a good reputation with one of the two wholesalers in his region. The other is a very large wholesaler whose very young buyer seems to consider Wilson an old jerk.

Through the course of the week, you give Wilson repeated verbal feedback on your observations and follow this up with a written report at the end of the week. At the beginning of the week, he is quite defensive about your feedback, but by week's end you notice that he is asking you for advice and encouragement. However, when late Friday afternoon arrives, you note that Wilson is getting somewhat anxious about what you're going to do.

What would you do?

A. Ask him to prepare a series of effort and performance commitments in light of the feedback you've given him. (GO TO 138)

B. Tell him that you expect him to work on the feedback you've given him. Be firm that you expect him to report next quarterly sales above 400 units or that you'll be forced to terminate him. (GO TO 184)

Decision Point 155

You decide to implement vertical loading with the cutters. After a careful analysis of their jobs, you conclude that the best way to do that is to delegate to them additional responsibility for determining the pace of their work and to have them perform their own quality control inspections. Once given this additional authority, however, problems begin to develop. The cutters like the break from their repetitive work that these additional tasks provide, but they are worried that they will lose their jobs if they make inadvertent errors. One cutter complains that he did not take this job to be a quality control person. Another cutter asks if she will be paid more now that her responsibilities have been expanded. After eight months, when you examine the results of this intervention, you are disappointed to note that absenteeism and turnover among the cutters have not markedly improved.

These problems are due to the choice you made about the QWL intervention. Vertical loading is most suitable to correct deficiencies in the autonomy of workers. The cutters suffered more from limited skill variety and task identity.

Re-evaluate your last decision. Circle the #155 you just wrote in your flow diagram. Then move to the last uncircled step in your flow diagram.

Your meeting with Virgil ends on a positive note, and you meet privately with Phyllis. You probe the interests that underlie her position, and like Virgil, you have to clarify your question several times to get her to open a bit. Finally she tells you that she has two interests besides the economic ones:

(1) getting Virgil's reports late means that her reports to headquarters will be late, and she is afraid that will make her look bad there; and

(2) getting Virgil's reports late means that she has to work late hours, and she has concerns about her safety when she leaves the plant late at night.

You end your meeting with Phyllis in much the same way you ended your meeting with Virgil.

When the three of you get back together, you open by asking them to consider two alternatives that occurred to you.

Alternative 1: Ivan should complete the paperwork for Virgil on Mondays while Virgil works on the Weber machine.

Alternative 2: Phyllis should get the headquarters staff responsible for setting weekly quotas to factor the likelihood of quality problems on the brush machines into their equations.

Although both voice some concerns, neither Phyllis nor Virgil reject the alternatives out-of-hand. In fact, as the discussion continues, you sense that you are close to an agreement, but you are also a bit concerned that you might lose momentum. What would you do now?

A. Ask your secretary to stop what she is doing so you can dictate a memo to her that outlines the specific responsibilities Phyllis, Virgil, and Ivan will have for implementing the two alternatives. (GO TO 171)

B. Announce that the two of them seem to be close to an agreement and ask if there is any reason they cannot go forward with the two alternatives. (GO TO 163)

Decision Point 157

You encourage John to do better, but his performance during the next quarter continues to be poor. Your conversation with John was fine except that you didn't nail down a specific performance commitment from him. In general, it is more effective to establish specific performance goals than goals that are vague such as, "Do the best you can."

Re-evaluate your last decision. Circle the #157 you just wrote in your flow diagram. Then move back to the first uncircled number above this one in your flow diagram.

Decision Point 158

You decide to implement QWL by opening feedback channels for the cutters. After a careful analysis of their jobs, you conclude that the best way to do that is by providing daily production figures to the group. This substitutes for the previous system of providing feedback on a monthly basis. In addition, you initiate a system that enables the cutters to get customer feedback when quality problems develop.

After two months, you examine the absenteeism and turnover figures for the group and note a slight improvement. After eight months, however, you note that these figures have returned to their previous levels.

These rather disappointing results are due to the choice you made about the QWL intervention. Opening feedback channels is most suitable to correct deficiencies in the task feedback of workers. The cutters suffered more from limited skill variety and task identity.

Re-evaluate your last decision. Circle the #158 you just wrote in your flow diagram. Then move to the last uncircled step in your flow diagram.

Decision Point 159

You decided to ask Phyllis and Virgil to prepare position papers to refer to in their meeting with you. This is unadvisable. If anything, preparing such documents will simply harden their positions on the issue. At this point your goal should be to move the two parties toward more flexible positions.

Re-evaluate your last decision. Circle the #159 you just wrote in your flow diagram. Then move back to the last uncircled step in your flow diagram.

You tell him he's being defensive. With that he totally clams up. Re-evaluate your last decision. Circle the #160 that you just wrote in your flow diagram. Then move back to the first uncircled number above this one in your flow diagram.

John Crosby's performance during the next quarter improves. He calls on 86 percent of the physicians in his territory, and his sales increase to 410 units, ten greater than standard.

He calls you after the quarterly performance report appears, and reminds you of your commitment to do something about the size of his territory. Since you do not want to go through a redistricting, you consult with your boss and others in the organization and find out that John could work part time with the company's market research group conducting "focus groups" of physicians in his territory. Available budgetary funds enable you to sweeten his "draw" (the salary he earns independent of his commission) for the extra responsibilities. This arrangement is a "one-shot deal," and you make that clear to John. He jumps at the offer, and his sales performance continues to be good (but not spectacular) while he works with the market research group.

Upon hearing of this situation, Susan Brown complains to you that she should have been given this special assignment; that is, she is now experiencing a perception of inequity. Luckily, however, you were careful to determine that the characteristics of the physicians in Crosby's district made them better candidates for focus groups than the physicians in other districts. Accordingly, you are able to convince Susan Brown that Crosby's special assignment was not given at her expense.

When you promised John that you would look into his assertion of inequity, you took a very serious chance. Had you done nothing, he would have felt you had gone back on your commitment. As it was, you risked creating inequity elsewhere among your reps. Congratulations! By bringing Crosby's perceived inequity back into line with realities, you successfully dealt with a volatile situation. You found that you had to identify a specific reference person to convince Crosby that his equity calculations were exaggerated. Additionally, you found you had to address Crosby's eroded belief that arose because of the inequity perception that his efforts would no longer matter. GO TO 122 to begin your analysis of the case of Jim Clemmons, the next of your employees in need of motivation.

Decision Point 162

You decide to implement QWL by forming natural work units for the cutters. After a careful analysis of their jobs, you conclude that the best way to do that is to divide the cutters into four product groupings, three for different styles of pants and one for denim jackets. This actually works quite well. The cutters were experiencing a deficiency in task identity, and this grouping of jobs allows them to identify better with the end-result of their labor. After eight months, however, when you examine the absenteeism and turnover figures, you note that the level of improvement is not what you expected. For a while there was improvement, but it has since returned to levels only slightly lower than before.

The reason for these disappointing results is that you chose an intervention that does not address the cutters need for more variety in their jobs.

Re-evaluate your last decision. Circle the #162 you just wrote in your flow diagram. Then move to the last uncircled step in your flow diagram.

Decision Point 163

Both Phyllis and Virgil agree that they do seem to be close to resolving their conflict. The discussion of the alternatives goes well. Although they continue to ask questions and propose modifications to alternative settlements, it is done in the spirit of problem-solving rather than arguing.

Virgil says that he does not want to give up his authority to complete the reports to Ivan. Since you know Virgil's need to seem "in control," you suggest that perhaps Ivan could assemble the numbers and Virgil could review them and approve the report. This seems to satisfy Virgil to some extent. He does state that it would be a lot easier to implement this if he had a week where he could work with Ivan to teach him how to complete the new assignment.

The discussion then turns to Alternative 2. Initially, Phyllis expresses pessimism that this will result in no change. You tell her that even if this happens, staff will see her as someone who takes efficiency seriously and wants to make the mathematical formulation even better. This disguised appeal to her interests is sufficiently persuasive that she agrees to try.

At this point, Virgil makes one additional proposal. He offers to provide Phyllis with some background information on the capabilities of the machines that will strengthen her arguments if she will agree that his report can be late next week so that he can work with Ivan. She agrees to this trade.

At this point, what would you do?

A. Thank the parties for their efforts and remind them of the commitments they have just made. (GO TO 148)

B. Dictate a memo to your secretary outlining the responsibilities of Phyllis, Virgil, and Ivan and send it to all parties (GO TO 123)

Decision Point 164

It is two days later and you are reading over the material Buff has given you. Looking at it, you are amazed at the extent of Buff's operation. He has involved most of his Omega clients in deals and many of their friends as well. Many of the doctors have invested with Buff for years.

The plan Buff provides for separating his real estate operations from his sales calls is unacceptable to you. In it he asks for a six-month "grace period" to "investigate" ways of reducing the overlap between his real estate deals and his sales calls. At the end of six-months, he says he will provide you with either a detailed plan for eliminating the "apparent conflict of interest" or his resignation. As you read over Buff's proposal, you become convinced that what he really wants to do is to set up his own real estate business but stay on your payroll for another six months while he does it.

You realize that the situation you are in presents you with a number of problems. First, Buff is clearly in violation of company policies and you can't tolerate that. Second, Buff has very good relations with the doctors in his territory (both through his pleasant personality and his real estate dealings), and you don't want to create ill will on the part of the doctors toward Omega. Third, the plan that Buff has presented you was not responsive to your request, and you strongly suspect that his entire purpose was to try to buy some time before leaving. Fourth, a potential replacement for Buff is just finishing training, but you think that it would be difficult to throw that person into Buff's district without more training and help than you can provide.

What actions would you now take?

A. Lay out the entire situation for your superior and ask him for advice in dealing with Buff. (GO TO 143)

B. Call Buff and attempt to find out why he wants six months to make his plans about resigning. (GO TO 130)

C. Discharge Buff and begin making plans for his replacement. (GO TO 109)

305

Decision Point 165

She tells you that she has already prepared such a list and hands it to you. Her preparation impresses you. The list is impressive, including a series of episodes that go back one full year. Apparently Virgil has not only been repeatedly late with his reports, but also has objected openly to her schedules. In one instance Virgil even argued with her in the presence of his crew. What would you say after reviewing her list?

A. Tell her that settling this issue is her responsibility. Let her know that you consider it important for her development as a new employee to try to work out these problems first before coming to you. Point out to her that a consideration in assessing the promotability of staff people is that they work well with line personnel. (GO TO 142)

B. Call Virgil into your office now to meet his accuser. (GO TO 210)

C. Acknowledge that her position in this conflict is an important one, but tell her that she is going to have to work with Virgil for a long time, so it is important that the three of you approach this situation with that in mind. (GO TO 248)

D. Inform her that you will instruct Virgil to be more cooperative. (GO TO 177)

Decision Point 166

You meet with your boss, give him a summary of Spaulding's performance, and tell him that you have heard a rumor about him conducting personal business with his Omega clients. He informs you that there is not much you can do on the basis of rumors, but that you should do something about Buff's substandard performance.

What would you now do?

A. Ask around the company discreetly to find out more about Buff's reputation as a salesman and how he is able to maintain his life-style when his earnings are so low. (GO TO 173)

B. Confront Buff with your hunch about his real estate deals, and ask if this is the cause of his poor performance. (GO TO 190)

C. Do nothing, since it seems your feedback on his sales efforts has led him to try harder. (GO TO 229)

Decision Point 167

Virgil is delighted with this decision. You work with Phyllis and arrange to pay her a special bonus to work overtime on Virgil's reports. One year later you assess the situation again and discover that the total cost of this decision in only $2,325. However, this cost was totally unnecessary. Somehow you got locked into the economics of the situation without considering how to move the positions of the parties closer together. Your decision cost the plant a considerable sum of money. It also established a precedent that you will settle conflicts by deciding whose stated position has the best short-run economic outcome.

Re-evaluate your last decision. Circle the #167 you just wrote in your flow diagram. Then move back to the last uncircled step in your flow diagram.

Decision Point 168

You decide to implement QWL by implementing flexitime in the cutters group. After consultation with the cutters and with other officials of the plant, you conclude that a core time of 9 a.m. to 3 p.m. is most suitable, allowing the cutters to begin as early as 7 a.m. and ending as late as 5 p.m. Although it takes a while to work out the supervision problems created by this new work schedule, the implementation actually goes quite well. Absenteeism improves dramatically. Unfortunately, however, turnover does not. In eight months, this nagging turnover problem has become even more critical as two cutter jobs have to remain unfilled for three weeks due to the unfavorable labor market in Eagle Point.

These mixed results and the lingering turnover problem were due to your choice to rely on flexitime to address the cutters' job design problem. The combination of the cutters' rather high growth need strength and their perceived deficiency in skill variety and task identity favored a different approach.

Re-evaluate your last decision. Circle the #168 you just wrote in your flow diagram. Then move to the last uncircled step in your flow diagram.

Decision Point 169

Jim's lower lip begins to quiver as he says, "I view life very differently now. My priorities are my life first, my family second, and my job third. For example, I find myself more involved in my son's activities. He's been in soccer for eight years, but I never got involved. Now I'm an assistant coach. My wife's been trying to get involved in my work. She goes with me on most of my trips, and as a nurse herself, she understands Omega's products. The biggest problem I have is making calls on rural physicians. I don't like to be away from home for more than two days, and that really makes certain doctors in my territory out of reach."

At this point, what would you say?

A. Acknowledge his comment but let him know that you think his performance is really low and that you would like to know exactly what he plans to do to improve it. (GO TO 146)

B. Ask Jim if he needs some time off to get himself together now that his personal crisis has passed. (GO TO 214)

C. Suggest that Jim may want to attend a sales seminar sponsored by the company next month. By coincidence, it is being conducted in the city where he lives. (GO TO 204)

D. Probe whether he really wants to continue as an Omega sales rep. (GO TO 105)

Decision Point 170

You and Lisa calculate that she requires a volume of 420 units to make the house payment. With that as a salient goal, Lisa enters the next quarter with renewed vigor. However, at the end of the quarter, her volume had dipped to 340 units (from 360). Discouraged and very frustrated, Lisa resigns.

Your analysis of Lisa's motivation revealed several things. Clearly Lisa has a strong belief that her efforts will pay off in terms of performance since she has a history of succeeding in nearly everything she has attempted. You can also be certain that Lisa believes that performance will be rewarded at Omega, since she is on an incentive pay system that relates her income directly to two indices of performance, volume and inventory. As for Lisa's particular preference for the her work outcomes, you know Lisa values the monetary outcomes of her job since she has indicated that she needs her commission check to make her first house payment. Given these factors, it is not surprising that Lisa's efforts are high (she called on 100 percent of her M.D.s, and each wholesaler twice). However, her performance is still low. In light of this assessment, think about what additional factor may account for her low performance.

Your approach did little more than reinforce what was already a strong belief that performance results in important outcomes. Thus, it was actually a rather redundant action that only added to Lisa's frustration level when she didn't improve.

Re-evaluate your last decision. Circle the #170 you just wrote in your flow diagram. Then move back to the first uncircled number above this one in your flow diagram.

Decision Point 171

As you begin dictating the memo to your secretary, both Virgil and Phyllis interrupt with objections about everything from the general idea to the specific words you are using. Within a short period of time, the agreement that you thought was imminent has completely broken down.

An important rule-of-thumb in mediation is not to rush parties into an agreement. It is frequently easier to gain commitment through a series of small steps than through one large request.

Write #163 as the next step in your flow diagram and turn to that decision point to continue the case assuming you had been more tentative in pushing for agreement.

Decision Point 172

You decide to implement QWL by implementing a concentrated work week in the cutters group. After consultation with the cutters and with other officials of the plant, you conclude that a four-day, forty-hour work week is most suitable. Although it takes a while to work out the supervision problems created by this new work schedule, the implementation actually goes quite well. Absenteeism improves dramatically. Unfortunately, however, turnover does not. In eight months, this nagging turnover problem has become even more critical as two cutter jobs remain unfilled for three weeks due to the unfavorable labor market in Eagle Point.

These mixed results and the lingering turnover problem were due to your choice to rely on a concentrated work week to address the cutter's job design problem. The combination of the cutters' rather high growth need strength and their perceived deficiency in skill variety and task identity favored a different approach.

Re-evaluate your last decision. Circle the #172 you just wrote in your flow diagram. Then move to the last uncircled step in your flow diagram.

Decision Point 173

Before meeting with Spaulding, you decide to gather information discreetly about his reputation and the conflict between his low earnings and abundant life-style. As a result, one staff person tells you that a doctor friend of his has shown him a flyer advertising a real estate partnership put together by Buff. The staff person says that it seems that all of Buff's Omega clients are receiving these and many are investing. You now feel that you have the "iron-clad" proof necessary to confront Buff. You know you must act.

What would you do now?

A. Consult with your superior about how to handle the situation. (GO TO 255)

B. Call Buff in and ask him if the rumors you have heard are true. (GO TO 179)

C. Call Buff in, lay out the evidence you have and tell him he must eliminate his outside deals and improve his performance. (GO TO 140)

Decision Point 174

You ask Phyllis and Virgil to brainstorm other options with you. In conducting the brainstorming process, how would you arrange the parties within your office?

A. Have Virgil and Phyllis sit across a table from one another. (GO TO 209)

B. Stand at the flip chart and position Phyllis and Vigil in chairs next to one another facing the flip chart. (GO TO 205)

C. Take three chairs away from the table and put them in a circle. (GO TO 271)

Decision Point 175

You accompany Spaulding on several calls and you are very surprised by the results. He demonstrates a fine knowledge of the company's products, and his approach is very effective throughout all the calls. Both wholesalers and doctors seem very responsive to his efforts.

After this dazzling performance, you let him know that he did an outstanding job and ask him to explain why his performance is so low when he clearly has such aptitude for the job. He asserts that he simply has been too casual about his performance but that now he understands that he had better improve.

As you are driving back to your office, you recall something that took place in one wholesaler's office. While Buff was making a count, the wholesaler asked if you were in on any of Buff's "little deals." When you responded with an uncertain look, the wholesaler said, "You know, condos." The conversation ended there as Buff and others came into the room; however, upon reflection, the wholesaler seemed to imply that Buff was putting together real estate deals with the customers he calls on. If true, this is a direct violation of company policy. There is no clear procedure for dealing with such infringements without "iron-clad" proof.

What would you do now?

A. Ask around the company discreetly to find out more about Buff's reputation as a salesman and how he is able to maintain his life-style when his earnings are so low. (GO TO 173)

B. Confront Buff with your hunch about his real estate deals and ask if this is the cause of his poor performance. (GO TO 190)

C. Consult with your supervisor about how to deal with this situation. (GO TO 166)

D. Do nothing, since it seems your feedback on his sales efforts has led him to try harder. (GO TO 229)

Decision Point 176

You decide to continue the existing pay scheme (individual piece rates) as a means to support your plan to rotate the cutters' jobs. This proves to be an unfortunate choice. When training begins, the cutters are very reluctant to attend since it takes them away from doing the work that affects their earnings. Even though you try to persuade them that the training will allow them to increase their earnings in the long run, attendance at the training sessions is poor.

Re-evaluate your last decision. Circle the #176 you just wrote in your flow diagram. Then move to the last uncircled step in your flow diagram.

Decision Point 177

You order Virgil to comply with Phyllis's need for timely information. Virgil reluctantly agrees to try to do better. The next week, he gets his report filed by Monday at 2 p.m. (two hours late). The following week goes better with Virgil submitting his report by 11. However, that week a major quality problem develops due to carelessness in setting up an extrusion machine. Virgil informs you that if he had not had to work on the report Monday, the problem would not have occurred. The problem cost the plant $6,000. You may have avoided this expense if you had handled the conflict differently.

You decided to side with Phyllis before even hearing Virgil's side of the story. As a result Virgil was not really committed to your solution, and he may have even created the quality problem as a way of showing his dissatisfaction. Your approach to this conflict is known as "arbitration" and is quite common in practice. However, it is less effective than mediation in bringing about satisfactory long-term resolutions to conflicts.

Re-evaluate your last decision. Circle the #177 you just wrote in your flow diagram. Then move back to the last uncircled step in your flow diagram.

Decision Point 178

Your conversation with Lisa is not yielding the type of information that you need to complete a motivational analysis. Re-evaluate your last decision, and consider how to get information that would be helpful in identifying the correct approach to motivating Lisa.

Re-evaluate your last decision. Circle the #178 you just wrote in your flow diagram. Then move back to the first uncircled number above this one in your flow diagram.

Decision Point 179

When you call Buff in, you begin the conversation with some pleasantries. After a few minutes, you tell him that you have heard rumors about his using his job primarily to develop his real estate interests. Buff responds by talking about the problems of teamwork in any company. As he continues, you get the strong impression that he is "ducking" the issue you are trying to raise. You finally interrupt him and tell him that you have two reliable reports of his dealings and that you are asking him straight out if he is involving his Omega clients in his real estate deals. Buff seems a bit surprised by your directness, but he admits to you that the allegations are true. When you ask Buff to give you the details of his deals, he lays out a story of real estate partnerships much broader than you thought possible. He has involved many doctors and wholesalers in a variety of partnerships. He says that his income from these deals is about the same as his salary. He also says that although some of these deals are risky, the potential payoff is great. You both know that he is in clear violation of company policy and that you must face it.

What would you do?

A.   Tell Buff that you have no choice but to discharge him. (GO TO 200)

B.   Tell Buff that he has a choice. He can either resign or end his real estate dealings. If he doesn't resign, you expect him to deliver a plan within 48 hours for ending his real estate involvements. (GO TO 164)

Decision Point 180

How would you define your own role in the negotiations at the meeting?

A.   You will hear both sides. and then announce your settlement. (GO TO 222)

B.   You will help the two parties explore alternatives so they can reach a satisfactory settlement . (GO TO 216)

C.   You prefer to mediate the conflict, but if the meeting ends in a stalemate, you will impose a solution that will probably displease one or both of the parties. (GO TO 117)

D.   You refuse to settle this situation for them. You will work with them to identify alternative settlements, but the ultimate decision must be theirs. (GO TO 245)

Decision Point 181

You decide to change the reward system from one based on piece rate to one that rewards seniority. Predictably, the senior cutters are delighted with the change, but the new cutters object. When the training begins, all the cutters attend, but some of the junior cutters openly object to having more work to perform without being adequately compensated for it. In three months, after you examine turnover and absenteeism figures, you note that they are on a par with what they were before the intervention. Apparently, changing the reward system the way you did was not the answer.

Re-evaluate your last decision. Circle the #181 you just wrote in your flow diagram. Then move to the last uncircled step in your flow diagram.

Decision Point 182

She responds that she wasn't prepared for the difficulty she's faced getting in to see doctors: "I'll tell you. It's tough even getting in the door. And when you do, the most you have is five minutes. And that's a very distracted five minutes, I'll tell you!"

How would you respond?

A. Ask her if she was disappointed with her commission check. (GO TO 129)

B. Indicate that physician calls are important, but that is equally important for her to build up wholesale inventory levels in her region. (GO TO 223)

C. Offer to help her in any way you can to build her sales volume. (GO TO 178)

Decision Point 183

Virgil very reluctantly agrees to try to do better. The next week he gets his report filed by Monday at 2 p.m. (two hours late). The following week goes better with Virgil actually submitting his report by 11. However, that week a major quality problem develops due to carelessness in setting up an extrusion machine. Virgil informs you that if he had not had to work on the report Monday, the problem would not have occurred. The problem cost the plant $6,000. You may have avoided this expense if you had handled the conflict differently. You were doing fine until you decided to side against Virgil. Actually, there is a resolution to this conflict situation that is satisfactory to both parties and to you.

Re-evaluate your last decision. Circle the #183 you just wrote in your flow diagram. Then move back to the last uncircled step in your flow diagram.

You decide not to have him participate in the development of an action plan. Instead you are firm that he should come up to an acceptable performance level. Generally it is preferable to use participation in the development of an action plan. You could have demanded the same performance level as part of that participative process.

Re-evaluate your last decision. Circle the #184 you just wrote in your flow diagram. Then move back to the first uncircled number above this one in your flow diagram.

You decide to consult with the cutters to see what change in the reward system they think is necessitated by the job rotation change. They tell you they think it is only fair that they are compensated in some way for the additional skills they must acquire to accommodate the intervention. You think this is a helpful suggestion, and you receive approval to implement a pay change to provide incentives on the acquisition of new skills.

You announce the changes to the cutters, and they begin rotating between cutting machines and blank assignments. This change immediately reduces absenteeism, but several cutters resign. Apparently, their growth need strength was not sufficient for them to see the advantages of the new job arrangements. Both of the individuals who leave work for the foreman who had expressed some reservations about job rotation, but six months later this foreman becomes converted when he notices that the cross-training of cutters allows him more flexibility in making assignments to make up for absent employees.

Your attention now turns to the sewers and finishers. Recall the questionnaire results for these two groups as follows:

Group	Low Perceived Job Characteristics	Growth Need Strength
Sewers	skill variety, autonomy, task significance	high
Finishers	skill variety, autonomy	moderate to high

You interview the members of these two groups and conclude that growth need strength is apparently quite high but the groups are not particularly cohesive--group members are much more interested in doing well as individuals than in working together as a group.

You know that one element of your QWL intervention should involve combining tasks because sewers and finishers believe their jobs are deficient in terms of skill variety. Is there any other QWL element that you should build into your QWL intervention?

A. Vertical loading. (GO TO 114)

B. Forming natural work units. (GO TO 196)

C. Flexitime. (GO TO 201)

D. Concentrated work week. (GO TO 207)

E. No other element. (GO TO 212)

Decision Point 186

Just because you have bruised Thomas's ego a bit is not reason to lower your expectations. Re-evaluate your last decision. Circle the #186 you just wrote in your flow diagram. Then move back to the first uncircled number above this one in your flow diagram.

Decision Point 187

You meet with your supervisor, give him a summary of Spaulding's performance, and tell him that you have heard a rumor about Spaulding's conducting personal business with his Omega clients. He informs you that there is not much you can do on the basis of rumors, but that you should do something about Buff's substandard performance.

What would you do?

A. Confront Buff with the rumor about his real estate deals and ask him if this is the cause of his poor performance. (GO TO 190)

B. Ask to accompany him on several sales calls, but don't mention the rumor you have heard. (GO TO 262)

Decision Point 188

You decided not to specify ground rules for your meeting with Phyllis and Virgil. This is unadvisable. Without ground rules, the meeting has a greater potential to deteriorate into a "free-for-all" or one that favors the party who shouts the loudest or is the most persuasive.

Re-evaluate your last decision. Circle the #188 you just wrote in your flow diagram. Then move back to the last uncircled step in your flow diagram.

Decision Point 189

You decided to pressure the parties to come up with alternatives by threatening to settle the conflict yourself. This was incorrect. As a rule, managers should not announce their intention to resort to arbitration. This often hardens the position of those who seem not to be benefiting from mediation. Saying nothing about arbitration does not preclude a manager arbitrating a deadlock.

Re-evaluate your last decision. Circle the #189 you just wrote in your flow diagram. Then move back to the last uncircled step in your flow diagram.

Decision Point 190

When you talk to Buff, you lay out his record of performance and tell him that it is not at an acceptable level. As you begin to discuss possible remedies for this low performance, you mention that there is a rumor floating around that he may be involved in some real estate deals which are taking him away from his work. As soon as you say this, he asks what you are talking about and challenges you to document your charges. Buff's approach puts you on the defensive and effectively ends the discussion about his low performance. In fact, by the time he leaves, he has so thoroughly manipulated the situation that you almost feel guilty for confronting him.

Re-evaluate your last decision. Circle the #190 you just wrote in your flow diagram. Then move back to the first uncircled number above this one in your flow diagram.

Decision Point 191

You decide to replace the piece-rate scheme with a salary plan that offers operators a base wage plus production bonuses. This change works reasonably well, although you have to be persuasive to convince the cutters that by taking the training, they will be able to earn more. The fact that the workers are guaranteed some income during their unproductive training time makes this a much more palatable plan.

The next month the training is completed and cutters begin rotating between cutting machines and blank assignments. This change immediately reduces absenteeism, but several cutters resign. Apparently, their growth need strength was not sufficient for them to see the advantages of the new job arrangements. Both of the individuals who leave worked for the foreman who had expressed some reservations about job rotation, but six months later this foreman becomes converted when he notices that the cross-training of cutters allows him more flexibility in making assignments to make up for absent employees.

Your attention now turns to the sewers and finishers. Recall the questionnaire results for these two groups as follows:

Group	Low Perceived Job Characteristics	Growth Need Strength
Sewers	skill variety, autonomy, task significance	high
Finishers	skill variety, autonomy	moderate to high

You interview the members of these two groups and conclude that growth need strength is apparently quite high but the groups are not particularly cohesive--group members are much more interested in doing well as individuals than in working together as a group. You know that one element of your QWL intervention should involve combining tasks because sewers and finishers believe their jobs are deficient in terms of skill variety. Is there any other QWL element that you should build into your QWL intervention?

A. Vertical loading. (GO TO 114)

B. Forming natural work units. (GO TO 196)

C. Flexitime. (GO TO 201)

D. Concentrated work week. (GO TO 207)

E. No other element. (GO TO 212)

You express concern that John is not giving his territory a chance. With that, John responds: "Why should I? You've dealt me a low hand. Even if I did call on 100 percent of my doctors, I couldn't make my quota."

At this point you challenge his observation, but he insists there is no use. What would you do now?

A.   Try to persuade John that the redistricting plan is equitable. Be prepared to compare his performance with Susan Brown's (such comparisons are not a problem since performance records are open within the company). (GO TO 236)

B.   Tell John that you do not like his attitude and that you will not give his new employers a good recommendation unless he improves his performance next quarter. (GO TO 221)

C.   Ask John what changes in redistricting he would suggest to correct the inequity he is experiencing. (GO TO 147)

D.   Mention to John that there may be some way to respond to his concerns, but you won't even talk about that until he demonstrates greater efforts to improve his sales (GO TO 100)

E.   Tell John you will be sorry to see him go but you understand that if he still thinks the redistricting is inequitable after your last comments, perhaps it is best that he leave the company. (GO TO 211)

F.   Ask John what things he likes about his present territory with the idea of trying to make the positive features he mentions more salient (obvious) compared with the negatives he seems to be emphasizing in his own mind. (GO TO 104)

You all work together in generating the financial estimates. After about 30 minutes of questioning and calculating, you come up with the following figures:

Estimated Loss Due to Procurement/Inventory Problems of Virgil's Position = $4,157/year

Estimated Loss Due to Quality Problems of Phyllis's Position = $11,319/year

Both parties seem to be giving you honest estimates, so you are sure that they are reasonably accurate.

What would you do at this point?

A. Settle the dispute by announcing that you are going to have to side with Virgil for purely economic reasons. Explore with Phyllis ways that she might work on reducing the costs of getting Virgil's reports late. (GO TO 167)

B. See if Virgil is willing to prepare his reports during his weekends at an additional salary adjustment of up to $4,157. (GO TO 111)

C. Tell both parties that these calculations have clarified the negotiations considerably, and that it is now time for all of you to work hard to identify alternative solutions that are less costly than these two. Ask the parties to brainstorm other options with you. (GO TO 174)

Decision Point 194

Jim is persuaded by this statement. He says: "You know, I really would miss those trips with my wife. In fact, do you think the two of us could share my job?"

This is an interesting idea. It would enable Jim to be with his son for more time and at the same time provide coverage for the rural portions of the territory. You and Jim invite his wife, Kathy, into the discussion. She is enthusiastic about the idea.

You follow up with a call to the Director of Employee Relations (at home) to be sure that this arrangement is possible. It is, and Jim's wife becomes scheduled for company training. This settled, you stress the necessity of making the standard 400 units per quarter. Both Jim and Kathy agree to coordinate their work to meet that figure.

One quarter later the resulting sales figures are better than your wildest dreams. Jim and his wife produce 525 units! Your questioning revealed that Jim's motivational problem was the value he placed on the outcomes offered by Omega. Because of a personal tragedy, Jim began to question the rewards (financial and otherwise) that he was getting from his job. You determined that, by problem-solving with Jim, you could turn his altered life-style into an advantage. Nice going! GO TO 249 to move on to your next motivational challenge.

You decided to ask Phyllis and Virgil which alternatives they like most. Predictably, Phyllis likes those that require Virgil to comply with her information needs, and Virgil likes those that require Phyllis to give him longer cycle times. You are now in a position where you want to try to break down the positions in this conflict. The only way to do this is to investigate the interests that underlie each party's position. Otherwise, you will be caught in this stalemate.

Re-evaluate your last decision. Circle the #195 you just wrote in your flow diagram. Then move back to the last uncircled step in your flow diagram.

You chose forming natural work units as a way of implementing QWL among the sewers and finishers. This works very poorly. Immediately, conflicts and work disagreements crop up. Ultimately, you have to abandon the scheme and return to the previous work configuration. Your observation that these workers were not very socially inclined should have indicated to you that this was not a good option.

Re-evaluate your last decision. Circle the #196 you just wrote in your flow diagram. Then move to the last uncircled step in your flow diagram.

When you ask Wilson to explain his low-effort figures, he is a bit taken aback by your question, but he recovers quickly.

"I always worked hard for this company. Five days a week, eight hours a day, I assure you. Do you want to look at my date-book? My territory is real spread out as you know, so I can't be expected to make 100 percent of my calls each quarter. As for my wholesale figures, I know they're low, but I called each one at least once during the quarter. I've been trying to tell you that our competitors are pulling out all the stops to take over in my territory. It's hard to beat them off with what you have given me."

How would you respond?

A. Review what you've done in the past to try and turn his performance around, and ask him to commit to do something about his "marginal performance." (GO TO 119)

B. Accompany him on a series of sales calls. (GO TO 154)

C. Schedule him for a training program that involves modern sales techniques. Warn him that this is his last chance. (GO TO 272)

D. Check to see if his job is really important to him. (GO TO 242)

E. Tell him that this is it and that you are at the end of your rope with him. Establish your willingness to help in any way you can, but either he comes up to standard next quarter or he's through with the company. (GO TO 151)

Decision Point 198

You chose to resolve the conflict by instructing the parties to generate a solution on their own. This provides the advantage of getting you out of the dispute. In conflicts like this one, their are many disadvantages to this approach, however. For example, they may not have the motivation or ability to generate an effective solution to the problem. Or, the decision may get made based on which one can intimidate or overwhelm the other.

Re-evaluate your last decision. Circle the #198 you just wrote in your flow diagram. Then move back to the last uncircled step in your flow diagram.

Decision Point 199

You decided to brainstorm alternatives at this point. This is a bit premature. There are two important things that you do not know at this point. One, you are unsure about just what is motivating Virgil and Phyllis to take the stands they have taken. And two, you are unclear why they cannot comply with one another's requests. After determining one or both of these things, you will be in a much better position to brainstorm the alternatives.

Re-evaluate your last decision. Circle the #199 you just wrote in your flow diagram. Then move back to the last uncircled step in your flow diagram.

Decision Point 200

Since Buff has violated company policy, you decide to terminate him. This has some negative repercussions for the district. First, you receive a substantial number of complaints from doctors and wholesalers in his district. Second, and more important, the new sales rep who replaces Buff has a difficult time establishing relationships with area doctors. Although terminating Buff may be appropriate given his poor performance, the close relationships that Buff developed had the potential to disrupt Omega's customer relationships. Under these circumstances it may be better to either work further with Buff or develop a plan for reducing the negative impact of his departure.

Given Buff's violation of policy, requiring him to leave Omega is appropriate and, in fact, the right thing to do. However, you might have been able to get Buff out without so many negative consequences. Therefore, re-evaluate your last decision with the idea of how you might terminate Buff in a less disruptive fashion. Circle the #200 you just wrote in your flow diagram. Then move back to the first uncircled number above this one in your flow diagram.

Decision Point 201

You chose flexitime as a way of implementing QWL among the sewers and finishers. After consultation with the workers and with other officials of the plant, you conclude that a core time of 9 a.m. to 3 p.m. is most suitable, allowing the workers to begin as early as 7 a.m. and ending as late as 5 p.m. Although it takes a while to work out the supervision problems created by this new work schedule, the implementation actually goes quite well. Absenteeism improves dramatically. Unfortunately, however, turnover does not. In eight months, this nagging turnover problem has become even more critical as two jobs remain unfilled for three weeks due to the unfavorable labor market in Eagle Point.

These mixed results and the lingering turnover problem were due to your choice to rely on flexitime to address the workers' job design problem. The rather high growth need strength of the sewers and finishers favored a different approach.

Re-evaluate your last decision. Circle the #201 you just wrote in your flow diagram. Then move to the last uncircled step in your flow diagram.

323

Decision Point 202

Virgil responds, "Well, that's your opinion, but I'll tell you that Ivan just doesn't have the ability or the confidence to handle setups on his machine himself. And there is no one else around who can work with him. It's a risk, but if you want to take it, fine; just order me to get my reports done, and I'll do it!"

What would you say now?

A. "As I understand it, your only concern is with quality. That is the only thing that keeps you from getting your reports in on time." (GO TO 106)

B. "Beside the possibilities of quality problems, what other negative things might happen if you were forced to get your reports in on time." (GO TO 265)

C. Tell Virgil you are willing to take the risk. Order him to get his reports in on time. (GO TO 183)

D. "Put yourself in Phyllis's shoes. What would you do if you were her?" (GO TO 226)

Decision Point 203

Jim's performance the next quarter continues to be poor. Inaction on your part was apparently predicated on the assumption that there was nothing you could do. However, such pessimism is premature. Re-evaluate your last decision. Circle the #203 you just wrote in your flow diagram. Then move back to the first uncircled number above this one in your flow diagram.

Decision Point 204

Jim jumps at the chance to attend the seminar. He especially likes the convenience of being able to attend it without leaving home. Upon completion of the seminar, Jim returns to work. However, his performance continues marginal. Though his wholesale inventory levels improve slightly, his calls on doctors continue very poor (67 percent). Clearly, Jim's performance did not benefit from the training.

Re-evaluate your last decision. Circle the #204 you just wrote in your flow diagram. Then move back to the first uncircled number above this one in your flow diagram.

324

Decision Point 205

You chose the best seating format for a mediation. It conveys that the parties' attention is focused on a shared problem (symbolized by the flip chart) rather than each other.

The meeting goes well. Although you occasionally have to enforce the "no criticism rule," the three of you come up with the following six alternatives (ruling out the obviously inappropriate ones):

1. Virgil could ask Ivan to complete the production reports for him while Virgil tends the machine.

2. Phyllis could complete Virgil's reports for him.

3. Phyllis could contact the headquarters office to see if they could factor the quality problems of the dental brush line into their calculations of weekly quotas.

4. You could complete Virgil's production report for him.

5. You could try to persuade the headquarters staff of the necessity of biweekly quotas for the dental brush line.

6. You could look into the possibility of getting Virgil a computer terminal, so he could finish his production reports more efficiently.

Having finished with brainstorming, what would you do now?

A. Call a two-hour recess with the idea that you will meet with each party privately to continue probing into each's concerns. (GO TO 227)

B. Ask Phyllis and Virgil to identify the alternative they favor. (GO TO 195)

C. Propose that the best options are 5 and 6 above. Agree to work in those directions. (GO TO 259)

Decision Point 206

Before meeting with Spaulding, you decide to gather information discreetly about his reputation and the conflict between his low earnings and opulent life-style. As a result, you hear a rumor from a staff person that Buff has been putting together real estate deals with many of the doctors he calls on. If these rumors are true, this is a direct violation of company policy. There is no clear procedure for dealing with such infringements, unless there is "iron-clad" proof.

What would you do now?

A.   Confront Buff with the rumor about his real estate deals and ask him if this is cause of his poor performance. (GO TO 190)

B.   Consult with your superior about how to deal with this situation. (GO TO 187)

C.   Ask to accompany him on several sales calls but not mention the rumor you have heard. (GO TO 262)

Decision Point 207

You chose a concentrated work week as a way of implementing QWL among the sewers and finishers. After consultation with the workers and with other officials of the plant, you conclude that a four-day, forty-hour work week is most suitable. Although it takes a while to work out the supervision problems created by this new work schedule, the implementation actually goes quite well. Absenteeism improves dramatically. Unfortunately, however, turnover does not. In eight months, this nagging turnover problem has become even more critical as two jobs remain unfilled for three weeks due to the unfavorable labor market in Eagle Point.

These mixed results and the lingering turnover problem were due to your choice to rely on a concentrated work week to address the job design problems of the sewers and finishers. The rather high growth need strength of the sewers and finishers favored a different approach.

Re-evaluate your last decision. Circle the #207 you just wrote in your flow diagram. Then move to the last uncircled step in your flow diagram.

Decision Point 208

Jim is notably nervous in responding, "I'm disturbed that I've let you down, believe me. I don't want to disappoint you, but I'm not sure what to suggest. I'll try harder, I promise." What would you say now?

A.   Nothing. Clemmons has committed himself to do better. (GO TO 121)

B.   Find out whether he realizes that his sales are probably suffering from the low inventory level being held by wholesalers in his region. (GO TO 251)

C.   Ask Jim if he needs some time off to get himself together now that his personal crisis has passed. (GO TO 214)

D.   Tell him you appreciate his willingness to try harder. Ask Jim how the death of his father has changed his outlook on his work. (GO TO 169)

E.   Press Jim for a specific performance commitment. (GO TO 124)

Decision Point 209

Your choice of a seating arrangement is not appropriate. You want to create an atmosphere that shows that the problem is the focus of attention, not each other.

Re-evaluate your last decision. Circle the #209 you just wrote in your flow diagram. Then move back to the last uncircled step in your flow diagram.

Decision Point 210

You decided to call Virgil into your meeting with Phyllis. This is premature. You should really not conduct a confrontational meeting until you have had a chance to interview both of the parties. Your decision would have been acceptable in an emergency, but there is no indication that this is truly an emergency.

Re-evaluate your last decision. Circle the #210 you just wrote in your flow diagram. Then move back to the last uncircled step in your flow diagram.

Decision Point 211

John seems taken aback by your statement, but he thanks you for your support. You ask him how you can help him with him job search. The remainder of the meeting seems relaxed as you problem-solve various approaches John is taking to get another job. As the meeting ends, you again promise your support but indicate forcefully that the company cannot afford to keep him in his territory while he conducts his job search unless he "acts in good faith" by continuing to complete his work.

You ask for his resignation effective in 30 days. In three weeks, he calls you and tells you of his new job. He also informs you that he has called 50 percent of the M.D.s in his territory (in this three-week period!).

Some people would assert that a manager should fight hard before "letting go" of an employee. In this instance, however, John Crosby was at best an average employee. In addition, he suffered from a motivational problem that was difficult for you to do anything about beyond the attempts you have already made. Luck would have it that it was relatively easy to replace him, and since John left with good feelings and a level of exit performance that was excellent, everything worked out for the best.

John suffered from a perception that his payment was inequitable. This was compounded by a belief (attributable to the perceived inequity) that effort didn't really matter. This was a difficult situation to reverse. You could have salvaged John but only at the expense of careful work and increased vigilance, and you apparently considered that not worth the effort. GO TO 122 to move along to your next employee to motivate, James Clemmons.

Decision Point 212

You decide that your plan to combine tasks is a sufficient way of implementing QWL among the sewers and finishers. Accordingly, you implement job enlargement. For a while, things proceed nicely. But the levels of absenteeism and turnover among the people in these groups does not decline as much as you expected. You conclude that the workers' desire for greater autonomy was more important than you thought.

Re-evaluate your last decision. Circle the #212 you just wrote in your flow diagram. Then move to the last uncircled step in your flow diagram.

Decision Point 213

You decide to maintain the present number of foremen for the sewers and finishers, but provide them with training in how to be more participative supervisors. This works reasonably well except that the foreman, once trained, find that they do not have much to do. Moreover, even with the training, they find it difficult to "let go" of some of their supervisory prerogatives.

Re-evaluate your last decision. Circle the #213 you just wrote in your flow diagram. Then move to the last uncircled step in your flow diagram.

Decision Point 214

Jim responds as follows: "Maybe that would be a good idea. A month off would be real helpful." You work out the details and Jim starts his leave of absence immediately. When he returns to work, however, his performance continues to be poor. Apparently the time off did not enable Jim to become more motivated himself.

Re-evaluate your last decision. Circle the #214 you just wrote in your flow diagram. Then move back to the first uncircled number above this one in your flow diagram.

Decision Point 215

Deciding when you much take over some of your subordinate's work is a difficult decision. Clearly, you can't do other people's work on a regular basis or over the long-term. In this situation, taking on a part of Wilson's job may be valuable. If the list of commitments you are asking from Wilson is substantial, asking him to "go it totally alone" may be overwhelming. It is important to keep the list of commitments attainable, and of all Wilson's objectives, improving his relationship with this wholesaler is perhaps unattainable. If an individual believes that goals are not reachable,

there will be little motivation to work to accomplish them. More over, by taking over this task, you may be able to improve Omega's reputation with this firm, and use this experience as a training tool for Wilson.

You will need to develop a timetable for making Wilson responsible for this task again. However, in this situation, your temporary help may pay big dividends.

Re-evaluate your last decision. Circle the #215 you just wrote in your flow diagram. Then move back to the first uncircled number above this one in your flow diagram.

Decision Point 216

You introduce the meeting by stating the ground rules and defining your role. The meeting begins with both parties stating their positions. Phyllis's voice cracks during her presentation, but Virgil seems a bit more controlled. Clearly, both are nervous. Disappointingly, no new information is revealed during the initial presentations except that the conflict appears much more emotional than you had first thought.

The part of the meeting where each party summarizes the positions of the other is very rocky. Neither side is initially satisfied with the other's attempt to summarize each's statements. So, it takes a great deal of your time and patience to finally get that part of the meeting completed.

At that point both Phyllis and Virgil turn to you. What would you say?

A.   "Okay, we understand where we all stand on this problem. Let's begin to explore alternative ways of solving it. Do either of you have any suggestions?" (GO TO 128)

B.   "At this point, I'd like to ask each of you to state what you want the other to do as simply and clearly as you can." (GO TO 244)

C.   "Well, it seems that we have two alternatives on the floor. One, proposed by Virgil, is that Phyllis refashion production schedules to cut back on setup time. The other, proposed by Phyllis, is for Virgil to turn in his production reports to her office by Monday at noon. At this point I'd like to ask each of you what impediments you are experiencing to keep you from doing what the other wants. Let's start with you, Virgil. Why can't you get your reports in on time?" (GO TO 101)

Decision Point 217

You decide to implement the job changes without taking any additional action about the foremen until problems develop. The implementation proceeds smoothly except that you notice that the foremen do not like their less powerful roles very much. One foreman applies for a transfer to another plant, and another complains to the plant manager that one machine was improperly maintained by an operator and that the entire QWL intervention will never work.

At first you thought that action targeting the foremen was unnecessary until problems showed up. Now that those problems have appeared, what would you do about it?

A.   Propose that the number of foremen governing the sewers and finishers be decreased in some humane way (through transfers or reassignments). Provide the remaining foremen with training in how to be more participative supervisors. (GO TO 268)

B.   Maintain the present number of foremen, but provide them with training in how to be more participative supervisors. (GO TO 213)

Decision Point 218

Your decision to encourage Lisa results in sales the next quarter similar to the last one. More frustrated than before, Lisa's efforts begin to wane, and she leaves the company.

When you talked to her, Lisa was at a critical point in her career. You were correct in encouraging her, because often sales of this kind lag a bit behind sales efforts and sales calls have a cumulative effect. However, she needed something more than pure encouragement.

Your analysis of Lisa's motivation revealed several important things. It is clear that Lisa has a strong belief that her efforts will pay off in terms of performance since she has a history of succeeding in nearly everything she has attempted. In addition, you can be certain that Lisa believes that performance will be rewarded at Omega, since she is on an incentive pay system that relates her income directly to two indices of performance, volume and inventory. As for Lisa's particular preference for her work outcomes, we can be sure that Lisa values the monetary outcomes of her job since she has indicated that she needs her commission check to make her first house payment. Given these factors, it is not surprising that Lisa's efforts are high (she called on 100 percent of her M.D.s, and each wholesaler twice). However, her performance is not up to expectations. In light of this assessment, think about what additional factor may account for her low performance.

By encouraging Lisa, you may have caused her belief that effort does result in performance to weaken in the following quarter. Perhaps she concluded that a particular obstetrician call makes little real difference in determining sales volume (the "drop in the bucket" idea). Pure encouragement may have reduced the sense of urgency that she showed in your conversation with her.

Re-evaluate your last decision. Circle the #218 you just wrote in your flow diagram. Then move back to the first uncircled number above this one in your flow diagram.

Decision Point 219

Jim says he understands your position completely, and he tells you that you will have his resignation. Jim Clemmons provided you with an extremely difficult motivational problem. As a person experiencing much inner conflict, Jim was reluctant to commit to much more than average performance, and that was not good enough for you. Fundamentally, Clemmons' motivational problem is that he doesn't value the outcomes of his work very much. The rewards offered by his job are not a sufficient inducement to do more than average work. Moreover, he is obtaining valued outcomes (being with his family) for not working. Thus, his problem is compounded by positive incentives for not performing.

About the only motivational strategy that works in such situations (assuming you cannot really lower the positive incentives on non-effort) is to (1) find out the outcomes he does value and increase them or (2) change the nature of the job to conform to his present level of motivation. In contrast, your action was to insist on performance without responding specifically to what he wants from work.

Re-evaluate your last decision. Circle the #219 you just wrote in your flow diagram. Then move back to the first uncircled number above this one in your flow diagram.

Decision Point 220

You decided to call Phyllis into your meeting with Virgil to hammer out a solution. This is a bit premature. Before inviting Phyllis to join you, it would have been better if you had "primed" Virgil's perspective a bit. Namely, research indicates that if one tries to get parties to approach conflicts from the viewpoint of a long-range relationship, they tend to approach the conflict more cooperatively.

Re-evaluate your last decision. Circle the #220 you just wrote in your flow diagram. Then move back to the last uncircled step in your flow diagram.

Decision Point 221

He responds that he does not like your attitude either, and he walks out of the meeting. In light of this, you phone the Personnel Department to discuss your disciplinary options. Accordingly, you send John a written warning on his low performance in conjunction with company procedures, since you cannot fire him without a written warning.

Three weeks into the next quarter, you call John to check on his performance. He doesn't return your call. You call two of the wholesalers in his territory, and they indicate that they have not seen him. You send him a registered letter indicating that if he doesn't phone you, he's fired. You don't hear from him, and you fire him.

The stern posture you took resulted in John leaving under adverse circumstances. Given that he was, at best, an average performer, he was not the worst person to leave, especially since he apparently was suffering from a perceived inequity problem that is difficult to resolve. However, his exit would have been much less costly had you been less threatening and more conciliatory. In addition, your options in this case included a strategy that would have turned John's performance around.

Re-evaluate your last decision. Circle the #221 you just wrote in your flow diagram. Then move back to the first uncircled number above this one in your flow diagram.

Decision Point 222

You decided to opt for an approach to resolving this conflict that resembles that of a judge. This is an appealing posture, but in this situation, mediation is called for. Generally, it is preferable if the conflicting parties come up with their own settlement. Consequently, you want to try to help them first to see if that is possible. You do not have to give up the option of ultimately "playing judge," but you do not want to preempt other possibilities by announcing your intentions too soon.

Re-evaluate your last decision. Circle the #222 you just wrote in your flow diagram. Then move back to the last uncircled step in your flow diagram.

Decision Point 223

She responds as follows: "But I called on each wholesaler twice during the quarter. And even though the average supply is only fifty days right now, that's up from forty-three when I started."

You were not aware of this improvement, which is fairly substantial. Therefore, you congratulate her for this accomplishment.

What would you say now?

A.   Offer to help her in anyway you can to build her sales volume. (GO TO 178)

B.   Try to ascertain if she is satisfied with her present level of sales. (GO TO 125)

Decision Point 224

You show your boss the logic behind the QWL intervention and point to the improvement in absenteeism and turnover. You calculate a payback period for the $50,000 investment he made for the consultant's report. He tells you that the investment is a sunk cost and a payback calculation is irrelevant.

Re-evaluate your last decision. Circle the #224 you just wrote in your flow diagram. Then move to the last uncircled step in your flow diagram.

Decision Point 225

A member of the Operations Research Group explains the redistricting formula to John's satisfaction, and he indicates that he will try harder next quarter. What would you do?

A.   Get John to commit himself to calling on specific number of M.D.s during the next quarter. (GO TO 132)

B.   Tell John that you are very pleased that he has agreed to improve. Encourage him to do the best he can. (GO TO 157)

C.   Negotiate a level of performance with John that you would consider an acceptable improvement for the next quarter. (GO TO 258)

Decision Point 226

Virgil responds that he guesses he would be fairly sore about not receiving the reports on time. You counter that you think she is concerned about the efficiency of the plant, and you do not think her motive is to be a troublemaker.

Now what would you say?

A.   "As I understand it, then, your only concern is with quality. That is the only thing that keeps you from getting your reports in on time." (GO TO 106)

B.   "Beside the possibilities of quality problems, what other negative things might happen if you were forced to get your reports in on time." (GO TO 265)

C. "I'll be honest with you, Virgil, I think your position here is rather flimsy. I believe that you are overreacting to the possibility that Ivan can't do the work himself." (GO TO 202)

Decision Point 227

Taking a recess is not always necessary when mediating a conflict. However, a recess does provide the opportunity for the mediator to do several things. A recess can be used to change the way the parties are viewing the conflict. It can be used to test possible settlements. Recesses are also useful to allow one or both parties to "cool off" if the conflict becomes emotionally charged. Most importantly, a recess can be a time for a mediator to learn *why* each individual is making a set of demands. An individual is much more likely to share this information in private than to announce it to the other person in the dispute. Once the mediator understands the reasons that lie behind the parties' positions, more options for resolving the conflict may become clear.

During the recess, you meet first with Virgil. You ask him what concerns underlie his position. He asks you what you mean. You say that behind each position in a conflict are interests that motivate these positions. You ask him what reasons he has for his position. Again he balks, "I've already told you that short production runs make my machines touchy. I can't be expected to do paperwork if that risks higher reject rates." What would you say now?

A. "As I understand it, then, your only concern is with quality. That is the only thing that keeps you from getting your reports in on time." (GO TO 106)

B. "Beside the possibilities of quality problems, what other negative things might happen if you were forced to get your reports in on time." (GO TO 265)

C. "I'll be honest with you, Virgil. I think your position here is rather flimsy. I believe that you are overreacting to the possibility that Ivan can't do the work himself." (GO TO 202)

D. "Put yourself in Phyllis's shoes. What would you do if you were her?" (GO TO 226)

Decision Point 228

You decide to try to deflect your boss's concerns about the differences between the QWL intervention and the consultant's report that cost him a considerable amount of money. He does not respond favorably to your efforts to deflect the question.

Re-evaluate your last decision. Circle the #228 you just wrote in your flow diagram. Then move to the last uncircled step in your flow diagram.

Decision Point 229

It is four weeks later, and Buff's performance figures are lower than ever. Waiting for Spaulding to improve is not the answer. Re-evaluate your last decision. Circle the #229 you just wrote in your flow diagram. Then move back to the first uncircled number above this one in your flow diagram.

Decision Point 230

You return in one month and notice some but not spectacular progress on Wilson's part. His sales calls are up, but you again have to coach him on managing his time. You note that he's altered his sales approach with the younger doctors, and you help him further refine his techniques.

The fact that you have taken over responsibility for the major wholesaler pays off. Druggist stock-outs are less frequent, and Wilson begins to see more results from his efforts. He accompanies you when you call on this troublesome wholesaler, and this serves as a model for him to copy.

In spite of these improvements, Thomas continues to be rather defensive about your criticism and he continually asks for approval in subtle ways.

With two months remaining in the quarter, you again schedule another visit to his region. This time you only stay two days, but again there is some progress. You begin to ease up a bit on the number of specific commitments you ask him to make.

At the end of the quarter, the performance figures come out and Thomas meets his quota: Sales = 400 units; M.D.s contacted = 93 percent; wholesale inventory level = 44 days.

Although Thomas will require more effort to reduce his need for your help and feedback, you have accomplished a difficult motivational assignment. Wilson Thomas is a classic plateaued performer who has developed poor work habits that he defends with excuses and closed-mindedness. In this situation, training will not suffice. He needs practice, firmness, encouragement, and frequent feedback. Your actions worked well. Congratulations! When you are ready, GO TO 137 for your last motivation problem, William Spaulding.

Decision Point 231

You call Phyllis to clarify her memo. She comes to your office and tells you her relationship with Virgil has deteriorated steadily since she joined your staff. She calls him an "obstructionist" and uses the words "uncooperative" and "unprofessional." She tells you that she has no problems with the other six supervisors.

How would you respond?

A.   Challenge her use of labels and ask her to prepare a specific list of situations with Virgil that she wants changed. (GO TO 165)

B.   Agree that Virgil can be a problem, but tell her that you intend to hear his side of the story before taking action. (GO TO 153)

C.   Tell her that settling this issue is her responsibility. Let her know that you consider it important for her development as a new employee to try to work out these problems before coming to you. Tell her that one consideration in assessing the promotability of staff people is that they work well with line personnel. (GO TO 142)

D.   Call Virgil into your office now to meet his accuser. (GO TO 210)

Decision Point 232

Wilson Thomas's phone calls are sporadic, and you are concerned that he is not living up to his commitments. What action would you take?

A.   You've done enough. If he does not live up to his commitment, terminate him. (GO TO 243)

B.   Go on even more sales calls with him in order to refine his action plan and give him feedback. (GO TO 230)

337

Decision Point 233

You decide to lay off the proper number of sewers to decrease the workflow unevenness. This creates severe morale problems. The remaining sewers slow down in order to protect their jobs, and significant conflicts begin to arise between the sewers and the finishers.

Re-evaluate your last decision. Circle the #233 you just wrote in your flow diagram. Then move to the last uncircled step in your flow diagram.

Decision Point 234

The next employee targeted for motivation is John Crosby. His performance record is shown on page 18. John has worked for Omega for six years. For five of those years, his performance record was average. Six months ago, to accommodate the addition of Lisa Dolan to your staff, you had to redistrict territories. This displaced four of your sales reps including John. The redistricting was done with the use of a computerized mapping formula developed by Omega's operations staff. The formula establishes equitable territories, and birth rate is one of many factors in the program. It is an award-winning model, and one that has been used throughout the industry. When the redistricting was announced, the three other sales reps affected accepted it, but not Crosby. He asserted that the birth rate in his new territory was too low. You explained that his new territory's birth rate was actually understated because it includes a large obstetric hospital (associated with a medical school) that does not report births in an ordinary way. This did not satisfy John. Susan Brown's territory was also affected (she was also given a territory with a large hospital), yet her last quarter sales were excellent. You decide to talk with John about his low figures. You ask for his side of the story.

He responds: "My greatest fears have come to pass. You gave me too small a district. I can't be expected to come up to my 400 unit quota in that territory. It will probably come as no surprise to you that I'm actively looking for another job right now." How would you respond?

A. Indicate that you are concerned that he has not given his new territory a chance. Point out that he only contacted 61 percent of the M.D.s in his region. (GO TO 192)

B. Try to persuade John that the redistricting plan is equitable. Be prepared to compare his performance with Susan Brown's (such comparisons are normal; performance records are open within the company). (GO TO 236)

C. Tell John that you do not like his attitude, and that you cannot give his future employer a good recommendation unless he improves his performance next quarter. (GO TO 221)

D. Ask John what changes in redistricting he would suggest to correct the inequity he is experiencing. (GO TO 147)

E. Mention to John that there may be some way to respond to his concerns, but you won't even talk about that until he demonstrates greater efforts to improve his sales efforts. (GO TO 100)

F. Tell John that you will be sorry to see him go but you understand that if he still thinks the redistricting is inequitable after your last discussion with him, then perhaps this is the best thing for him to do. (GO TO 211)

G. Ask John what things he likes about his present territory, with the idea of reminding him of the positive features of his job compared with the negative things he seems to be emphasizing in his own mind. (GO TO 104)

Decision Point 235

You decided to call Virgil into your office at this juncture to hear his side of the conflict. This invitation is a bit premature. All you have to "go on" is the memo from Phyllis. Since this document does not detail specific areas of concern, it is too early to involve Virgil in this issue. Involving him now runs the risk that if Phyllis's accusations are unwarranted, the relationship between Virgil and Phyllis will be permanently harmed. Re-evaluate your last decision. Circle the #235 you just wrote in your flow diagram. Then move back to the last uncircled step in your flow diagram.

Decision Point 236

You try to convince John that his perception that the redistribution plan is inequitable is false. He disagrees at first, but when you describe Susan Brown's performance, he modifies his position slightly. At the same time, he persists that the redistricting is unfair. John pulls out his quarterly sales report (the same one as in your initial description of the situation). He states, "Look at Brown's standard-over-birth-rate--10.92. Now look at mine--13.39--the highest in your region. Do you still say the territories are fair?"

At this point what would you do?

A. Tell John that you do not like his attitude, and that you cannot give his future employers a good recommendation unless he improves his performance next quarter. (GO TO 221)

B. Ask John what changes in redistricting he would suggest to redress the inequity he is experiencing. (GO TO 147)

C. Indicate to John that you will look into the territorial question, but that you can't guarantee anything. Insist that he bring his effort up as a sign of good faith. (GO TO 100)

D. Tell John that you will be sorry to see him go but you understand that if he still thinks the redistricting is inequitable after your comments to him, perhaps this is the best thing for him to do. (GO TO 211)

E. Ask John what things he likes about his present territory with the idea of trying to make the positive features he mentions more salient (obvious) compared with the negatives he seems to be emphasizing in his own mind. (GO TO 104)

F. Persist with your argument. Call in a member of the Operations Research Group that developed the redistricting formula to explain it to John. (GO TO 225)

Decision Point 237

You consult with the corporate industrial engineer about how to handle the situation of unevenness in the workflow. The engineer sends a senior engineer to the plant to investigate. Unfortunately, this person has a negative attitude about QWL. Accordingly, his presence has a very negative effect on some of the other people at the plant (mostly front-office managers). Ultimately, he decides that it is the QWL intervention that is the problem.

This experience with the industrial engineer is not necessarily a common one, but in this instance it was better to handle the situation yourself rather than call in an unknown expert.

Re-evaluate your last decision. Circle the #237 you just wrote in your flow diagram. Then move to the last uncircled step in your flow diagram.

Decision Point 238

You meet with Virgil to try to formulate an action plan with him. He reluctantly agrees to try to do better. The next week he gets his report filed by Monday at 2 p.m. (two hours late). The following week goes better, with Virgil actually submitting his report by 11. However, that week a major quality problem develops due to carelessness in setting up an extrusion machine. Virgil informs you that if he had not had to work on the report Monday, the problem would not have occurred. The problem cost the plant $6,000.

You may have avoided this expense if you had handled the conflict differently. You decided to side with Phyllis before even hearing Virgil's side of the story. As a result, Virgil was not really committed to your solution and may have even created the quality problem as a way of showing his dissatisfaction.

Your approach to this conflict is "arbitration" and is quite common in practice. However, it is seldom effective in bringing about satisfactory long-term resolutions to conflicts.

Re-evaluate your last decision. Circle the #238 you just wrote in your flow diagram. Then move back to the last uncircled step in your flow diagram.

Decision Point 239

Your analysis of Lisa's motivational circumstances revealed some important information. First, you may conclude that Lisa has a strong belief that her efforts would pay off in terms of performance because throughout her life she succeeded in everything she attempted. In addition, it is probable that she also believes that monetary outcomes are linked to performance since much of her earnings are directly related to sales volume and inventory levels. Clearly, monetary outcomes are important to her because she is counting on her commission check to make her first house payment. It is not surprising that Lisa's efforts are high (she called on 100 percent of her M.D.s and each wholesaler twice). However, her performance, particularly regarding her obstetrician calls, is not yet satisfactory. In light of this assessment, think through what additional factors may account for her low performance. Your approach did little more than remind her of what was already a strong belief that performance is linked to outcomes. Therefore, it was actually a rather redundant action, and it added little except frustration when Lisa's performance did not improve.

Re-evaluate your last decision. Circle the #239 you just wrote in your flow diagram. Then move back to the first uncircled number above this one in your flow diagram.

Decision Point 240

He states, "All I ever get from Phyllis is pressure. She doesn't understand that my machines are very touchy. Every time we set one up, we have to watch it like a hawk to be sure it stays plumb. Her schedules don't account for these things, and I've told her that again and again. She just doesn't understand machinery."

You press him for specifics, and he offers the same general excuse for each situation on Phyllis' list: her schedules call for a great deal of difficult machine setups, and since her weekly quotas repeat runs completed the week before, Virgil thinks larger runs are possible.

How would you respond now?

A. Call Phyllis into the meeting at this juncture to hammer out a solution. (GO TO 220)

B. Tell Virgil that his position sounds reasonable but emphasize how important it is that the two of them work more cooperatively in the future. Schedule a meeting between Virgil and Phyllis as soon as possible. (GO TO 261)

C. Tell Virgil that he has a weak case. Side with Phyllis, and tell him to get his reports to her on time. (GO TO 177)

D. To show empathy for Virgil's position, describe your experience as a line manager working with staff people. End by indicating that your experience is that line managers should accept working with staffers as an unavoidable part of their jobs. Tell him that you are going to schedule a meeting between the two of them as soon as possible. (GO TO 254)

Decision Point 241

You decide to let the situation take care of itself. The sewers soon run out of fabric (from the cutters), as you expected, and they have to slow down. The problem is that the plant manager complains that productivity is too low and something better happen because people from corporate headquarters are scheduled to make a plant tour soon.

Re-evaluate your last decision. Circle the #241 you just wrote in your flow diagram. Then move to the last uncircled step in your flow diagram.

Decision Point 242

He responds: "What do you think? My wife and I are looking forward to retirement in four years. We've got a place down in Orlando." Now what?

A.   Tell him he is dangerously close to being terminated unless he turns his performance around. Be precise about just what level of performance is necessary to keep you from taking this action. (GO TO 151)

B.   Ask him if he has considered an early retirement. (GO TO 266)

C.   Review what you've done in the past to try and turn his performance around, and ask him for a renewed commitment to do something about his "marginal" performance. (GO TO 119)

D.   Accompany him on a series of sales calls. (GO TO 154)

E.   Schedule him for a training program that involves modern sales techniques. Warn him that this is his last chance. (GO TO 272)

F.   Tell him that this is it; that you are at the end of your rope with him. Establish your willingness to help in any way you can, but either he comes up to standard next quarter, or he's through with Omega. (GO TO 151)

Decision Point 243

He agrees to try again, but his quarterly figures continue poor (320 units; 83 percent of doctors contacted; 41 days inventory). You follow through on your promise and terminate him.

Wilson Thomas offered perhaps the most challenging motivational assignment any manager ever faces--the plateaued performer. There is no one remedy in cases like these, but there is one in this situation. While you might argue that Wilson Thomas is not worth salvaging as an employee, re-evaluate your last decision. Circle the #243 you just wrote in your flow diagram. Then move back to the first uncircled number above this one in your flow diagram.

Decision Point 244

You asked them to state what they want the other party to do for a second time. This is unnecessary. It is not only redundant, but it serves to harden positions. Flexibility in the positions of the parties is something that you should be particularly concerned about right now.

Re-evaluate your last decision. Circle the #244 you just wrote in your flow diagram. Then move back to the last uncircled step in your flow diagram.

Decision Point 245

You decided to tell Phyllis and Virgil that the responsibility for handling this conflict is theirs. You said that while you will help them identify alternatives, they are the ones who must choose a solution. This statement is inadvisable since it restricts your options. At this stage you do not want to preclude the possibility of arbitrating the settlement should the negotiations deadlock or intervening to assure that the settlement is in the best interests of the organization.

Re-evaluate your last decision. Circle the #245 you just wrote in your flow diagram. Then move back to the last uncircled step in your flow diagram.

Decision Point 246

You decide to redesign the jobs of the office staff by combining tasks. After a careful analysis of all the jobs in the office, you conclude that job enlargement makes much more sense than job rotation. Accordingly, you add tasks to each job. This change is greeted by a great deal of resistance even though you gave careful consideration to the implementation of organizational changes. As a result, absenteeism grows worse and tardiness becomes a problem.

It was not your choice of job enlargement over job rotation that did you in here. It was the low growth need strength of the office staff. Low growth need strength impedes the effectiveness of a QWL that addresses the work itself.

Re-evaluate your last decision. Circle the #246 you just wrote in your flow diagram. Then move to the last uncircled step in your flow diagram.

Decision Point 247

You choose to debate Wilson Thomas on the type of sales approach that is most effective in selling pharmaceuticals. He reacts defensively to your comments, and comes very close to calling you a liar on several occasions.

Wilson Thomas is a very anxious and defensive person. He wants to salvage some self-respect, and your approach doesn't enable him to do that.

You are walking a tightrope with this individual. You deserve to be firm, but you also have to be somewhat acknowledging. In general, it is much easier to walk this tightrope by talking about specific behavior in specific situations than engaging in abstract debates. Re-evaluate your last decision. Circle the #247 you just wrote in your flow diagram. Then move back to the first uncircled number above this one in your flow diagram.

Decision Point 248

Phyllis asks you how you intend to approach this matter. What would you say?

A. "I'm going to talk to Virgil to get his side of the story, then I will make my decision." (GO TO 222)

B. "I am going to show Virgil your list and work out an action plan with him that hopefully will get him to be more cooperative." (GO TO 238)

C. "I will interview Virgil to get his side of the story, then the three of us will get together to come up with a satisfactory solution." (GO TO 134)

D. Tell her that settling this issue is her responsibility. Let her know that you consider it important for her development as a new employee to try to work out these problems before coming to you. Tell her that one consideration in assessing the promotability of staff people is that they work well with line personnel. (GO TO 142)

E. "I'm not sure yet. Let me talk to Virgil first to see what his side of the story is." (GO TO 269)

Decision Point 249

Wilson Thomas has worked for Omega for 21 years, but since you arrived, his performance has been quite poor. Wilson's present sales figures are on page 18.

His poor performance has been exasperating for you. For the past three years, you have "tried everything" to turn his performance around. You have sent him to company training and refresher courses. You tried skill building. However, Wilson seems to consider his old-fashioned, laid-back, soft-sell approach better than any approach he's been taught. You've tried warning him, and at one point issued him two written warnings on his performance. You stopped short of firing him only because he came up to standard nine months ago. Too often Wilson's defense is that factors outside his control are against him. He is an expert at denying personal responsibility, and will latch onto any convenient excuse to hold onto his present practices and overinflated self-image. This time, however, you are determined to give him only one more chance.

How would you approach your conversation with him?

A. Review what you've done in the past to try and turn his performance around, and ask him for a renewed commitment to do something about his "marginal" performance. (GO TO 119)

B. Accompany him on a series of sales calls. (GO TO 154)

C. Schedule him for a training program that involves modern techniques. Warn him that this is his last chance. (GO TO 272)

D. Check to see if his job is really important to him. (GO TO 242)

E. Ask him to explain his poor figures (77 percent M.D.s contacted; 38 days inventory). (GO TO 197)

F. Tell him this is it; you are at the end of your rope with him. Establish your willingness to help in any way you can, but either he comes up to standard next quarter or he's through with Omega. (GO TO 151)

Decision Point 250

You decide to implement a compressed work week for the office staff at the Eagle Point plant. After consultation with the workers and with other officials of the plant, you conclude that a four-day, forty-hour work week is most suitable. You stagger the days off to cover all five days.

Unanticipated problems immediately pop up. First, some of the younger office employees have problems adjusting their day-care arrangements. Second, the older workers grow tired and unproductive working ten-hour days. So serious are these problems that you find it necessary to scrap the plan in three weeks. Concentrated work weeks were appropriate to the low growth need strength of the office staff. However, the peculiar demographic mix of the staff made this less effective than one of your other options.

Re-evaluate your last decision. Circle the #250 you just wrote in your flow diagram. Then move to the last uncircled step in your flow diagram.

Decision Point 251

Jim tells you that he is aware that the wholesale inventory levels are very low. He says that he realizes that he will have to make many more calls on wholesalers if he stays on with Omega.

How would you respond?

A.   Ask Jim if he needs some time off now that his personal crisis has passed. (GO TO 214)

B.   Ask Jim if he is considering resigning. (GO TO 133)

C.   Ask him why he was able to contact only 73 percent of the doctors in his territory last quarter. (GO TO 260)

D.   Ask Jim how the death of his father has changed his outlook on his work. (GO TO 169)

Decision Point 252

You decided to ask other supervisors whether they have difficulty getting their reports in on time. As a result, Virgil learns through the grapevine that you are about to side with Phyllis in his conflict. Accordingly, he begins to try to persuade other supervisors that they really should help him "win his battle" with Phyllis. As your questioning continues, more and more supervisors begin to criticize Phyllis' work.

Your action has caused the conflict to escalate to other employees. As a rule one should be very careful in "asking around" while one is working to solve an employee conflict. Often other people know about the conflict and know that you are involved in settling it. Others may also have interests in how you solve it. For these reasons managers should have a low profile when it comes to information gathering during the conflict-management process.

Re-evaluate your last decision. Circle the #252 you just wrote in your flow diagram. Then move back to the last uncircled step in your flow diagram.

Decision Point 253

You decide not to try to improve the quality of worklife of the office staff. Absenteeism continues to be a problem, and tardiness becomes more common. The plant manager asks you to do something about the situation.

You had a better option than to just do nothing. Re-evaluate your last decision. Circle the #253 you just wrote in your flow diagram. Then move to the last uncircled step in your flow diagram.

Decision Point 254

You schedule a meeting between Phyllis and Virgil. What ground rules would you set for the beginning of the meeting?

A. Each person must first state his or her position on the issue, starting with Phyllis. After each party has presented his or her position, the other must summarize this position in his or her own words until the first is satisfied that he or she is understood. (GO TO 180)

B. Before the meeting, each person must prepare a position paper in writing including specific requests of changes in the other's behavior. At the outset of the meeting, each party presents his or her position paper, giving a copy to the other so there is little possibility for misunderstanding. (GO TO 159)

C. No specific ground rules. Play it by ear. (GO TO 188)

You lay out the evidence that you have collected. Your supervisor agrees that you do have "iron-clad" proof that Spaulding has been using his Omega job to foster his real estate business. He says that you need to deal with Spaulding's actions but that you will want to make sure that your actions don't create more difficulties with customers than necessary. Now what?

A.   Call Buff in and ask him if the rumors that you have heard are true. (GO TO 179)

B.   Call Buff in, lay out the evidence you have, and tell him that he must eliminate his outside deals and improve his performance. (GO TO 140)

You have decided to tell Virgil that his case is rather weak. This is likely to make him more pessimistic about the outcome. This is particularly dangerous since, if you now hesitate in making a final decision, Virgil may take some serious risks in getting you to change your position. This could result in severe escalation of the conflict.

In general, it is unadvisable to make the parties to a mediation pessimistic about their chances.

An additional problem with your statement to Virgil is that you negatively evaluated the interests that are behind his position. This was inappropriate because your probing aimed at doing just that. When probing into the interests that lie behind a position, it is important to try to be neutral about them. That way you can successfully probe during a subsequent occasion without fear of only hearing what someone thinks you want to hear.

Re-evaluate your last decision. Circle the #256 you just wrote in your flow diagram. Then move to the last uncircled step in your flow diagram.

You were correct in choosing combining tasks as your QWL intervention. Their moderate to high growth need strength makes the cutters good candidates for job redesign of some kind, and combining tasks is a reasonable type of intervention to correct the problematic factors of skill variety and task identity.

As you consider how to combine the tasks of the cutters into larger task clusters, two options occur to you: job rotation and job enlargement. You rule out job enlargement since cutters' jobs cannot be enlarged without taking over tasks performed by shipping and receiving or the sewers. Since rotation would necessitate working on different machines and on different geometric problems of setting up blanks, rotation would certainly create more skill variety.

Before you approach the workers with the job rotation option, you work through the management issues with the two foremen involved. One of them is quite positive about the plan; the other expresses reservations but agrees to "try it."

You estimate that the additional training required to allow for job rotation will cost about $18,500. You get approval from the Plant Manager for that expenditure on the promise that turnover and absenteeism costs will go down by that amount in three years.

You also need to consider how the present incentive pay scheme should be adjusted to accommodate job rotation. How would you adjust it for the cutters?

A.   Continue the incentive pay scheme (individual piece rates) as is. (GO TO 176)

B.   Provide some additional incentives for acquiring skills but maintain the individual piece-rate system. (GO TO 108)

C.   Change the reward system to one that places more incentive on seniority than on performance. (GO TO 181)

D.   Consult the workers as to whether the incentive scheme should be changed. (GO TO 185)

E.   Replace the piece-rate scheme with a salary plan that offers operators a base wage plus production bonuses. (GO TO 191)

Decision Point 258

John Crosby's performance during the next quarter turns around positively. He calls on 86 percent of the physicians in his territory, and his performance improves to 410 units, ten greater than the standard.

Congratulations! By bringing his perceived inequity back into line with realities, you successfully dealt with a volatile situation. You found you had to identify a specific reference person to convince Crosby that his equity calculations were faulty.

Additionally, you found you had to address his problem of not believing that his efforts would pay off.

GO TO 122 to begin your analysis of the motivational needs of Jim Clemmons, the next employee in a sub-par performance situation.

Decision Point 259

You have worked hard to specify the alternatives available to the three of you. You decided to totally take responsibility in a very personal way for the outcome of this conflict. Unfortunately, this sets a dangerous precedent. If you think about it, Virgil and Phyllis have been rewarded by taking strong and unyielding positions here. They now know what to do if they ever have conflicts with colleagues in the future. They will come to you, be assertive and inflexible, and you will exert effort yourself in solving it. Actually, there is a resolution to this incident that involves far less effort on your part and more work for the parties involved. To discover it, however, you must look behind the positions of Phyllis and Virgil to their motivations.

Re-evaluate your last decision. Circle the #259 you just wrote in your flow diagram. Then move back to the last uncircled step in your flow diagram.

Decision Point 260

Jim tells you that he is embarrassed by that figure. He says that he knows he'll have to raise that figure for your sake.

How would you respond?

A. Ask Jim how the death of his father has changed his outlook on his work. (GO TO 169)

B. Let him know that you think his performance is really seriously low, and you would like to know exactly what he plans to do about it. (GO TO 208)

C. Find out whether he realizes that his sales are probably suffering from the low inventory levels presently being held by wholesalers in his territory. (GO TO 251)

D. Ask Jim whether he needs some time off now that his personal crisis has passed. (GO TO 214)

E.   Suggest that Jim may want to attend a sales seminar sponsored by the company. Coincidentally, it is being conducted in the city where Jim lives. (GO TO 204)

F.   Ask to accompany Jim on a sales call. (GO TO 110)

Decision Point 261

You schedule a meeting between Phyllis and Virgil. What ground rules would you set for the beginning of the meeting?

A.   Each person must first state his or her position on the issue, starting with Phyllis. After each party has presented his or her position, the other must summarize this position in his or her own words until the first is satisfied that he or she is understood. (GO TO 180)

B.   Before the meeting, each person must prepare a position paper in writing including specific requests of changes in the other's behavior. At the outset of the meeting, each party presents his or her position paper, giving a copy to the other so there is little possibility for misunderstanding. (GO TO 159)

C.   No specific ground rules. Play it by ear. (GO TO 188)

Decision Point 262

You accompany Spaulding on several calls, and you are very surprised by the results. He demonstrates a fine knowledge of the company's products, and his demeanor is very effective throughout the call. Both wholesalers and doctors seem very responsive to his efforts.

After this dazzling performance, you tell him that he did an outstanding job and ask him to explain why his performance is so low when he clearly has so much aptitude for his work. He tells you that he simply has been too casual about his work but he now understands that he had better improve.

About two weeks later, you receive a call from one of the doctors you visited with Buff. He tells you that Buff is a terrific sales rep and asks you to be understanding with him. You wonder whether Spaulding has asked him to call you. A few days later one of your sales reps calls you to relay some interesting information. It seems that one of this rep's obstetrician clients knows another doctor who asked whether you are "out to get" Buff Spaulding. Further, this client indicated that Spaulding and this other doctor have several real estate deals together and that the doctor is concerned that Buff may not be able to make a mortgage payment on some property if he loses his job. You now feel that you have the "iron clad proof" necessary to confront Buff. You know that you must act. What would you now do?

A.   Consult with your boss about how to handle the situation. (GO TO 255)

B.   Call Buff in and ask him if the rumors you had heard are true. (GO TO 179)

C.   Call Buff in, lay out the evidence you have and tell him that he must eliminate his outside deals and improve his performance or resign. (GO TO 140)

Decision Point 263

You have decided to tell Virgil that his case is rather weak before you have a clear understanding of it. This is likely to make him more pessimistic about the outcome. Unfortunately, this may lead him to do something risky, to try to change your mind, or to expand the conflict with Phyllis to other areas where he feels like he might "win."

In general, it is unadvisable to make either side to a mediation pessimistic about their chances.

Re-evaluate your last decision. Circle the #263 you just wrote in your flow diagram. Then move back to the last uncircled step in your flow diagram.

Decision Point 264

Lisa attends the program, and her next quarter's sales are only modestly better. Apparently this training effort was not the answer to her performance problem.

Your analysis of Lisa's motivation revealed several important things. It is clear that Lisa has a strong belief that her efforts will pay off in terms of performance since she has a history of succeeding in nearly everything she has attempted. In addition, you can be certain that Lisa believes that performance will be rewarded at Omega, since she is on an incentive pay system that relates her income directly to two indices of performance, volume and inventory. As for Lisa's particular preference for the her work outcomes, we can be sure that Lisa values the monetary outcomes of her job since she has indicated that she needs her commission check to make her first house payment. Given these factors, it is not surprising that Lisa's efforts are high (she called on 100 percent of her M.D.s, and each wholesaler twice). However, her performance is not up to expectations. In light of this assessment, think about what additional factor may account for her low performance.

Your decision to give Lisa additional training was consistent with an appraisal that she needed abilities and skills not developed in the formal training program she completed with the company. However, you know little about just what Lisa's specific training needs are at this point. Re-evaluate your last decision. Circle the #264 you just wrote in your flow diagram. Then move back to the first uncircled number above this one in your flow diagram.

Decision Point 265

Virgil responds, "Okay, I understand what you are getting at. Listen, if you side with Phyllis on this issue, my crew is really going to think that I have no influence whatever in this organization. I can't afford to lose their respect, believe me. There is nothing worse than a supervisor whose crew thinks he has 'lost control.'"

"Furthermore," he continues, "paperwork is a real pain in the neck for me. When I come in Monday morning, I want to get my hands dirty; I don't want to pansy around shuffling papers!" In effect, Virgil has just told you that he has two interests beside the risk of quality problems: (1) he wants to appear in control with his crew; and (2) he does not like doing paperwork on Mondays.

As your private meeting with Virgil ends, what would you say?

A. "While I agree with you that seeming in control is important to every manager, I don't accept your reasons for not doing paperwork on Mondays. Doing paperwork is part of your job, and if that's what your job is, you should do it. I don't think there is any room for personal preferences in these negotiations. When we get back together I hope you will keep that in mind." (GO TO 256)

B. "This meeting has been really helpful, Virgil. When we get back together, let's focus on alternatives that reflect all your interests. For example, think about finding an alternative that will not result in your losing the respect of your crew." (GO TO 156)

354

Thomas indicates that he might be interested in early retirement if a satisfactory financial arrangement could be reached. You call the Director of Employee Relations and get a figure. You share that information with Wilson, and he refuses it outright. You warn him that it might be better to take the offer and remove the threat, but he is firm.

What would you do now?

A.   Tell him he is dangerously close to being terminated unless he turns his performance around. Be precise about just what level of performance is necessary to keep you from taking this action. (GO TO 151)

B.   Review what you've done in the past to try and turn his performance around, and ask him for a renewed commitment to do something about his "marginal performance." (GO TO 119)

C.   Accompany him on a series of sales calls. (GO TO 154)

D.   Schedule him for a training program that involves modern sales techniques. Warn him that this is his last chance. (GO TO 272)

E.   Ask him to explain his poor figures--77 percent of doctors contacted, 38 days inventory. (GO TO 197)

Your meeting with Spaulding goes better than you anticipated. He apologizes for his performance, and quickly (perhaps too quickly) agrees to a set of performance objectives that you consider reasonable. You also inform Spaulding that you will monitor his performance closely.

A few weeks later, you check Buff's log and the records from his region. Nothing seems to have changed regarding his performance. Later that day you receive a call from an obstetrician in Buff's territory. He tells you that Buff is a terrific sales rep, and asks you to be understanding with him. You wonder whether Spaulding asked him to contact you. After some independent checking you find out that this doctor is one of Spaulding's frequent golf partners. Three days later you hear from another client, this time a wholesaler, who tells you that Spaulding is one of the best reps who calls on him and that he has just decided to place a huge order that would bring his stock of Omega drugs up to 75 days.

You are surprised by this call and mention it to one of your colleagues. He says that he has heard that this wholesaler "owes" Spaulding and is repaying a favor. He also told you that he doubts if the alleged order would ever be booked. He seems to be correct, as two weeks have passed and the order has not been received. What would you now do?

A. Since his performance has not improved, begin the process of terminating Spaulding. (GO TO 200)

B. Ask to accompany Spaulding on several of his sales calls. (GO TO 175)

C. Ask around the company discreetly to find out more about Buff's reputation as a salesman and how he is able to maintain his life-style when his earnings are so low. (GO TO 206)

Decision Point 268

You decided to relocate the necessary number of foremen into staff positions or through transfers to other plants. This was a good move since under-worked supervisors often interfere with a QWL intervention.

Three months later, all is going quite well with the two QWL changes you have introduced. Absenteeism continues to drop in the sewers and finishers group, and has leveled off at an acceptable level in the cutters group. You receive a visit from the vice-president of operations (your boss), and he is thrilled by the results of the intervention to date. He comments, however, that the sewers and cutters seem to be using procedures that are at odds with those recommended by the consulting firm in its $50,000 report.

How would you respond to his concerns?

A. Show him the logic behind the intervention and point to the improvement in absenteeism and turnover. Calculate a payback period for the $50,000 investment. (GO TO 224)

B. Show him the logic behind the intervention and point to the improvement in absenteeism and turnover. Invite him to speak with the operators about their reaction to the new system. (GO TO 120)

C. Deflect his concerns and hope he does not press the issue. (GO TO 228)

Decision Point 269

Phyllis leaves your office, and you ask Virgil to come in. After exchanging plea-santries, you open the discussion of his conflict with Phyllis and invite him to comment. He responds: "I guess I am in the doghouse again, huh? Well, okay, I'll try harder to work with 'Miss Smarty-pants.'" What would you say?

A. "Yes you are in the doghouse. From what Phyllis tells me, you have been rather uncooperative." (GO TO 263)

B. "Let's soft-pedal the name-calling, Virgil. I want your side of the story. Here's a list of situations that Phyllis has prepared. Now then, describe these situations as you see them." (GO TO 139)

C. "You're not in the doghouse, Virgil. You are a vital member of this organiza-tion. I'm trying to get to the bottom of what is going on between the two of you. Name-calling is not going to get us anywhere." (GO TO 240)

Decision Point 270

He shrugs his shoulders and completes a rather detailed set of commitments. He balks, though, when it comes to implementing your suggestion regarding interacting with the large wholesaler with which he's had difficulty.

In light of the fact that Thomas is considered an "old jerk" and already has made a substantial series of commitments, would you assume responsibility for interacting with this wholesaler yourself for one quarter?

A. Yes. (GO TO 112)

B. No. (GO TO 215)

Decision Point 271

Your choice of a seating arrangement is not appropriate. You want to create an atmosphere that shows that the problem is the focus of attention, not each other.

Re-evaluate your last decision. Circle the #271 you just wrote in your flow diagram. Then move back to the last uncircled step in your flow diagram.

Decision Point 272

You schedule Wilson Thomas for a training program that involves sales skill building. You also warn him that this is his last chance. He attends the program, but much to your chagrin, you receive the following letter from him:

"I have completed the program you scheduled me to take, and I want you to know that it was a total waste of time. Nothing covered was new, and I fail to see why a professional approach is now out of date. The trainers of the program couldn't answer that to my satisfaction."

How would you respond?

A. Review what you've done in the past to try and turn his performance around, and ask him for a renewed commitment to do something about his "marginal" performance. (GO TO 119)

B. Accompany him on a series of sales calls. (GO TO 154)

C. Tell him that you think he's being defensive. (GO TO 160)

D. Tell him that this is it; you are at the end of your rope with him. Establish your willingness to help in any way you can, but either he comes up to standard next quarter or he's through with Omega. (GO TO 151)

E. Tell him his sales approach may be correct but he can't make it work unless he improves his effort. Remind him that he only contacted 77 percent of the doctors in his territory and that his inventory figure (38 days) is very low. (GO TO 197)

F. Confront the differences between his stated sales approach and the sort of approach you know works well for the highest performing reps in your region. (GO TO 247)

G. Check to see if his job is really important to him. (GO TO 242)

Decision Point 273

Sam Blakestone was manager of the Automation Systems Group for five years, and he was with the Division for seven. Now with a competing firm, Sam jumps at the chance to express his opinion when you phone him.

"It sounds like Fenwick finally got his way. He's been trying to get the monkey off his back for years. He's no professional, I'll tell you that! He's probably been getting heat for inventory costs, so he invents a policy to put the heat elsewhere. Typical, real typical. You are just lucky he's planning to retire in one year!"

Unfortunately, this is not the type of information that you can really act upon. The opinions of a former employee are not really relevant here. While you were not in error for talking with Blakestone, re-evaluate your last decision. Circle the #273 you just wrote in your flow diagram, and move to the last uncircled step in your flow diagram.

Decision Point 274

You decide to use the Nominal Group Technique. You tell the group the steps involved in the process:

1. Team members work alone and in silence, writing down all their topic ideas.

2. Members share their ideas using a round-robin procedure, during which members are encouraged to add items to their list of topic ideas.

3. Participants discuss each recorded idea in order to clarify its meaning and intent and to provide initial evaluation.

4. Task force members use rank-voting to indicate their feelings concerning the importance of the ideas. Group output is then determined by summing the ranked votes.

5. Members discuss the results of the initial voting and take a final vote.

You tell the task force that you will work through steps 1 through 4, but will reserve 5 for another meeting. You and your group begin with step 1--the individual work. While you had intended to spend at least 10 minutes on this stage, Lyle Seashore gets up and walks around to Harrison Gump, whispers something in his ear, and leaves the room. Gump begins to stand up.

What would you do?

A. Look downward and model the sort of behavior you want Gump and the other task force members to act out. (GO TO 389)

B.   Tell Gump to get to work and leave the room and ask Seashore to return. (GO TO 439)

Decision Point 275

Your confrontation with Duckworth, Brown, and Johnson backfires. In the following one month period, Johnson and Duckworth both resign to join your predecessor in his consulting firm (you discover that they had standing offers from him all the time). You are now seriously under-staffed in the face of having to complete three one-month assignments in three months. The results are predictably bad. Your team fails to make all three deadlines, and the quality of the work reflects the under-staffing.

Re-evaluate your last decision. Circle the #275 you just wrote in your flow diagram. Then go back in your flow diagram to the first uncircled number above this step.

Decision Point 276

Your opening question to Bill Banquet results in the following answer: "When I first heard of the new policy, I really tried putting the damper on it. But Fenwick had a lot of influence with Billingsworth. With the upcoming cuts in Product Planning, he had no choice. Somebody had to take on the planning responsibility Product Planning used to have, and I sure didn't want Manufacturing to call the shots.

"Now we're under a microscope. If we can show that we can plan well, we'll be able to keep production schedules responsive to the market. My concern is that if we resist this thing, or water it down, the pressure on inventory costs will mean more stock-outs when we really need product."

At this point what would you do?

A.   Deliver your proposal as planned. (GO TO 438)

B.   Center the discussion on the alternatives of shorter planning periods and training for the sales engineers. (GO TO 357)

C.   Abandon your efforts to find relief from the policy and, after telling your people what Banquet just said, ask them to live with the policy. (GO TO 429)

Decision Point 277

You tell the group that you plan to use the Nominal Group Technique as a method of deriving alternative topics for the seasonal issue. While this method may be well--suited to the first aspect of your charter, it is really premature to announce it. You should have opened the meeting by summarizing the decisions made at the first meeting and asking Gump and Seashore to report on what they have discovered from their survey of ongoing topic assignments within the Editorial Department. Let's assume you had done that and resume the interactive case at that point.

Gump hands out a list of topics that are presently being worked on in the Editorial Department by various reporters. This done, you need to instruct the group as to what technique is appropriate for the task force to use.

What technique would you use?

A.   Nominal Group Technique. (GO TO 274)

B.   Ordinary group discussion. (GO TO 309)

C.   Subgroups engaged in ordinary group discussion. (GO TO 415)

D.   Brainstorming. (GO TO 299)

Decision Point 278

Your decision to open meetings up to group discussion seriously bogs the group down. You have given the group an assignment that is already quite taxing in terms of workflow. By opening the meetings, you are essentially making the workflow even more complicated. Since your group is not yet in a P-1 condition, this is premature.

Re-evaluate your last decision. Circle the #278 you just wrote in your flow diagram. Then go back in your flow diagram to the first uncircled number above this step.

Decision Point 279

You have an opportunity to chat with three of your peers (Amy Holcott is out of town). All of them expressed irritability with the new policy, but none seemed put out enough to fight it. Don James' (Sales Manager--Pneumatic Products) opinion was typical:

"I don't know if my people are good enough planners for us to make our estimates within the 20% window. I suspect that they are, but there's no telling. Right now, with the market so sour, most of our business is repeat business. My hunch is that simply keeping our estimates to the high side of historical figures should suffice. That's what I am telling my people to do. They're sure not going to like the extra paperwork, that I can assure you. But most of my sales engineers are still jittery about being laid off, so it shouldn't be too hard a sell."

What would you do now?

A. Speak with Bill Banquet (your boss) about his "reading" of the new policy. (GO TO 385)

B. Phone a friend of yours who works as a financial analyst at the corporate level (Blake-Emerson, the parent company) for his perspective on how to respond to this policy change. (GO TO 298)

C. Call your predecessor (now with another firm) for his perspective on how to handle this situation. (GO TO 273)

D. Wait and bring this issue up at a weekly staff meeting of the sales managers (chaired by Bill Banquet). (GO TO 420)

E. Diplomatically oppose the new policy as it applies to your unique circumstances. Petition for an exemption. (GO TO 329)

F. Instruct your subordinates what to do about the new policy. (GO TO 333)

Decision Point 280

You ask each member to rank order the ideas from 1 to 52. This is a very difficult assignment. It is far too complex for anyone to rank order such a large number of items without breaking them into more manageable categories first.

Re-evaluate your last decision. Circle the #280 you just wrote in your flow diagram. Then move to the last uncircled step in your flow diagram.

It is one month later, and your personal position with your team is stronger. Bob Alton responded to your stern warning by leaving the company, and this gave you the opportunity to promote Luke Spurior to Alton's position (Employment Manager). You also bring in an individual who you have known for years into Spurior's former position (Employment Analyst). Her name is Sandy Schaeffer, and while not accepted immediately into the group, she and Jane Duckworth seem to get along satisfactorily.

In spite of these changes, the level of team morale seems quite low. Some individuals seem to have accepted your leadership (notably Best, Bennet, and Spurior) while others continue to be cool toward you (Duckworth, Brown, and Johnson). Halfway through the last month, Jane Duckworth approached you and confessed feeling disturbed that the once "family feeling" in the Department is no longer there. You persuaded her not to leave the company.

Since it is now three months until your three departmental assignments are due, you must now decide what assignment to complete first. Which assignment would you give now?

A. Assignment 1 -- Preparation for Labor Negotiations. In five months your department begins negotiations with the Sheetmetal Workers Union for the first time in two years. Since the contract will affect each department member's specialty, you will solicit everyone's input. Bunkie Brown will draw up a list of probable union demands. He will send these to other department members for an assessment of economic and administrative impact. You will then aggregate these assessments into an integrated impact report that will serve to determine the company's negotiating strategy (GO TO 296).

B. Assignment 2 -- Development of an Integrated Personnel Policy. Top management has asked you to assess existing departmental policies. It is due in five months. Preparing this document will involve intensive meetings of all department members (GO TO 425).

C. Assignment 3 -- Creation of an Annual Staffing Plan. In five months the staffing planning for the next fiscal year is due. This is a serial process beginning with Roy Best who estimates promotions and transfers. This then goes to Bob Alton's group (Alton, Duckworth, and Spurior) who calculate new staffing needs. It then travels on to George Bennet who justifies these figures into the affirmative action plan. Finally, Floyd Banks transposes these estimates into a budget form (GO TO 327).

Decision Point 282

No matter how diplomatic you are, this course of action is entirely too premature. You work for a person who has been in his job for a short time, and you have found him to be cautious. Declaring yourself opposed to this policy change now would lead to uncertain results at best. You need more information before committing yourself (even if it is a commitment to comply).

When policies like this are announced, especially policies that require 100% compliance to be effective and that were not arrived at democratically, those responsible are likely to be in a defensive posture. That is, those who have publicly committed themselves are unlikely to reverse their position even when the force of logic is compelling. Clearly, you should gather more information before deciding how best to respond to this situation.

Re-evaluate your last decision. Circle the #282 you just wrote in your flow diagram, and move to the last uncircled step in your flow diagram.

Decision Point 283

You identified an excellent combination of talent. Since your assignment requires a creative approach, you needed a task force with a heterogeneous composition. This meant that the two members who came from outside Editorial should ideally be from different departments. This ruled out combinations like Smithers/Fitzgerald and Leybolt/Jones.

Another issue worth considering was the style of each member. Ideally a task force should have some combination of task- and people-oriented members. Since any two of your Editorial people are task-oriented, you needed someone who was more socially inclined. Michael Smithers was ideal in this respect.

This left two possibilities:

B. Gump, Seashore, Smithers, Foy, or
E. Seashore, Patrick, Smithers, Leybolt.

You were correct to choose B because the combination of Leybolt and Smithers would be too easily dominated by the two Editorial members. Leybolt couldn't hold his own without some support of Smithers, and Smithers couldn't have given him that support.

Your next problem is to put an agenda together. It seems to you that you should begin with a discussion of the objectives for the issue. Personally, you hope the group identifies an increase in circulation as an objective, but you realize that will not be greeted with enthusiasm among the Editorial people who are always reluctant to "sell out" to commercial interests. However, you think it will be impossible to get anywhere unless the group agrees to this objective.

How would you deal with this problem?

A. Meet with members of the task force individually before the first meeting to "feel them out" on objectives. (GO TO 398)

B. Have the publisher come to the first meeting and announce that one of the objectives is to increase circulation. (GO TO 319)

C. Conduct the first meeting with objectives as the first agenda item. (GO TO 287)

Decision Point 284

In making this assignment and in conducting yourself in weekly departmental meetings and at other public occasions, what would you do?

A. Say that it is important for the department to "play this assignment by the book." Suggest that they propose no increases in the Human Resources staffing budget, as this is premature. State that you think the long-term prospects for such an increase and for the department as a whole appear good, but say that you think it's wise for the group to maintain a low profile with top management for a while (GO TO 335).

B. Publicly congratulate those specific individuals (Floyd Banks, Bunkie Brown, and Steve Johnson) who did such a fine job on the last assignment (GO TO 375).

C. Change the format of weekly departmental meetings to allow more group discussion where members have concerns (GO TO 278).

Decision Point 285

Sterling Cartwright is a man of about 40 who has been with the company for only three weeks. You ask him about Banquet's opinion of the way the new policy is

365

working. He responds: "Bill is concerned. He really is. He doesn't like the way it puts the burden on you. Just the other day he met with Mr. Billingsworth about it."

You ask him what Banquet is doing about this situation. "Bill has a plan, and I'm sure it will work in time, but with the cuts in product planning, things are a bit uncertain. I'm sure you can expect something in the next few months."

What would you do now? (Bill Banquet is out of town.)

   A.   Go see Mildred Barnes of the Product Planning Department. (GO TO 397)

   B.   Meet privately with Brian Robinson to work out a strategy for addressing this policy problem. (GO TO 348)

   C.   Phone William Barstow, your friend at the corporate headquarters. (GO TO 359)

   D.   Instruct your subordinates about what to do now. (GO TO 429)

Decision Point 286

By pressing Bill Banquet for a decision, you are implicitly handing complete control of the situation over to him. You have given him the rationale for an exemption. However, he has signaled you indirectly that he is unprepared for anything as bold as what you have proposed (an all-out exemption).

Re-evaluate your last decision. Circle the #286 you just wrote in your flow diagram, and then move to the last uncircled step in your flow diagram.

Decision Point 287

You decide to conduct the first meeting with objectives as the first agenda item. Under normal circumstances this would be very smart. However, this is a potentially controversial issue, and it's probably better to talk to task force members before raising the issue as a means of gauging just how much disagreement there is.

Let's assume you have done that and resume the interactive case from that point. Your first meeting is with Lyle Seashore. True to form, he objects to any objective for the issue that "smacks" of narrow, commercial interests. Yet when you meet with Harrison Gump, you are surprised to find him willing to select a topic for the seasonal edition that will have "broad appeal." Knowing Gump as you do, you realize that is as close to agreeing with commercial appeal as an objective as you are likely to get.

When you raise the issue with Smithers and Foy, they have no problem with the idea of an increase in circulation as a specific objective. Clearly Seashore is in the minority, but you are concerned that if you raise the issue in your first meeting, he may be able to win Gump over on a matter of principle and deadlock the task force.

How would you proceed from this point?

A.   Raise the issue of objectives at your first meeting and be prepared to guide the group to the resolution that you and the publisher want. (GO TO 313)

B.   Return to Lyle Seashore and explore with him what objectives he can live with. Be prepared to tell him that if he can't live with a commercial objective, you may have to ask someone else to serve on the task force. (GO TO 311)

C.   Have your boss (the publisher) talk with Seashore to persuade him of the importance of circulation. (GO TO 293)

Decision Point 288

Your statement solves a problem your group has been having with your leadership-- they were not sure whether your allegiance was to them or the opposition (top management). By announcing your charter, you place yourself clearly in top management's corner. The results are predictable. You are shut off from upward communication and treated as a "lackey." Surely, you cannot remedy this negative impression for some time.

Re-evaluate your last decision. Circle the #288 you just wrote in your flow diagram. Then go back in your flow diagram to the first uncircled number above this step.

Decision Point 289

You ask if you should have the publisher talk with the members' bosses about the importance of the task force, thus freeing them from other conflicting responsibilities. They indicate that would be helpful. You call the publisher's office, and the secretary says that she will have the publisher sign a memo to that effect.

Back at the meeting you next want to give a few remarks on the political sensitivities of serving on the task force. What would you say in this regard?

A.   "With the quality of people on this task force, I'm very optimistic about being able to put together a superb seasonal issue. However, I am a bit concerned that we keep to ourselves. Please, let's keep our deliberations confidential, and if you are having a problem with the way anything is done on this task force, see me before you talk about it with people not in the group. Is that agreeable to everyone?" (GO TO 421)

B.   "I'm convinced that, with the people on this task force, we cannot fail. However, our assignment is a challenging one, and it is very likely that we will step on each other's toes from time to time. For that reason, I would like to ask all of you to keep whatever conflicts arise in this room in confidence." (GO TO 448)

C.   "All of you have been carefully selected to represent your constituencies on this task force. It is very imperative that you bring the points of view of your departments to our deliberations so we can be sure that the special issue is acceptable to all involved." (GO TO 445)

Decision Point 290

How do you know if compliance to this policy is necessary? Obviously it affects your unit in a negative way. Yet, you have not gauged others' reactions to it. Deciding to comply presumes that no one but Emerson Billingsworth has any influence over policy. Further, if you plan to tell your subordinates to partially comply with this policy, how do you know this will work without first finding out what others are going to do? Clearly, you should first gather more information before deciding what to do. Blind obedience or precipitous reaction is rarely as effective as an informed, deliberate move.

Re-evaluate your last decision. Circle the #290 you just wrote in your flow diagram, and move to the last uncircled step in your flow diagram.

Decision Point 291

You decide to call off the session since it is clear to you that the group has exhausted its creative potential. This is unfortunate. Typically periods of silence do emerge in every brainstorming session, and often the most imaginative and useful ideas come up right after these periods. Therefore, it is generally useful to wait out at least a few silent periods during brainstorming. Let's assume you had done that and rejoin the interactive case from that point.

You wait out the silence, and the first few ideas that emerge are truly fabulous. This stimulates a second burst of ideas from the group that lasts almost five minutes. A second silence overcomes the group, and you wait through that one as you did the first. However, few ideas of any merit arise.

With the task force rather tired and the scheduled end of the meeting approaching, you decide to call an end to this session. A total of 52 different topic ideas have been generated. You instruct your assistant to duplicate and distribute the results of the brainstorming meeting to the participants.

What instructions would you give the members?

A.   Ask them to look over the list of prospective topics that came out of this meeting and put them into categories that make sense. (GO TO 395)

B.   Tell them that the meeting was very productive, and you will follow up with the discussion at the next meeting. (GO TO 332)

C.   Ask each member to rank order the ideas that have been derived on the basis of 1 = best and 52 = worst. (GO TO 280)

Decision Point 292

It is three weeks later, and in checking on the progress of the assignment, you realize that it is behind schedule. A closer examination reveals that Bunkie Brown and Steve Johnson got their assumptions to other team members one week late. In addition, Bob Alton, Jane Duckworth, and Luke Spurior have yet to even begin their work on it. The others (Roy Best, George Bennet, and Floyd Banks) are close to completion. When you confront Alton about the delay, he offers a believable excuse, but you are wonder whether he is really committed to the schedule.

What would you do about this?

A.   Confront Alton again privately. Let him know that you expect his cooperation, but you will not tolerate any trouble with him (GO TO 396).

B.   At the next weekly staff meeting, deliver a speech that emphasizes your confidence in everyone in the group. Stress the need for everybody to work toward objectives that are both professionally worthwhile and relevant to the needs of the company (GO TO 422).

C.   Announce the charter that you were given by top management at the next weekly staff meeting. State your resolve to bring the department back into line with the needs of the organization (GO TO 288).

D.   Mention at a weekly staff meeting that you are pleased that Brown and Johnson gave so much thought to their assumptions and that Best, Bennet, and Banks have been making excellent progress on the assignment. Say nothing about Alton, Duckworth, and Spurior (GO TO 323).

Decision Point 293

You ask your boss to speak with Seashore to persuade him of the importance of circulation. Your boss declines, saying that he feels you should handle the matter.

What now?

A.   Raise the issue of objectives at your first meeting and be prepared to guide the group to the resolution that you and the publisher want. (GO TO 313)

B.   Return to Lyle Seashore and explore with him what objectives he can live with. Be prepared to tell him that if he can't live with a commercial objective, you may have to ask someone else to serve on the task force. (GO TO 311)

Decision Point 294

The first time you send Fenwick a memo detailing expected deviations, he sends you back the following memo:

Memorandum

TO: YOU
FR: JUSTIN FENWICK
RE: PRODUCT PLANNING

I received your recent memo detailing expected deviations from this month's product plan. I hope you appreciate that production planning is a highly complex endeavor.

With our shrinking staff, we simply cannot integrate these deviations into this month's plan. Accordingly, there is no need for you to send us these data. Presumably, they will be useful for your own internal purposes.

I certainly hope you did not send us these unrequested figures as a sign of unwillingness to fully cooperate with the new policy. As you no doubt appreciate, Mr. Billingsworth expects total cooperation with the policy. Anything short of that and we cannot guarantee product availability. I know I can count on you to make this new system a success.

cc: E. Billingsworth; B. Banquet

As well intentioned as your action might have been, it certainly back-fired. Re-evaluate your last decision. Circle the #294 you just wrote in your flow diagram, and move to the last uncircled step in your flow diagram.

Decision Point 295

You go to Gump and confess the difficulty you are having convincing your boss. While this is certainly truthful, it may be a bit premature. Part of your job as the leader of this team is to buffer your team from the rest of the organization. Communicating the publisher's concerns before you really understood them may unnecessarily distract the group from its task.

Re-evaluate your last decision. Circle the #295 you just wrote in your flow diagram. Then move to the last uncircled step in your flow diagram.

Decision Point 296

In making this assignment and in conducting yourself in weekly departmental meetings and at public occasions, what would you do?

A.   Suggest that these labor negotiations are a real opportunity for the department to regain its credibility with top management. Note that it will take a coordinated effort to overcome what will surely be a tough bargaining stand by the union (GO TO 407).

B.   Change the format at weekly departmental meetings to allow more group discussion where members have concerns (GO TO 452).

C.   Take every chance to reinforce and publicly acknowledge any efforts in line with top management's concern that Human Resources become more relevant to the realities of the firm (GO TO 419).

D.   Be tough privately and individually with Duckworth, Brown and Johnson to neutralize their opposition to your leadership (GO TO 275).

Decision Point 297

Foy and Smithers say very little in the ensuing discussion. However, Foy seems to be becoming convinced by the diatribes of Gump and Seashore. Finally, when you intervene, it appears too late. Foy expresses a "deep reservation" about whether the task force can proceed without more independence from "management."

Re-evaluate your last decision. Circle the #297 you just wrote in your flow diagram. Then move to the last uncircled step in your flow diagram.

Decision Point 298

You have known William Barstow for years. You attended the same university together. When you tell him of the policy directive, he gives you some interesting information:

"I haven't heard anything about the policy, but I can tell you that the Fluid Products Division is getting a lot of heat to get its costs under control. The word is that Billingsworth's argument that his division has strong profit potential is no longer credible until he can produce the numbers. The division is now under considerable pressure not to cut its line personnel, but rather its staff. One view from these lofty heights is that the axe is due to fall soon on just about every staff unit in the Division."

If true, this would mean that Justin Fenwick's group is in for some cuts, but your group should not be affected.

What would you do now?

A.   Speak with Bill Banquet (your boss) about his "reading" of the new policy. (GO TO 363)

B. Call your predecessor (now with another firm) for his perspective on how to handle this situation. (GO TO 273)

C. Wait and bring this issue up at a weekly staff meeting of the sales managers (chaired by Bill Banquet). (GO TO 420)

D. Diplomatically oppose the new policy as it applies to your unique circumstances. Petition for an exemption. (GO TO 329)

E. Instruct your subordinates what to do about the new policy. (GO TO 333)

Decision Point 299

You decide to use brainstorming. You tell the group the ground rules:

1. Criticism is ruled out. Judgment or evaluation of ideas must be withheld until a later time.

2. Freewheeling is welcomed. The wilder or more radical the idea, the better.

3. Quantity of ideas is wanted. The more alternative topics, the better.

4. Combination and improvement is desirable. Task force members should suggest how the ideas of others can be turned into other ideas.

    How would you keep track of the ideas generated?

A. Ask the group if it has any objections if you ask your personal assistant to keep track of the ideas. Position him at the flip chart. (GO TO 344)

B. Take notes yourself on a note pad. (GO TO 371)

C. Use a flip chart to write down the ideas yourself. (GO TO 355)

D. Tape record the session. (GO TO 364)

Decision Point 300

It is one month later, and the team is evidently getting used to your style of management. On several occasions, you have publicly recognized excellent performance and called for a need for improvement. While the group still is unsure toward you

373

personally, you note that there is much less talk about the firm "putting down" a professional approach to human resources. In addition, you sense that Alton is losing his influence with the team. While Duckworth and Spurior are still loyal to him, Brown and Johnson seem more uncommitted to his leadership. One thing that troubles you, though, is that Alton is being very quiet at meetings, and you have heard that he secretly criticized some of your statements and actions.

By working *individually* with group members, you are creating stronger bonds between the employees and you than they have between each other. This has the effect of decreasing the cohesiveness of the group, i.e., from P-4 to P-3.

There are now four months left until your team's three one-month assignments are due. What would you do now?

A.   Assignment 1 -- Preparation for Labor Negotiations. In five months your department begins negotiations with the Sheetmetal Workers Union for the first time in two years. Since the contract will affect each department member's specialty, you will solicit everyone's input. Bunkie Brown will draw up a list of probable union demands. He will send these to other department members for their assessments of the economic and administrative impact. You will then aggregate these assessments into an integrated impact report that will serve to determine the company's negotiating strategy (GO TO 361).

B.   Assignment 2 -- Development of an Integrated Personnel Policy. Top management has asked you to assess existing departmental policies. It is due in five months. Preparing this document will involve intensive meetings of all department members (GO TO 393).

C.   Assignment 3 -- Creation of an Annual Staffing Plan. In five months the staffing plan for the next fiscal year is due. This is a serial process beginning with Roy Best who estimates promotions and transfers. This then goes to Bob Alton's group (Alton, Duckworth, and Spurior) who calculates new staffing needs. Then it travels on to George Bennet who justifies these figures into the affirmative action plan. Finally, Floyd Banks transposes these estimates into a budget form (GO TO 428).

D.   Hold off from making an assignment for one more month (GO TO 378).

Decision Point 301

You ask the group if anyone has any more ideas. This question elicits no further ideas, so you are left with no option but closing this part of the meeting. This is unfortunate. Typically periods of silence do emerge in every brainstorming session, and often the most imaginative and useful ideas come up right after these periods. Therefore, it is generally useful to wait out at least a few silent periods during brainstorming. Let's assume you had done that and rejoin the interactive case from that point.

You wait out the silence, and the first few ideas that emerge are truly fabulous. This stimulates a second burst of ideas from the group that lasts almost five minutes. A second silence overcomes the group, and you wait through that one as you did the first. However, few ideas of any merit arise.

With the task force becoming rather tired and the scheduled end of the meeting approaching, you decide to call an end to this session. A total of 52 different topic ideas have been generated. You instruct your assistant to duplicate and distribute the results of the brainstorming meeting to the participants.

What instructions would you give the members?

A.   Ask them to look over the list of prospective topics that came out of this meeting and put them into categories that make sense to them. (GO TO 395)

B.   Tell them that the meeting was very productive, and you will follow up with the   discussion at the next meeting. (GO TO 332)

C.   Ask each member to rank order the ideas that have been derived on the basis of 1 = best and 52 = worst. (GO TO 280)

Decision Point 302

There are several ways for you to diplomatically oppose this new policy. Which option would you choose?

A.   Ask Bill Banquet to use his influence to earn an exemption from this policy requirement in light of your group's special circumstances. (GO TO 453)

B.   Go directly to Justin Fenwick and petition him for an exemption from this policy requirement. (GO TO 382)

C.   Send a memo to Emerson Billingsworth (the announcement came from him, so it is proper) detailing in explicit form your case for an exemption from this new policy. (GO TO 405)

Decision Point 303

You decide to say nothing about the arrangement your boss has with the Vice President of Operations. As a result, this subgroup makes no special plans to get copy to Operations early. This has disastrous consequences. The Vice President of Operations complains to your boss, and he gives you a verbal tongue-lashing.

Re-evaluate your last decision. Circle the #303 you just wrote in your flow diagram. Then move to the last uncircled step in your flow diagram.

Decision Point 304

The group struggles with this assignment. It seems that you were too optimistic about the level of commitment in the group. It spite of the success with the last assignment, there is still ill-feeling about top management. The group is also still uncertain toward you. Given this, opening the sensitive topic of personnel policies is ill-advised. The team labors long and hard on the subject, but conflicts arise between those committed to your leadership and those who have little confidence in you. Unfortunately, the resulting document lacks the direction you wanted. It also takes 2 months to complete. This lateness compounds your problem with top management and clouds your future ability to forge a team spirit.

You have worked hard to move the group from its original P-4 condition to its present P-2 state. Of the two available assignments, you chose the one with the highest degree of workflow complexity.

Re-evaluate your last decision. Circle the #304 you just wrote in your flow diagram. Then go back in your flow diagram to the first uncircled number above this step.

Decision Point 305

Your upbeat closing remarks fall short of the mark. Generally, at the end of each meeting, you should reiterate who is expected to do what before the next meeting and get an explicit commitment from those involved.

Re-evaluate your last decision. Circle the #305 you just wrote in your flow diagram. Then move to the last uncircled step in your flow diagram.

Will Barstow has much to say, "Well, by now you've heard about the personnel cuts in Product Planning. My hunch is that these are the last cuts. This quarter's earnings are up, and it now appears that we are about as lean as we can be.

"I've checked with some of my contacts. It's clear that your policy problem is not without precedent in the corporation. Two other divisions in Atlanta and Trenton have their salespeople estimate product demand as part of the planning effort. Marketing managers there gave their salespeople extensive training in statistical estimation procedures. Each has access to a computer terminal so they can report deviations from the plan in real time."

As you hang up the phone, Mildred Barnes of the Product Planning Department appears in the doorway of your office. Mildred Barnes and you have established a pleasant relationship during the past month. Through mutual and harmless teasing, you have built a rapport that both of you relish. When you ask her views of the policy, she has much to say.

"You know why the policy was created, don't you? Well, Billingsworth was facing significant pressure from corporate headquarters to cut staff personnel. Justin (Fenwick) had been successful in protecting us until then. But when the axe fell, we could no longer do all the product planning for manufacturing. You know we had been analyzing sales trends and setting manufacturing requirements accordingly. Well, the new policy was followed by a 22 percent cut in our staff. Jack Collins was the last of these cuts, and he left just last week. I was really lucky to survive this purge, believe me...

"Your group and Robinson's are the most hard-hit. But that's not really surprising. When we were doing the product forecasting, your two units were always the hardest to predict. Don't quote me, but you are getting screwed in all this.

"If you ask me, product scheduling is going toward shorter time frames. Now we are asking for projections one month ahead. In the next few months with the computer models we are playing with, we should be able to shorten that to two weeks."

Later in the conversation she says, "...If your people are having a rough time, there is one thing I could do--training. I've been teaching planning methods at a junior college where I live. I'd be more than willing to work with your salespeople to give them tools to use in figuring their product requirements."

What would you do now?

A.   Talk to your peers about their experiences with the new policy. (GO TO 441)

B.   Instruct your subordinates about what to do now. (GO TO 429)

Decision Point 307

You chose the combination of Seashore, Patrick, Smithers, and Leybolt. This is not the best composition for your task force. Leybolt lacks the sort of credibility that would enable him to hold his own with the two representatives from the Editorial Department.

Re-evaluate your last decision. Circle the #307 you just wrote in your flow diagram. Then move to the last uncircled step in your flow diagram.

Decision Point 308

It is one month later, and your team is evidently getting used to your style of management. On several occasions, you have congratulated those who have done well and have pointed to a need for improvement. Although your team still cool toward you, there is less talk about top management's opposition to professional standards. Alton's popularity is declining. While Duckworth and Spurior are still loyal to him, Brown and Johnson are less so. One thing that bothers you is that you have heard that Alton secretly criticizes some of your actions and comments.

By working *individually* with group members, you are creating stronger bonds between the employees and you than they have between each other. This has the effect of decreasing the cohesiveness of the group, i.e., from P-4 to P-3.

There are now four months left until your team's three assignments are due. What would you do now?

A.   Assignment 1 -- Preparation for Labor Negotiations. In five months your department begins negotiations with the Sheetmetal Workers Union for the first time in two years. Since the contract will affect each department member's specialty, you will solicit everyone's input. Bunkie Brown will draw up a list of probable union demands. He will send these to other department members for their assessment of economic and administrative impacts. You will then aggregate these assessments into an integrated impact report that will serve to determine the company's negotiating strategy (GO TO 361).

B.   Assignment 2 -- Development of an Integrated Personnel Policy. Top management has asked you to assess departmental policies. It is due in five months.

378

Preparing this document will involve intensive meetings of all department members (GO TO 393).

C. Assignment 3 -- Creation of an Annual Staffing Plan. In five months the staffing plan for the next fiscal year is due. This is a serial process beginning with Roy Best who estimates promotions and transfers. This then goes to Bob Alton's group (Alton, Duckworth, and Spurior) who calculates new staffing needs. It then travels on to George Bennet who justifies these figures into the affirmative action plan. Finally, Floyd Banks transposes these estimates into a budget form (GO TO 428).

D. Hold off from making an assignment for one more month (GO TO 339).

Decision Point 309

You have decided to use an ordinary group discussion to develop alternative topics for the seasonal issue. Unfortunately, there are many better methods for meeting this objective than the typical group format.

Re-evaluate your last decision. Circle the #309 you just wrote in your flow diagram. Then move to the last uncircled step in your flow diagram.

Decision Point 310

You have known William Barstow for years. You attended the same university together. When you tell him of the policy directive, he gives you some interesting information:

"I haven't heard anything about the policy, but I can tell you that the Fluid Products Division is getting a lot of heat to get its costs under control. The word is that Billingsworth's argument that his division has strong profit potential is no longer credible until he can produce the numbers. The division is now under considerable pressure not to cut its line personnel, but rather its staff. One view from these lofty heights is that the axe is due to fall soon on just about every staff unit in the Division."

If true, this would mean that Justin Fenwick's group is in for some cuts, but your group should not be affected.

What would you do now?

A. Call your predecessor (now with another firm) for his perspective on how to handle this situation. (GO TO 273)

B. Wait and bring this issue up at a weekly staff meeting of the sales managers (chaired by Bill Banquet). (GO TO 420)

C. Diplomatically oppose the new policy as it applies to your unique circumstances. Petition for an exemption. (GO TO 302)

D. Instruct your subordinates what to do about the new policy. (GO TO 400)

Decision Point 311

You return to Lyle Seashore to discuss the matter of the objectives further. During this meeting, you discover that he has several ideas for the issue that would have a very powerful positive impact on circulation. You conclude that he will be positively inclined toward topics that will be popular, but negatively inclined toward going on record that that is the objective. You thus decide not to force the issue and leave the objectives implicit. By exploring the issue with Seashore in private, you avoided the risk of creating a conflict and polarizing the group at its first meeting.

You call the first meeting. You know that the members of your task force do not know each other very well (with the exception of Gump and Seashore). What would you do to "break the ice"?

A. Send each member a brief one-page biography (available through the Human Resource office) on each member before the meeting, and ask the task force members to introduce themselves at the beginning of the meeting. (GO TO 342)

B. At the first meeting, introduce the members yourself, highlighting those elements of their personal histories that have common elements, and then have coffee brought in to facilitate conversations during an unscheduled break. (GO TO 362)

Decision Point 312

Your "pep talk" is greeted with almost no reaction. Later during the same day, however, you learn "through the grapevine" that several group members expressed cynicism about what you said. Although you are not sure, you suspect that this negativity comes from Bob Alton.

The principle that governed this unfortunate outcome is that it is almost impossible for a manager to transform a P-4 group into a P-3 group simply by giving a speech.

What would you do now?

A.   Take a tough stand with Bob Alton. Let him know privately that you expect him to cooperate and that you expect no trouble from him (GO TO 443).

B.   Let others in the group know privately that you think that Alton must have been disappointed about being passed over for your job. Tell group members that you are looking forward to working with him. Express a willingness to support those who work for the Department and to oppose those who work against it (GO TO 369).

C.   Meet with each team member individually to discuss his/her career goals and aspirations. Express your support for these goals if there is evidence of a commitment for departmental goals and performance. Begin to single out individual efforts aligned with your plans (GO TO 308).

D.   Announce the charter that you were given by top management at the next weekly staff meeting. State your resolve to bring the department back into line with the needs of the organization (GO TO 390).

Decision Point 313

You decide to raise the issue of objectives at your first meeting. This results in a very heated discussion that seriously polarizes the task force. Seashore delivers a very passionate speech on the importance of editorial independence, and you are left with few alternatives, none of them particularly appealing.

Re-evaluate your last decision. Circle the #313 you just wrote in your flow diagram, and then move to the last uncircled step in your flow diagram.

Decision Point 314

You have an opportunity to chat with three of your peers (Amy Holcott is out of town). All of them expressed irritability with the new policy, but none seemed put out enough to fight it. Don James' (Sales Manager--Pneumatic Products) opinion was typical:

"I don't know if my people are good enough planners for us to make our estimates within the 20% window. I suspect that they are, but there's no telling. Right now, with the market so sour, most of our business is repeat business. My hunch is that simply keeping our estimates to the high side of historical figures should suffice, at least that's what I am telling my people to do. They're sure not going to like the extra paperwork, that I can assure you. But most of my sales engineers are still jittery about being laid off, so it shouldn't be too bad."

What would you do now?

A. Call your predecessor (now with another firm) for his perspective on how to handle this situation. (GO TO 273)

B. Wait and bring this issue up at a weekly staff meeting of the sales managers (chaired by Bill Banquet). (GO TO 420)

C. Diplomatically oppose the new policy as it applies to your unique circumstances. Petition for an exemption. (GO TO 302)

D. Instruct your subordinates what to do about the new policy. (GO TO 400)

Decision Point 315

By not further clarifying your charter, you risk proceeding without a thorough understanding of what your boss wants.

Re-evaluate your last decision. Circle the #315 you just wrote in your flow diagram. Then move to the last uncircled step in your flow diagram.

Decision Point 316

You have decided to give the group an assignment. The results are very disappointing. Not only is the impact report finished late, but it contained assumptions that top management found unacceptably naive. Apparently, you expected too much too soon from a team that neither accepted you as leader nor the new directions you were hired to lead the department in. Your evaluation of the social conditions in your team should have concluded that the team is presently in a P-4 condition: high cohesiveness and antagonistic work norms. As such, you were ill-advised to give them an assignment that required more complex work relationships than in their regular work. Instead, you should have held off for a while until you had an opportunity to begin to

382

alter the social conditions of the group.

Re-evaluate your last decision. Circle the #316 you just wrote in your flow diagram. Then go back in your flow diagram to the first uncircled number above this step.

Decision Point 317

This part of the session proceeds efficiently, although you have to remind your assistant to use the precise words given by each member in his abbreviated listing. When each member of the task force has exhausted his individual list, a total of 52 ideas have been generated.

You then distribute 3 X 5 cards and ask task force members to vote for their favorites using whatever criteria they want, giving a "1" to their favorite, a "2" to their next favorite, etc., through "7." You then tally these votes and come up with the following:

1.   regional development problems (the highest rated),
2.   police inadequacies in dealing with minor theft,
3.   disillusionment of the middle-class and alternative life-styles,
4.   justice for the underclass--farm workers, the homeless and indigent,
5.   organized crime and real estate scams,
6.   child abuse and alcoholism,
7.   overcrowding at the county prison.

This initial voting concluded, the meeting ends. You ask each member to reflect on these results and return prepared to discuss them further and come up with the final decision.

Three days later at the next scheduled meeting, you realize that you must now confront the issue of evaluative criteria. Before the first task force meeting, you had decided to delay the issue of decision criteria because of the publisher's rather controversial concern that the topic have circulation potential. You can delay no longer, so you open the issue of criteria.

The discussion is tense at first, with the two people from Editorial sparring with the others on the matter of journalistic independence and circulation potential without mentioning either. At that point Lyle Seashore begins dominating the discussion. He makes his point with story after story that support the notion that circulation should not serve as the guiding force in editorial decisions.

What would you say to Seashore to regain control over this meeting?

A.   "Lyle, I think all of us understand your point of view. In all fairness, we should now give someone else a chance to be heard on the matter." (GO TO 360)

B.   "Lyle, that's enough. You are beginning to repeat yourself." (GO TO 340)

C.   "Am I the only one who disagrees with Lyle on this point?" (GO TO 324)

Decision Point 318

Bill Banquet is out of town. This gives you time to gather other information. The following information sources are available to you.

Which would you choose first?

A.   Your peers. (GO TO 343)

B.   Mildred Barnes of the Product Planning Department. (GO TO 391)

C.   Sterling Cartwright (Bill Banquet's new administrative assistant). (GO TO 367)

D.   William Barstow, your friend at the corporate headquarters. (GO TO 408)

Decision Point 319

You decide to ask the publisher to attend the first meeting to announce that one of the objectives of the seasonal edition is to increase circulation. He declines this invitation, preferring you to handle the situation yourself.

Now what?

A.   Meet with members of the task force individually before the first meeting to "feel them out" on objectives. (GO TO 398)

B.   Conduct the first meeting with objectives as the first agenda item. (GO TO 287)

Decision Point 320

This admission has the effect of personalizing an issue that your team considers vitally important from a professional viewpoint. It also casts suspicion on your motives and ambitions. The subsequent policy discussions are strained and unproductive. Finished one month late, the policy document lacks focus and direction. Your team members lack commitment to its contents.

Re-evaluate your last decision. Circle the #320 you just wrote in your flow diagram. Then go back in your flow diagram to the first uncircled number above this step.

Decision Point 321

Your decision to say nothing about the fact that your boss intends to approve the topic has very negative consequences. Gump and Seashore "get wind" that your boss has made that statement, and your credibility with the task force is seriously eroded when Gump asks you if what he has heard is true.

Re-evaluate your last decision. Circle the #321 you just wrote in your flow diagram, and then move to the last uncircled step in your flow diagram.

Decision Point 322

Mildred Barnes and you have established a pleasant relationship during the past month. Through mutual and harmless teasing, you have built a rapport that both of you relish. You ask her views on the new policy.

"You know why the policy was created, don't you? Well, Billingsworth was facing significant pressure from corporate headquarters to cut staff personnel. Justin (Fenwick) had been successful in protecting us until then. When the axe fell, it was obvious that we could no longer do all the product planning for manufacturing. You know, we had been analyzing sales trends and setting manufacturing requirements accordingly. Well, the new policy was followed by a 22% cut in our staff. Jack Collins was the last of these cuts, and he left just last week. I was really lucky to survive this purge, believe me...

"Your group and Robinson's are the most hard-hit. But that's not really surprising. When we were doing the product forecasting, your two units were always the hardest to predict. Don't quote me, but you are getting screwed in all this."

"If you ask me, product scheduling is going toward shorter time frames. Now we are asking for projections one month ahead. In the next few months with our new computer models, we can probably shorten that to two weeks."

Later in the conversation she says, "If your people are having a rough time, there is one thing I could do--training. I've been teaching planning methods at a junior college where I live, and I'd be more than willing to work with your salespeople to give them tools to use in figuring their product requirements."

As you are leaving Mildred's office, her secretary slips you a note that William Barstow, your friend in the corporate office is trying to reach you by phone. You ask to use a phone in a deserted office and phone him. He tells you that he wanted to get back to you with the latest gossip:

"Well, by now you've heard about the personnel cuts in Product Planning. My hunch that personnel cuts are now a thing of past is a conviction. This quarter's earnings are up, and it now appears that we are about as lean as we can be.

"I've checked with some of my contacts. It's clear that your policy problem is not without precedent in the corporation. Two other divisions in Atlanta and Trenton have their salespeople estimate product demand as part of the planning effort. Marketing managers there gave their sales people extensive training in statistical estimation procedures. Each has access to a computer terminal so they can report deviations from the plan in real time."

What would you do now?

A.   Since Bill Banquet is out of town, talk to Sterling Cartwright (his new administrative assistant). (GO TO 432)

B.   Meet privately with Brian Robinson to work out a strategy for addressing this policy problem. (GO TO 414)

C.   Instruct your subordinates about what to do now. (GO TO 429)

Decision Point 323

In spite of your public statement, it takes Alton, Duckworth, and Spurior one more month to finish their assignment. Along the way, you receive more excuses. When you finally put together the inputs from team members (it takes you a week), you look at the results. Somehow, the assumptions do not "add up." Yet, because it took your team twice as long to complete the assignment as you originally thought, you do not consider this issue serious enough to pursue further, and you submit the report to top management.

As for departmental morale, your personal position in the group is stronger. The high level of team spirit has eroded, but some people have clearly sided with you (e.g., Best, Bennet, Banks, Brown, and Johnson). You are unsure about Duckworth and Spurior, but Alton continues quiet and sullen in public. Halfway though the last month, Luke Spurior came in to see you and confessed feeling disturbed that the "family feeling" in the Department seems to have disappeared. You persuaded him that things would get better.

Top management reacts negatively to the impact report you gave them. They label it "too optimistic" and "too theoretical, as usual." You challenge these labels, and express confidence in your people.

At this point, would you?

A. At a departmental meeting announce that top management has challenged the report, and ask everyone to go over their assumptions. Be prepared to revise the report accordingly (GO TO 353).

B. Check the figures and assumptions yourself. Speak privately with Bunkie Brown to assure yourself that he based them on reasoning that you understand and accept. Take the revised report to top management and challenge them if they criticize it again (GO TO 440).

C. Agree with top management that the report may be too optimistic and theoretical. Ask them for more time to "whip your team into shape." (GO TO 437).

Decision Point 324

You try to control Seashore by asking, "Am I the only one who disagrees with Lyle on this point?" This backfires. No one expresses a contrary position. In trying to get equitable participation in a discussion, it is preferable to invoke the norm of fairness.

Re-evaluate your last decision. Circle the #324 you just wrote in your flow diagram. Then move to the last uncircled step in your flow diagram.

Decision Point 325

Sterling Cartwright is a man of about 40 who has been with the company for only three weeks. You ask him about Banquet's opinion of the way the new policy is working. He responds: "Bill is concerned. He really is. He doesn't like the way it puts the burden on you. Just the other day he met with Mr. Billingsworth about it."

You ask him what Banquet is doing about this situation. "Bill has a plan, and I'm sure it will work in time, but with the cuts in product planning, things are a bit uncertain. I'm sure you can expect something in the next few months."

What would you do now? (Bill Banquet is out of town.)

A. Meet with your peers to learn about their experience with the new policy. (GO TO 441)

B. Instruct your subordinates about what to do now. (GO TO 429)

Decision Point 326

He tells you that he is still committed to having at least two representatives on the task force from Editorial. He warns you, though, that you will have to "control their creative juices."

Your conversation is then interrupted by his intercom, and his secretary informs him that the mayor is waiting to see him. He stands up and points you to a side door. What would you do?

A. Leave his office and get to work with your task force. (GO TO 412)

B. Ask him, "What involvement do you personally want on this project?" (GO TO 451)

Decision Point 327

You have decided to give your work team an assignment that requires a moderate level of required interaction. The results are not good. A serious bottleneck occurs when the staffing plan moves from Roy Best to Duckworth, Spurior, and Schaeffer. Due to Spurior's inexperience and Schaeffer's newness to the team, they simply cannot agree on a set of assumptions that you consider feasible. Desperate, you intervene and press the issue. Jane Duckworth resigns over the "interference." The assignment is completed three weeks later, and top management rejects it as unrealistic. Since you now have to go back and trace the difficulties, you are forced to delay other assignments. The results are disastrous for building the credibility of the Department.

Your previous action of holding off making an assignment until absolutely necessary was correct. It gave you the opportunity to work on the social fabric of the team. Results were encouraging. Your actions have moved a group that was firmly in a P-4 condition to one that is now P-3. However, your choice of a particular assignment was incorrect. The Annual Staffing plan assignment requires more complex interaction among team members than one of the other alternatives.

Re-evaluate your last decision. Circle the #327 you just wrote in your flow diagram. Then go back in your flow diagram to the first uncircled number above this step.

Decision Point 328

Gump arms you with some very persuasive information, and you return to your boss's office. You make "the best presentation of your career," and he gives you approval conditional on your ability to do a good job with the coordination issues. You believe this "condition" was more a face-saving gesture than a real requirement, but you are concerned that everything go smoothly. You recall that he told you several weeks ago that you had to get all the background material to Operations 36 hours in advance. You understand that means that whatever you do, you should make sure that Operations is "well taken care of." Clearly this will require you to exercise some persuasion with Editorial. At the next meeting of the task force, Lyle Seashore is very late. You tell the other members that the topic has been approved as soon as they arrive, but after 15 minutes elapse and Seashore is still late, you have to decide what to do.

What would you do?

A. Ask your secretary to phone Seashore and remind him that the meeting is scheduled. (GO TO 352)

B. Go ahead anyway, with the idea that Gump can brief Seashore on the next step. (GO TO 442)

Decision Point 329

In deciding to act before consulting your boss, you are risking taking action that your boss would disagree with. This policy seems to have negative effects on your unit, so there is good reason to oppose it. However, the policy came from a level above your boss, so you do not want to oppose it without getting your boss' guidance. To remedy this situation, read the results of a discussion with Bill Banquet that appear below and then decide what to do.

Your meeting with Bill Banquet was unexpectedly short. Bill confessed to being distracted by Bob Jenson's resignation. Jenson was his administrative assistant. Jenson was known to be looking for another position, but the timing of his decision seemed to have taken Banquet by surprise.

You: "Did you see the memo about the new product planning policy?"
Bill: "Yes, I've seen it. I wasn't consulted on it in advance, but I was told that it was coming. I know the sales people are not going to like it."
You: "Not only that, but I doubt if my people can be expected to estimate their product needs within the 20% window. You know that our situation is different from the other groups."
Bill: "I know; I know. Listen, I've got to go. I've got to get over to Human Resources to sign the authorization forms to replace Jenson before my flight to Toledo. Look, do the best you can with the policy. I'll see you in a week."

What would you do now?

  A.   If you have not done so yet, phone a friend of yours who works as a financial analyst at the corporate level (Blake-Emerson--the parent company) for his perspective on how to respond to this policy change. (GO TO 310)

  B.   If you have not done so yet, call your predecessor (now with another firm) for his perspective on how to handle this situation. (GO TO 273)

  C.   Wait and bring this issue up at a weekly staff meeting of the sales managers (chaired by Bill Banquet). (GO TO 420)

  D.   Diplomatically oppose the new policy as it applies to your unique circumstances. Petition for an exemption. (GO TO 302)

  E.   Instruct your subordinates what to do about the new policy. (GO TO 400)

Decision Point 330

You tell your task force members that it is up to them to get the necessary relief from other responsibilities to devote time to the task force. This does not work very well.

Three members must miss the next meeting because of other commitments, after which tardiness becomes a serious problem. You miss several milestones, and the task force flounders significantly. One of the responsibilities of a task force chairman is to assure that task force members have the necessary time to devote to it. You failed this responsibility.

Re-evaluate your last decision. Circle the #330 you just wrote in your flow diagram. Then move to the last uncircled step in your flow diagram.

Decision Point 331

It is three weeks later, and in checking the progress of the assignment, you realize that it is behind schedule. A closer examination reveals several things. Brown and Johnson got their assumptions to other team members only one week late. Alton, Duckworth, and Spurior have yet to even begin their work on the assignment. The other team members are ready for the inputs of Alton's group, so a bottleneck has developed. When you confront Alton about the delay, he offers a somewhat believable excuse, but you are skeptical about whether his motives are honorable. What would you do about this?

A. Confront Alton again privately. Let him know that you expect his cooperation, and you will not tolerate any trouble from him (GO TO 396).

B. At the next weekly staff meeting, deliver a speech that emphasizes your confidence in everyone in the group. Reiterate the need for everybody to work toward objectives that are both professionally worthwhile and relevant to the needs of the company (GO TO 422).

C. Announce the charter that you were given by top management at the next weekly staff meeting. State your resolve to bring the department back into line with the needs of the organization (GO TO 288).

D. Mention at a weekly department meeting that you are pleased that Brown and Johnson gave so much thought to their assumptions and that Best, Bennet, and Banks have been excellent progress on the assignment. Say nothing about Alton, Duckworth, and Spurior (GO TO 323).

Decision Point 332

You tell your task force members that the meeting was productive and that you will follow up at the next meeting. The problem with this action is that the product of this meeting needs simplification. People have difficulty dealing with 52 separate items without simplifying them into categories of some type.

Re-evaluate your last decision. Circle the #332 you just wrote in your flow diagram. Then move to the last uncircled step in your flow diagram.

Decision Point 333

In deciding to act before consulting your boss, you are risking taking action that your boss would disagree with. This policy seems to have negative effects on your unit, so there is good reason to oppose it. However, the policy came from a level above your boss, so you do not want to oppose it without getting your boss' guidance. To remedy this situation, read the results of a discussion with Bill Banquet that appear below and then decide to do.

Your meeting with Bill Banquet was unexpectedly short. Bill confessed to being distracted by Bob Jenson's resignation that morning. Jenson was his administrative assistant. Jenson was known to be looking for another position, but the timing of his decision seemed to have taken Banquet by surprise.

You: "Did you see the memo about the new product planning policy?"
Bill: "Yes, I've seen it. I wasn't consulted on it in advance, but I was told that it was coming. I know the sales people are not going to like it."
You: "Not only that, but I doubt if my people can be expected to estimate their product needs within the 20% window. You know that our situation is different from the other groups."
Bill: "I know; I know. Listen, I've got to go. I've got to get over to Human Resources to sign the authorization forms to replace Jenson before my flight to Toledo. Look, do the best you can with the policy. I'll see you in a week."

What would you do now?

A. If you have not done so yet, phone a friend of yours who works as a financial analyst at the corporate level (Blake-Emerson--the parent company) for his perspective on how to respond to this policy change. (GO TO 310)

B. If you have not done so yet, call your predecessor (now with another firm) for his perspective on how to handle this situation. (GO TO 273)

C. Wait and bring this issue up at a weekly staff meeting of the sales managers (chaired by Bill Banquet). (GO TO 420)

D. Diplomatically oppose the new policy as it applies to your unique circumstances. Petition for an exemption. (GO TO 302)

E. Instruct your subordinates what to do about the new policy. (GO TO 400)

Decision Point 334

You decide to return to the members and tell them that the publisher has rejected their topic. There is no reason to do this until you have exhausted every possible way to persuade him. Hang tough.

Re-evaluate your last decision. Circle the #334 you just wrote in your flow diagram. Then move to the last uncircled step in your flow diagram.

Decision Point 335

The staffing plan is completed, but one week behind schedule. This does not cause serious problems, but it does raise a few eyebrows among top management. They are pleased, though, that for the first time in several years, your department proposes no staffing increases.

In tracing the delay, you find out that Luke Spurior and George Bennet had a minor dispute over an interpretation in affirmative action guidelines. Bennet wanted to include an interpretation of the guidelines that he knew top management would object to, and Spurior convinced him to be less contrary.

There are now only three weeks left to complete the most difficult assignment of all--the new personnel policies. How would you organize the meetings to accomplish this assignment?

A. Serve as chair of the meetings yourself and assume responsibility for setting the agenda and directing the meetings. Allow other members to volunteer for other roles (taking notes, maintaining files, making the final presentation to top management, and performing necessary research) (GO TO 356).

B. Appoint Spurior the chair, and work with him privately on the agenda (GO TO 413).

Decision Point 336

Much to your surprise, Seashore expresses nothing negative after hearing about the need to get background material to Operations 36 hours before press time. Instead, he and Foy work very closely during the next four weeks to see to it that everything involved in the project between Operations and Editorial runs smoothly. Operations does in fact get nearly all of the background within the agreed-on time limit.

When the special seasonal issue hits the streets, it is extremely successful. All three local television stations quote the edition in their prime-time news programs, and the next month, thanks to a two-for-one special subscription offer (timed by the external subgroup), circulation is up over 6 percent!

Congratulations! You have successfully completed the Managing a Task Force Interactive Case.

Decision Point 337

You have an opportunity to chat with three of your peers (Amy Holcott is out of town). All of them expressed irritability with the new policy, but none seemed put out enough to fight it. Don James' (Sales Manager--Pneumatic Products) opinion was typical:

"I don't know if my people are good enough planners for us to make our estimates within the 20% window. I suspect that they are, but there's no telling. Right now, with the market so sour, most of our business is repeat business. My hunch is that simply keeping our estimates to the high side of historical figures should suffice, at least that's what I am telling my people to do. They're sure not going to like the extra paperwork, that I can assure you. But most of my sales engineers are still jittery about being laid off, so it shouldn't be too bad."

What would you do now?

A. Speak with Bill Banquet (your boss) about his "reading" of the new policy. (GO TO 363)

B. Call your predecessor (now with another firm) for his perspective on how to handle this situation. (GO TO 273)

C. Wait and bring this issue up at a weekly staff meeting of the sales managers (chaired by Bill Banquet). (GO TO 420)

D. Diplomatically oppose the new policy as it applies to your unique circumstances. Petition for an exemption. (GO TO 329)

E. Instruct your subordinates what to do about the new policy. (GO TO 333)

Decision Point 338

You ask your the members if they would like to hear from the publisher. They all indicate that would be helpful. You excuse yourself from the meeting and call the publisher's office. His secretary tells you that he is in a meeting after which he is leaving for an extended trip to Washington, DC and Eastern Europe. You know it will be at least two weeks before you can get the publisher to attend a meeting. You tell the group what you have learned. Now what?

A. Let the discussion continue to see if Foy and Smithers can counter Seashore and Gump. (GO TO 297)

B. Make the statement, "I don't think it's the task force's role to redefine the charter given to us by the publisher." (GO TO 427)

C. Say, "I understand your position, Lyle, but I really believe the publisher's involvement is a function of his interests and not an intention of interfering. My sense is that if we do approach him with this, that's what he will say. Why don't we proceed with our assignment and see?" (GO TO 424)

Decision Point 339

During this second one month period when you have given your department no group assignment, what would you do?

A. Take a tough stand with Bob Alton. Let him know privately that you expect his cooperation, and you will not tolerate any trouble from him (GO TO 410).

B. Let others in your group know privately that you think that Alton must have been disappointed about being passed over for your job. Tell him you look forward to working with him. Express a willingness to support those who work for the Department and to oppose those who do not (GO TO 416).

C. At the next weekly staff meeting, deliver a speech that emphasizes your confidence in everyone in the group. Reiterate the need for everybody to work toward objectives that are both professionally worthwhile and relevant to the needs of the company (GO TO 350).

D.   Announce the charter that you were given by top management at the next weekly staff meeting. State your resolve to bring the department back into line with the needs of the organization (GO TO 365).

Decision Point 340

You try to control a dominating member by "taking him on." This approach may work on occasion, but it frequently distracts the group or creates animosity.

Re-evaluate your last decision. Circle the #340 you just wrote in your flow diagram. Then move to the last uncircled step in your flow diagram.

Decision Point 341

You have a chance to "buttonhole" several of the other sales managers. Their comments follow:

Sandra Smith (Sales Mgr--Hydraulic Products): "I'll tell you one thing. My sales engineers certainly don't like the extra paperwork, but we've done pretty well making the 20% window. In fact (she winks), it feels good moving from #4 to #2! All kidding aside, I think it's good that we now require our salespeople to plan their product needs. After all, the personnel people are always harping that we should prepare them for moving into the managerial ranks."

Brian Robinson (Sales Mgr--Delivery Systems): "All that sounds fine and good, but the fact remains that the policy penalizes those of us who have uncertain demand or complex lines. No, this thing is stupid. The strategic plan for this year identifies my line as vitally important, and then they turn around and discourage our development of new accounts because one can never plan them systematically. I've talked to Banquet about this and he agrees, but he hasn't done anything about it!"

Don James (Sales Mgr--Pneumatic Products): "My sales engineers have had a helluva time getting their numbers right. Even with our standard lines, they consistently overestimated their needs. I suspect that they will get better and that the product will be available. It's creating hell with our volume, I'll tell you."

What would you do now? (Bill Banquet is out of town.)

A.   Talk with Sterling Cartwright, Bill Banquet's new administrative assistant. (GO TO 432)

B.   Meet privately with Brian Robinson to work out a strategy for addressing this policy problem. (GO TO 414)

C.   Instruct your subordinates about what to do now. (GO TO 429)

Decision Point 342

You send members a one-page biography of their new colleagues and ask them to introduce themselves at the beginning of the meeting. This works acceptably until the public introductions. At that point Seashore and Gump give glowing introductions of themselves and Foy and Smithers say very little. This dominance by the Editorial Department people carries over into the initial discussions, and you conclude that you should have used some other device for the initial introductions.

Re-evaluate your last decision. Circle the #342 you just wrote in your flow diagram, and then move to the last uncircled step in your flow diagram.

Decision Point 343

You have a chance to "buttonhole" several of the other sales managers. Their comments follow:

Sandra Smith (Sales Mgr--Hydraulic Products): "I'll tell you one thing. My sales engineers certainly don't like the extra paperwork, but we've been able to do pretty well making the 20% window. In fact (she winks), it feels good moving from #4 to #2! All kidding aside, I think it's good that we now require our salespeople to plan their product needs. After all, the personnel people are always harping that we should prepare them for moving into the managerial ranks."

Brian Robinson (Sales Mgr--Delivery Systems): "All that sounds fine and good, but the fact remains that the policy penalizes those of us who have uncertain demand or complex lines. No, this thing is stupid. The strategic plan for this year identifies my line as vitally important, and then they turn around and discourage our development of new accounts because one can never plan them systematically. I've talked to Banquet about this and he agrees, but he hasn't done anything about it!"

Don James (Sales Mgr--Pneumatic Products): "My sales engineers have had a helluva time getting their numbers right. Even with our standard lines, they consistently overestimated their needs. I suspect that they will get better and that the product will be available. It's creating hell with our volume, I'll tell you."

What would you do now? (Bill Banquet is out of town.)

A. Go see Mildred Barnes of the Product Planning Department. (GO TO 322)

B. Since Bill Banquet is out of town, talk with Sterling Cartwright (his new administrative assistant). (GO TO 285)

C. Phone William Barstow, your friend at the corporate headquarters. (GO TO 417)

D. Meet privately with Brian Robinson to work out a strategy for addressing this policy problem. (GO TO 348)

E. Instruct your subordinates about what to do now. (GO TO 429)

Decision Point 344

You invite your assistant in to man the flip chart and the group begins brainstorming. The ideas come rapidly at first, so fast that your assistant has difficulty keeping up. Then when Smithers suggests the topic of the marketing of baby formula on the local Indian reservation, Gump breaks in and says, "That's very old news. The Tucson Gazette had a story on that last year."

This remark violates the rules of brainstorming. Would you interrupt to remind Gump of the rules?

A. Yes. (GO TO 430)

B. No, let it ride this time. (GO TO 374)

Decision Point 345

Your statement is taken as a signal that the policy assignment is unimportant ("only words"). Several Department members put forth little effort on the assignment. Most seriously, when you hand the President's secretary the completed report, she asks you if it is "just words for stodgy old management?"

Re-evaluate your last decision. Circle the #345 you just wrote in your flow diagram. Then go back in your flow diagram to the first uncircled number above this step.

Decision Point 346

You instruct your subordinates to ignore the policy. Two days after the planning reports are due you receive a call from Justin Fenwick's secretary. He says that unless you submit them at once, you cannot expect adequate supplies of product to meet sales. You are now left with no option but to comply. Now, however, you have been identified as uncooperative and resistant to change, and this label reduces your ability to mount a campaign for an exemption.

Re-evaluate your last decision. Circle the #346 you just wrote in your flow diagram, and move to the last uncircled step in your flow diagram.

Decision Point 347

You chose the combination of Gump, Seashore, Fitzgerald, and Smithers. There is only one thing wrong with this combination. You opted to include two members of the Sales/Marketing Department. This prevents you from representing Operations. Since the objective here is creativity and coordination, you want much more diversity on your task force. Moreover, the fact that Fitzgerald and Smithers do not get along well (from Fitzgerald's point of view) makes this particular combination not very appealing. If you had to choose between them, Smithers is probably a better choice (for his social skills and his more established reputation).

Re-evaluate your last decision. Circle the #347 you just wrote in your flow diagram. Then move to the last uncircled step in your flow diagram.

Decision Point 348

You meet privately with Brian Robinson to discuss how you might approach the policy problem together. You agree that your first step should be information gathering. Robinson agrees to talk with Sterling Cartwright if you will contact Mildred Barnes and William Barstow. You first contact Mildred Barnes. Mildred Barnes and you have established a pleasant relationship during the past month. Through mutual and harmless teasing you have built a rapport that both of you relish. When you ask her opinions about the new policy, she replies:

"You know why the policy was created, don't you? Well, Billingsworth was facing significant pressure from corporate headquarters to cut staff personnel. Justin (Fenwick) had been successful in protecting us until then. When the axe fell, we could no longer do all the product planning for manufacturing like we had been doing. You know, we had been analyzing sales trends and setting manufacturing requirements accordingly. Well, the new policy was followed by a 22% cut in our staff. Jack Collins was the last of these cuts, and he left just last week. I was really lucky to survive this purge, believe me...

"Your group and Robinson's are the most hard-hit. But that's not really surprising. When we were doing the product forecasting, your two units were always the hardest to predict. Don't quote me, but you are getting screwed in all this. If you ask me, product scheduling is headed toward shorter time frames. Now we are asking for projections one month ahead. In the next few months with our new computer models, we can shorten that to two weeks."

Later in the conversation she says, "If your people are having a rough time, there is one thing I could do--training. I've been teaching planning methods at a junior college where I live. I'd be more than willing to work with your salespeople to give them tools to use in figuring their product requirements."

You next contact William Barstow. He says:

"Well, by now you've heard about the personnel cuts in Product Planning. My hunch that personnel cuts are now a thing of past is a conviction. This quarter's earnings are up, and it now appears that we are about as lean as we can be.

"I've checked with some of my contacts. It's clear that your policy problem is not without precedent in the corporation. Two other divisions in Atlanta and Trenton have their salespeople estimate product demand as part of the planning effort. Marketing managers there gave their sales people extensive training on statistical estimation procedures. Each has access to a computer terminal so they can report deviations from the plan in real time."

When you meet Brian Robinson again, he characterizes his conversation with Cartwright as totally worthless: "The guy's a spineless lackey who will never express an independent thought. He just wants to protect his boss, that's all. He's a jerk."

From these inputs, it seems that you two have three major alternatives: (1) lobby for an exemption for strategically important units (your unit and Robinson's are strategically important), (2) lobby for planning period reduction from one month to one or two weeks, or (3) lobby for training for your sales engineers. You both agree that alternative (1) is the most preferred, (2) is the second best, and (3) is the worst. You now have to decide how to go forward with your proposals for policy modifications.

Which would you do?

A. Once he returns, propose alternative (1) to Banquet, being prepared to settle for alternatives (2) or (3) if he does not think it feasible. (GO TO 438)

B. Same as A above except begin by asking Banquet his assessment of how well the policy is working. (GO TO 276)

Decision Point 349

You decide to say nothing at this point about your boss's desire that the topic chosen has market appeal. This is a serious mistake. Although you realize that Seashore will object, it is important to give your task force a complete assignment at the outset of its deliberations. Otherwise it is likely to select a topic that will be unacceptable to the publisher.

Re-evaluate your last decision. Circle the #349 you just wrote in your flow diagram. Then move to the last uncircled step in your flow diagram.

Decision Point 350

You have elected to give a pep talk to try to create an over-riding goal that will replace the antagonistic norms with supportive norms. The result is very disappointing. "Professional" norms die hard, and your superordinate goal is not very compelling. Consequently, the group thinks you have "sold out" to a manufacturing orientation that is "the enemy."

The group is not yet stable in a P-3 position. You should continue to work on the group to make sure that cohesiveness declines around its antagonistic norms.

Re-evaluate your last decision. Circle the #350 you just wrote in your flow diagram. Then go back in your flow diagram to the first uncircled number above this step.

Decision Point 351

The group responds very negatively to the new policy. They grouse at having to process more paperwork and express pessimism at trying to forecast their needs with the required accuracy. Their first month's estimates are very uneven. Some of your people spend a great deal of effort on their plans and some approach it in entirely too cavalier a fashion. The estimates are accordingly among the least accurate in the Marketing Department. While you expected miscalculations, you did not expect this.

Re-evaluate your last decision. Circle the #351 you just wrote in your flow diagram, and move to the last uncircled step in your flow diagram.

Decision Point 352

Seashore comes rushing into the meeting and apologizes for his lateness. He seems delighted to learn that the publisher has approved the topic. You then outline the charge to the two coordination subcommittees, one made up of Smithers and Gump (for external coordination) and one composed of Seashore and Foy (for internal coordination).

You are much less concerned about the external coordination group than the internal one, since the latter involves work with Operations, and you are worried that Seashore may object to the deal the publisher made with Operations about having background copy available to Operations 36 hours in advance of press time.

How would you deal with this issue?

A. Tell Foy privately of the deal that the publisher made with his boss (the Vice President of Operations) and instruct him to advise you if it is in jeopardy as the subgroup proceeds with its activities. Say nothing to Seashore about the arrangement. (GO TO 392)

B. Meet with Foy and Seashore together (but separate from the task force) and tell them both of the agreement the Publisher has with the Vice President of Operations. (GO TO 336)

C. Say nothing to anyone at this point, but monitor the progress of the internal coordination subgroup closely. (GO TO 303)

Decision Point 353

Your statement that top management has challenged the assessment report stimulates an outpouring of resentment and alienation. Brown is defensive. Duckworth expresses her anti-manufacturing attitudes, and the others reflect anger and frustration. Under these circumstances, the performance on subsequent assignments is marginal, and top management continues dissatisfied with your Department's work.

You have missed a tremendous opportunity to give the group (now in a P-2 condition) an experienced group success. Instead, you have created an enemy in top management. A more diplomatic approach would have yielded a more successful outcome.

Re-evaluate your last decision. Circle the #353 you just wrote in your flow diagram. Then go back in your flow diagram to the first uncircled number above this step.

Decision Point 354

You have a chance to "buttonhole" several of the other sales managers.

Sandra Smith (Sales Mgr--Hydraulic Products): "I'll tell you one thing. My sales engineers certainly don't like the extra paperwork, but we've done pretty well making the 20% window. In fact (she winks), it feels good moving from #4 to #2! All kidding aside, I think it's good that we now require our salespeople to plan their product needs. After all, the personnel people are always harping that we should prepare them for moving into the managerial ranks."

Brian Robinson (Sales Mgr--Delivery Systems): "All that sounds fine and good, but the fact remains that the policy penalizes those of us who have uncertain demand or complex lines. No, this thing is stupid. The strategic plan for this year identifies my line as vitally important, and then they turn around and discourage our development of new accounts because one can never plan them systematically. I've talked to Banquet about this and he agrees, but he hasn't done anything about it!"

Don James (Sales Mgr--Pneumatic Products): "My sales engineers have had a helluva time getting their numbers right. Even with our standard lines, they consistently overestimated their needs. I suspect that they will get better and that the product will be available. It's creating hell with our volume, I'll tell you."

What would you do now? (Bill Banquet is out of town.)

A. Go see Mildred Barnes of the Product Planning Department. (GO TO 397)

B. Phone William Barstow, your friend at the corporate headquarters. (GO TO 359)

C. Meet privately with Brian Robinson to work out a strategy for addressing this policy problem. (GO TO 348)

D. Instruct your subordinates about what to do now. (GO TO 429)

Decision Point 355

You stand at the flip chart and play the role of recorder yourself. This does not work very well. You find that you are so busy writing you don't have any inputs to the listing. This in effect reduces the size of the group from five to four, and the group comes up with only 31 ideas.

Re-evaluate your last decision. Circle the #355 you just wrote in your flow diagram, and move to the last uncircled step in your flow diagram.

Decision Point 356

How would you give your team its assignment?

A.   Review the progress of the Department since you became Director, and congratulate everyone specifically for their contribution. Indicate that the policy statement should be conservative. Persuade them that this will not jeopardize longer-range concerns that are infeasible today. Tell them that a radical document will make future reforms impossible (GO TO 404).

B.   Acknowledge the sensitivity around developing a human resources policy. Be honest in labelling top management as conservative and stodgy. Tell them that the only way to judge the accomplishments of the Department is in actions not words (GO TO 345).

C.   Admit your own need to have a document that will be something that is credible and realistic (GO TO 320).

Decision Point 357

You present your proposal, and it goes well. Banquet agrees to lobby with Fenwick and Billingsworth to explore the possibility of shorter time frames for certain products, especially those that are strategically important. This proposal is appealing to both parties. It is a practice used in other divisions of the corporation, and it allows Fenwick to argue effectively for restoring some of his staff cuts. Banquet also agrees to free up $2,500 from his discretionary budget for training to cover the time it requires to take your case to Billingsworth and Fenwick. Both actions bear fruit. Two months later the policy is modified to suit your unit's needs, and all but one product plan falls within the 20% window. No customers are lost due to the inventory underage contingency.

In order to successfully oppose the new policy, you had to develop a coalition and build a rational case for modifying the policy. This was possible only because you were able to collect information before expressing your opposition publicly and irrevocably. Congratulations! You have just completed the Organizational Politics Interactive Case.

Decision Point 358

You wait out the silence, and the first few ideas that emerge are truly fabulous. This stimulates a second burst of ideas from the group that lasts almost five minutes. A second silence overcomes the group, and you wait through that one as you did the first. However, few ideas of any merit arise.

With the task force becoming rather tired and the scheduled end of the meeting approaching, you decide to call an end to this session. A total of 52 different topic ideas have been generated. You instruct your assistant to duplicate and distribute the results of the brainstorming meeting to the participants.

What instructions would you give the members?

A. Ask them to look over the list of prospective topics that came out of this meeting and put them into categories that make sense to them. (GO TO 395)

B. Tell them that the meeting was very productive, and you will follow up with the discussion at the next meeting. (GO TO 332)

C. Ask each member to rank order the ideas that have been derived on the basis of 1 = best and 52 = worst. (GO TO 280)

Decision Point 359

Will Barstow has much to say, "Well, by now you've heard about the personnel cuts in Product Planning. My hunch is that these are the last cuts. This quarter's earnings are up, and it now appears that we are about as lean as we can be.

"I've checked with some of my contacts. It's clear that your policy problem is not without precedent in the corporation. Two other divisions in Atlanta and Trenton have their salespeople estimate product demand as part of the planning effort. Marketing managers there gave their salespeople extensive training in statistical estimation procedures. Each has access to a computer terminal so they can report deviations from the plan in real time."

As you hang up the phone, Mildred Barnes of the Product Planning Department appears in the doorway of your office. Mildred Barnes and you have established a pleasant relationship during the past month. Through mutual and harmless teasing, you have built a rapport that both of you relish. When you ask her views of the policy, she has much to say.

"You know why the policy was created, don't you? Well, Billings-worth was facing significant pressure from corporate to cut staff personnel. Justin (Fenwick) had been successful in protecting us until then. When the axe fell, we could no longer do all the product planning for manufacturing. You know we had been analyzing sales trends and setting manufacturing requirements accordingly. Well, the new policy was followed by a 22% cut in our staff. Jack Collins was the last of these cuts, and he left just last week. I was really lucky to survive this purge, believe me...

"Your group and Robinson's are the most hard-hit. But that's not really surprising. When we were doing the product forecasting, your two units were always the hardest to predict. Don't quote me, but you are getting screwed in all this.

"If you ask me, product scheduling is going toward shorter time frames. Now we are asking for projections one month ahead. In the next few months with our new computer models, we can shorten that to two weeks."

Later in the conversation she says, "...If your people are having a rough time, there is one thing I could do--training. I've been teaching planning methods at a junior college where I live. I'd be more than willing to work with your salespeople to give them tools to use in figuring their product requirements."

What would you do now?

A.   Meet privately with Brian Robinson to work out a strategy for how to address this policy problem. (GO TO 414)

B.   Instruct your subordinates about what to do now. (GO TO 429)

Decision Point 360

This works very well. Seashore recedes from the discussion a bit and Foy, Gump, and you begin discussing the issue of evaluative criteria. However, you notice that Smithers is saying nothing.

What would you say to draw him into the discussion?

A. "Smithers, we haven't heard from you for awhile. What is your position on the question of criteria?" (GO TO 403)

B. "I hope by the time we are finished with this discussion, everyone who has something to say feels that they have had a chance to make their feelings known." (GO TO 436)

Decision Point 361

In making this assignment and in conducting yourself in weekly department meetings and at public occasions, what would you do?

A. Suggest that these labor negotiations are a real opportunity for the Department to regain its credibility with top management. State that it will take a coordinated effort to overcome what will surely be a tough bargaining stand by the union (GO TO 292).

B. Change the format of weekly department meetings to allow more group discussion where members have concerns (GO TO 372).

C. Take every opportunity to reinforce and publicly acknowledge any efforts in line with top management's concern that Human Resources become more relevant to the realities of the firm (GO TO 331).

Decision Point 362

Your technique of having task force members get to know each other works very well. By emphasizing common elements in the personal backgrounds of your members in your introductions, you find that Seashore and Smithers (an unlikely pair) were graduates of the same college and that Foy and Gump share a love for hiking in wilderness parks.

The break at its end, you now face the need to give the task force its charter. You map out your experiences chairing the last six special edition task forces and express your genuine hope that this coming special edition will be truly significant. You detail two major goals of the task force: to identify a topic for the seasonal edition that will be a contribution to the community and region and to facilitate the coordination problems associated with the special edition.

You also announce that, as in the past, the task force will operate as a whole at the beginning until an acceptable topic is arrived at. After that the task force will break into two subunits--one for internal coordination and the other for external coordination. (It is your experience that one subcommittee can be responsible for coordinating between Editorial and Sales/Marketing [external coordination] and the other for coordinating between Editorial and Operations [internal coordination].) Tentatively, you plan to assign Smithers and Gump to the group that is responsible for external affairs and Foy and Seashore to the group that is concerned with internal coordination.

You have already decided to sidestep the issue of objectives, but when you give the task force its charter from your boss, what will you tell them?

A.   Your boss's concern that the topic chosen has market appeal, the ample budget, and your boss's desire to approve the topic. (GO TO 368)

B.   Your boss's concern that the topic chosen has market appeal and the ample budget. Say nothing at this point of your boss's desire to approve the topic. (GO TO 321)

C.   Your boss's concern that the topic chosen has market appeal and his desire to approve the topic. Say nothing at this point about the budget he has given you. (GO TO 386)

D.   Your budget and your boss's desire to approve the topic. Say nothing at this point about your boss's concern that the topic chosen have market appeal. (GO TO 349)

Decision Point 363

Your meeting with Bill Banquet was unexpectedly short. Bill confessed to being distracted by the resignation that morning of Bob Jenson, his administrative assistant. Jenson was known to be looking for another position, but the timing of his decision seemed to have taken Banquet by surprise.

You: "Did you see the memo about the new product planning policy?"
Bill: "Yes, I've seen it. I wasn't consulted on it in advance, but I was told that it was coming. I know the sales people are not going to like it."
You: "Not only that, but I doubt if my people can be expected to estimate their product needs within the 20% window. You know that our situation is different from the other groups."

Bill: "I know; I know. Listen, I've got to go. I've got to get over to Human Resources to sign the authorization forms to replace Jenson before my flight to Toledo. Look, do the best you can with the policy. I'll see you in a week."

What would you do now?

A.   Call your predecessor (now with another firm) for his perspective on how to handle this situation. (GO TO 273)

B.   Wait and bring this issue up at a weekly staff meeting of the sales managers (chaired by Bill Banquet). (GO TO 420)

C.   Diplomatically oppose the new policy as it applies to your unique circumstances. Petition for an exemption. (GO TO 302)

D.   Instruct your subordinates what to do about the new policy. (GO TO 400)

Decision Point 364

You decide to tape-record the session. This has two rather negative results. First, the presence of the tape recorder has a chilling effect. Even though the members are professionals used to having their words transcribed, it does hold down especially "wild" ideas, and the proceedings take on the appearance of a much more businesslike meeting than most brainstorming sessions should. In addition, since the participants cannot see your notes, there is much less piggy-backing of ideas.

Re-evaluate your last decision. Circle the #364 you just wrote in your flow diagram. Then move to the last uncircled step in your flow diagram.

Decision Point 365

Your statement solves a problem your group has been having with your leadership--they were not sure whether your allegiance was to them or the "opposition" (top management). By announcing your charter, you place yourself clearly in top management's corner. The results are predictable. You are cut off from upward communication and treated as a "lackey." Surely, you cannot remedy this negative impression for some time.

Re-evaluate your last decision. Circle the #365 you just wrote in your flow diagram. Then go back in your flow diagram to the first uncircled number above this step.

Decision Point 366

You leave your boss's office feeling a bit defeated but resolved to put together the most persuasive presentation possible at your next meeting with him. You know that Harrison Gump and his reporters are already working on the topic, and you believe that if you are to convince your boss, you need some of the facts that they are uncovering. The problem is that you don't want to let the group know you are having problems convincing the publisher that the task force's topic is satisfactory.

How would you handle this situation?

A. Go directly to the reporters involved and get the information from them. (GO TO 377)

B. Go to Harrison Gump directly and confess that you are having some difficulty convincing your boss and ask his help. (GO TO 295)

C. Go to Gump and ask his help in "making the best case you can" for the topic that the task force has chosen, but say nothing about the publisher's initial resistance to the idea. (GO TO 328)

Decision Point 367

Sterling Cartwright is a man of about 40 who has been with the company for only three weeks. You ask him about Banquet's opinion of the way the new policy is working. He responds: "Bill is concerned. He really is. He doesn't like the way it puts the burden on you. Just the other day he met with Mr. Billingsworth about it."

You ask him what Banquet is doing about this situation. "Bill has a plan, and I'm sure it will work in time, but with the cuts in product planning, things are a bit uncertain. I'm sure you can expect something in the next few months."

What would you do now? (Bill Banquet is out of town.)

A. Talk to your peers about their experience with the new policy. (GO TO 354)

B. Go see Mildred Barnes of the Product Planning Department. (GO TO 447)

C. Phone William Barstow, your friend at the corporate headquarters. (GO TO 306)

D. Instruct your subordinates about what to do now. (GO TO 429)

You decide to tell your task force everything you know about your task force's charter, its budget, and the involvement the publisher wants. By doing this, you provide the members with all the information that will have to be a part of their decisions. You also begin to establish the norm that group members should be honest with each other. However, your statement beings a very heated discussion at this, your first meeting.

Foy: "Wow, that's a lot of money. The old man really wants to throw money at this issue."

Seashore: "My concern is that he's trying to buy us off for his involvement. I can tell you that the people in Editorial are not going to like this . . . not one bit."

Gump: "That's for sure. You can't run a newspaper without offering reporters more independence than that. I was concerned when he nixed a story on toxic waste, but I'm beginning to feel just this side of outrage."

Smithers: "Harrison, Harrison, you're going to burst an artery."

Foy: "Just because he's asking to see our topic before we proceed doesn't mean that he's going to veto it."

Seashore: "That's not the point. I don't know about you, but I don't want to have to consider how the old man will react to every topic we come up with. That's ludicrous!"

Gump (turning to Seashore): "You are the master of understatement, my friend."

You are concerned that Gump and Seashore perceive the independence of the task force to be a matter of principle and may escalate the issue to the Vice President of the Editorial Department.

What would you do at this point?

A.   Don't intervene at this point. Let the discussion unfold a bit more to see if Foy and Smithers can counter Seashore and Gump. (GO TO 297)

B.   Break into the discussion with the statement, "I don't think it's the task force's role to redefine the charter given to us by the publisher." (GO TO 427)

C.   Say, "I understand your position, Lyle, but I really believe the publisher's involvement is a function of his interests and not an intention of interfering.

My sense is that if we do approach him with this, that's what he will say. Why don't we proceed with our assignment and see?" (GO TO 424)

D.   Say, "Would you like me to ask the Publisher what his intentions are?" (GO TO 338)

Decision Point 369

It is one month later, and your team is evidently getting used to your style of management. On several occasions, you have publicly recognized excellent performance and called attention to a need for improvement where it was necessary. While the group seems ambivalent toward you, there is less talk about top management being overly conservative. In addition, you sense that Alton is losing his influence with the team. Although Duckworth and Spurior continue to be loyal to him, Brown and Johnson seem increasingly indifferent to his leadership. One thing that troubles you is that Alton is being very quiet at department meetings. You have heard that he has quietly ridiculed some of your statements and actions.

By working *individually* with group members, you are creating stronger bonds between the employees and you than they have between each other. This has the effect of decreasing the cohesiveness of the group, i.e., from P-4 to P-3.

There are now four months left until your department's three assignments are due. What would you do now?

A.   Assignment 1 -- Preparation for Labor Negotiations. In five months your department begins negotiations with the Sheetmetal Workers Union for the first time in two years. Since the contract will affect each department member's specialty, you will solicit everyone's inputs. Bunkie Brown will draw up a list of probable union demands. He will send these department members for their assessment of economic and administrative impacts. You will then aggregate these assessments into an integrated impact report that will serve to determine the company's negotiating strategy (GO TO 361).

B.   Assignment 2 -- Development of an Integrated Personnel Policy. Top management has asked you to assess departmental policies. It is due in five months. Preparing this document will involve intensive meetings of all department members (GO TO 393).

C.   Assignment 3 -- Creation of an Annual Staffing Plan. In five months the staffing plan for the next fiscal year is due. This is a serial process beginning with Roy Best who estimates promotions and transfers. This then goes to Bob Alton's group (Alton, Duckworth, and Spurior) who calculates new staffing needs. Then it travels on to George Bennet who justifies these figures into the affirmative action plan. Finally, Floyd Banks transposes these estimates into a budget form (GO TO 428).

D.   Hold off on making an assignment for one more month (GO TO 378).

Decision Point 370

In deciding to act before consulting your peers, you now lack adequate information about the potential force that might be mobilized in opposition to this policy. Accordingly, your last decision was not correct. To remedy this situation, the results of a discussion with your peers are shown below.

You have an opportunity to chat with three of your peers (Amy Holcott is out of town). All of them expressed irritability with the new policy, but none seemed put out enough to fight it. Don James' (Sales Manager--Pneumatic Products) opinion was typical:

"I don't know if my people are good enough planners for us to make our estimates within the 20% window. I suspect that they are, but there's no telling. Right now, with the market so sour, most of our business is repeat business. My hunch is that simply keeping our estimates to the high side of historical figures should suffice, at least that's what I am telling my people to do. They're sure not going to like the extra paperwork, that I can assure you. But most of my sales engineers are still jittery about being laid off, so it shouldn't be too bad."

What would you do now?

A.   If you have not done so yet, phone a friend of yours who works as a financial analyst at the corporate level (Blake-Emerson--the parent company) for his perspective on how to respond to this policy change. (GO TO 310)

B.   If you have not done so yet, call your predecessor (now with another firm) for his perspective on how to handle this situation. (GO TO 273)

C.   Wait and bring this issue up at a weekly staff meeting of the sales managers (chaired by Bill Banquet). (GO TO 420)

413

D. Diplomatically oppose the new policy as it applies to your unique circumstances. Petition for an exemption. (GO TO 302)

E. Instruct your subordinates what to do about the new policy. (GO TO 400)

Decision Point 371

You decide to takes notes yourself on a note pad. This arrangement does not work well. You find that you are so busy writing you don't have any inputs to the listing. This in effect reduces the size of the group from five to four, and the group only comes up with 31 ideas. In addition, since the participants cannot see your notes, there is much less piggy-backing of ideas.

Re-evaluate your last decision. Circle the #371 you just wrote in your flow diagram, and move to the last uncircled step in your diagram.

Decision Point 372

At the first meeting where you call for discussion of concerns, there is little response. At the next meeting, however, Jane Duckworth delivers a passionate speech that expresses her strong professional values in contrast to the "narrow thinking in manufacturing." Other team members express similar attitudes and even sorrow over the "firing" of your predecessor. At this point you intervene, but it is too late.

Essentially, by opening weekly meetings to a discussion of concerns, you have in effect created conditions of more complex work relationships. Since your team is presently in at best a P-3 state, your action is premature. All you have done is provide a forum for expressing a sense of powerlessness that may restore the antagonistic norms that are beginning to erode.

Re-evaluate your last decision. Circle the #372 you just wrote in your flow diagram. Then go back in your flow diagram to the first uncircled number above this step.

Decision Point 373

You have known William Barstow for years. You attended the same university together. When you tell him of the policy directive, he gives you some interesting information:

"I haven't heard anything about the policy, but I can tell you that the Fluid Products Division is getting a lot of heat to get its costs under control. The word is that Billingsworth's argument that his division has strong profit potential is no longer credible until he can produce the numbers. The division is now under considerable pressure not to cut its line personnel, but rather its staff. One view from these lofty heights is that the axe is due to fall soon on just about every staff unit in the Division."

If true, this would mean that Justin Fenwick's group is in for some cuts, but your group should not be affected.

What would you do now?

A. Talk with your peers (the other sales managers who report to Bill Banquet) to gauge their reaction to the new policy. (GO TO 314)

B. Call your predecessor (now with another firm) for his perspective on how to handle this situation. (GO TO 273)

C. Wait and bring this issue up at a weekly staff meeting of the sales managers (chaired by Bill Banquet). (GO TO 420)

D. Diplomatically oppose the new policy as it applies to your unique circumstances. Petition for an exemption. (GO TO 426)

E. Instruct your subordinates what to do about the new policy. (GO TO 370)

Decision Point 374

Gump continues to make evaluative remarks, and in time Foy also begins signaling his displeasure with body language and sighs.

Brainstorming requires compliance with its no-evaluation rule. You should have enforced that rule as soon as the first violation appeared. Let's assume you had done so and proceed with the case.

The brainstorming begins again, and sheet after sheet of flip chart paper is filled and taped to the walls of your conference room. This goes on for about 20 minutes, and then there is a prolonged lull in the group.

At this point what would you do?

A.   Wait out the silence. (GO TO 358)

B.   Call off the session since it is clear that the group has exhausted its creative potential. (GO TO 291)

C.   Ask if anyone has any more ideas. (GO TO 301)

Decision Point 375

You publicly congratulate Floyd Banks, Bunkie Brown, and Steve Johnson on a job well done on the staffing plan. However, Roy Best and George Bennet had done good work too. Because of this oversight, Best and Bennet take a minor role in the next assignment. Consequently, the policy document lacks direction and focus in their areas of concern.

You have worked hard to move the group from its initial P-4 condition to its position in P-2 or P-3. However, by singling out some individuals and not others, you have kept the group from building cohesiveness that would have had a positive impact on performance.

Re-evaluate your last decision. Circle the #375 you just wrote in your flow diagram. Then go back in your flow diagram to the first uncircled number above this step.

Decision Point 376

You decided to act before consulting either your boss or your peers. This was incorrect. First, in deciding to act before consulting your peers, you now lack adequate information about the potential force that might be mobilized in opposing this policy. To remedy this situation, the results of a discussion with your peers is shown below.

You have an opportunity to chat with three of your peers (Amy Holcott is out of town). All of them expressed irritability with the new policy, but none seemed put out enough to fight it. Don James' (Sales Manager--Pneumatic Products) opinion was typical:

"I don't know if my people are good enough planners for us to make our estimates within the 20% window. I suspect that they are, but there's no telling. Right now, with the market so sour, most of our business is repeat business. My hunch is that simply keeping our estimates to the high side of historical figures should suffice, at least that's what I am telling my people to do. They're sure not going to like the extra paperwork, that I can assure you. But most of my sales engineers are still jittery about being laid off, so it shouldn't be too bad."

Your second error was choosing to act before consulting your boss. In doing so, you were running the risk of implementing a policy that he may want to oppose or to implement in a way that is beneficial to the goals of the sales force. To remedy this situation, read the results of a discussion with Bill Banquet shown below.

Your meeting with Bill Banquet was unexpectedly short. Bill confessed being distracted by the resignation that morning of Bob Jenson, his administrative assistant. Jenson was known to be looking for another position, but the timing of his decision seemed to have taken Banquet by surprise.

You: "Did you see the memo about the new product planning policy?"
Bill: "Yes, I've seen it. I wasn't consulted on it in advance, but I was told that it was coming. I know the salespeople are not going to like it."
You: "Not only that, but I doubt if my people can be expected to estimate their product needs within the 20% window. You know that our situation is different from the other groups."
Bill: "I know; I know. Listen, I've got to go. I've got to get over to Human Resources to sign the authorization forms to replace Jenson before my flight to Toledo. Look, do the best you can with the policy. I'll see you in a week."

What would you do now?

A.   If you have not done so yet, phone a friend of yours who works as a financial analyst at the corporate level (Blake-Emerson, the parent company) for his perspective on how to respond to this policy change. (GO TO 310)

B.   If you have not done so yet, call your predecessor (now with another firm) for his perspective on how to handle this situation. (GO TO 273)

C.   Wait and bring this issue up at a weekly staff meeting of the sales managers (chaired by Bill Banquet). (GO TO 420)

D.   Diplomatically oppose the new policy as it applies to your unique circumstances. Petition for an exemption. (GO TO 302)

E.   Instruct your subordinates what to do about the new policy. (GO TO 400)

Decision Point 377

You decided to go directly to the reporters involved in the topic and get the information you needed to make your appeal to your boss. This did not work very well. Harrison Gump (the reporters' boss) found out about your request, and informed the other members of the task force what you were up to. The resulting rumors got back to your boss, and he remained rigid in his rejection of the topic.

Whenever you move around a task force member, you invite this sort of reaction. The benefits are simply not worth the risks.

Re-evaluate your last decision. Circle the #377 you just wrote in your flow diagram. Then move to the last uncircled step in your flow diagram.

Decision Point 378

During this second month period when you have given your team no group assignment, what would you do?

A.   Take a tough stand with Bob Alton. Let him know privately that you expect his cooperation, and you will not tolerate any trouble from him (GO TO 281).

B.   At the next weekly staff meeting, deliver a speech that emphasizes your confidence in everyone in the group. Reiterate the need for everybody to work toward objectives that are both professionally worthwhile and relevant to the needs of the company (GO TO 350).

C.   Meet with each team member individually to discuss his/her career goals and aspirations. Indicate your support for these goals if there is commitment toward departmental goals and performance (GO TO 416).

D.   Announce the charter that you were given by top management at the next weekly staff meeting. State your resolve to bring the department back into line with the needs of the organization (GO TO 365).

Decision Point 379

The following information sources are available to you. Which would you choose first?

A. Talk with your peers (the other sales managers who report to Bill Banquet) to gauge their reaction to the new policy. (GO TO 279)

B. Speak with Bill Banquet (your boss) about his "reading" of the new policy. (GO TO 450)

C. Phone a friend of yours who works as a financial analyst at the corporate level (Blake-Emerson, the parent company) for his perspective on how to respond to this policy change. (GO TO 444)

D. Call your predecessor (now with another firm) for his perspective on how to handle this situation. (GO TO 273)

E. Wait and bring the issue up at a weekly staff meeting of the sales managers (chaired by Bill Banquet). (GO TO 420)

Decision Point 380

You summarize the decisions made at the first meeting and ask Seashore and Gump for their report. Gump hands out a list of topics that are presently being worked on in the Editorial Department by various reporters. This done, you need to instruct the group as to what technique is appropriate for the task force to use to derive topics for the seasonal issue.

What technique would you use?

A. Nominal Group Technique. (GO TO 274)

B. Ordinary group discussion. (GO TO 309)

C. Use of subgroups engaged in ordinary group discussion. (GO TO 415)

D. Brainstorming. (GO TO 299)

Decision Point 381

You decided to give the group an assignment. The results are very disappointing. Not only is the impact report finished late, but it contains assumptions that top management finds unacceptable. Apparently, you expected too much too soon from a team that neither accepted you as leader nor the new departmental directions you were hired to promote.

You should have concluded that your team was a P-4 group. Cohesiveness was high because your team members socialized regularly. The antagonistic norms were evident from the difference between what the group valued and what top management valued. It is ill-advised to give a P-4 group an assignment that required more complex work relationships than in their regular work. Instead, you should have held off for a while until you had an opportunity to begin to alter the social conditions of the group.

Re-evaluate your last decision. Circle the #381 you just wrote in your flow diagram. Then go back in your flow diagram to the first uncircled number above this step.

Decision Point 382

Your meeting with Justin Fenwick is strained, and Fenwick responds to your petition defensively, re-explaining the logic of the policy and attempting to persuade you to go along. He is unyielding even when you outline your reservations.

Several days after your meeting, you hear through the grapevine that as far as the Product Planning Group is concerned, you are a trouble-maker.

Re-evaluate your last decision. Circle the #382 you just wrote in your flow diagram, and move to the last uncircled step in your flow diagram.

Decision Point 383

You chose the combination of Gump, Patrick, Leybolt, and Foy. While this is a representative composition, it puts an "unassuming" person on the task force who lacks organizational credibility. There is a better combination.

Re-evaluate your last decision. Circle the #383 you just wrote in your flow diagram. Then move to the last uncircled step in your flow diagram.

Decision Point 384

George Bennet reacts angrily and resigns on the spot to attend law school full time. Roy Best follows suit joining your predecessor's consulting firm. The situation is the group deteriorates rapidly, and with your Department seriously understaffed, you are unable to meet any of the deadlines top management gave you.

Apparently, your approach was a bit extreme given the volatile situation in the Department. One can effectively confront an informal group leader when a team is in a P-4 condition. However, one must be careful not to act to create oneself as a "common enemy." Otherwise, you simply intensify the resistance to your leadership. By confronting Bennet as well as Alton, you have done just that.

Re-evaluate your last decision. Circle the #384 you just wrote in your flow diagram. Then go back in your flow diagram to the first uncircled number above this step.

Decision Point 385

Your meeting with Bill Banquet was unexpectedly short. Bill confessed being distracted by the resignation that morning of Bob Jenson, his administrative assistant. Jenson was known to be looking for another position, but the timing of his decision seemed to have taken Banquet by surprise.

You: "Did you see the memo about the new product planning policy?"
Bill: "Yes, I've seen it. I wasn't consulted on it in advance, but I was told that it was coming. I know the sales people are not going to like it."
You: "Not only that, but I doubt if my people can be expected to estimate their product needs within the 20% window. You know that our situation is different from the other groups."
Bill: "I know; I know. Listen, I've got to go. I've got to get over to Human Resources to sign the authorization forms to replace Jenson before my flight to Toledo. Look, do the best you can with the policy. I'll see you in a week."

What would you do now?

A. Phone a friend of yours who works as a financial analyst at the corporate level (Blake-Emerson, the parent company) for his perspective on how to respond to this policy change. (GO TO 310)

B. Call your predecessor (now with another firm) for his perspective on how to handle this situation. (GO TO 273)

C. Wait and bring this issue up at a weekly staff meeting of the sales managers (chaired by Bill Banquet). (GO TO 420)

D. Diplomatically oppose the new policy as it applies to your unique circumstances. Petition for an exemption. (GO TO 302)

E. Instruct your subordinates what to do about the new policy. (GO TO 400)

Decision Point 386

You decide to say nothing about the budget your boss has given you. This is a mistake. It is a piece of information that your task force should have in deciding a topic and in working out coordination details.

Re-evaluate your last decision. Circle the #386 you just wrote in your flow diagram. Then move to the last uncircled step in your flow diagram.

Decision Point 387

You decided to give the group an assignment. The results are very disappointing. Not only is the impact report finished late, but it contains assumptions that top management finds unacceptable. Apparently, you expected too much too soon from a team that neither accepted you as leader nor the new departmental directions you were hired to promote.

You should have concluded that your team was a P-4 group. Cohesiveness was high because your team members socialized regularly. The antagonistic norms were evident from the difference between what the group valued and what top management valued. It is ill-advised to give a P-4 group an assignment that required more complex work relationships than in their regular work. Instead, you should have held off until you had an opportunity to begin to alter the social conditions of the group.

Re-evaluate your last decision. Circle the #387 you just wrote in your flow diagram. Then go back in your flow diagram to the first uncircled number above this step.

Decision Point 388

You have a chance to "buttonhole" several of the other sales managers. Their comments follow:

Sandra Smith (Sales Mgr--Hydraulic Products): "I'll tell you one thing. My sales engineers certainly don't like the extra paperwork, but we've done pretty well making the 20% window. In fact (she winks), it feels good moving from #4 to #2! All kidding aside, I think it's good that we now require our salespeople to plan their product needs. After all, the personnel people are always harping that we should prepare them for moving into the managerial ranks."

Brian Robinson (Sales Mgr--Delivery Systems): "All that sounds fine and good, but the fact remains that the policy penalizes those of us who have uncertain demand or complex lines. No, this thing is stupid. The strategic plan for this year identifies my line as vitally important, and then they turn around and discourage our development of new accounts because one can never plan them systematically. I've talked to Banquet about this and he agrees, but he hasn't done anything about it!"

Don James (Sales Mgr--Pneumatic Products): "My sales engineers have had a helluva time getting their numbers right. Even with our standard lines, they consistently overestimated their needs. I suspect that they will get better and that the product will be available. It's creating hell with our volume, I'll tell you."

What would you do now? (Bill Banquet is out of town.)

A.   Since Bill Banquet is out of town, talk with Sterling Cartwright (his new administrative assistant). (GO TO 432)

B.   Meet privately with Brian Robinson to work out a strategy for addressing this policy problem. (GO TO 414)

C.   Instruct your subordinates about what to do now. (GO TO 429)

Decision Point 389

Seeing you concentrated in work, Gump sits back down and continues adding to his list of prospective ideas. Time passes and Seashore returns to the room, and seeing the others working, also returns to his yellow pad.

Ten more minutes pass, and after all pencils are stop moving, you move onto the next step--the sharing of ideas in a round-robin fashion.

How would you keep track of the ideas generated?

A.   Ask the members if they have any objections if you ask your personal assistant to keep track of the ideas. Position him at the flip chart. (GO TO 317)

B.   Take notes yourself on a note pad. (GO TO 371)

C.   Use a flip chart to write down the ideas yourself. (GO TO 355)

D.   Tape-record the session. (GO TO 364)

Decision Point 390

After your statement, George Bennet asks if you think that the Department has a responsibility to lead the organization to a level of professionalism befitting "the times." You respond that it is true that top management does not have an enlightened view of what a Human Resources department should be as many professionals have. However, you assert, there is no way the department can hope to lead the organization without first building its credibility.

A few days later, the factory superintendent (a position at the same organizational level as your's) mentions that he heard about your aim to build credibility so your department can put in place an activist set of human resources policies. He informs you that such politicking will never work at the company.

You have been victimized by an end-run at the hands of Bunkie Brown and Bob Alton. Your credibility with top management has suffered a severe setback. And, since you have yet not established yourself as the leader of your group, the situation is virtually irretrievable.

In thinking about where you went wrong, consider that your group is presently in a P-4 social condition: high cohesiveness, antagonistic work norms. Your statement that your charter is to confront these antagonistic norms, while true, serves only to unify the group against you as a common enemy. In general, it is advisable to avoid appearing to take sides publicly when one's P-4 team members oppose you. It is better to handle the group individually, making it clear that there are some behaviors that you want and others that you do not want.

Re-evaluate your last decision. Circle the #390 you just wrote in your flow diagram. Then go back in your flow diagram to the first uncircled number above this step.

Decision Point 391

Mildred Barnes and you have established a pleasant relationship during the past month. Through mutual and harmless teasing, you have built a rapport that both of you relish. You ask her views on the new policy.

"You know why the policy was created, don't you? Well, Billingsworth was facing significant pressure from corporate to cut staff personnel. Justin (Fenwick) had been successful in protecting us until then. When the axe fell, we could not keep doing all the product planning for manufacturing. You know, we had been analyzing sales trends and setting manufacturing requirements accordingly. Well, the new policy was followed by a 22% cut in our staff. Jack Collins was the last of these cuts, and he left just last week. I was really lucky to survive this purge, believe me...

"Your group and Robinson's are the most hard-hit. But that's not really surprising. When we were doing the product forecasting, your two units were always the hardest to predict. Don't quote me, but you are getting screwed in all this.

"If you ask me, where product scheduling is going is toward shorter time frames. Now we are asking for projections one month ahead. In the next few months with our new computer models, we can shorten that to two weeks."

Later in the conversation she says, "If your people are having a rough time, there is one thing I could do--training. I've been teaching planning methods at a junior college where I live. I'd be more than willing to work with your salespeople to give them tools to use in figuring their product requirements."

As you are leaving Mildred's office, her secretary slips you a note that William Barstow, your friend in the corporate office is trying to reach you by phone. You ask to use a phone in a deserted office and phone him. He tells you that he wanted to get back to you with the latest gossip:

"Well, by now you've heard about the personnel cuts in Product Planning. My hunch that personnel cuts are now a thing of past is a conviction. This quarter's earnings are up, and it now appears that we are about as lean as we can be.

"I've checked with some of my contacts. It's clear that your policy problem is not without precedent in the corporation. Two other divisions in Atlanta and Trenton have their salespeople estimate product demand as part of the planning effort. Marketing managers there gave their sales people extensive training in statistical estimation procedures. Each has access to a computer terminal so they can report deviations from the plan in real time."

What would you do now?

A.   Since Bill Banquet is out of town, talk with Sterling Cartwright (his new administrative assistant). (GO TO 325)

B.   Talk with your peers about their experience with the new policy. (GO TO 388)

C.   Instruct your subordinates about what to do now. (GO TO 429)

425

Decision Point 392

Your tactic of telling one task force member something you have not told another backfires. Lyle Seashore hears of your "deception" and resigns from the task force. Clearly, at this point, there is no need for selectively telling task force members things.

Re-evaluate your last decision. Circle the #392 you just wrote in your flow diagram. Then move to the last uncircled step in your flow diagram.

Decision Point 393

You have decided to give the group an assignment requiring the highest complexity of required interaction. The results are extremely disappointing. Not only is the policy statement finished late, but it contained assumptions that top management found unacceptably naive. Apparently, you expected too much too soon of a team that neither accepts you as their leader nor the new directions you were hired to lead the department in.

During the first month, you did act successfully to decrease group cohesiveness a bit as evidenced by Alton's loss of influence. However, the group is in at best a P-3 condition. Accordingly, you acted prematurely in requiring them to perform well at such a high complexity of required interaction.

Re-evaluate your last decision. Circle the #393 you just wrote in your flow diagram. Then go back in your flow diagram to the first uncircled number above this step.

Decision Point 394

You decided to act before consulting either your boss or your peers. This was incorrect. First of all, in deciding to act before consulting your peers, you now lack adequate information about the potential force that might be mobilized in opposition to this policy. To remedy this situation, the results of a discussion with your peers is shown below.

You have an opportunity to chat with three of your peers (Amy Holcott is out of town). All of them expressed irritability with the new policy, but none seemed put out enough to fight it. Don James' (Sales Manager--Pneumatic Products) opinion was typical:

"I don't know if my people are good enough planners for us to make our estimates within the 20% window. I suspect that they are, but there's no telling. Right now, with the market so sour, most of our business is repeat business. My hunch is that simply keeping our estimates to the high side of historical figures should suffice, at least that's what I am telling my people to do. They're sure not going to like the extra paperwork, that I can assure you. But most of my sales engineers are still jittery about being laid off, so it shouldn't be too bad."

Your second error was choosing to act before consulting your boss. In doing so, you were running the risk of implementing a policy that he may want to oppose or to implement in a way that is beneficial to the goals of the sales force. To remedy this situation, read the results of a discussion with Bill Banquet shown below.

Your meeting with Bill Banquet was unexpectedly short. Bill confessed being distracted by the resignation that morning of Bob Jenson, his administrative assistant. Jenson was known to be looking for another position, but the timing of his decision seemed to have taken Banquet by surprise.

You: "Did you see the memo about the new product planning policy?"
Bill: "Yes, I've seen it. I wasn't consulted on it in advance, but I was told that it was coming. I know the salespeople are not going to like it."
You: "Not only that, but I doubt if my people can be expected to estimate their product needs within the 20% window. You know that our situation is different from the other groups."
Bill: "I know; I know. Listen, I've got to go. I've got to get over to Human Resources to sign the authorization forms to replace Jenson before my flight to Toledo. Look, do the best you can with the policy. I'll see you in a week."

What would you do now?

A.   If you have not done so yet, phone a friend of yours who works as a financial analyst at the corporate level (Blake-Emerson, the parent company) for his perspective on how to respond to this policy change. (GO TO 310)

B.   If you have not done so yet, call your predecessor (now with another firm) for his perspective on how to handle this situation. (GO TO 273)

C.   Wait and bring this issue up at a weekly staff meeting of the sales managers (chaired by Bill Banquet). (GO TO 420)

D.   Diplomatically oppose the new policy as it applies to your unique circumstances. Petition for an exemption. (GO TO 302)

E.   Instruct your subordinates what to do about the new policy. (GO TO 400)

Decision Point 395

As your third task force meeting begins, it appears that there is a new sense of togetherness in the group. Smithers, whom you wanted on the team for his social skills, is actually rather quiet in the minutes just before the meeting when all the members are present. Instead, Foy and Gump are exchanging stories and engaging in boisterous laughter.

Seashore sits alone, and you try to strike up a conversation, but to no avail. His thoughts are elsewhere, and you find yourself hoping that his pensiveness has nothing to do with the task force.

You begin the meeting by asking members to report on the categories they have been able to identify from the results of the last meeting. When all the individual reports are completed, it is clear that the alternative topics fall into the following seven categories:

1. regional development problems (the highest rated),
2. police inadequacies in dealing with minor theft,
3. disillusionment of the middle-class and alternative life-styles,
4. justice for the underclass--farm workers, the homeless and indigent,
5. organized crime and real estate scams,
6. child abuse and alcoholism,
7. overcrowding at the county prison.

You must now decide how to evaluate each of these categories. Before the first task force meeting you had decided to delay the issue of decision criteria because of the publisher's rather controversial concern that the topic have circulation potential. You can delay no longer, so you open the issue of criteria.

The discussion is tense at first, with the two people from Editorial sparring with the others on the matter of journalistic independence and circulation potential without mentioning either. At that point Lyle Seashore begins dominating the discussion. He makes his point with story after story that all support the notion that circulation should not serve as the guiding force in editorial decisions. What would you say to Seashore to regain control of this meeting?

A. "Lyle, I think all of us understand your point of view. In all fairness, we should now give someone else a chance to be heard on the matter." (GO TO 360)

B. "Lyle, that's enough. You are beginning to repeat yourself." (GO TO 340)

C. "Am I the only one who disagrees with Lyle on this point?" (GO TO 324)

Your tough stand with Alton backfires. Duckworth and Spurior feel equally disciplined. Alton and Duckworth both quit joining your predecessor's consulting firm. Apparently, Doc Stevens had given them standing offers to join the firm even before you became Director. You are now seriously under-staffed in the face of having to complete three one month assignments in three months. The results are dreadful. Your team fails to make all of its deadlines, and the quality of the work reflects the under-staffing.

While you were correct in concluding that some action on the individuals was appropriate to further decrease cohesiveness, your tough action again Alton is unwarranted for several reasons. First, although you are skeptical, Alton's excuses are believable. Second, now that you are underway with your assignments, you should appreciate that you are now dependent on your team, i.e., if they become uncommitted, you will look bad. For these reasons, it is probably more prudent to single individuals out with praise, not "tough stands."

Re-evaluate your last decision. Circle the #396 you just wrote in your flow diagram. Then go back in your flow diagram to the first uncircled number above this step.

Mildred Barnes and you have established a pleasant relationship during the past month. Through mutual and harmless teasing, you have built a rapport that both of you relish. You ask her views on the new policy.

"You know why the policy was created, don't you? Well, Billingsworth was facing significant pressure from corporate headquarters to cut staff personnel. Justin (Fenwick) had been successful in protecting us until then. When the axe fell we could no longer do all the product planning for manufacturing. You know, we had been analyzing sales trends and setting manufacturing requirements accordingly. Well, the new policy was followed by a 22% cut in our staff. Jack Collins was the last of these cuts, and he left just last week. I was really lucky to survive this purge, believe me...

"Your group and Robinson's are the most hard-hit. But that's not really surprising. When we were doing the product forecasting, your two units were always the hardest to predict. Don't quote me, but you are getting screwed in all this.

"If you ask me, where product scheduling is going is toward shorter time frames. Now we are asking for projections one month ahead. In the next few months with our new computer models, we can shorten that to two weeks."

Later in the conversation she says, "If your people are having a rough time, there is one thing I could do--training. I've been teaching planning methods at a junior college where I live. I'd be more than willing to work with your salespeople to give them tools to use in figuring their product requirements."

As you are leaving Mildred's office, her secretary slips you a note that William Barstow, your friend in the corporate office is trying to reach you by phone. You ask to use a phone in a deserted office and phone him. He tells you that he wanted to get back to you with the latest gossip:

"Well, by now you've heard about the personnel cuts in Product Planning. My hunch that personnel cuts are now a thing of past is a conviction. This quarter's earnings are up, and it now appears that we are about as lean as we can be.

"I've checked with some of my contacts. It's clear that your policy problem is not without precedent in the corporation. Two other divisions in Atlanta and Trenton have their salespeople estimate product demand as part of the planning effort. Marketing managers there gave their sales people extensive training in statistical estimation procedures. Each has access to a computer terminal so they can report deviations from the plan in real time."

What would you do now?

A.   Meet privately with Brian Robinson to work out a strategy for addressing this policy problem. (GO TO 414)

B.   Instruct your subordinates about what to do now. (GO TO 429)

Decision Point 398

You decide to meet individual members of the task force before the first meeting to feel them out on objectives. Your first meeting is with Lyle Seashore. True to form, he objects to any objective for the issue that "smacks" of narrow, commercial interests. Yet when you meet with Harrison Gump, you are surprised to find him willing to select a topic for the seasonal edition that will have "broad appeal." Knowing Gump, you realize that is as close to agreeing with commercial appeal as an objective as you are likely to get. When you raise the issue with Smithers and Foy, they have no problem with the idea of an increase in circulation as a specific objective. Clearly Seashore is in the minority, but you are concerned that if you raise the issue in your first meeting, he may be able to win Gump over on a matter of principle and deadlock the task force. How would you proceed from this point?

A. Raise the issue of objectives at your first meeting and be prepared to guide the group to the resolution that you and the publisher want. (GO TO 313)

B. Return to Lyle Seashore and explore with him what objectives he can live with. Be prepared to tell him that if he can't live with a commercial objective, you may have to ask someone else to serve on the task force. (GO TO 311)

C. Have your boss (the publisher) talk with Seashore to persuade him of the importance of circulation. (GO TO 293)

Decision Point 399

In making this assignment and in conducting yourself in weekly department meetings and other public occasions, what would you do?

A. Suggest that these labor negotiations are a real opportunity for the Department to regain its credibility with top management. State that it will take a coordinated effort to overcome what will surely be a tough bargaining stand by the union (GO TO 407).

B. Change the format of weekly department meetings to allow for more group discussions on issues of concern (GO TO 452).

C. Take every chance to reinforce and publicly acknowledge any efforts in line with top management's concern that Human Resources becomes more relevant to the realities of the firm (GO TO 419).

Decision Point 400

There are several ways for you to instruct your subordinates to respond to this new policy. Which option would you choose?

A. Tell your subordinates to ignore the policy directive and the product planning forms for the time being until you have a chance to appeal for an exemption. (GO TO 346)

B. Instruct your subordinates to comply with the new policy. When they resist, be prepared to defend the need for better product planning but assure them that you are working to bring the new policy into line with your group's special circumstances. (GO TO 351)

431

C.	Ask for your group's advice as to how to implement this new policy requirement. Be prepared to justify the logic behind the policy should the group advocate resistance. (GO TO 411)

D.	Instruct your subordinates to comply with the new policy but to report to you any significant deviations from the monthly product plan as they arise. By reporting these deviations to Justin Fenwick as addenda to each plan, you will have grounds to argue against penalties imposed against your group for inaccurate estimates. (GO TO 294)

Decision Point 401

How would you open the next meeting?

A.	Summarize what was decided at the last meeting and ask for a report from Gump and Seashore. (GO TO 380)

B.	Tell the group that you plan to use brainstorming as a method of deriving alternative topics for the seasonal issue. (GO TO 406)

C.	Tell the group that the task force will use the Nominal Group Technique for developing alternative topics for the seasonal issue. (GO TO 277)

Decision Point 402

Your meeting with Bill Banquet was unexpectedly short. Bill confessed being distracted by the resignation that morning of Bob Jenson, his administrative assistant. Jenson was known to be looking for another position, but the timing of his decision seemed to have taken Banquet by surprise.

You: "Did you see the memo about the new product planning policy?"
Bill: "Yes, I've seen it. I wasn't consulted on it in advance, but I was told that it was coming. I know the sales people are not going to like it."
You: "Not only that, but I doubt if my people can be expected to estimate their product needs within the 20% window. You know that our situation is different from the other groups."
Bill: "I know; I know. Listen, I've got to go. I've got to get over to Human Resources to sign the authorization forms to replace Jenson before my flight to Toledo. Look, do the best you can with the policy. I'll see you in a week."

What would you do now?

A. Talk with your peers (the other sales managers who report to Bill Banquet) to gauge their reactions to the new policy edict. (GO TO 314)

B. Call your predecessor (now with another firm) for his perspective on how to handle this situation. (GO TO 273)

C. Wait and bring this issue up at a weekly staff meeting of the sales managers (chaired by Bill Banquet). (GO TO 420)

D. Diplomatically oppose the new policy as it applies to your unique circumstances. Petition for an exemption. (GO TO 426)

E. Instruct your subordinates what to do about the new policy. (GO TO 370)

Decision Point 403

You try to draw Smithers into the discussion by calling on him. Sometimes that works, but this time it doesn't. He simply clams up all the more, and the discussion moves on without his involvement. Initially, it is preferable to speak more indirectly to the entire group about the unevenness of the participation. You might have said, "I hope by the time we are finished with this discussion, everyone who has something to say feels that they have had a chance to make their feelings known." Let's assume you had made that statement and proceed with the interactive case from that point.

Finally, Smithers says, "You know, I get the feeling that Harrison and Lyle think that the rest of us want to force some second-rate topic down their throats. Personally, I want a topic that will help people. Compassion not exploitation sells newspapers." This remarks breaks the impasse. The group quickly agrees that an effective topic will have the following attributes:

(1) It should increase circulation by arousing compassion in the community;
(2) It should meet the highest standards of journalistic work; and
(3) It should play into the strengths of the Editorial Department.

These criteria identified, the group assesses each of the seven broad topic areas and the clear favorite is police inadequacies in dealing with minor crime (auto burglary, shoplifting, vandalism, etc.). Harrison Gump reports that two members of his staff have been conducting some preliminary research on the topic and discovered that 61 percent of the citizenry are touched by such minor crimes each year, and that police indifference may be due to the fact that most of the community's opinion leaders have insurance. There are many facets to the issue, and the task force is really quite enthusiastic.

433

As the meeting comes to a close, you ask the members to return prepared to address the coordination issues associated with this topic. Seashore then asks you if you are going to talk with the publisher about the topic. You promise to do that before the next meeting.

The meeting ends, and you enter your boss's office planning to have a pretty easy time convincing him that the topic your task force has chosen is a good one. Much to your surprise, he is very unimpressed by your committee's choice. You try to persuade him, but he remains firm that the topic will have little readership appeal. Now you are in a real jam. What would you do?

A.   Ask to talk with him more about this issue at a later time. (GO TO 366)

B.   Return to your task force and tell them of the publisher's rejection of the topic it has chosen. (GO TO 334)

Decision Point 404

Your team works harmoniously in hammering out a statement of personnel policies. Top management approves it, and two months later, you receive authorization for a healthy budget increase. Congratulations! Your actions have forged a new team spirit and developed your credibility with a skeptical top management. This completes the Work Teams Interactive Case.

Decision Point 405

Approaching Emerson Billingsworth at this point produces disastrous consequences. He informs your boss of your action and takes no action to relieve your unit of responsibility to complete the product planning task.

Re-evaluate your last decision. Circle the #405 you just wrote in your flow diagram, and return to the last uncircled step in your flow diagram.

Decision Point 406

You tell the group that you plan to use brainstorming as a method of deriving alternative topics for the seasonal issue. While this method may be well suited to the first aspect of your charter, it is really premature to announce it. You should have opened the meeting by summarizing the decisions made at the first meeting and asking Gump and Seashore to report on what they have discovered from their survey of ongoing topic assignments within the Editorial Department. Let's assume you had done that and resume the interactive case at that point.

You summarize the decisions made at the first meeting and ask Seashore and Gump for their report. Gump hands out a list of topics that are presently being worked on in the Editorial Department by various reporters. This done, you need to instruct the group as to what technique is appropriate for the task force to use to derive topics for the seasonal issue.

What technique would you use?

A.   Nominal Group Technique. (GO TO 274)

B.   Ordinary group discussion. (GO TO 309)

C.   Use of subgroups engaged in ordinary group discussion. (GO TO 415)

D.   Brainstorming. (GO TO 299)

Decision Point 407

It is one month later, and the team completed its assignment on schedule. You received the inputs of each team member, and you formulated an impact report that you have some confidence in. You are not certain of the validity of the assumptions, but you think they are sound. Upon submitting the report to top management, they react that it is much too optimistic and too theoretical "as usual." Would you?

A.   At the next department meeting announce that top management has challenged the report, and ask each team member for a reassessment of their inputs. Plan to take any revised figures back to top management to challenge their statements that the report is too optimistic (GO TO 353).

B.   Check the figures yourself. Speak privately with Bunkie Brown to assure yourself that he has based his figures on reasoning you understand and accept. Plan to take the resultant figures back to top management to challenge their statements that the report is too optimistic (GO TO 440).

C.   Agree with top management that the report may be too optimistic and theoretical, but say that you need more time to "whip the team into shape" (GO TO 437).

Decision Point 408

Will Barstow has much to say, "Well, by now you've heard about the personnel cuts in Product Planning. My hunch is that these are the last cuts. This quarter's earnings are up, and it now appears that we are about as lean as we can be.

"I've checked with some of my contacts. It's clear that your policy problem is not without precedent in the corporation. Two other divisions in Atlanta and Trenton have their salespeople estimate product demand as part of the planning effort. Marketing managers there gave their salespeople extensive training in statistical estimation procedures. Each has access to a computer terminal so they can report deviations from the plan in real time."

As you hang up the phone, Mildred Barnes of the Product Planning Department appears in the doorway of your office. Mildred Barnes and you have established a pleasant relationship during the past month. Through mutual and harmless teasing, you have built a rapport that both of you relish. When you ask her views of the policy, she has much to say.

"You know why the policy was created, don't you? Well, Billingsworth was facing significant pressure from corporate to cut staff personnel. Justin (Fenwick) had been successful in protecting us until then. When the axe fell, we could no longer do all the product planning for manufacturing. You know we had been analyzing sales trends and setting manufacturing requirements accordingly. Well, the new policy was followed by a 22% cut in our staff. Jack Collins was the last of these cuts, and he left just last week. I was really lucky to survive this purge, believe me...

"Your group and Robinson's are the most hard-hit. But that's not really surprising. When we were doing the product forecasting, your two units were always the hardest to predict. Don't quote me, but you are getting screwed in all this.

"If you ask me, product scheduling is going toward shorter time frames. Now we are asking for projections one month ahead. In the next few months with our new computer models, we can shorten that to two weeks."

Later in the conversation she says, "...If your people are having a rough time, there is one thing I could do--training. I've been teaching planning methods at a junior college where I live. I'd be more than willing to work with your salespeople to give them tools to use in figuring their product requirements."

What would you do now?

A. Talk to your peers about their experience with the new policy. (GO TO 341)

B. Since Bill Banquet is out of town, talk with Sterling Cartwright (his new administrative assistant). (GO TO 325)

C. Instruct your subordinates about what to do now. (GO TO 429)

Decision Point 409

You chose the combination of Seashore, Patrick, Foy, and Fitzgerald. This is not the best composition. When you examine the descriptions of all four of these individuals carefully, you will notice that none of them has anything but a tough, efficiency-conscious, businesslike demeanor. The problem with this is that task forces operate best with compositions that have a balance between individuals who bring a businesslike orientation and those who are more socially inclined. Of all the candidates, Michael Smithers is about the only individual who has a social orientation.

Re-evaluate your last decision. Circle the #409 you just wrote in your flow diagram. Then move to the last uncircled step in your flow diagram.

Decision Point 410

Your tough stand with Alton comes as a complete shock to him and to those who continue to support his informal leadership (Duckworth and Spurior). Apparently, your previous action of discussing career goals with each individual did not show that you planned to be so firm. After all, you had at best suspicions about Alton's motives supported only by an unsubstantiated rumor.

Because of your action, Alton quits joining your predecessor's consulting firm. To make matters worse, you hear that Duckworth has decided to see an attorney about suing her former boss for sexual harassment.

Your actions to date have been correct in terms of holding off from making an assignment. However, this last action solidified opposition to you as a common enemy of the team.

Re-evaluate your last decision. Circle the #410 you just wrote in your flow diagram. Then go back in your flow diagram to the first uncircled number above this step.

437

Decision Point 411

You directed your subordinates to comply with the new policy for the time being. However, you asked them for their advice about how to implement the policy. The resulting discussion is rocky, but it does develop the group sentiment that they are in it together and they should make the best of it.

Since the new policy came from a level above your boss, talking with your boss before taking action was critical. In addition, by talking with other people within the company, you have learned some information that would have helped you in planning how to approach the situation.

Two months later the effects of the new policy have had an opportunity to be felt, and felt they were. Your unit failed to make the 20% planning window on 30% of the products sold. As a result, four orders are delayed, two of which are cancelled by customers due to the delay. Additionally, fifteen parts are over-ordered leading to a decrease by 17% of the reported sales volume credited to your unit. This results in your unit falling from the number two position in sales volume to the number three position.

Your sales engineers complain bitterly about the new policy, especially when their estimates over- or undershoot actual product requirements. Accounting for penalties, all but one of your sales engineers failed to meet their volume goals, and all expressed concern that their merit pay would be adversely affected.

Because of your heavy travel schedule during the month, you have had little opportunity to interact with your boss, your peers, or with others outside your immediate sphere of responsibility. The sole exception is Mildred Barnes, an analyst in the Product Planning Department. Barnes reports directly to Justin Fenwick and is the analyst responsible for translating your unit's product plans into production schedules.

At this point, what would you do?

A. Tell your boss your concerns to elicit his help in moderating the policy. (GO TO 318)

B. Gather information about how others in the organization view this policy now that it has been in place for two months. (GO TO 435)

C. Instruct your subordinates about what to do now. (GO TO 429)

You leave your boss's office without ascertaining what involvement he wants on the topic for the seasonal edition. This is a mistake. Without this sort of clarification, you cannot be certain that your boss wants the same level of involvement you assume he does.

Re-evaluate your last decision. Circle the #412 you just wrote in your flow diagram. Then move to the last uncircled step in your flow diagram.

Luke Spurior tries very hard as chair but is unable to earn the respect of the others in the group. Moreover, once others sense that you are the "behind-the-scenes" chair, Spurior's credibility drops considerably. As a result, the assignment takes a very long time to complete, and several members of the team resent your "manipulations."

For the first time you can see that team members are enforcing work norms on one another than support your definition of performance. Therefore, you can be fairly sure that your team is in a P-2 position (low cohesiveness; supportive norms). Your decision to make Spurior the chair will keep the group from moving to a P-1 position. Spurior does not want the position, and it is not the preferred assignment of the group.

Re-evaluate your last decision. Circle the #413 you just wrote in your flow diagram. Then go back in your flow diagram to the first uncircled number above this step.

After discussing strategy with Robinson in some detail, you consider three major alternative actions:

(1) Lobby for an exemption for strategically important units (your unit and Robinson's are considered strategically important).

(2) Lobby to reduce the planning period from one month to one or two weeks.

(3) Lobby for training for your sales engineers.

You both agree that alternative (1) is the most preferred, (2) is the second best, and (3) is the worst. You now have to decide how to go forward with your proposals for policy modifications. Which would you do?

A. When he is back from his trip, propose alternative (1) to Bill Banquet being prepared to settle for alternative (2) or (3) if he does not think it feasible. (GO TO 438)

B. Same as A above except begin by asking Banquet his assessment of how well the policy is working. (GO TO 276)

Decision Point 415

You have chosen subgroups as a method of developing alternative topics for the seasonal issue. This is an inappropriate group decision-making method for developing alternatives since there is no evidence that there would be any advantage in using subgroups. Subgroups are typically used when the responsibility given to the group at large is divisible into coherent parts and when some members have interests or abilities that reflect this division.

Re-evaluate your last decision. Circle the #415 you just wrote in your flow diagram. Then move to the last uncircled step in your flow diagram.

Decision Point 416

It is one month later, and your personal position in the group is stronger. Unfortunately, however, the high level of group spirit you observed when you first arrived has been seriously eroded. Some individuals have sided with you (e.g., Best, Bennet, Banks, Brown, and Johnson) and others continue to be cool toward you (Duckworth and Spurior). Alton is still quiet and sullen in public. Halfway through the month, Spurior approached you and confessed feeling troubled that the "family feeling" in the Department was gone. You persuaded him that things would get better in time.

Since it is now three months until your three departmental assignments are due, you must now decide what assignment to complete first. Which would you choose?

A. Assignment 1 -- Preparation for Labor Negotiations. In five months your department begins negotiations with the Sheetmetal Workers Union for the first time in two years. Since the contract will affect each department member's

440

specialty, you will solicit everyone's inputs. Bunkie Brown will draw up a list of probable union demands. He will send these to department members for their assessment of economic and administrative impacts. You will then aggregate these assessments into an integrated impact report that will serve to determine the company's negotiating strategy (GO TO 399).

B. Assignment 2 -- Development of an Integrated Personnel Policy. Top management has asked you to assess departmental policies. It is due in five months. Preparing this document will involve intensive meetings of all department members (GO TO 425).

C. Assignment 3 -- Creation of an Annual Staffing Plan. In five months the staffing plan for the next fiscal year is due. This is a serial process beginning with Roy Best who estimates promotions and transfers. It then goes to Bob Alton's group (Alton, Duckworth, and Spurior) who calculates new staffing needs. It then travels on to George Bennet who justifies these figures into the affirmative action plan. Finally, Floyd Banks transposes these estimates into a budget form (GO TO 446).

Decision Point 417

Will Barstow has much to say, "Well, by now you've heard about the personnel cuts in Product Planning. My hunch is that these are the last cuts. This quarter's earnings are up, and it now appears that we are about as lean as we can be.

"I've checked with some of my contacts. It's clear that your policy problem is not without precedent in the corporation. Two other divisions in Atlanta and Trenton have their salespeople estimate product demand as part of the planning effort. Marketing managers there gave their salespeople extensive training in statistical estimation procedures. Each has access to a computer terminal so they can report deviations from the plan in real time."

As you hang up the phone, Mildred Barnes of the Product Planning Department appears in the doorway of your office. Mildred Barnes and you have established a pleasant relationship during the past month. Through mutual and harmless teasing, you have built a rapport that both of you relish. When you ask her views of the policy, she has much to say.

"You know why the policy was created, don't you? Well, Billingsworth was facing significant pressure from corporate headquarters to cut staff personnel. Justin

(Fenwick) had been successful in protecting us until then. When the axe fell, we could no longer do all the product planning for manufacturing. You know we had been analyzing sales trends and setting manufacturing requirements accordingly. Well, the new policy was followed by a 22% cut in our staff. Jack Collins was the last of these cuts, and he left just last week. I was really lucky to survive this purge, believe me...

"Your group and Robinson's are the most hard-hit. But that's not really surprising. When we were doing the product forecasting, your two units were always the hardest to predict. Don't quote me, but you are getting screwed in all this.

"If you ask me, product scheduling is going toward shorter time frames. Now we are asking for projections one month ahead. In the next few months with our new computer models, we can shorten that to two weeks."

Later in the conversation she says, "...If your people are having a rough time, there is one thing I could do--training. I've been teaching planning methods at a junior college where I live. I'd be more than willing to work with your salespeople to give them tools to use in figuring their product requirements."

What would you do now?

A.   Since Bill Banquet is out of town, talk with Sterling Cartwright (his new administrative assistant). (GO TO 432)

B.   Meet privately with Brian Robinson to work out a strategy for how to address this policy problem. (GO TO 414)

C.   Instruct your subordinates about what to do now. (GO TO 429)

Decision Point 418

This arrangement works well. You talk with the vice presidents and get their cooperation. Back at the meeting, you next want to make a few remarks on the political sensitivities of serving on the task force.

What would you say in this regard?

A.   "With the quality of people on this task force, I'm very optimistic about being able to put together a superb seasonal issue. However, our assignment is a

442

challenging one, and it is very likely that we will step on each other's toes from time to time. Please, let's keep our deliberations confidential, and if you are having a problem with the way anything is done on this task force, see me before you talk about it with people not in the group. Is that agreeable to everyone?" (GO TO 421)

B. "I'm convinced that, with the people on this task force, we cannot fail. We should be able to work together well without much disagreement. If, by chance, we have conflicts, I would like to ask you to keep them in this room." (GO TO 448)

C. "All of you have been carefully selected to represent your constituencies on this task force. It is very imperative that you bring the points of view of your departments to our deliberations so we can be sure that the special issue is acceptable to all involved." (GO TO 445)

Decision Point 419

It is one month later, and the team completed its assignment on schedule. You received the inputs of each team member, and you formulated an impact report that you have some confidence in. You are not sure of all of the assumptions, but they appear sound to you. Upon submitting the report to top management, they react that it is too optimistic and too theoretical "as usual." Would you?

A. At the next department meeting announce that top management has challenged the report, and ask each team member for a reassessment of their inputs. Plan to take any revised figures back to top management to challenge their statements that the report is too optimistic (GO TO 353).

B. Check the figures yourself. Speak privately with Bunkie Brown to assure yourself he based his conclusions on reasoning you understand and accept. Plan to take the resultant figures back to top management to challenge their statements that the report is too optimistic (GO TO 440).

C. Agree with top management that the report may be too optimistic and theoretical, but say that you need more time to "whip the team into shape" (GO TO 437).

Decision Point 420

Bill Banquet returns from Toledo and promptly calls a regular staff meeting. You bring up the policy at the meeting, and this opens up a gripe session that causes Bill Banquet to wince. Forced to make a public declaration, he throws his weight behind the policy. He says that managers should try the new system for a while to see if it will bring down inventory costs without jeopardizing sales. When pressed for how long this trial period would be, Banquet says, "three months."

The problem with this action is that you have chosen a forum for information gathering that (1) is outside your control, and (2) forces your boss into making commitments he may not be prepared to make. The results speak for themselves. Bill Banquet's hand was forced, and now you face the certainty of three months of compliance. You might have been able to do better for your unit. You have also created a situation where your boss has had to appear weak in the face of this edict.

Re-evaluate your last decision. Circle the #420 you just wrote in your flow diagram and move to the last uncircled step in your flow diagram.

Decision Point 421

Lyle Seashore asks whether reporting the involvement of the publisher in the selection of the seasonal edition topic violates the norm of confidentiality. You respond that you think it does and indicate that the group has decided to take a wait-and-see posture. With that, all the members agree that confidentiality makes sense.

That behind you, you then address one last issue: you think the task force would benefit from knowing what long-term investigative work is under way in the Editorial Department that may have the potential of serving as the basis for the task force's choice of a topic. You ask Gump and Seashore to report to the task force at the next scheduled task force meeting on these developments. They agree to do so. How would you end the meeting?

A. "Well, we're off to a good start. Let's see, at the next meeting we will begin work on the topic. See you then." (GO TO 305)

B. "At the next meeting, we will begin work on the topic for the special issue. You all may want to think about that in preparation for the meeting. And my understanding is that Harrison and Lyle will be bringing us some inputs. Is that correct?" (GO TO 401)

Decision Point 422

The group gives no reaction to your "pep talk." Later, during the same day, you learn through the grapevine that it stimulated a great deal of cynicism. While you are not sure, you suspect that this negativity comes from Bob Alton.

What would you do now?

A.   Take a tough stand with Bob Alton. Let him know privately that you expect him to cooperate and that you expect no trouble from him (GO TO 396).

B.   Announce the charter that you were given by top management at the next weekly staff meeting. State your resolve to bring the department back into line with the needs of the organization (GO TO 288).

C.   Mention at a weekly department meeting that you are pleased that Brown and Johnson gave so much thought to their assumptions and that Best, Bennet, and Banks have made excellent progress on their part of the assignment; say nothing about Alton, Spurior, or Duckworth (GO TO 323).

Decision Point 423

You have an opportunity to chat with three of your peers (Amy Holcott is out of town). All of them expressed irritability with the new policy, but none seemed put out enough to fight it. Don James' (Sales Manager--Pneumatic Products) opinion was typical:

"I don't know if my people are good enough planners for us to make our estimates within the 20% window. I suspect that they are, but there's no telling. Right now, with the market so sour, most of our business is repeat business. My hunch is that simply keeping our estimates to the high side of historical figures should suffice, at least that's what I am telling my people to do. They're sure not going to like the extra paperwork, that I can assure you. But most of my sales engineers are still jittery about being laid off, so it shouldn't be too bad."

What would you do now?

A.   Phone a friend of yours who works as a financial analyst at the corporate level (Blake-Emerson--the parent company) for his perspective on how to respond to this policy change. (GO TO 310)

B. Call your predecessor (now with another firm) for his perspective on how to handle this situation. (GO TO 273)

C. Wait and bring this issue up at a weekly staff meeting of the sales managers (chaired by Bill Banquet). (GO TO 420)

D. Diplomatically oppose the new policy as it applies to your unique circumstances. Petition for an exemption. (GO TO 302)

E. Instruct your subordinates what to do about the new policy. (GO TO 400)

Decision Point 424

Your comment seems to put the issue to rest for the time being. Seashore remains disturbed, but Gump agrees that the task force ought to take a wait-and-see posture. He adds: "I'll be watching his so-called involvement very carefully. If he starts managing our efforts from a distance, you will have my resignation from this effort."

You then lay out a number of procedures similar to the ones you have used with previous task forces. You tell them you will be responsible for producing and distributing minutes as a vehicle for keeping the members posted. You give them a schedule of milestones that will have to be met.

Your schedule is greeted by a chorus of groans. Each member reacts negatively to the timing of certain milestones. All but Foy argue that their other responsibilities are going to seriously interfere with their ability to make the necessary commitment to the task force.

How would you react to this development?

A. "Gentlemen, all of us are busy, but the publisher is committed to this special issue. It is really up to you to negotiate with your respective bosses to be freed up sufficiently from your other duties to give 100 percent to this assignment." (GO TO 330)

B. "Talk with your prospective bosses about this first. If you don't get the necessary slack from them, let me know, and I'll talk with them myself." (GO TO 418)

C. "Would you like me to ask the publisher to talk with your bosses about freeing up your time for this?" (GO TO 289)

446

You have decided to give your work team a highly complex assignment. Such a task will most likely lead to heated discussions during a time that your team is anything but "together." The results are unfortunate. The discussions emphasize the differences between individual opinions, and even the existing factions disintegrate. Deadlines are missed, and the resultant document lacks focus. You watch the credibility of the Department with top management go down.

Your previous action of holding off making an assignment until absolutely necessary was correct. It gave you the opportunity to work on the social conditions in the group. The results for the most part were encouraging. Your actions resulted in the team moving from an initial P-4 condition to the P-3 condition that you observed when you made your last decision. The Integrated Personnel Policy assignment requires the highest level of complexity in required interaction. Clearly, you should have held off giving this assignment until much later.

Re-evaluate your last decision. Circle the #425 you just wrote in your flow diagram. Then go back in your flow diagram to the first uncircled number above this step.

In deciding to act before consulting your peers, you now lack adequate information about the potential force that might be mobilized in opposition to this policy. Accordingly, your last decision was not correct. To remedy this situation, the results of a discussion with your peers are shown below.

You have an opportunity to chat with three of your peers (Amy Holcott is out of town). All of them expressed irritability with the new policy, but none seemed put out enough to fight it. Don James' (Sales Manager--Pneumatic Products) opinion was typical:

"I don't know if my people are good enough planners for us to make our estimates within the 20% window. I suspect that they are, but there's no telling. Right now, with the market so sour, most of our business is repeat business. My hunch is that simply keeping our estimates to the high side of historical figures should suffice, at least that's what I am telling my people to do. They're sure not going to like the extra paperwork, that I can assure you. But most of my sales engineers are still jittery about being laid off, so it shouldn't be too bad."

What would you do now?

A. If you have not done so yet, phone a friend of yours who works as a financial analyst at the corporate level (Blake-Emerson--the parent company) for his perspective on how to respond to this policy change. (GO TO 310)

B. If you have not done so yet, call your predecessor (now with another firm) for his perspective on how to handle this situation. (GO TO 273)

C. Wait and bring this issue up at a weekly staff meeting of the sales managers (chaired by Bill Banquet). (GO TO 420)

D. Diplomatically oppose the new policy as it applies to your unique circumstances. Petition for an exemption. (GO TO 302)

E. Instruct your subordinates what to do about the new policy. (GO TO 400)

Decision Point 427

You say, "I don't think it's the task force's role to redefine the charter given to us by the publisher." Gump strongly objects. He says, "The publisher is a reasonable man, and I think he will be interested in what the task force thinks." Your statement was ill advised, for it gives the impression that the charter was given in a "take it or leave it" fashion.

Re-evaluate your last decision. Circle the #427 you just wrote in your flow diagram. Then move to the last uncircled step in your flow diagram.

Decision Point 428

You have decided to give your team an assignment that involves a moderate level of complexity in required interaction. The results are extremely disappointing. Not only is the staffing plan finished late, but it contained figures that top management challenged. Apparently, you expected too much too soon from a group that neither accepts you as a leader nor the new directions you were hired to lead the Department in.

During the first month, you did act successfully to decrease group cohesiveness a bit as evidenced by Alton's loss of influence. However, the group is presently at best in a P-3 condition. Consequently, your assignment required more complex interactions than the group was ready for. Re-evaluate your last decision. Circle the #428 you just wrote in your flow diagram. Then go back in your flow diagram to the first uncircled number above this step.

Decision Point 429

It is premature for you to give your subordinates directions as to how to proceed. You simply do not know at this point whether some sort of modification more favorable to your unit can be worked out.

Re-evaluate your last decision. Circle the #429 you just wrote in your flow diagram, and move to the last uncircled step in your flow diagram.

Decision Point 430

Gump responds well to your intervention and does not offer judgmental remarks again.

The brainstorming begins again, and sheet after sheet of flip chart paper is filled and taped to the walls of your conference room. This goes on for about 20 minutes, and then there is a prolonged lull in the group.

At this point what would you do?

A. Wait out the silence. (GO TO 358)

B. Call off the session since it is clear that the group has exhausted its creative potential. (GO TO 291)

C. Ask if anyone has any more ideas. (GO TO 301)

Decision Point 431

During the one month period when you have decided to give your team no group assignment, what would you do?

A. Take a tough stand with Bob Alton. Let him know privately that you expect his cooperation and that you will not tolerate any trouble from him (GO TO 434).

B. Let others in the group know privately that you know that Bob Alton must have been very disappointed about being passed over for your job. Tell him that you look forward to working with him. Express a willingness to support those who work for the Department and to oppose those who work against it (GO TO 369).

C.   At the next weekly staff meeting, deliver a speech that emphasizes your confidence in everyone in the group. Reiterate the need for everybody to work toward objectives that are both professionally worthwhile and relevant to the needs of the company (GO TO 312).

D.   Meet with each team member individually to discuss his/her career goals and aspirations. Express support for those who appear committed to your vision of the Department. Begin to single out individual efforts aligned with your plans (GO TO 308).

E.   Announce the charter that you were given by top management at the next weekly staff meeting. State your resolve to bring the department back into line with the needs of the organization (GO TO 390).

Decision Point 432

Sterling Cartwright is a man of about 40 who has been with the company for only three weeks. You ask him about Banquet's opinion of the way the new policy is working. He responds: "Bill is concerned. He really is. He doesn't like the way it puts the burden on you. Just the other day he met with Mr. Billingsworth about it."

You ask him what Banquet is doing about this situation. "Bill has a plan, and I'm sure it will work in time, but with the cuts in product planning, things are a bit uncertain. I'm sure you can expect something in the next few months."

What would you do now? (Bill Banquet is out of town.)

A.   Meet privately with Brian Robinson to work out a strategy for how to address this policy problem. (GO TO 414)

B.   Instruct your subordinates about what to do now. (GO TO 429)

Decision Point 433

You chose the combination of Gump, Patrick, Fitzgerald, and Jones. This composition has two problems. First, Fitzgerald does not as yet have the stature and credibility that is required for an effective task force member. Second, when you examine the descriptions of all four of these individuals carefully, you will notice that none of them has anything but a tough, efficiency-conscious, businesslike demeanor. The problem with this is that task forces operate best with compositions that have a balance between individuals who bring a businesslike orientation and those who are more socially inclined. Of all the candidates, Michael Smithers is about the only individual who has a social orientation.

Re-evaluate your last decision. Circle the #433 you just wrote in your flow diagram. Then move to the last uncircled step in your flow diagram.

Decision Point 434

Bob Alton reacts little to your tough stand except to say that he has no intention of causing you trouble. Later in the week, however, you sense that other members of your team are growing very cool to your leadership. Your secretary informs you that Alton has been telling others that you threatened him for no reason and that you lack "professional polish." Two days later, when walking down the corridor, you overhear George Bennet referring to you in the same way while talking with Bunkie Brown. What would you do now?

A. At the next weekly staff meeting, deliver a speech that emphasizes your confidence in everyone in the group. Reiterate the need for everybody to work toward objectives that are both professionally worthwhile and relevant to the needs of the company (GO TO 443).

B. Meet with each team member individually to discuss his/her career goals and aspirations. Express support for those who appear committed to your vision of the Department. Begin to single out individual efforts aligned with your plans (GO TO 300).

C. Announce the charter that you were given by top management at the next weekly staff meeting. State your resolve to bring the department back into line with the needs of the organization (GO TO 390).

D. Confront George Bennet, and take a tough stand with him (as you did with Bob Alton) (GO TO 384).

Decision Point 435

The following information sources are available to you. Which would you choose?

A. Your peers. (GO TO 343)

B. Mildred Barnes of the Product Planning Department. (GO TO 391)

C. Since Bill Banquet is out of town, Sterling Cartwright (his new administrative assistant). (GO TO 367)

D. William Barstow, your friend at the corporate headquarters. (GO TO 408)

Decision Point 436

Finally, Smithers says, "You know, I get the feeling that Harrison and Lyle think that the rest of us want to force some second-rate topic down their throats. Personally, I want a topic that will help people. Compassion not exploitation sells newspapers."

This remarks breaks the impasse. The group quickly agrees that an effective topic will have the following attributes:

(1) It should increase circulation by arousing compassion in the community;
(2) It should meet the highest standards of journalistic work;
(3) It should play to the particular strengths of the Editorial Department.

These criteria identified, the group assesses each of the seven broad topic areas and the clear favorite is police inadequacies in dealing with minor crime (auto burglary, shop-lifting, vandalism, etc.). Harrison Gump reports that two members of his staff have been conducting some preliminary research on the topic and discovered that 61 percent of the citizenry are touched by such minor crimes each year, and that police indifference may be due to the fact that most of the community's opinion leaders have insurance. There are many facets to the issue, and the task force is really quite enthusiastic.

As the meeting comes to a close, you ask the members to return prepared to address the coordination issues associated with this topic. Seashore then asks you if you are going to talk with the publisher about the topic. You promise to do that before the next meeting.

The meeting ends, and you enter your boss's office planning to have a pretty easy time convincing him that the topic your task force has chosen is a good one. Much to your surprise, he is very unimpressed by your committee's choice. You try to persuade him, but he remains firm that the topic will have little readership appeal.

Now you are in a real jam. What would you do?

A.   Ask to talk with him more about this issue at a later time. (GO TO 366)

B.   Return to your task force and tell them of the publisher's rejection of the topic it has chosen. (GO TO 334)

Decision Point 437

Your statement to top management works its way into the grapevine and into the Department via Bunkie Brown. The "whip the group into shape" phrase passes through the Department like wildfire, and everyone now sees you as a "lackey" of manufacturing. This unfortunate label hurts you and severely suppresses the commitment of your team to your goals.

By accepting top management's indictment of work you had "some confidence in," you missed an opportunity to quietly orchestrate an experienced group success so helpful in this P-2 condition. Some sort of upward influence is called for. Otherwise, you will unify the group, again in opposition to top management.

Re-evaluate your last decision. Circle the #437 you just wrote in your flow diagram. Then go back in your flow diagram to the first uncircled number above this step.

Decision Point 438

Banquet listens carefully to your proposal, but reacts negatively to your first alternative (an exemption). When you try to emphasize the other alternatives as a fall back position, he keeps reintroducing the infeasibility of an exemption. Even when you agree that an exemption would be out of the question, Banquet seems to hold onto the view that the other alternatives would be perceived by "the powers that be" as a sign that the original policy was ill-conceived.

Your negotiation posture has caused your alternatives to be seen as versions of the same overall action--resistance. Clearly you need a different negotiation strategy with Bill Banquet.

Re-evaluate your last decision. Circle the #438 you just wrote in your flow diagram, and return to the first uncircled step in your flow diagram.

Decision Point 439

You tell Harrison Gump to get to work, and leave the room to ask Seashore to return. This alienates both these task force members. In situations like this, it is initially far better to model the behavior you want, rather than being too heavy-handed.

Re-evaluate your last decision. Circle the #439 you just wrote in your flow diagram. Then move to the last uncircled step in your flow diagram.

Decision Point 440

You convince top management that the impact report is based on sound thinking. Bunkie Brown hears of your defense of the team through the grapevine, and your support grows within the group. Even Jane Duckworth begins to show commitment. You remain unsure, though, if these developments are sufficient to conclude that the group is now unified behind you.

Since there are two months to go before you must complete two assignments, you must select the next assignment to give the team. Which would you choose?

A.   Assignment 2 -- Development of an Integrated Personnel Policy. Top management has asked you to assess existing departmental policies. It is due in five months. Preparing this document will involve intensive meetings of all department members (GO TO 304).

B.   Assignment 3 -- Creation of an Annual Staffing Plan. In five months the staffing plan for the next fiscal year is due. This is a serial process beginning with Roy Best who estimates promotions and transfers. This then goes to Bob Alton's group (Alton, Duckworth, and Spurior) who calculates new staffing needs. It then travels on to George Bennet who justifies these figures into the affirmative action plan. Finally, Floyd Banks transposes these estimates into a budget form (GO TO 284).

You have a chance to "buttonhole" several of the other sales managers. Their comments follow:

Sandra Smith (Sales Mgr--Hydraulic Products): "I'll tell you one thing. My sales engineers certainly don't like the extra paperwork, but we've made the 20% window. In fact (she winks), it feels good moving from #4 to #2! All kidding aside, I think it's good that we now require our salespeople to plan their product needs. After all, the personnel people are always harping that we should prepare them for moving into the managerial ranks."

Brian Robinson (Sales Mgr--Delivery Systems): "All that sounds fine and good, but the fact remains that the policy penalizes those of us who have uncertain demand or complex lines. No, this thing is stupid. The strategic plan for this year identifies my line as vitally important, and then they turn around and discourage our development of new accounts because one can never plan them systematically. I've talked to Banquet about this and he agrees, but he hasn't done anything about it!"

Don James (Sales Mgr--Pneumatic Products): "My sales engineers have had a helluva time getting their numbers right. Even with our standard lines, they consistently overestimated their needs. I suspect that they will get better and that the product will be available. It's creating hell with our volume, I'll tell you."

What would you do now? (Bill Banquet is out of town.)

A. Meet privately with Brian Robinson to work out a strategy for addressing this policy problem. (GO TO 414)

B. Instruct your subordinates about what to do now. (GO TO 429)

You decide to go ahead with the meeting without Seashore and ask Gump to brief him. This results in a serious communication problem. You should have tried to contact him before proceeding with this important meeting.

Re-evaluate your last decision. Circle the #442 you just wrote in your flow diagram. Then move to the last uncircled step in your flow diagram.

Decision Point 443

The team now opposes your leadership. Your combination of giving your subordinates a pep talk and giving the informal leader a reprimand gives your team members a mixed message. Giving a pep talk is likely to arouse cynicism and, if anything, create more cohesiveness when you should be trying to decrease cohesiveness. Your action was inappropriate to a P-4 group.

Re-evaluate your last decision. Circle the #443 you just wrote in your flow diagram. Then go back in your flow diagram to the first uncircled number above this step.

Decision Point 444

You have known William Barstow for years. You attended the same university together. When you tell him of the policy directive, he gives you some interesting information:

"I haven't heard anything about the policy, but I can tell you that the Fluid Products Division is getting a lot of heat to get its costs under control. The word is that Billingsworth's argument that his division has strong profit potential is no longer credible until he can produce the numbers. The division is now under considerable pressure not to cut its line personnel, but rather its staff. One view from these lofty heights is that the axe is due to fall soon on just about every staff unit in the Division."

If true, this would mean that Justin Fenwick's group is in for some cuts, but your group should not be affected.

What would you do now?

A. Talk with your peers (the other sales managers who report to Bill Banquet) to gauge their reaction to the new policy edict. (GO TO 337)

B. Speak with Bill Banquet (your boss) about his "reading" on the new policy. (GO TO 402)

C. Call your predecessor (now with another firm) for his perspective on how to handle this situation. (GO TO 273)

D. Wait and bring this issue up at a weekly staff meeting of the sales managers (chaired by Bill Banquet). (GO TO 420)

E.   Diplomatically oppose the new policy as it applies to your unique circumstances. Petition for an exemption. (GO TO 394)

F.   Instruct your subordinates what to do about the new policy. (GO TO 376)

Decision Point 445

You emphasize the need for the members to represent their departments on the task force. This creates real problems for the task force. Discussions easily polarize, and members take time between meetings to check with their bosses and other members of their departments for approval for their inputs.

In general, it is important to keep a task force free from outside pressures. You want representatives, but not representatives subjected to a great deal of pressure to represent.

Re-evaluate your last decision. Circle the #445 you just wrote in your flow diagram. Then move to the last uncircled step in your flow diagram.

Decision Point 446

You have decided to give your work team an assignment that requires a moderate level of required interaction. The results are not good. A serious bottleneck occurs when the staffing plan moves from Roy Best to Duckworth, Spurior, and Alton. They simply cannot agree on a set of assumptions that you consider feasible. Desperate, you intervene and press the issue. Jane Duckworth resigns over the "interference." The group completes the assignment three weeks later, but top management rejects it as unrealistic. Since you now have to go back and trace the difficulties, you are forced to delay other assignments. The results are disastrous for building the credibility of the Department.

Your previous action of holding off making an assignment until absolutely necessary was correct. It gave you the opportunity to work on the social fabric of the team. The results were encouraging. Your actions have moved a group that was firmly in a P-4 condition to one that is now P-3. However, your choice of a particular assignment was incorrect. The Annual Staffing plan assignment requires more complex interaction among team members than one of the alternatives.

Re-evaluate your last decision. Circle the #446 you just wrote in your flow diagram. Then go back in your flow diagram to the first uncircled number above this step.

457

Decision Point 447

Mildred Barnes and you have established a pleasant relationship during the past month. Through mutual and harmless teasing, you have built a rapport that both of you relish. You ask her views on the new policy.

"You know why the policy was created, don't you? Well, Billingsworth was facing significant pressure from corporate headquarters to cut staff personnel. Justin (Fenwick) had been successful in protecting us until then. When the axe fell, we could no longer do all the product planning for manufacturing. You know, we had been analyzing sales trends and setting manufacturing requirements accordingly. Well, the new policy was followed by a 22% cut in our staff. Jack Collins was the last of these cuts, and he left just last week. I was really lucky to survive this purge, believe me...

"Your group and Robinson's are the most hard-hit. But that's not really surprising. When we were doing the product forecasting, your two units were always the hardest to predict. Don't quote me, but you are getting screwed in all this.

"If you ask me, where product scheduling is going is toward shorter time frames. Now we are asking for projections one month ahead. In the next few months with our new computer models, we can shorten that to two weeks."

Later in the conversation she says, "If your people are having a rough time, there is one thing I could do--training. I've been teaching planning methods at a junior college where I live. I'd be more than willing to work with your salespeople to give them tools to use in figuring their product requirements."

As you are leaving Mildred's office, her secretary slips you a note that William Barstow, your friend in the corporate office is trying to reach you by phone. You ask to use a phone in a deserted office and phone him. He tells you that he wanted to get back to you with the latest gossip:

"Well, by now you've heard about the personnel cuts in Product Planning. My hunch that personnel cuts are now a thing of past is a conviction. This quarter's earnings are up, and it now appears that we are about as lean as we can be.

"I've checked with some of my contacts. It's clear that your policy problem is not without precedent in the corporation. Two other divisions in Atlanta and Trenton have their salespeople estimate product demand as part of the planning effort. Marketing managers there gave their sales people extensive training in statistical estimation procedures. Each has access to a computer terminal so they can report deviations from the plan in real time."

What would you do now?

A. Talk to your peers about their experiences with the new policy. (GO TO 441)

B. Instruct your subordinates about what to do now. (GO TO 429)

Decision Point 448

You emphasize the need for group harmony in your little speech. This had little positive effect. One of the attributes of the diverse task force you have mobilized is conflicting opinions. By emphasizing the need for harmony, you are contradicting yourself.

Re-evaluate your last decision. Circle the #448 you just wrote in your flow diagram. Then move to the last uncircled step in your flow diagram.

Decision Point 449

Your tough stand with Alton, Duckworth, and Spurior backfires. Alton and Duckworth both quit joining your predecessor's consulting firm. You learn that he had given them an open job offer when he left your company. You are now seriously understaffed in the face of having to complete three one-month assignments in three months. The results are dreadful. Your team fails to make all three deadlines, and the quality of work of your team reflects the under-staffing.

Re-evaluate your last decision. Circle the #449 you just wrote in your flow diagram. Then go back in your flow diagram to the first uncircled number above this step.

Decision Point 450

Your meeting with Bill Banquet was unexpectedly short. Bill confessed being distracted by the resignation that morning of Bob Jenson, his administrative assistant. Jenson was known to be looking for another position, but the timing of his decision seemed to have taken Banquet by surprise.

You: "Did you see the memo about the new product planning policy?"
Bill: "Yes, I've seen it. I wasn't consulted on it in advance, but I was told that it was coming. I know the sales people are not going to like it."

You: "Not only that, but I doubt if my people can be expected to estimate their product needs within the 20% window. You know that our situation is different from the other groups."

Bill: "I know; I know. Listen, I've got to go. I've got to get over to Human Resources to sign the authorization forms to replace Jenson before my flight to Toledo. Look, do the best you can with the policy. I'll see you in a week."

What would you do now?

A. Talk with your peers (the other sales managers who report to Bill Banquet) to gauge their reactions to the new policy. (GO TO 423)

B. Phone a friend of yours who works as a financial analyst at the corporate level (Blake-Emerson, the parent company) for his perspective on how to respond to this policy change. (GO TO 373)

C. Call your predecessor (now with another firm) for his perspective on how to handle this situation. (GO TO 273)

D. Wait and bring this issue up at a weekly staff meeting of the sales managers (chaired by Bill Banquet). (GO TO 420)

E. Diplomatically oppose the new policy as it applies to your unique circumstances. Petition for an exemption. (GO TO 426)

F. Instruct your subordinates what to do about the new policy. (GO TO 370)

Decision Point 451

You asked your boss what involvement he wants in your task force. Confirming the role your boss wishes to play is an important first step. Without a clear understanding of the expectations of the task force sponsor, the group could find itself facing problems later.

In answer to your question, he tells you that he wants to approve the topic your task force chooses before you proceed with the coordination portion of your activity. This is a departure from tradition and one that will not be particularly popular with a number of task force members, especially those from Editorial. However, with all the money he is throwing in your direction, the request is understandable.

You decide that the best size for the task force is five. The dynamics in an odd size group may be marginally easier to manager than in an even sized group. In addition, a five person group is large enough to represent significant points of view, yet small enough to be easy to manage.

You now have to determine the specific makeup of your task force. Since last season's topic involved sports, you decide that your two representatives from Editorial should come from the following:

Harrison Gump (Feature Editor)--Hard-nosed, irascible, and a bit abrasive, a real no-nonsense person. Cut out of the mold of the typical crusty city editor.

Lyle Seashore (News Editor)--Pulitzer Prize-winning investigative reporter turned editor. Arrogant workaholic and defender of the Editorial Department's prerogatives when it comes to the selection of topics for the seasonal issue.

Myra Patrick (Business Editor)--The youngest business editor at any major newspaper in the U.S. and still finding her way. Known to be incredibly imaginative but very serious. Closely controls her own staff but has yet to earn the respect of her peers.

Your choice of the other candidates is very important. In the past, the representatives from Editorial have dominated the task force, and this has caused problems working out the coordination details with the other departments. The candidates for the other two positions are

Michael Smithers (Director of Circulation)--Community activist; articulate, amusing conversationalist; unswerving promoter of the Register in Madison.

Elaine Fitzgerald (Director of Consumer Advertising)--Efficient, intelligent, does not respect Smithers on the grounds that she thinks he is "vacuous." New to the Register (two years).

Baron Leybolt (Director of Human Resources)--Unassuming, diligent, earnest, and eager to please; doesn't yet have much credibility in the organization.

Peter Foy (Director of Information Systems)--Extremely knowledgeable of internal operations; tough-minded (perhaps even severe); persuaded only with facts.

Haley Jones (Treasurer)--Brisk, aloof, super-rational, and businesslike.

Which of the following combinations of members would you choose?

A.   Gump, Seashore, Fitzgerald, Smithers. (GO TO 347)

461

B.   Gump, Seashore, Smithers, Foy. (GO TO 283)

C.   Gump, Patrick, Leybolt, Foy. (GO TO 383)

D.   Gump, Patrick, Fitzgerald, Jones. (GO TO 433)

E.   Seashore, Patrick, Smithers, Leybolt. (GO TO 307)

F.   Seashore, Patrick, Foy, Fitzgerald. (GO TO 409)

Decision Point 452

At the first meeting where you call for an open discussion of concerns, there is little response. At the next meeting, however, Jane Duckworth delivers a passionate speech that indicates her strong preference for professional values over the "narrow thinking in manufacturing." Others join the discussion expressing their sorrow over the dismissal of your predecessor. At this point you intervene, but it is too late.

Essentially, by opening the team to an open discussion of shared concerns, you have in effect created conditions of very complex required interaction. Since your team is presently in a P-3 condition, this is entirely too premature.

Re-evaluate your last decision. Circle the #452 you just wrote in your flow diagram. Then go back in your flow diagram to the first uncircled number above this step.

Decision Point 453

You ask Bill Banquet to use his influence to earn an exemption. He says, "I understand that you may have difficulties abiding by this policy. However, it's not at all clear to me that you can't make it work."

You respond with facts that your sales group uses a more complex array of products and experiences a more uncertain demand than Banquet's other units. Further, you indicate the morale problems that will be created if your unit is adversely penalized due to the unique nature of the business it does. He then asks you for your recommendation, and you propose an exemption. He reacts:

"Well, we'll have to see about that. I understand your concerns, but we have to be very sure before we propose anything that far-reaching."

How would you respond to this?

A. Say that you will direct your subordinates to comply with the policy for the time being, and that you will keep him up to date on how successful your people are at estimating their product requirements. (GO TO 400)

B. Ask Bill what exactly it is that he wants you to do. (GO TO 286)

C. Go to Emerson Billingsworth and petition your case there. (GO TO 405)

Decision Point 454

Bill's relationship with this new person provides him with an excellent anchor for completing his integration. Through this relationship, Bill and his wife learn how to become active in the rural education district. Bill purchases a four-wheel drive vehicle at the urging of his new friend, and his commuting problems soon disappear. Your decision was correct because Bill was having problems integrating work and his personal life, a final predictable stage of a new employee's socialization. Bill needed help to overcome this problem, and someone else was in a better position to mentor Bill since the two of you had very different lifestyles, and he was facing challenges you had never personally encountered.

Congratulations! You have just completed the New Employee Interactive Case.

Decision Point 455

You appoint an implementation committee made up of professional librarians and aides known to be at least indifferent to the computerization effort. You chair the committee to make sure that it stays "on target." However, from the beginning you have problems working out the details of the plan with the group. Although you "stacked" the committee, the meetings become endless discussions of details that stimulate petty disagreements. In addition, committee members become targets of blunt comments from their colleagues not on the committee. Two members become so disillusioned with the seeming pointlessness of the meetings and the snipes they receive from their colleagues that they ask to leave the committee.

Using delegation in this instance was inadvisable for several reasons: (1) There is little relevant expertise in the workforce. You were the one most qualified to determine the implementation plan. (2) LCLD employees are not used to participation. Ms.

B's maternalistic approach made them unfamiliar with participative management. (3) Time is very tight with this change. (4) The LCLD's accreditation crisis is known to everyone. This is a public agency, so LCLD's problems with the state have been in the news.

Re-evaluate your last decision. Circle the #455 you just wrote in your flow diagram. Then move to the first uncircled step above this one in your flow diagram.

Decision Point 456

You feel that there are still some issues that need to be resolved with Robin. When you meet him, which approach would you take?

A. Stress to Robin the importance of everyone working together on this project. Point out that everyone in the group had input and now is the time to move on to implementation. (GO TO 522)

B. Probe Robin to see why he raised the objections he did. (GO TO 548)

Decision Point 457

You decided to call the Human Resources Department to find out what disciplinary options are available to you. You are told that the disciplinary sequence runs as follows:

> 1st offense--written warning (filed with Human Resources)
>
> 2nd offense--second written warning (filed with Human Resources and carrying an automatic one-day suspension without pay)
>
> 3rd offense--termination

Human Resources also informs you that chronic absenteeism is a relevant offense.

What would you do?

A. Write Frank up for chronic absenteeism and leave a copy of the warning in an envelope on his desk for him to see when he comes in. (GO TO 487)

B. Ask Human Resources if there are other departments that need people with Frank's qualifications so you can transfer him there. (GO TO 514)

464

C. Talk to some of Frank's co-workers to see if they have any idea what might be causing Frank's absences. (GO TO 499)

D. Check with Frank's previous supervisor to see what his past attendance record was like. (GO TO 594)

E. Do nothing. Wait until Frank returns and have a talk with him. (GO TO 618)

F. Discuss the matter with your manager in order to get her advice and input in handling the matter. (GO TO 469)

Decision Point 458

You have just lost a potentially valuable member of the organization because you protected him too long from more challenging assignments. As a result, Bill delivered you an ultimatum that you apparently were unwilling to accept. Bill's resignation creates significant political problems for you. K. C. Wong complains over your treatment of Bill, and you hear through the grapevine that the division manager is very displeased that you lost him. It appears that he had personally stuck his neck out to get Bill's high salary offer approved. Under these circumstances, you should have gracefully given in to his ultimatum (You could have made the assignment temporary to save face).

In order to make progress, new employees need initial assignments that will both challenge them and allow them to grow. Re-evaluate your last decision. Circle the #458 you just wrote, and move to the last uncircled step in your flow diagram.

Decision Point 459

You decided to hire Sloan Kilgore as your Director of Library Information Systems. This was a good choice. Sloan will have to work very closely with this change, and generally change agents require both technical credibility and social skills. Of the two professionally credentialed (MLS degree) and therefore credible applicants, Sloan was the most socially gifted.

You now must decide precisely what to say to your staff during your public announcement. You have already decided that you will complete the implementation in phases. You will also announce the elimination of the Director of Community Service position and the appointment of Sloan Kilgore.

Since some of the staff may not understand how severe the present situation is, how would you discuss this issue during your announcement?

A. Emphasize that the change is necessary largely for external reasons. Tell them how LCLD will suffer without accreditation. (GO TO 473)

B. Emphasize that the change is necessary largely for internal reasons. Develop an argument that computerization will bring about more efficiency in the district and better long-run service for patrons. (GO TO 517)

C. Emphasize both the internal and external need for change. (GO TO 497)

Decision Point 460

Bill strongly disagrees with your statement, and, in a rare show of temper, leaves your office and slams the door behind him. You call him in the next day to clear the air.

Bill needs information and background to learn and grow, not just advice. What would you say now?

A. Show how he could have better assessed this situation in terms of Sam's fundamental weaknesses, the team leader's responsibilities, and the particular client involved. (GO TO 599)

B. Tell Bill that clients should be allowed to say whatever they want even if it is uncomplimentary and that one important role of a Venus employee is to be a flak-catcher. (GO TO 615)

Decision Point 461

Keeping the position of Director of Community Service has two flaws. First, it leaves the responsibility for the technical aspects of the change fully on your shoulders. This is troublesome since you have many responsibilities in your position. Second, keeping the position would create an advocate for community service during a time when LCLD will have to temporarily compromise service.

Re-evaluate your last decision. Circle the #461 you just wrote in your flow diagram. Then move to the first uncircled step above this one in your flow diagram.

At the next meeting of your team, you sit in. The meeting seems to lack any direction. The discussion shifts back and forth over the same ground, and you are not sure what direction the group wants to take. Shortly before the meeting is scheduled to break up, you mention that the "flexible assembly" approach was suggested by Eugene. Directly after this, Marilyn says that the flexible assembly idea seems pretty good. Larry immediately agrees with her and Robin adds support as well. Quickly everyone seems to agree that this approach ought to be pursued. As the meeting breaks up, you are a bit unsure about your next step. While you are happy with the group's decision, you are not certain that your group is truly committed to it or that everyone thinks that it is the best choice.

What would you do?

A.   Before the meeting breaks up, poll the team members to see if "flexible assembly" is really their choice. (GO TO 544)

B.   Accept the group's recommendation and tell them that you will develop a set of plans for implementing flexible assembly. (GO TO 569)

C.   Accept the group's recommendation and ask them to develop a set of implementation recommendations. (GO TO 556)

D.   Schedule another meeting for the group to discuss their recommendation. (GO TO 581)

Frank Wilson has a severe personal problem. He is absent on Mondays not by choice, but because of factors largely outside his control. Under these circumstances, it is not surprising that Frank is irritable in response to anything but sensitive treatment.

Had you given Frank reason to confide in you, he would have told you: "The problem is my wife. We just got together again after we had been separated for eight months. She found out that she has an incurable kidney disease, and she wanted to come back on account of Eric, that's our son. Anyway, she has dialysis treatments three times a week, Mondays, Wednesdays, and Fridays. The toughest day of the week is Sunday, since she's on her second day without dialysis, and her body chemistry is all off. She gets real irritable, and she, Eric, and I always get in a fight over one thing or another. Mostly, it's Eric. He blames me for our first breakup, and when Barbara is weak, he just piles it on. The last two Sundays he just walked out.

"Last Monday I had to bail him out of jail all the way over in Clay County. It was 9:00 a.m. before we got home. Now that he's back at home without a driver's license, Sundays are going to mighty tough. If he acts up, Barbara is going to need me more than ever, and her dialysis appointment isn't until noon Mondays. I've talked with her doctor about her Sunday mood problems, but he says he doesn't want to give her any more drugs."

If you were sitting across from Frank when he told you this, how would you react?

A. "Well, it's real helpful to know what's been troubling you. Now, then, you must realize that I am being held responsible for production, so to be fair to the company, I am going to have to give you a formal warning on your attendance. I will pull it from your file if you are able to work the next four Mondays in a row. Otherwise, I am going to have to give you a second warning, and you know what that means." (GO TO 582)

B. "I understand. It sounds to me that you realize how important it is to improve your attendance record. I know now that you have got a tricky problem on your hands. I just want you to know that you've got my support. Do the best you can with your absences, and I'll cover for you as long as I can." (GO TO 481)

C. "I think I understand your situation, but you know my situation as well. I am getting pressure for production, and your absences are troublesome. We need to work out a plan that will result in a level of production that is your fair share. Do you have any ideas that we might put to use?" (GO TO 574)

D. "I know someone who is a professional family counselor. He's a neighbor of mine, and he is really good. Here's his phone number. If you need help with this thing, you should see a professional." (GO TO 622)

Decision Point 464

Your daily meetings with Bill go well, but they are very time consuming. He begins bringing up even the most trivial issues, and occasionally, you even find yourself doing his work. The meetings grow in duration until one day, you cut it off and firmly suggest that Bill try to get along without your help for a while. Cut loose, Bill flounders again, misses deadlines on important tasks, and completes unimportant ones with more "flair" than necessary. You conclude that Bill is not seeing the forest for the trees. What would you do now?

A. Tell Bill that it's probably best to stick it out. Bolster his sagging confidence and suggest that he talk to someone in the *Solaris* design team about a good reference book in aeronautics. (GO TO 472)

B. Reassign Bill to one of the other assignments you had originally considered for him, and replace him with another person. Bolster his sagging confidence by assuming full responsibility for his misplacement. (GO TO 488)

C. Move another person from your department onto the *Solaris* team to relieve some pressure on Bill. Talk to K. C. Wong about the importance of pacing Bill so he can regain his confidence, but not at the expense of meeting *Solaris* milestones. (GO TO 583)

D. Tell K. C. Wong that he is responsible for Bill's effectiveness in the group. Tell K. C. that you do not want him to sacrifice the objectives of the *Solaris* project, but that you think Bill deserves more of his time. (GO TO 619)

Decision Point 465

Linda Hemingway tells you that she heard a rumor that the Crystal Lake Branch will have to close to accommodate computerization. You have no plans to close the Branch, nor does anyone else that you know of. You ask Linda to trace the rumor for you. But because she expresses some initial reluctance, you decide not to put her on the spot.

How would you react to this situation?

A. Ask Linda to tell all the people in the Crystal Lake Branch that there are absolutely no plans to close the Branch in the foreseeable future. (GO TO 604)

B. Try to find out the source of the rumor yourself before proceeding further. (GO TO 608)

C. Attend a weekly meeting of all Crystal Lake personnel (scheduled the next day) and clarify this matter. (GO TO 588)

Decision Point 466

Bill and this other person really hit it off. They become very close friends, but his colleagues continue to reject him. His co-workers now seem to feel that he lacks real interest in them, and they begin to give him the "cold shoulder."

469

Three weeks later, Bill sends you a memo that says he would like to transfer to the division where his new friend works. You are convinced that granting the transfer would hurt you, Bill, and ultimately the entire organization.

What went wrong here is that you were not careful in assigning Bill his new mentor. Not only should mentors be socially skilled and have sufficient time and resources to invest in this role, they must also have the experience to provide useful advice. You found Bill a colleague, not someone who could help him learn about his new situation.

What would you do now?

A.   Grant his request for the transfer because you do not think Bill can possibly earn the approval of his group under these circumstances. (GO TO 502)

B.   Discourage Bill from taking the transfer and urge him to withdraw his request. (GO TO 500)

Decision Point 467

Your decision to change the position and fill it with a computer system specialist is a correct one. It brings in another specialist to assist you in the introduction and maintenance of the system. It reduces your dependence on a person (Alice Bishop) who has told you she has some questions about the practicality of the system. Your decision also reinforces the high visibility necessary when implementing a top-down change.

You interview three outside candidates. Which is best qualified?

A.   Bob Bramsen--Professional librarian. Ambitious, upwardly mobile though somewhat abrasive person formerly in a university library; experienced in implementing computer systems in urban settings. (GO TO 565)

B.   Marcia Gamble--Master's degree in computer science, bachelor's in English; very personable and sociable; wrote her master's thesis on merging library files using *BIBLIOTEK*. (GO TO 521)

C.   Sloan Kilgore--Professional librarian; was a consultant to the firm that originally developed *BIBLIOTEK*; very diplomatic and socially skilled. (GO TO 459)

You return to your team with Eugene's specific concerns. The members react very negatively. You settle them down, but Robin is particularly upset. Even though some of Eugene's concerns appear legitimate to you, Robin openly ridicules them. You adjourn the meeting with no real progress made.

At the next meeting the group continues to be immobilized by its frustrations over Eugene's actions. You decide to go back to Eugene to explore the basis for his opposition. When you enter his office, he says, "How are things going with the super-team plan?" You answer that that's what you are there to talk about. He interrupts, "Gordon Garvin thinks your plan is terrific. He says the timing couldn't be better from his viewpoint. What did you want to talk to me about?"

Apparently Eugene has changed his position 180 degrees. "Good news," you think to yourself. Yet when you return to your group, it takes the news very sullenly. The rumor has spread that Garvin saved the plan, not you, and the group has lost respect for your leadership. Its future actions lack real enthusiasm.

Re-evaluate your last decision. Circle the #468 you just wrote in your flow diagram. Then move to the first uncircled step above this one in your flow diagram.

You have decided to discuss the problem with your manager before taking any other action. She says: "No, I don't know Wilson, but I do know that we are behind on our schedule. I just got out of a staff meeting, and people were all over my case. It was embarrassing! I don't care what you do, but get some life into that team of yours, and get them back on schedule. It looks like we're going to have to use more overtime again. That is really playing hell with my budget."

What would you do now?

A. Talk to some of Frank's co-workers to see if they have any idea what might be causing Frank's absences. (GO TO 499)

B. Check with Frank's previous supervisor to see what his past attendance record was like. (GO TO 594)

C. Do nothing. Wait until Frank returns and have a talk with him. (GO TO 618)

D. Call the Human Resources Department to see what disciplinary options are open to you. (GO TO 457)

E. Call the Human Resources Department to see if there are other departments that need people with Frank's qualifications so you can transfer him there. (GO TO 514)

F. Write Frank up for chronic absenteeism and leave a copy of the warning in an envelope on his desk for him to see when he comes in. (GO TO 487)

Decision Point 470

You decided to let K. C. Wong handle this situation. K. C. feels he should tell Bill that Sam needs practice dealing with problems like this and that Bill should stay out of it next time. Bill disagrees strongly with K. C.'s position and storms out of his office muttering something about loyalty. Clearly, K. C. was the wrong person to assign the mentoring role since he apparently lacked the social skills and patience to do the job.

Bill enters your office the next day still hot over the issue. After settling him down, what would you do?

A. Suggest how he could have better assessed the situation between Sam and the client in terms of Sam's fundamental weaknesses, K. C.'s responsibilities in this instance, and the attributes of the client involved. (GO TO 599)

B. Inform Bill that Sam needs practice bailing himself out of situations like this, and that Bill should not get involved in Sam's development. (GO TO 460)

C. Tell Bill that clients should be allowed to say whatever they want, even if it is uncomplimentary and that one important role of a Venus employee is to be a flak-catcher. (GO TO 615)

D. Tell Bill that his actions in this situation are irresponsible, and that you cannot tolerate any more difficulties of this nature. (GO TO 516)

Decision Point 471

It is better to implement a change in phases than to do it all at once. However, you have selected a sequence that is not advisable. Starting with the Main Branch has two

472

major problems. First, the organization chart indicates that Main Branch is the largest and its operations the most complex. It is not necessary to confront such a comparatively difficult situation right from the start. Second, it is best to sequence the phases to be certain of early success. You will note that the Main Branch (while headed by someone in favor of computerization) is staffed with many detractors of the plan. The Live Oak Branch is a more logical choice for this first test.

Re-evaluate your last decision. Circle the #471 you just wrote in your flow diagram. Then move to the first uncircled step above this one in your flow diagram.

Decision Point 472

The bad situation with Bill continues to grow. He botches a critical test given him with inadequate instructions, and the other two members of his team "jump all over him." Too embarrassed to tell you, Bill sulks for two days before signing a resignation letter. Bill never took the time to get a good reference book in aeronautics.

Unfortunately, Bill needs substantial advice and feedback in order to understand the technical challenges of his new job. Therefore, re-evaluate your last decision. Circle the #472 you just wrote and move to the last uncircled step in your flow diagram.

Decision Point 473

Successful change managers emphasize both the external and internal conditions that create the need for change. Re-evaluate your last decision. Circle the #473 you just wrote in your flow diagram and move to the first uncircled step above this one in your flow diagram.

Decision Point 474

You decide to include Randy Winslow in your plans. This backfires. In the period before he leaves for England, he is particularly prone to defending the interests of his group of engineering technicians. Immediately after your conversation with him, he informs both the leader of his techs and his boss, Gordon Garvin (Director of Engineering), that you are trying to take over Engineering. As a result, your change program suffers an enormous political setback. Eugene is pressured from several sides to call you off, and finally when he senses growing opposition, he does so.

Re-evaluate your last decision. Circle the #474 you just wrote in your flow diagram. Then move to the first uncircled step above this one in your flow diagram.

Decision Point 475

You invite Frank into your office, and Frank explodes into a verbal tirade: "I'm really mad about this. I've put in three years in this damn company, and I certainly deserve to be told to my face if there's a problem! Okay, okay, so I've been absent. I've got a problem at home, okay? You just get off my back, or so help me . . . " You interrupt him at this point.

What would you say in this situation?

A. "Wait a minute, Frank, who do you think you are talking to? I'm writing you up for insubordination. Now get out of here and get back to work!" (GO TO 606)

B. "Frank, I can see that you're pretty angry, but I think you'd better settle down a little before you say something you'll regret later. I'll tell you what, why don't you sit here in my office and cool down while I give Janet some paperwork. Help yourself to some coffee, and I'll be back in about 20 minutes." (GO TO 549)

C. "Okay, Frank, take it easy. I gave you the warning because with our production schedules, we just can't afford to support people who are absent all the time. What's this about a problem at home?" (GO TO 519)

Decision Point 476

Bill apologizes for being so aggressive with the client and goes back to work. Two weeks later, you overhear Bill making disparaging remarks about several design engineers who "think they know more about control systems" than his project team. Later that day, Bill engages in verbal bantering in the company cafeteria with a design engineer. The bantering escalates into name calling and ends when Bill calls the designer "a jerk who should design with a crayon."

Fearing that this attitude may endanger the necessary work relationship between the team and the designers, you decide to intervene.

What would you say to Bill?

A. Suggest how he could have better handled the situation. Point out the necessity of good relationships between the designers and his team. Tell him he must deal with such conflicts in a more diplomatic way. And brief him on the particular attributes of the design group involved. (GO TO 599)

B. Tell Bill that he should let K. C. Wong deal with the designers for a while until things cool off. (GO TO 494)

C. Verify the story of the cafeteria incident with K. C. Wong before calling Bill in. (As it is now 4:30 p.m., this will require a one day delay.) (GO TO 591)

Decision Point 477

If you do not address the issue of employment insecurity, the change is likely to arouse fears that may immobilize the entire effort. Even though the members of LCLD have civil service protection, they are still prone to feelings of insecurity that you should be anticipate and acknowledge.

Re-evaluate your last decision. Circle the #477 you just wrote in your flow diagram. Then move to the first uncircled step above this one in your flow diagram.

Decision Point 478

You decided not to ask Bill for his assignment preference. Although getting Bill's preference might provide you with better information and build his commitment to the new assignment, asking him his preference is risky. He might have chosen an assignment not right for him. Which assignment would you give him?

A. Assignment 1. Junior Control Engineer, *Dart* Project. Join a team of four members to test a ballistics control system for a *Dart* missile. Bob Blair is the project manager. The *Dart* missile is like other systems except that the new control system requires several standards never required before. Smythe's senior thesis dealt with ballistics control systems. Likelihood of Bill making a contribution to the team - Good. Value to Bill's development if he is personally successful - Fair. (GO TO 623)

B. Assignment 2. Junior Control Engineer, *Solaris* Project. Join a team of three members to test the propulsion control system for a *Solaris* booster. K. C. Wong heads the team. Wong is very enthusiastic about Bill joining the team. Wong graduated from the same engineering school as Bill. The *Solaris* project will require a unique control system that has never been implemented before. The project is presently behind schedule because of the novelty of its design. It would offer a fantastic learning opportunity for any junior engineer. Likelihood of Bill making a contribution to the team - Fair. Value to Bill's development if he is personally successful - Very Good. (GO TO 626)

C. Assignment 3. Junior Control Engineer, Systems Test Group. Act as your administrative assistant. Perform several studies regarding planning and scheduling in preparation for upcoming budget negotiations. While this assignment has only a modest technical component, it is a great way for Bill to learn the inner workings of your department. It may allow him to find his own technical place in the group. Likelihood of Bill making a contribution to the team - Excellent. Value to Bill's development if he is personally successful - Marginal. (GO TO 628)

D. Assignment 4. Junior Control Engineer, Systems Test Group and member, *Micascope* Divisional Task Force. Join a task force of seven members conducting a manufacturing feasibility study of *Micascope*, a laser-refracting targeting system. The task force is chaired by the assistant to the divisional manager. The feasibility study proposed is controversial, with some task force members committed to manufacturing and some dead set against it. The division manager is said to favor manufacturing, but he has agreed to "let the chips fall where they may." While he hand-picked the members of the task force from other departments, he asked you to appoint the department member of your choice. Since all of your other people are busy with project work, Bill seems like a natural. Likelihood of Bill making a contribution to the team - Fair. Value to Bill's development if he is personally successful - Very Good. (GO TO 557)

Decision Point 479

Computerization will force fundamental changes in the organizational culture of LCLD. Ms. B's emphasis on service over professionalism did more than shape expectations; it created habits and entire patterns of thinking. Cultural changes require events that signal an end to the old and a birth of the new. There is no reason to opt for a muted occasion. A dramatic point of departure is better, and an announcement with significant visibility does just that. High visibility also demonstrates your resolve to "go the distance." Your people may be tempted into believing that you are really not committed if you chose a more low-key alternative

Re-evaluate your last decision. Circle the #479 you just wrote in your flow diagram. Then move to the first uncircled step above this one in your flow diagram.

Decision Point 480

You and Eugene spend five hours assessing the three alternatives under consideration. Early on, "flexible assembly" seems to be the most viable plan. At the end of that time, you are clear on the steps that need to be taken to implement the change. You realize that each member of your group has an important role to play if the process is to be successful. Marilyn will have to have much more flexible scheduling procedures. She will also have to shift from handling large quantities of relatively few parts to handling smaller quantities of a larger number of parts. Larry will have to reorganize his assembly lines, train his lead supervisors in the new process, and integrate most of the engineering techs into his group. Robin will absorb a number of the new techs and will also have to decide how to handle increased parts testing and more specialized warranty work.

When you give each person his or her assignment, there is a bit of grumbling. You remind the team that this project is important. Two weeks later when you check back with your team, there is little progress and the group seems to be generally resistant to your direction.

At this point in time you are faced with few options, none of which is very attractive. By embarking upon a change without involving your team in important decisions about it, you have forced a top-down implementation pattern on a situation more appropriate to delegation: (1) the change does not require immediate action; (2) the problem the change addresses is not commonly recognized throughout the organization; (3) knowledge relevant to the change is dispersed throughout the organization; and (4) your team has been successful when you have offered them a voice in decisions in the past.

Re-evaluate your last decision. Circle the #480 you just wrote in your flow diagram. Then move to the first uncircled step above this one in your flow diagram.

Decision Point 481

You have urged Frank to do the best he could to improve his attendance habits. As a result, Frank is absent for the following three Mondays, and you are left with no choice but to dismiss him. This causes severe problems because of declining production levels, co-worker dissatisfaction, and what you think may be the feeling among your people that you have been unfair. Your boss is growing less and less satisfied with your work.

Apparently, the method you chose of trying to get Frank to correct his attendance habits did not work.

Re-evaluate your decision. Circle the #481 you just wrote in your flow diagram. Then go back in your flow diagram to the first uncircled number above this step.

Decision Point 482

Your coaching of Bill pays off to some extent. He becomes more assertive in asking for help, and his once-cluttered desk is more orderly. However, he still has apparently not grasped the sense of priorities he needs to have to manage his own work well. You even notice that he is taking more work home at times when there is a relative lull in the project.

What would you do now?

A. Take time to remind others in your group of helping Bill adapt to his job is important.(GO TO 611)

B. Agree to meet daily with Bill to coach him on how to handle the specific, day-to-day problems that come up in his work. (GO TO 511)

C. Remind Bill of his agreement that he would take initiative if he had questions or was having difficulties. Suggest that he will not succeed unless he begins to ask questions, tells Bob Blair of his problems, and takes control of his own situation. (GO TO 595)

D. Begin to give Bill a detailed account of how to contend with the challenges and problems of his work. Agree to meet with him in three days to review his progress and advise him on new situations. (GO TO 534)

E. Tell Bob Blair that he is responsible for Bill's performance on the team. Tell Bob that you do not want him to sacrifice the objectives of the *Dart* test system, but that you think Bill deserves more of his time. (GO TO 575)

Decision Point 483

It is now three months after your announcement, and the personnel changes you made in the wake of Simmons' resignation are working well. You are optimistic that Hemingway will be a much better catalyst for change in the Crystal Lake Branch than an unknown quantity (the outsider). After all, she has been in on the early stages of the change, and you know she has been supportive of computerization from the start. While the staffing changes are working well, the Live Oak implementation hits a serious snag. An unforeseen software problem delays progress for two weeks.

More seriously, two Crystal Lake Branch aides complain to you that the new system has caused cut-backs in the "Children's Story Hour." You remind them that the cuts are only temporary. However, they express worry that the loss of patrons may severely affect their monthly circulation (Crystal Lake is the smallest branch).

What would you do?

A.   Reiterate your statement and ask their patience. (GO TO 512)

B.   Call Linda Hemingway (Crystal Lake librarian) and ask her to keep you posted on the attitude of her aides. (GO TO 612)

C.   Call Linda Hemingway and ask her if there are other reasons for her aides' concerns. (GO TO 465)

Decision Point 484

You and Bill have a problem-solving discussion. The two of you identify several alternatives to his commuting problem and his school problem. You give him several suggestions (carpooling; transfer the children to a suburban private school).

Two months pass and Bill's performance goes down again. At his performance appraisal interview, you express concern over his declining effort, and Bill breaks down. He and his wife have separated. A "city person," she never fully adapted to the country lifestyle. She apparently made few friends and suffered from "cabin fever." Apparently, your problem-solving meeting with Bill did not go far enough to address his problems of integrating his personal life with his career.

It is difficult to mentor individuals about things you have not experienced personally. Since Bill is facing challenges you have not had to deal with, it is unlikely that you can be an effective mentor at this point. Therefore, re-evaluate your last decision. Circle the #484 you just wrote, and move to the last uncircled step in your flow diagram.

Decision Point 485

Your choice of a new motto is not the best option. Banners and mottos can be powerful symbols in a top-down change. Effectively constructed, they are compelling and superordinate. Compelling means that they are attractive and energizing. Superordinate means that they are appreciated by groups that might differ on other issues.

"Where Service Is Always Professional" is neither compelling nor superordinate. It is not compelling because it implies cold, impersonal interactions between patrons and library staff. It is not superordinate because LCLD has a history of periodic conflict between professionally oriented staff and community-service-oriented staff. Rather than healing these old schisms, your new motto seems to declare one winner in an old contest.

Re-evaluate your last decision. Circle the #485 you just wrote in your flow diagram. Then move to the first uncircled step above this one in your flow diagram.

Decision Point 486

Your second meeting with Eugene is short and to the point. He authorizes the funds necessary for the change and tells you he will take care of Gordon Garvin (Director of Engineering). He then informs you that it is true that Randy Winslow (the manager of the technicians currently doing the custom work in Engineering) will be moving to England, and that that was one of the reasons he wants you to begin thinking about the change now. When you follow up with a question about his time preference, Eugene tells you that he expects the market to take an important turn (toward customization) in two years, so you ought to have completed the change within 18 months. Thus, Eugene isn't thinking about this change in crisis proportions.

Clarifying your concerns with Eugene was important in that it allowed you to answer a number of questions you had about the change that needed to be implemented. Not having a clear sense of the situation could have led you to make incorrect choices about how to proceed.

As you leave Eugene's office, you are comfortable now with the charter he has given you. Clearly this is an important matter that has far-reaching effects. You look over the three alternatives once again and begin to sketch out some of the issues that will have to be addressed before implementation can proceed. The more you think about the issue, the more appealing the "flexible assembly" option seems.

What would you do now?

A.   Go back to Eugene and together decide which alternative (flexible assembly, super-teams, contracting) should be implemented. (GO TO 480)

B.   Call a meeting with the members of your team (Larry Beeson, Robin Broderick, and Marilyn Wilson) in order to study the issue of how to incorporate custom production into your department. (GO TO 605)

Decision Point 487

The next morning, when you arrive for work, you find Frank waiting outside your office with the warning in his hand. He looks angry. He belligerently says, "What the hell is this? I really want to talk this over with you now!"

You resent the tone he is taking, and you feel that you have been careful to follow all disciplinary guidelines.

What would you do at this point?

A.   Politely but firmly tell Frank that the warning covers everything that needs to be said and suggest that you both get to work. (GO TO 541)

B.   Tell Frank that since he feels so strongly about this you will talk to him now. (GO TO 475)

C.   Arrange to meet Frank later that morning. (GO TO 549)

Decision Point 488

What assignment would you give him?

A.   *Assignment 1.* Junior Control Engineer, *Dart* Project. Join a team of four members to test a ballistics control system for a *Dart* missile. Bob Blair is the project manager. The *Dart* missile is like other systems except that the new control system requires several standards never required before. Smythe's senior thesis dealt with ballistics control systems. Likelihood of Bill making a contribution to the team - Good. Value to Bill's development if he is personally successful - Fair. (GO TO 623)

B.   *Assignment 3.* Junior Control Engineer, Systems Test Group. Act as your administrative assistant. Perform several studies regarding planning and scheduling in preparation for upcoming budget negotiations. While this assignment has only a modest technical component, it is a great way for Bill to learn the inner workings of your department It also may allow him to find his own technical place in the group. Likelihood of Bill making a contribution to the team - Excellent. Value to Bill's development if he is personally successful - Marginal. (GO TO 628)

481

C. *Assignment 4.* Junior Control Engineer, Systems Test Group and member, *Micascope* Divisional Task Force. Join a task force of seven members conducting a manufacturing feasibility study of *Micascope*, a laser-refracting targeting system. The task force is chaired by the assistant to the divisional manager. The feasibility study proposed is controversial, with some task force members committed to manufacturing and some dead set against it. The division manager is said to favor manufacturing, but he has agreed to "let the chips fall where they may." While he hand-picked the members of the task force from other departments, he asked you to appoint the department member of your choice. Since all of your other people are busy with project work, Bill seems like a natural. Likelihood of Bill making a contribution to the team - Fair. Value to Bill's development if he is personally successful - Very Good. (GO TO 557)

Decision Point 489

You decide to hire someone from the outside to replace Mel Simmons. The results are unfortunate. While familiar with *BIBLIOTEK*, she is unfamiliar with the operations of LCLD. Accordingly when it comes time for the Crystal Lake Branch to come "on line," she makes several judgment errors that jeopardize the entire change effort. Moreover, since her subordinates are not all supportive of the change, she decides to appear tough in order to earn their respect. The net effect is that you have created a new set of problems for yourself.

Re-evaluate your last decision. Circle the #489 you just wrote in your flow diagram. Then move to the first uncircled step above this one in your flow diagram.

Decision Point 490

Some people think that giving a new recruit a candid assessment of the social skills of his or her co-workers is dangerous. If it is done discreetly and carefully, however, it provides a new employee with exactly the sort of information he or she needs to progress through this stage.

It is one month later, and there are several signs that Bill is now considered a legitimate member of the team. He is seldom excluded from the group's informal activities. He has even been included in a Friday night poker party organized by a co-worker who initially had been hard on him. So completely has Bill been integrated into his team that he has begun to show defensiveness whenever an outsider or client criticizes the team or any member of it.

One situation is particularly important. One of Bill's team members, Sam Scanlon, is a very capable engineer but is socially very meek and self-conscious. Unfortunately, this trait has caused him to be the least visible and most uninfluential member of your entire work group--a distinction that is some concern to you. Two days ago Sam was briefing a panel of clients on the *Solaris* project. Everyone on the project team was present. Sam's presentation was technically sound but lacked polish in delivery. A member of the panel, who you know to be caustic in such situations, interrupted Sam in the midst of his monotone and severely criticized his conclusions. Sam struggled for a response, but was failing miserably. His attacker pressed the matter. Sam struggled some more. K. C. Wong interrupted and clarified the logic. Seemingly satisfied the client eased up. But later, he repeated his concerns. With that, Bill let loose with a pointed, almost personal attack on the client that stopped him but put a pall over the rest of the meeting.

What would you do now?

A. Let K. C. Wong handle the matter. (GO TO 470)

B. Tell Bill how he could have better assessed the situation in terms of Sam's fundamental weaknesses, K. C. Wong's responsibilities, and the particular personality of this client. (GO TO 599)

C. Inform Bill that Sam needs practice bailing himself out and that he should not get involved in his development. (GO TO 538)

D. Tell Bill that clients should be allowed to say whatever they want even if it is uncomplimentary and that one important role of a Venus employee is to be a flak-catcher. (GO TO 476)

E. Tell Bill that his actions in this situation are irresponsible and that you cannot tolerate more difficulties of this nature. (GO TO 516)

Decision Point 491

You dealt with the question of professional control very effectively. Professional organizations are very difficult settings for changes that seem to erode "professional autonomy." Doctors, lawyers, architects, and engineers often object to any change that constrains their options at work. Your response dealt well with the question, for it mentioned the benefits of the new system and included assurances that professional prerogatives were not compromised.

It is now two weeks after your speech. You have completed your public relations campaign emphasizing the benefits of a computerized library information system. It has generated a great deal of community interest. However, some district office people are not learning *BIBLIOTEK* very rapidly. When they are confronted, they offer the excuse that they have community service chores to do. They also remind you that your earlier speech said that LCLD's should not lose its service philosophy. Apparently, you have not adequately differentiated your overriding philosophy from Ms. B's.

What would you do now?

A. Make it clear that top priority should be given to the computerization program even if service activities have to suffer a bit in the short run. (GO TO 616)

B. Contact Ms. B to earn her endorsement for the computerization effort. Encourage her to speak out on the benefits of computerization on service to the community in the long run. (GO TO 561)

C. Announce a new motto that differentiates your philosophy from Ms. B's. (GO TO 627)

Decision Point 492

When you meet next with your group, you spell out the general problems of how to integrate the engineering techs into your work group. You mention that this may be difficult because you must maintain current production as well as develop the ability to shift to heavier use of single item production within the next couple of years. At this point Marilyn mentions that it seems to her that flexible assembly may be a good long-run solution to a change in the market, but not a very good approach over the short run because it will disrupt all the assembly teams.

As the meeting draws to a close, you feel you have a good sense of where your team stands. They all see the need for the change and realize that over the long run it will radically change the way production is carried out. As well, you are aware that they are concerned about the potential disruptiveness of the flexible assembly approach.

The group agrees that the problem is much as you describe it. After a short discussion, Larry suggests that since it will be two years before the complete implementation of "flexible assembly" is necessary, one intermediate step might be to implement the "super-team" approach initially. Larry suggests that this will isolate the techs and give you an opportunity to phase in the changes. Marilyn and Robin both speak up to support his idea.

As the group discusses this idea, you become more and more convinced of its reasonableness. As well, you sense genuine excitement on your team. You accept the recommendation and agree to take it to Eugene for his approval. Eugene's first reaction is negative. He expresses concern that you seem to be acting too conservatively and that he's never heard of a "super-team" before.

How would you react?

A.   Gently try to persuade Eugene that your team's recommendation makes a great deal of sense. Provide detail that makes the case compelling. (GO TO 609)

B.   Defend your team's decision. Indicate that the idea of a "super-team" is only an interim move. Tell Eugene that your team's analysis was thorough. (GO TO 536)

C.   Ask Eugene what his specific concerns are with the idea so that you can return to discuss them with your team. (GO TO 468)

Decision Point 493

In discussing Frank's absences with him, which general approach would you be most likely to take?

A.   Tell him that your boss is on your back for more productivity, and ask for his help in correcting his attendance problem. (GO TO 578)

B.   Explain the necessity of good attendance if production goals are to be met and point out to him how much his attendance is adversely affecting production. Urge him to do better. (GO TO 481)

C.   Mention to him in as positive a way as you can that if he doesn't improve you will be forced to give him a written warning. (GO TO 509)

D.   Ask him what difficulty he is having. (GO TO 563)

E.   Ask him if he is feeling better today. (GO TO 570)

Decision Point 494

Bill discusses the situation with his team leader, and the two of them agree that Bill should "stay out of the way" of the design group. In spite of this distance, the designers retaliate and take the matter up the chain of command to a common manager. Top management sends you a pointed memo that says in effect "Keep that kid of yours in tow, or else!"

While taking a coffee break in the cafeteria, a design engineer talks loudly about top management's reprimand so that Bill can overhear it. Bill flies off the handle again and threatens to punch the engineer in the nose. Bill's project leader breaks up the confrontation and takes Bill aside for a scolding. Bill resigns the next morning.

Re-evaluate your last decision. Circle the #494 you just wrote, and move to the last uncircled step in your flow diagram.

Decision Point 495

You are correct in phasing the implementation. This will enable you to demonstrate a small victory, which will add to the momentum of the change effort. Choosing the Live Oak Branch as your test site is also correct, for the personnel there seem least resistant to it at the outset.

Now you face the decision about how to announce the change. It occurs to you that you could introduce it with different levels of visibility and fanfare. Which of the following would you choose?

A. High visibility--Call a meeting of all personnel and announce your plan for the implementation of the computer system. Simultaneously send out a press release to county newspapers that details the plan and promises better service after the system is operational. Solicit invitations to speak to community service groups (e.g., Lions Club, Rotary, etc.) about the change. (GO TO 507)

B. Moderate visibility--Call a meeting of all personnel and announce your plan for the implementation of the computer system. (GO TO 479)

C. Low visibility--Tell the professional librarians your plans and ask them to communicate this to their aides and assistants. (GO TO 568)

Your daily meetings with Bill go well, but they are very time consuming. He begins bringing up even the most trivial issues, and occasionally you even find yourself doing his work. The meetings grow in duration until one day you cut it off and firmly suggest that Bill try to go it alone for a while. Cut loose, Bill flounders again, misses deadlines on important tasks, and completes unimportant ones with more "flair" than necessary. You conclude that Bill is not seeing the forest for the trees.

What would you do now?

A. Tell K. C. Wong that he is responsible for Bill's performance. Tell K. C. that you do not want him to sacrifice the objectives of the *Solaris* system, but that you think Bill deserves more of his time. (GO TO 564)

B. Begin again to give Bill a detailed account of how to contend with the challenges and problems of his work. Agree to meet with him in three days to review his progress and advise him on new situations. (GO TO 571)

C. Talk to K. C. Wong about sharing responsibility for breaking Bill in. (GO TO 567)

In your speech, you need to decide what if anything you should say to ease the feelings of employment insecurity that are likely to be caused by your announcement. Obviously, some of those who oppose computerization feel that threatens their jobs. You know from experience that computerizing a library generally results in somewhere between 10% and 20% in voluntary attrition. So, it would not be dishonest to tell them that the people who want to remain after computerization will have some job within the LCLD.

A. Nothing. There is no reason to deal with this issue in advance. (GO TO 477)

B. Tell them that specific staffing cuts are not foreseen but that no guarantees can be made. (GO TO 510)

C. Say that you realize the hard work that all will have to do to make computerization a success. In a non-threatening way, tell them that you will do everything you can to ensure that the job of everyone who supports the computerization effort is safe. (GO TO 515)

D. Promise that no one will lose his or her job because of computerization. (GO TO 620)

E. Acknowledge that the LCLD is currently over-staffed but say that you are reasonably confident that this problem will be solved through natural attrition. (GO TO 624)

Decision Point 498

You call a meeting of your team to consider the three options you have come up with. Your group jumps at the chance to take on this problem, but there is a subtle uneasiness on two counts: (a) Marilyn and Robin remain unconvinced that change is really called for; and (b) it is unclear how the group's recommendations are going to be used in decision making. After considerable discussion, your team decides to deal with this issue as a hypothetical question. This is not really a satisfactory posture, but it is the only one you can exercise leadership around. Apparently you brought a charge to your team without a very clear charter from your boss. This resulted in your group having to take on an academic frame of reference.

Re-evaluate your last decision. Circle the #498 you just wrote in your flow diagram. Then move to the first uncircled step above this one in your flow diagram.

Decision Point 499

You decide to ask others in your group if they know what Frank's problem might be. You go to his co-workers and ask if they think they know why he is missing so much work. No one seems to be willing to discuss the matter with you. You finally ask one of your newest employees if she knows anything. She says that a friend of hers who works in data processing told her that he saw Frank and some woman in a car headed out of town that morning (Monday). Further, her friend told her that Frank looked drunk. You know that your company has a good alcoholism counseling program. What would you do now?

A. Check with Frank's previous supervisor to see what his past attendance record was like. (GO TO 594)

B. Call Frank aside upon his return and have a talk with him. (GO TO 493)

C. Discuss the matter with your manager in order to get her advice and input in handling the situation. (GO TO 469)

D. Call the Human Resources Department to see what disciplinary options are open to you. (GO TO 457)

E. Call the Human Resources Department to see if there are other departments that need people with Frank's qualifications so you can transfer him there. (GO TO 514)

F. Instruct Frank to report to the company counseling center when he returns to work since you don't feel competent to cope with his drinking. (GO TO 586)

G. Write Frank up for chronic absenteeism and leave a copy of the warning in an envelope on his desk for him to see when he comes in. (GO TO 487)

Decision Point 500

Convinced by your arguments, Bill withdraws his request for a transfer. Unfortunately, however, the rumor that Bill wants out of the group begins to spread throughout his project team. This results in Bill being given "the silent treatment" for a couple of days, and Bill comes in again with the idea of a transfer.

What is happening here is that Bill is having difficulty finding out how to fit into his group. What would you do now?

A. Grant his request for a transfer because you do not think Bill can possibly earn the acceptance of his group under these circumstances. (GO TO 502)

B. Give Bill a candid, accurate assessment of the social strengths and weaknesses of the other members of his work team, and advise him of specific actions he might take to gain more acceptance into the group. Monitor his social performance closely. (GO TO 530)

C. Talk privately to other members of Bill's team and encourage each of them to serve as a mentor to Bill. (GO TO 579)

D. Ask his team leader to allow Bill to be a spokesperson for the team in an upcoming meeting with divisional management (at which all will be present) so that he will have a chance to earn his team's approval. (GO TO 603)

Decision Point 501

You decide to implement the change through delegation. You call all employees together in a meeting. You point out the need for computerization in your opening remarks and throw the subject open for suggestions concerning how to implement the change. The suggestions from the floor are diverse and contradictory. Some suggest delaying the change indefinitely. Others recommend an implementation schedule that is much too optimistic. By the end of the meeting, you realize that opening up the topic to full and open dialogue was unwise. All that it accomplished was to splinter the employees into coalitions that are unwilling to negotiate or compromise. To keep the momentum of the meeting, you appoint a panel of the most active participants to serve as the implementation committee. Sharply divided, the committee is unable to agree on a plan until after important deadlines have passed.

Using participation in this instance is inadvisable for several reasons: (1) Expertise about computers is not dispersed in the work force. You were the one most qualified to design the implementation plan. (2) LCLD employees are not used to participation. Ms. B's maternalistic approach made them unfamiliar with participative management. (3) Time is a serious constraint with this change. (4) The LCLD's accreditation crisis is known to everyone. This is a public agency, so LCLD's problems with the state have been in the news.

Re-evaluate your last decision. Circle the #501 you just wrote in your flow diagram. Then move to the first uncircled step above this one in your flow diagram.

Decision Point 502

Bill transfers and your fears are realized. He runs into technical problems again, his new supervisor asks you why you sent her a "turkey," and Bill ultimately leaves the company.

Re-evaluate your last decision. Circle the #502 you just wrote, and move to the last uncircled step in your flow diagram.

Decision Point 503

The decision you should make before your speech is what to do about a motto or theme for the "new LCLD." Ms. B consistently articulated the theme "The County Is Served When We Make the Time to Listen."

In your speech, how would your address the issue of symbols?

A.   Postpone developing a new motto for the time being. Instead, argue that computerization is totally consistent with LCLD's historical emphasis on service. Accordingly, Ms. B's old motto will work just fine. (GO TO 596).

B.   Announce a new motto: "Where Service Is Always Professional." Arrange to have all stationery and library cards embossed with that new motto. (GO TO 485)

C.   Announce a new motto: "Looking for Better Ways to Serve You Best." Arrange to have all stationery and library cards embossed with that new motto. (GO TO 547)

Decision Point 504

Providing your team with detailed information was important in helping them understand the need to change and increasing their motivation to work on the problem.

You begin the next meeting with your team by providing a detailed summary of your initial conversation with Eugene and a report of what Tom told you. You try to make clear to the group the necessity of the change and the importance it holds for the Production group. After you provide your summary, you get a number of questions from Larry and Robin which seem to indicate that they don't feel it is particularly necessary to integrate the technicians doing custom work into the Production Department. You reiterate the importance of the change and offer to arrange for your group to receive a firsthand report of the shift in the PBX market. As you continue to talk, you begin to notice that the group is becoming less resistant to the ideas you are presenting. Larry and Marilyn make comments that suggest that they are quite concerned about how to cope with the new market conditions. Even Robin admits that the scenario you describe could be a real threat if Arion does not respond to it.

At this point you feel that your team is motivated to respond to the situation you outlined. You know that you now need to spell out what your team will need to do to develop the capability to increase custom production.

What would you do now?

A.   Give members a progress report on the analysis you have done so far and tell them that you will continue analyzing alternatives and report back to them. (GO TO 589)

B. Lay out the "flexible assembly" plan and ask the group to develop procedures for implementing it. (GO TO 526)

C. Provide the group with the information you have collected about the three alternatives and tell the group to provide you with a set of recommendations. (GO TO 552)

D. Give members the information you have assembled, and tell them to develop a workable plan and implement it. (GO TO 625)

Decision Point 505

"The problem is my wife. We just got together again after she and I had been separated for eight months. She found out that she has an incurable kidney disease, and she wanted to come back on account of Eric, that's our son. Anyway, she has dialysis treatments three times a week, Mondays, Wednesdays, and Fridays. The toughest day of the week is Sunday, since she's on her second day without dialysis, and her body chemistry is all off. She gets real irritable, and she, Eric, and I always get in a fight over one thing or another. Mostly, it's Eric. He blames me for our first breakup, and when Barbara is weak, he just piles it on. The last two Sundays he just walked out.

"Last Monday I had to bail him out of jail all the way over in Clay County. It was 9:00 a.m. before we got home. Now that he's back at home without a driver's license, Sundays are going to be mighty tough. If he acts up, Barbara is going to need me more than ever, and her dialysis appointment isn't until noon Mondays. I've talked with her doctor about her Sunday mood problems, but he says he doesn't want to give her any more drugs."

At this point what would you say?

A. "Well, it's real helpful to know what's been troubling you. Now, then, you must realize that I am being held responsible for production, so to be fair to the company, I am going to have to give you a formal warning on your attendance. I will pull it from your file if you are able to work the next four Mondays in a row. Otherwise, I am going to have to give you a second warning, and you know what that means." (GO TO 582)

B. "I understand. It sounds to me that you realize how important it is to improve your attendance record. I know now that you have got a tricky problem on your hands. I just want you to know that you've got my support.

Do the best you can with your absences, and I'll cover for you as long as I can." (GO TO 481)

C. "I think I understand your situation, but you know my situation as well. I am getting pressure for production, and your absences are troublesome. We need to work out a plan that will result in a level of production that is your fair share. Do you have any ideas that we might put to use?" (GO TO 574)

D. "I know someone who is a professional family counselor. He's a neighbor of mine, and he is really good. Here's his phone number. If you need help with this thing, you should see a professional." (GO TO 622)

Decision Point 506

You learn that Bill has committed himself to try the suggestions given him by both the men, a commitment he cannot possibly follow. Before you can talk to Bill, he is absent for three days and resigns on the fourth.

Apparently having two mentors has put Bill in a box he could not get out of. With his credibility on the line, and desperate to gain the acceptance from his fellow workers, he felt no other option but to quit.

Re-evaluate your last decision. Circle the #506 you just wrote, and move to the last uncircled step in your flow diagram.

Decision Point 507

A highly visible campaign of announcing your intentions leaves little doubt as to your resolve for getting the system up and operational in a year. Anything less than this, and people may be apt to test your resolve or underestimate it. You chose correctly.

You now need to decide what to do with the position of Community Service Director. Recall that this position was vacated by Ms. B's husband when the two of them retired. One option is to fill the position with a person who will continue to serve as the primary liaison between LCLD and the community. Thus, the new person would spearhead such efforts as the Joy of Reading Program and the Children's Story Hour Program. This individual would also be responsible for arranging new cooperative ventures with other libraries in the county. Computerization facilitates such ventures, for it will ultimately lead to the entire county being linked by an integrated information resource system). Another way of dealing with the position is to change it to a position to Director of Library Information Systems.

This will require a change in civil service classification, but you have good reason to believe that this could be done without delay or opposition. The implications of these two options are as follows:

Option 1: Replace Ms. B's husband with a new Director of Community Relations. You will need to ask Alice Bishop to serve as the primary detail person regarding computer implementation. She is familiar with the operational details of the *BIBLIOTEK* system, so she possesses the necessary technical skills to act in this capacity. However, you will have to be very involved with the change to the point of having to delegate almost all responsibility for community service to the new director. This option will enable the LCLD to maintain a high profile in its concern for community service.

Option 2: Change the position to Director of Library Information Systems and fill it with a professional. This will enable you to bring in an expert on library computer systems. He or she will be prepared to handle the details of the change and the linkages to other library systems. This will free you to be more visible in the community and allow you more flexibility in dealing with your responsibilities.

Which option would you choose?

A.   Option 1. (GO TO 461)

B.   Option 2. (GO TO 467)

Decision Point 508

You have decided to provide a sketchy outline of the importance of this project for Arion's future. The outcome of this is to increase the "nervousness" of your team. Unfortunately, this anxiety is not channeled into constructive effort. Rather, it comes out as a general mistrust of you and the organization.

Two weeks later the group has not made any progress on the assignment. The only outcome seems to be that you have heard rumors that Marilyn is looking for a new job because she doesn't think there is much of a future at Arion.

Re-evaluate your last decision. Circle the #508 you just wrote in your flow diagram. Then move to the first uncircled step above this one in your flow diagram.

Decision Point 509

You have decided that this situation is best dealt with by using the system of discipline used in the company. However, it doesn't work in this case. Frank continues his habit of Monday absences through the final warning and he ultimately is terminated. Now you face the job of recruiting a replacement and dealing with the growing dissatisfaction of your boss and your people.

It is not that formal discipline systems like this one are poorly designed, it is that they must be administered carefully. Careful administration means moving beyond enforcing the relationship between undesired behavior and punitive outcomes.

Re-evaluate your decision. Circle the #509 you just wrote in your flow diagram. Then go back in your flow diagram to the first uncircled number above this step.

Decision Point 510

You plan to announce that you foresee no specific staffing cuts but that you can make no guarantees. While it is good that you say something about whether computerization will lead to staff cuts, your statement will do little to allay fears. Those concerned realize that you cannot make absolute guarantees. However, they would like to have stronger assurances that you do not have specific people targeted for cuts.

Re-evaluate your last decision. Circle the #510 you just wrote in your flow diagram. Then move to the first uncircled step about this one in your flow diagram.

Decision Point 511

Your daily meetings with Bill go well, but they are very time consuming. He begins bringing up even the most trivial issues, and occasionally you even find yourself doing his work. The meetings grow in duration until one day you cut it off and firmly suggest that Bill try to go it alone for a while. Cut loose, Bill flounders again, misses deadlines on important tasks, and completes unimportant ones with more "flair" than necessary. You conclude that Bill is not seeing the forest for the trees. Even though you are spending time with Bill, he is not receiving the kind of mentoring that will help him adapt.

What would you do now?

A. Tell Bob Blair that he is responsible for Bill's performance. Tell Bob that you do not want him to sacrifice the objectives of the *Dart* system, but that you think Bill deserves more of his time. (GO TO 575)

B. Begin again to give Bill a detailed account of how to contend with the challenges and problems of his work. Agree to meet with him in three days to review his progress and advise him on new situations. (GO TO 534)

C. Talk to Bob Blair about sharing responsibility for breaking Bill in. (GO TO 550)

D. Take time to remind others in your group that helping Bill adapt to his job is important. (GO TO 611)

Decision Point 512

You decide to reiterate your position and ask for their patience. Under some circumstances, this may be enough. In this case, you really needed to investigate the causes of this mild resistance. You should consider the complaints as a signal that the branch people may resist more firmly unless you convince them otherwise. You may learn something if you look into the matter more thoroughly. There could be a basis in fact for their concerns that they are not stating directly. The best action is to see if there are concerns beyond their stated concerns. Otherwise, the resistance will probably snowball.2

Re-evaluate your last decision. Circle the #512 you just wrote in your flow diagram. Then move to the first uncircled step about this one in your flow diagram.

Decision Point 513

Each member of the team gives a very general statement about the need to respond to the changing market. However, you continue to wonder about the strength of the group's commitment.

At this point what would you do?

A. Lay out an implementation plan for flexible assembly. (GO TO 559)

B. Conclude that you are probably worrying over nothing. Instruct the group to develop procedures for implementing "flexible assembly." (GO TO 562)

C. Assign one team member to develop and present an argument for flexible assembly and another member to play "devil's advocate" and present counter-arguments. Once those arguments are all out, lead a general discussion. (GO TO 601)

Decision Point 514

You have decided to ask the Human Resources Department about the possibilities of transferring Frank. Human Resources tells you that there is an opening in the Research Department for someone with Frank's qualifications. Since the position offers more money, you conclude that Frank would probably welcome the change. Certainly, the pressure on productivity is not nearly as great there as it is in your department.

What would you do at this juncture?

A. Talk to Frank about the transfer when he returns. (GO TO 553)

B. Talk with some of Frank's co-workers to see if they have any idea what might be causing Frank's absences. (GO TO 499)

C. Check with Frank's previous supervisor to see what his past attendance was like. (GO TO 594)

D. Call Frank aside upon his return without the intention of discussing the transfer. (GO TO 493)

E. Discuss the matter with your manager in order to get her advice and input in handling his absenteeism. (GO TO 469)

F. Call Human Resources to see what disciplinary options are open to you. (GO TO 457)

Decision Point 515

Your plan to deal with the employment insecurity issue is excellent. While you make no guarantees, you promise to fight for their security because you realize you are asking them to work hard to make computerization work. That is a nice quid pro quo: "I'm asking you to scratch my back, so I'll scratch yours in return." Promises of reciprocation usually allay fears of insecurity.

You now must decide what you will say in your speech about the specifics of the implementation plan. What would you do?

A.   Outline a specific timetable for the change specifying training objectives and implementation targets. Arrange time targets for early stages that are pessimistic to "guarantee" early perceived successes. (GO TO 503)

B.   Outline a specific timetable for the change specifying training objectives and implementation targets. Arrange time targets for all stages based on "most likely" outcomes. (GO TO 535)

C.   Stay clear of specifying a timetable so you can keep your options open. (GO TO 580)

Decision Point 516

You decided to take a tough stand with Bill. He reacts very negatively to your comments, and his resignation letter appears on your desk at the end of the day.

Re-evaluate your last decision. Circle the #516 you just wrote, and move to the last uncircled step in your flow diagram.

Decision Point 517

Successful change managers emphasize both the external and internal conditions that create the need for change. Re-evaluate your last decision. Circle the #517 you just wrote in your flow diagram. Then move to the first uncircled step about this one in your flow diagram.

Decision Point 518

You have decided to meet with Eugene and discuss the major political, cost, and timetable factors surrounding his decision to bring the technicians into your department. You have identified three specific points that you want to cover:

1.   You are concerned about how Randy Winslow's boss, Gordon Garvin (Director of Engineering), will react to this change. You and Gordon have occasionally had difficulty cooperating in the past, and you want Eugene to coordinate the transition with Gordon.

2. You estimate that it will take about one week to redesign the manufacturing process and move equipment, no matter what approach is chosen. As well, you think that it will be another two weeks to get the performance of the assembly group back to current levels.

3. The direct costs of the reorganization, including new equipment and overtime, are likely to be between $60,000 and $87,500. You are not sure where that money will come from.

After you lay out these points, Eugene quickly shifts the discussion. He says that the market is changing, moving away from the standard PBX system you have been manufacturing toward more customized systems. He expresses confidence in your ability to meet the challenge brought about by this market change. At that point he ends the meeting by saying that he has another very important appointment, but that he could see you later that afternoon if you felt it was really necessary.

What would you do now?

A. Schedule a meeting with Eugene for later that afternoon. (GO TO 486)

B. Take Eugene's comments as a signal that he is unprepared to deal with the points that you have raised until you have made more progress. Arrange to meet with your group soon to begin the process of analyzing which alternative (flexible assembly, super-teams, contracting) to choose. (GO TO 498)

C. Do nothing. Clearly Eugene does not consider this a priority, so wait until he brings it up again. (GO TO 540)

Decision Point 519

You have asked Frank about his personal problem during a rather tense conversation. Under the circumstances, Frank would probably say, "My problem at home is my own business," or something like that. You have simply not given Frank any reason to trust or even respect you.

Re-evaluate your last decision. Circle the #519 you just wrote in your flow diagram. Then go back in your flow diagram to the first uncircled number above this step.

Decision Point 520

You ask Bill for his preference for an assignment. Although getting Bill's preferences might provide you with better information and build his commitment to his new assignment, this was risky. He might have requested an assignment that would not be right for him. As it is, he tells you that he really wants to work on *Solaris*.

Which assignment would you give him?

A.   Assignment 1. Junior Control Engineer, *Dart* Project. Join a team of four members to test a ballistics control system for a *Dart* missile. Bob Blair is the project manager. The *Dart* missile is like other systems except that the new control system requires several standards never required before. Bill's senior thesis dealt with ballistics control systems. Likelihood of Bill making a contribution to the team - Good. Value to Bill's development if he is personally successful - Fair. (GO TO 623)

B.   Assignment 2. Junior Control Engineer, *Solaris* Project. Join a team of three members to test the propulsion control system for a *Solaris* booster. K. C. Wong is the project manager. Wong is very enthusiastic about Bill joining the team. Wong graduated from the same engineering school as Bill. The *Solaris* project will require a unique control system that has never been implemented before. The project is presently behind schedule because of the novelty of its design. It would offer a fantastic learning opportunity for any junior engineer. Likelihood of Bill making a contribution to the team - Fair. Value to Bill's development if he is personally successful - Very Good. (GO TO 626)

C.   Assignment 3. Junior Control Engineer, Systems Test Group. Act as your administrative assistant. Perform several studies regarding planning and scheduling in preparation for upcoming budget negotiations. While this assignment has only a modest technical component, it is a great way for Bill to learn the inner workings of your department. It may also allow him to find his own technical place in the group. Likelihood of Bill making a contribution to the team - Excellent. Value to Bill's development if he is personally successful - Marginal. (GO TO 628)

D.   Assignment 4. Junior Control Engineer, Systems Test Group and member, *Micascope* Divisional Task Force. Join a task force of seven members conducting a manufacturing feasibility study of *Micascope*, a laser-refracting targeting system. The task force is chaired by the assistant to the divisional manager. The feasibility study proposed is controversial, with some task force members committed to manufacturing and some dead set against it. The division manager is said to favor manufacturing, but he has agreed to "let the chips fall where they may." While he hand-picked the members of the task

500

force from other departments, he asked you to appoint the department member of your choice. Since all of your other people are busy with project work, Bill seems like a natural. Likelihood of Bill making a contribution to the team - Fair. Value to Bill's development if he is personally successful - Very Good. (GO TO 557)

Decision Point 521

Marcia Gamble is not the best candidate. Change agents ideally have both high social skills and technical credibility. Marcia lacks technical credibility. In a professional organization, technical credibility begins with a professional degree, e.g., M.D., J.D., Ph.D., R.N., etc. Marcia's master's degree just does not measure up because it is not a M.L.S. (master's of library science, the "union card" for librarians).

Re-evaluate your last decision. Circle the #521 you just wrote in your flow diagram. Then move to the first uncircled step about this one in your flow diagram.

Decision Point 522

You instruct your team to begin to develop an implementation plan for "flexible assembly." The group works hard and develops a detailed set of procedures. All seems to be going well until the techs are actually moved into their new quarters. Although Larry has few initial problems, the situation in Robin's "shop" is dreadful. Two of the tech's assigned to him quit, and Gordon Garvin begins taking "pot shots" at your plan. Apparently you didn't do enough to assure yourself that Robin was on board before you moved the team to implementation questions.

Re-evaluate your last decision. Circle the #522 you just wrote in your flow diagram. Then move to the first uncircled step above this one in your flow diagram.

Decision Point 523

You ask directly if his problem has something to do with alcohol. He says, "It most certainly does not!" What would you say to Frank's denial?

A.   "Frank, I have reason to believe that it is, and I should tell you that it is affecting your work. If it continues, it may cost you your job. Now I want to help. Why don't you go down there and talk to the people in the center. They are really equipped there to help you." (GO TO 586)

501

B. "Frank, if it isn't alcohol, then what is it?" (GO TO 549)

C. "Okay, you say it's not alcohol, but tell me honestly, Frank, have you really been sick for the last three Mondays out of four, or is it something else?" (GO TO 537)

Decision Point 524

Bill and this other person really hit it off. They become very close friends, but his fellow group members continue to reject Bill. His co-workers now seem to feel that he lacks real interest in them, and they begin to give him the "cold shoulder." The lesson here is that not everyone has the skills nor job slack to be an effective mentor.

Three weeks later, Bill sends you a memo insisting that he would like to transfer to the division where his new friend works. You are convinced that granting the transfer would hurt you, Bill, and ultimately the entire organization.

What went wrong here is that you were not careful in assigning Bill his new mentor. Not only should mentors be socially skilled and have sufficient time and resources to invest in this role, they must also have the experience to provide useful advice. You found Bill a colleague, not someone who could help him learn about his new situation.

What would you do now?

A. Grant his request for the transfer because you do not think Bill can possibly earn the approval of his group under these circumstances. (GO TO 502)

B. Discourage Bill from taking the transfer and urge him to withdraw his request. (GO TO 554)

Decision Point 525

While this situation certainly calls for action, you do not need to threaten the security of people who has been working hard for you by bringing in an outsider. In general, it is better to bring in new people at the beginning of a change program than the end. Remember, too, that it will take more time to find, orient, and train a person from the outside than an intern from within.

Re-evaluate your last decision. Circle the #525 you just wrote in your flow diagram. Then move to the first uncircled step about this one in your flow diagram.

You instruct your team to begin to plan the implementation of the flexible assembly option. The group works hard and develops a detailed set of plans. Marilyn develops a plan for more flexible scheduling procedures. As well, she prepares for shifting inventory from large counts of a relatively few parts to small counts of more parts. Larry completes a plan for reorganizing his assembly lines and training his lead supervisors. Robin completes a set of plans for dealing with changing warranty repairs.

When the techs are moved into the Production group, the changes are much more complicated than anyone anticipated. The techs still think of themselves as engineers and have a difficult time fitting into assembly functions. Worse, the presence of the techs disrupts your assembly workers and interferes with your group's ability to complete its normal production runs.

Overall, there are many more problems than you anticipated. Costs are higher than you forecast, and it is clear that you will not be able to bring them under control. In short, this change was more than the group could take. Just this morning Robin expressed his intention to quit Arion as a result of this situation.

Re-evaluate your last decision. Circle the #526 you just wrote in your flow diagram. Then move to the first uncircled step above this one in your flow diagram.

The plan you have worked out with Frank accomplishes several objectives. Frank's attendance does improve. He does miss the next two Mondays, but he attends regularly after that time. In addition, since you have already administered the second warning by the time Frank's attendance improves, this "protects the company" from his falling back into his old habits. The cost of this protection, though, is three days of lost production (two Mondays and a one-day suspension on the second warning). There are instances where this loss is justified and instances where it is not.

You did an excellent job. Congratulations! This completes the Problem Employee Interactive Case.

Decision Point 528

The problem with your decision is that continuing as your administrative assistant was insufficiently challenging to help Bill get beyond his need to establish himself technically.

As a result, Bill grows so dissatisfied with the limited technical nature of his work that he contacts a firm that heavily recruited him. They again offer him a job at a higher salary than he is being paid at Venus.

Job offer in hand, Bill confronts tells you he will resign unless you assign him to the *Solaris* project, even though he likes Venus and you.

What would you do now?

  A.   Assign him to the *Solaris* project. (GO TO 626)

  B.   Wish him well with the other firm. (GO TO 458)

Decision Point 529

It is now nine months since the implementation began. The system is up and operational in the Live Oak Branch and 75 percent operational in the Main Branch. Crystal Lake is ahead of schedule. But, just as you are feeling comfortable with how things are unfolding, Emmet Smith drops a bombshell by resigning. As the assistant librarian of the Main Branch, Smith was somewhat skeptical of computerization at the beginning. However, Emmet was the person most responsible for 75% implementation at the Main Branch, and he really seemed to be a source of enthusiasm. His timing could not be worse! The progress of the entire implementation at Main Branch is presently at a very delicate stage and one that is unique to Main Branch.

What would you do about the vacancy left by King's exit?

  A.   Fill it with an intern "from the outside." (GO TO 572)

  B.   Fill it with a professional from the outside (this will risk having to let someone from the full-time staff go at the end of the year unless another professional voluntarily leaves in the next three months). (GO TO 525)

  C.   Fill it with the intern you hired into the district office seven months ago. Replace this intern with another intern from the "outside." (GO TO 551)

A risk in giving Bill a candid assessment of the social skills of others is that it might betray confidences, be tantamount to speaking behind peoples' backs, or be misunderstood by others. Nevertheless, it is a good approach. Consider that at this point in his development Bill needs the specific social understandings that you and perhaps you alone can give him. If done delicately and sensitively, it will not violate the expectations others have, and it will help Bill over this important developmental hurdle.

It is one month later, and there are several signs that Bill is now considered a legitimate member of the team. He is seldom excluded from informal group activities. The group even includes him in a Friday night poker party organized by a man who had initially been hard on him.

So completely has Bill been integrated into his team that he has begun to show defensiveness whenever an outsider or client criticizes the team or any member of it. One situation is particularly important. One of Bill's team members, Sam Scanlon, is a very capable engineer but is socially very meek and self-conscious. Unfortunately, this trait has caused him to be the least visible and most uninfluential member of your entire work group--a distinction that is some concern to you. Two days ago Sam was briefing a panel of clients on the *Dart* project. Everyone on the project team was present. Sam's presentation was technically sound but lacked polish in delivery. One member of the panel, who you know as caustic in such situations, interrupted Sam in the midst of his monotone and severely criticized his conclusions. Sam struggled for a response, but was failing miserably. His attacker pressed the matter. Sam struggled some more. Bob Blair interrupted and clarified the logic. Seemingly satisfied the client eased up. But later he repeated his concerns. With that, Bill let loose with a pointed, almost personal attack on the client that stopped him but put a pale over the rest of the meeting.

What would you do now?

A. Let Bob Blair handle the matter. (GO TO 587)

B. Suggest to Bill how he could have better assessed the situation in terms of Sam's fundamental weaknesses, Bob Blair's responsibilities, and the particular personality of this client. (GO TO 599)

C. Inform Bill that Sam needs practice bailing himself out and that he should not get involved in his development. (GO TO 460)

D. Tell Bill that clients should be allowed to say whatever they want, even if it is uncomplimentary, and that one important role of a Venus employee is to be a flak-catcher. (GO TO 615)

Decision Point 531

You delegate the decision as to whether to implement computerization to the entire group. The outcome of this effort parallels your interviews: some are in favor and some against. Opening up this issue to public debate, however, hardens positions and polarizes the work force. County officials call you frequently about the progress of computerization. Your options are few at this point.

Using delegation in this instance is inadvisable for several reasons: (1) Expertise about computers is not dispersed in the work force. You were the one most qualified to design the implementation plan. (2) LCLD employees are not used to participation. Ms. B's maternalistic approach made them unfamiliar with participative management. (3) Time is a serious constraint with this change. (4) The LCLD's accreditation crisis is known to everyone. This is a public agency, so LCLD's problems with the state have been in the news.

Re-evaluate your last decision. Circle the #531 you just wrote in your flow diagram. Then move to the first uncircled step above this one in your flow diagram.

Decision Point 532

You lay out the advantages and disadvantages of each of the three alternatives with Eugene. After a lengthy discussion, the two of you decide that "flexible assembly" offers the greatest net advantages. You then arrange for the implementation of this alternative. Immediately you run into resistance. The members of your team are miffed by not being included in the process, and Larry Beeson tells you that he has had considerable experience with "flexible assembly" at another firm--experience that would have led Arion in another direction.

Re-evaluate your last decision. Circle the #532 you just wrote in your flow diagram. Then move to the first uncircled step above this one in your flow diagram.

Decision Point 533

You tell Frank that he will be written up if he doesn't report for counseling. He tells you that he doesn't need counseling, but what he does need is for you to "get off my back" and "out of my personal life." He goes on to say, "I'm not going to see some shrink, and if you don't like it, go ahead and write me up." With that, he starts to walk out the door. What would you do now?

506

A. Wait until Frank returns and ask him to meet with you later that day. (GO TO 549)

B. Call Frank back and tell him that either he goes to counseling or he faces discharge. (GO TO 606)

C. Fill out a written warning on Frank for refusal to go to the counseling center. Send one copy to Frank and one to Human Resources. (GO TO 509)

Decision Point 534

You become Bill's mentor by default. No one else could guide Bill through the predictable crises he will face, so you must take on this role. As a mentor, you can provide Bill with information about the organization, give him advice and give him feedback about how he is progressing.

Bill responds well to the periodic meetings you and he set up. This closer monitoring and more frequent coaching begin to show in Bill's confidence and technical performance. Yet other problems begin to show up. You notice that he still is hesitant to initiate contact with his other team members when he is having a problem. And when he does ask for help, other team member misunderstand them or perceive them as an annoying call for reassurance. What is particularly disturbing is that Bill has yet to be accepted as a real member of the team. He is frequently excluded from lunches with the other members, and he has been given some mild hazing by one co-worker.

How would you react to this?

A. Start going to lunch with him regularly. (GO TO 542)

B. Set up an informal meeting between Bill and a new recruit from another division who has been more successfully accepted as a member of his team. (GO TO 466)

C. Give Bill a candid, accurate assessment of the social strengths and weaknesses of the other members of his work team. Advise him of specific strategies that he might use to gain acceptance into the group. Monitor his social performance closely. (GO TO 530)

D. Talk privately to the other members of Bill's team and encourage each of them to serve as Bill's mentor. (GO TO 579)

E.   Ask his team leader to allow Bill to be the spokesperson for the team in an upcoming meeting with division management (at which all department members will be present), so that he will have a better chance to earn his team's acceptance. (GO TO 603)

Decision Point 535

It is important to orchestrate the phasing of the change so that you have an early success. Using "most likely time estimates" is going to guarantee only a 50 percent success rate. You want a higher rate than that to make sure you have a success to celebrate.

Re-evaluate your last decision. Circle the #535 you just wrote in your flow diagram. Then move to the first uncircled step about this one in your flow diagram.

Decision Point 536

Your rather "direct" approach with Eugene works well. He gives you the green light for implementation. He agrees to clear things with Gordon Garvin and gives you a budget number for the funds you need for implementation. He also compliments you and your group for its careful work and creative solution.

It is now about two months later. The "super-team" is up and running well. The only difficulty is that the "engineering values" of the techs still create a bit of conflict with the manufacturing people. This level of conflict convinces you that you made a good decision in not throwing everyone together at once.

You are certain that when you phase in "flexible assembly," the process will be smooth. Larry, Robin, and Marilyn have begun to develop ways of phasing in the changes necessary. You are sure that your team is working more effectively now than ever! Given that you were convinced that you team had done a careful analysis, it became your responsibility to "sell" the solution to the rest of the organization, including your boss.

You have mobilized your team to implement a difficult change. Congratulations!

You asked Frank if he has really been ill. He says, "Look, I know the rules. They say that either illness or the illness of someone in your immediate family is allowable as sick leave. And it's been one of the two, I assure you!"

What would you do now?

A. Explain to Frank that his absences are causing real problems in production, and urge him to do better. (GO TO 481)

B. Ask Frank what the difficulty is. (GO TO 549)

C. Tell Frank that you don't like his attitude, and that if he is such an expert on the rules, then he knows that you can nail him any time you want. (GO TO 606)

Bill disagrees strongly with your statement, and in a rare show of temper slams the door when he leaves your office. You call him in the next day to clear the air. What should you do now?

A. Suggest how Bill could have better assessed the incident in terms of Sam's fundamental weaknesses, K. C. Wong's responsibilities in this situation, and the attributes of this client. (GO TO 599)

B. Tell Bill that clients should be allowed to say whatever they want, even if it is uncomplimentary, and that one important role of a Venus employee is to be a flak-catcher. (GO TO 615)

C. Tell Bill that it is unprofessional to show his temper to a client, his team leader, or you. Insist that he try to control himself. (GO TO 516)

Your answer is unresponsive to a latent issue that is likely to be the basis of the question--control. In general, administrative changes are more resisted than technical changes simply because they realign control and power relationships. As a change, computerization has an administrative component, so this question originates with a

509

concern about a loss of power and control. Specifically, computerization often scares professionals because they fear that it will result in more restrictions to their autonomy and less influence in the organization.

Re-evaluate your last decision. Circle the #539 you just wrote in your flow diagram. Then move to the first uncircled step above this one in your flow diagram.

Decision Point 540

You go on with your normal duties, in effect ignoring Eugene's concern about "flexible assembly." Three weeks pass and nothing else happens. Then you happen to see one of Eugene's friends in the hallway near your office. She greets you with the following comments, "Oh, Eugene has been telling me how well you are doing in planning the move Arion is making toward more customization. He's really counting on you, you know. My, he had such good things to say about you."

Clearly Eugene has expectations for your efforts that you did not accurately sense. Now that you know this is a high priority with him, what would you do?

A.   Schedule a meeting with Eugene for later that afternoon. (GO TO 486)

B.   Take Eugene's earlier comments as a signal that he is unprepared to deal with the points that you have raised until you have made more progress. Arrange to meet with your group soon to begin the process of analyzing which alternative (flexible assembly, super-teams, contracting) to choose. (GO TO 498)

Decision Point 541

After your comment to Frank, he doesn't say anything, but goes directly back to work. That afternoon, one of the men tells you that Frank has been telling other employees that you treated him unfairly. Later that same afternoon, as you pass Frank, you catch a glimpse of a gesture he makes behind your back. The other employees laugh. When you turn around, Frank is back at work. What would you do now?

A.   Ask the employees who laughed to tell you what they saw. (GO TO 590)

B.   Warn Frank that he had better stick to work and forget about making "smart" comments toward you. (GO TO 606)

510

C. Call Frank over to a more private place, and ask him what is on his mind. (GO TO 549)

Decision Point 542

You have decided to go to lunch with Bill regularly. He is a pleasant lunch companion, and you discover that this is a good chance to catch up on what is happening with him. After about two weeks, you notice that Bill begins to expect your luncheon meetings to continue indefinitely. He arrives every day at noon, and shows disappointment any time you have made other plans.

What is worse, Bill's lack of social acceptance by his peers is really becoming a problem. They now are apparently growing resentful of all the attention you are giving him. It is clearly time for you to break the umbilical cord with Bill. What would you do now?

A. Set up an informal meeting between Bill and a new recruit from another division who has been more successfully accepted as a member of his team. (GO TO 466)

B. Give Bill a candid, accurate assessment of the social strengths and weaknesses of the other members of his work team. Advise him of specific strategies that he might use to gain acceptance into the group. Monitor his social performance closely. (GO TO 530)

C. Talk privately to the other members of Bill's team and encourage each of them to serve as Bill's mentor. (GO TO 579)

D. Ask his team leader to allow Bill to be the spokesperson for the team in an upcoming meeting with division management (at which all department members will be present), so that he will have a better chance to earn his team's acceptance. (GO TO 603)

Decision Point 543

It is a better idea to phase an implementation than to attempt it all at once. Phasing facilitates the implementation of change for two reasons. First, it allows a demonstration effect that shows the benefits of the change on a small scale. Second, it galvanizes opinion in favor of the change, since observers now have evidence of its efficacy.

Re-evaluate your last decision. Circle the #543 you just wrote in your flow diagram. Then move to the first uncircled step above this one in your flow diagram.

Decision Point 544

Since you are not sure that the group is really convinced of its decision, you decide to poll each member individually. As you go around your team, everyone gives what you see as "lukewarm" support of flexible assembly.

At this point what would you do?

A. Accept the group's recommendation and tell it that you will develop a set of plans for implementing flexible assembly. (GO TO 569)

B. Accept the group's recommendation and ask it to develop a set of implementation recommendations. (GO TO 556)

C. Schedule another meeting for the group to discuss its recommendation. (GO TO 581)

Decision Point 545

You have told Frank that you understood him to say that his attendance is important to him but he may not want to talk about it. In return, he says, "It's a family problem," and lowers his eyes. Now what would you say?

A. "Frank, if it's a family problem, there's really no one here at the company who can help you with it. I do know someone who is a professional family counselor. He's a neighbor of mine, and he's very good. Here's his phone number. If you need help with this, you should see a pro." (GO TO 622)

B. "A family problem?" (GO TO 505)

C. "Does the problem involve alcohol, Frank?" (GO TO 523)

D. "Okay, Frank, if it's a family matter, then I don't want to butt in. I have to tell you though that I have to give you a formal warning on your attendance. I'll pull it from your file if you are able to work the next four Mondays. Otherwise, I'm afraid I'll have to give you a second warning, and you know what that means." (GO TO 582)

You have decided to go to lunch with Bill regularly. He is a pleasant lunch companion, and you discover that this is a good chance to catch up on what is happening with him. After about two weeks, you notice that Bill begins to expect your luncheon meetings to continue indefinitely. He arrives every day at noon, and shows disappointment any time you have made other plans.

What is worse, Bill's lack of social acceptance by his peers is really becoming a problem. They now are apparently growing resentful of all the attention you are giving him. It is clearly time for you to break the umbilical cord with Bill. What would you do now?

A. Set up an informal meeting between Bill and a new recruit from another division who has been more successfully accepted as a member of his team. (GO TO 466)

B. Give Bill a candid, accurate assessment of the social strengths and weaknesses of the other members of his work team. Advise him of specific strategies that he might use to gain acceptance into the group. Monitor his social performance closely. (GO TO 490)

C. Talk privately to the other members of Bill's team and encourage each of them to serve as Bill's mentor. (GO TO 579)

D. Ask his team leader to allow Bill to be the spokesperson for the team in an upcoming meeting with division management (at which all department members will be present), so that he will have a better chance to earn his team's acceptance. (GO TO 603)

Your speech goes well. In the question-and-answer session that follows, only one question emerges from the floor: "Does computerization mean that I will have to follow regulations on fines, returns, and maximum withdrawal levels that I have been waiving for some of my elderly patrons?" How would you respond?

A. "Computerization means increased service, not more restrictive controls on professionals. All of us make judgments about the administration of rules on our patrons. While the computer will give the District Office a more thorough record, increased controls will occur only if practices are excessive." (GO TO 576)

B.   "The new system will better serve patrons like this. The computer will automatically inform them by mail of their overdue withdrawals. That should save you from having to make waiver decisions." (GO TO 539)

C.   "If the rules at LCLD are outdated, then we should have a look at them." (GO TO 592)

Decision Point 548

As you begin to talk with Robin, you start to think about why people might resist change. You know that people will resist a change if the new procedures will threaten their jobs or adversely affect their economic situation. But as Robin begins to talk, his resistance seems to center on the problems of dealing with the engineering techs. He tells you that he thinks it will be hard to convince the new techs to focus on production issues rather than engineering problems. He ends by saying that he fears that the new techs will subvert all the hard work he spent turning his techs around. Robin finally says that he knows that within a couple of years the nature of the production will have to change, but that just mixing the engineering techs into the group may be more disruptive than necessary. You thank him for his frankness. Now what?

A.   Meet with your entire group and share this general problem. (GO TO 492)

B.   Have your group develop procedures for implementing flexible assembly. (GO TO 526)

C.   Go to Eugene Marshall with the group's recommendation and ask for his approval. (GO TO 573)

Decision Point 549

Your meeting with Frank seems tense and strained. You ask Frank what difficulty he is having. He says, "Look, all I need is some support from you right now. I'm working through a very difficult personal problem right now, and you are not making it any easier for me. I know I've been absent a lot lately, but damn it, I've given this company over three years of my life, and it seems that I deserve more consideration."

What would you say now?

A. Tell him you consider his statement insubordination and you are going to write him up for it. (GO TO 606)

B. Say, "Okay, okay, I guess I have been a little hard on you. It's just that I'm really getting heat from my boss, and I don't know why you've been absent so much. If there is something I can do that would help you with your problem so the absenteeism straightens out, I want you to know that I'll do what I can." (GO TO 578)

C. Ask him what his personal problem is. (GO TO 519)

D. Say, "Tell me honestly, Frank, have you really been sick for the last three Mondays out of four, or is it something else?" (GO TO 537)

E. Ask him if his problem has something to do with alcohol. (GO TO 523)

F. Say, "Okay, Frank, if it's personal, then I don't want to butt in. I have to tell you though that I have to give you a warning on your attendance. I'll pull it from your file if you are able to work the next four Mondays. Otherwise, I'm afraid I'll have to give you a second warning, and you know what that means!" (GO TO 509)

Decision Point 550

Bob Blair agrees to give him two hours a week, and you give him two hours a week as well. This works well until, without either of you knowing, Bill gets conflicting advice from you and Bob on how to deal with a sensitive issue with a client. Bob's advice reflects a superior approach because of his better knowledge of the project, but Bill follows your suggestion. As a result, Bob publicly "dresses him down" at a team meeting for not following his advice. Two days later, Bill leaves the company without even talking to you about it.

It can create problems for some new employees when more than one person serves as a mentor. Accordingly, re-evaluate your last decision. Circle the #550 that you just wrote, and move to the last uncircled step in your flow diagram.

Decision Point 551

The intern works out extremely well. He knows the inner workings of the LCLD and can start immediately. Excellent choice.

It is now 342 days after your introductory speech. You have done well. All three branches have their systems up and operational, and your effort has been recognized in the county, the profession, and with the accreditation agency. Congratulations! You have successfully completed the Managing Change I Interactive Case.

Decision Point 552

You spend the rest of the meeting providing the group with the data you collected relating to the "super-team," "flexible assembly," and "contracting" alternatives. Also, you tell the group that there are probably lots of other good alternatives that you haven't considered. After answering questions and having a general discussion about the change, you tell the group to get back to you within two weeks with a recommendation for you to consider.

A week later, at a regularly scheduled staff meeting, you ask your people for a progress report. Larry says that progress is "real slow" and that they seem to be stalled. Both Marilyn and Robin echo these concerns. When you check with your team about why this is occurring, your staff indicates that it has been meeting but just can't seem to make much headway.

At this point what would you do?

A. Have Randy Winslow (the head of the engineering technicians) join the group to stimulate things (he is in town for two weeks). (GO TO 585)

B. Encourage the group and remind members of the importance of the task. (GO TO 621)

C. Arrange to join your team at its next meeting. (GO TO 462)

Decision Point 553

You decide to talk to Frank about the transfer. He is delighted by the prospect of more money, and he impresses the Research people during his transfer interviews. By Thursday, he is no longer a member of your department.

The consequences of the decision, though, are not good. Your team's performance continues lackadaisical. Frank apparently provided a spark to teamwork, and petty squabbles now emerge among your people. Your manager continues to hound you for higher productivity. You have had real difficulty replacing Frank, more than you

516

anticipated when you made the decision to transfer him. And, if all that isn't bad enough, you just received a call from Frank's supervisor in the Research Department asking you about Frank's attendance problem. He got pretty steamed about the fact that you sent him "a lemon," as he put it.

Clearly, transferring Frank is not the best solution to the problem under these circumstances. If you want a second chance, circle the #553 you just wrote in your flow diagram, and move back in your flow diagram to the first uncircled number above this step.

Decision Point 554

Convinced by your arguments, Bill withdraws his request for a transfer. Unfortunately, however, the rumor that Bill wants out of the group begins to spread throughout his project team. This results in Bill being given the "silent treatment" for a couple of days, and Bill comes in again with the idea of a transfer.

What would you do now?

A. Grant his request for a transfer because you do not think Bill can possibly earn the acceptance of his group under these circumstances. (GO TO 502)

B. Give Bill a candid, accurate assessment of the social strengths and weaknesses of the other members of his work team, and advise him of specific actions he might take to gain more acceptance into the group. Monitor his social performance closely. (GO TO 490)

C. Talk privately to other members of Bill's team and encourage each of them to serve as a mentor to Bill. (GO TO 560)

D. Ask his team leader to allow Bill to be a spokesperson for the team in an upcoming meeting with divisional management (at which all will attend), so that he will have a chance to earn his team's approval. (GO TO 603)

Decision Point 555

It is now two months later. The change is going very well. Together you and Sloan Kilgore have successfully brought the system nearly up at the Live Oak Branch. At this point it appears that you will beat the timetable by one month (as you predicted). All the news is not good, however. Mel Simmons, Head Librarian at the Crystal Lake

Branch, has just resigned. Thus, you face the problem of replacing the head of a branch where the resistance to computerization is the strongest. What would you do now?

A. Hire someone from the outside who has experience with *BIBLIOTEK* to replace Simmons. (GO TO 489)

B. Replace Simmons with Linda Hemingway, promote Dave Seagate to Hemingway's old position (reference librarian), and replace Seagate with an intern. This option will free funds that can be used for new hardware and streamlined software. It will also make Seagate's position more secure. (GO TO 483)

Decision Point 556

You instruct the group to develop procedures for implementing "flexible assembly." The group accepts this assignment somewhat grudgingly but begins work on procedures. Two weeks later you expect a report from the group that will present procedures for implementation. At the end of that period your group presents you with a report that can only be described as sloppy and incomplete.

At this point what would you do?

A. Schedule a meeting to re-evaluate "flexible assembly." (GO TO 581)

B. Develop the implementation procedures yourself. (GO TO 569)

C. Give the report back to the group with specific instructions as to how to make it more useful. (GO TO 562)

Decision Point 557

Unaware of the underlying political nature of the feasibility study, Bill is courted by proponents and opponents of the laser-refracting targeting system. This reminds Bill of the treatment he was given by the various recruiters who tried to entice him to join their firms when he was in college. Mistaking this attention for a vote of confidence in his ability, Bill sides with the opposition group. His stand is based on publicly stated but faulty technical reasoning, and it flaws the case of the opposition group. The division manager predictably sides against Bill's group, and Bill becomes the scapegoat for those opposing the decision. Bill leaves the company two days later.

Putting a new employee in the middle of a conflict is a problem. Re-evaluate your last decision. Circle the #557 you just wrote, and move to the last uncircled step in your flow diagram.

Decision Point 558

You have correctly decided that a top-down implementation scheme is best. You now face several decisions about how to do this. Your first need to decide how to phase the change. Three options occur to you. Which would you choose?

A.   Implement the change so that it is operational in the Live Oak Branch first and then in the Main Branch and finally in the Crystal Lake Branch. (GO TO 495)

B.   Implement the change so that it is operational in all the branches simultaneously. (GO TO 543)

C.   Implement the change so that it is operational in the Main Branch first and then in the Live Oak Branch and finally in the Crystal Lake Branch. (GO TO 471)

Decision Point 559

You have given your group the assignment to implement a decision to which it is not really committed. As the group continues working on the assignment, you find yourself being forced to spend more and more time working on implementation. Under these circumstances, the long-run success of the change program is remote. Essentially your team is suffering from group-think. Little in the way of real incisive analysis is going on, and the group is looking for a way to make an easy decision.

Re-evaluate your last decision. Circle the #559 you just wrote in your flow diagram. Then move to the first uncircled step above this one in your flow diagram.

Decision Point 560

Surprisingly this appeal really works, and two members of Bill's team begin coaching Bill, taking him under their wing. You are delighted to see that the group finally accepts Bill. In general, assigning the mentoring role to an entire group does not work out since different people often give different advice. Here, the disagreement concerns the advice his two mentors give him about how to deal with a problem with the team leader. Unsure how to go on, Bill comes to you.

What would you do now?

A.   Give Bill a candid assessment of the social strengths and weaknesses of the other members of his work team and advise him of specific strategies he might use to solve his problem with his boss without upsetting either of his mentors. (GO TO 490)

B.   Talk to the two mentors privately and see if you can mediate this problem for Bill. (GO TO 506)

Decision Point 561

Flattered by the statements in the press that you made about her outstanding contribution and pleased that you had not altered her overriding philosophy, Ms. B graciously accepts your invitation. At a staff meeting, she speaks out on behalf of computerization. You seize this initiative to again reinforce the notion that short-term deficits in service will be more than made up in the future.

Time passes. It is now two months later. The change is going very well. Together you and Sloan Kilgore have successfully brought the system nearly up at the Live Oak Branch. At this point it appears that you will beat the timetable by one month (as you predicted).

All the news is not good, however. Mel Simmons, Head Librarian at the Crystal Lake Branch, resigns. Now you face the problem of replacing the head of a branch where the resistance to computerization is the strongest.

What would you do?

A.   Hire someone from the outside who has experience with *BIBLIOTEK* to replace Simmons. (GO TO 489)

B.   Replace Simmons with Linda Hemingway, promote Dave Seagate to Hemingway's old position (reference librarian), and replace Seagate with an intern. This option will free funds that can be used for new hardware and streamlined software. It will also make Seagate's position more secure. (GO TO 483)

The group comes back with a set of procedures that you think are satisfactory. However, when it is time to try out the new procedures, things don't seem to work out. Your people just seem to be "going through the motions." When the engineering techs are introduced into the system, confusion results. Integrating the techs is going to be difficult and you are now not optimistic about the chances for success.

Re-evaluate your last decision. Circle the #562 you just wrote in your flow diagram. Then move to the first uncircled step above this one in your flow diagram.

Your meeting with Frank seems relatively relaxed. You ask Frank what problem he is having, and he says, "Well, it's rather personal, and I'm not sure I want to talk about it. I know I can't go on being absent like this."

What would you say now?

A. "I'm glad you realize how important it is that you improve your attendance record. Do the best you can to make it to work, okay?" (GO TO 481)

B. "Tell me honestly, Frank, have you really been sick for the last three Mondays out of four, or is it something else?" (GO TO 537)

C. "Okay, Frank, if it's personal, then I don't want to butt in. I have to tell you though that I have to give you a formal warning on your attendance. I'll pull it from your file if you are able to work the next four Mondays. Otherwise, I'm afraid I'll have to give you a second warning and you know what that means." (GO TO 582)

D. "Frank, do you have an alcohol problem?" (GO TO 523)

E. "If you don't want to talk about it, that's fine, but we need to work out a plan that will result in the level of production we need from you. Do you have any ideas that we might put to use?" (GO TO 598)

F. "I see, you think it's important to improve your attendance, but you are not sure you want to talk about what is causing the attendance problem." (GO TO 545)

Decision Point 564

K. C. Wong does not work out as Bill's mentor. He is entirely too busy to give Bill all the attention he deserves, and he sometimes grows impatient when Bill does not catch on quickly.

Bill continues to show an inability to set correct priorities to his work tasks. In addition, he is beginning to show signs of a loss of confidence again. Therefore, you decide to become more involved in mentoring Bill.

What would you do now?

   A.   Agree to meet daily with Bill to coach him on how to handle the specific, day-to-day problems that come up in his work. (GO TO 496)

   B.   Begin yourself to give Bill a detailed account of how to contend with the challenges and problems in his work. Agree to meet with him in three days to review his progress and advise him on new situations. (GO TO 571)

   C.   Talk to K. C. Wong about sharing responsibility for breaking Bill in. (GO TO 567)

Decision Point 565

Bob Bramsen is not the best candidate. Change agents ideally have both high social skills and technical credibility. While he has the technical credentials necessary to do well, his social skills are questionable. Specifically, he is going to have to get the cooperation of others to be successful. Ambitious and upwardly-mobile Bramsen is a bit too abrasive for this assignment.

Re-evaluate your last decision. Circle the #565 you just wrote in your flow diagram. Then move to the first uncircled step above this one in your flow diagram.

Decision Point 566

You have decided to make decisions yourself about this situation before refining your charter from your boss. This is unwise. He gave you a very cryptic assignment in an informal encounter, and the assignment has far-reaching consequences for the entire company. Certainly you want to clarify what he is asking you to do and what problem or opportunity he is responding to.

Re-evaluate your last decision. Circle the #566 you just wrote in your flow diagram. Then move to the first uncircled step above this one in your flow diagram.

Decision Point 567

K. C. Wong agrees to give him two hours a week, and you agree to give him two hours a week as well. This works out well, until without your knowledge, you and K. C. give him different advice about how to deal with a problem with a client. K. C.'s advice is better, for it reflects a better understanding of the specific situation. However, Bill follows your suggestion.

As a result, K. C. publicly "dresses him down" at a team meeting for not following his advice. Two days later, Bill leaves the company without even talking to you.

Sometimes giving a new employee two mentors can put the person in a difficult spot. Therefore, re-evaluate your last decision. Circle the #567 you just wrote, and move to the last uncircled step in your flow diagram.

Decision Point 568

Computerization will force fundamental changes in the organizational culture of LCLD. Ms. B's emphasis on service over professionalism did more than shape expectations; it created habits and entire patterns of thinking. There seem to be people ready to consider other priorities for LCLD, but it is unlikely that a meek approach will get the needed attention. Remember, these are civil servants who have considerable employment security. You should consider a dramatic point of departure. Anything less than total commitment on your part may be seen as half-hearted. It invites others to test your resolve and attempt to discover just how committed you are.

Re-evaluate your last decision. Circle the #568 you just wrote in your flow diagram. Then move to the first uncircled step above this one in your flow diagram.

Decision Point 569

Based on the group's recommendation, you begin to develop a way of implementing the plan. You spend five days diagramming the revised assembly lines, determining personnel assignments, and planning new equipment. Each member of the team has an important role to carry out if the process is to be successful. Marilyn will have to have much more flexible scheduling procedures. She also will have to shift from handling large quantities of relatively few parts to handling smaller quantities of a larger number of parts. Larry has to reorganize his assembly lines, train his lead supervisors in the new process, and integrate most of the engineering techs into his group. Robin will absorb a number of new techs and will also have to make plans as to how to handle increased parts testing and more specialized warranty work.

As your team starts to make these changes, things seem to take much longer than you estimated. When you are finally ready to test the new procedures, things don't work as well as anticipated. In addition, you don't sense that your team is really motivated to make things work. By involving the group in making the decision but not really getting their commitment, you lost some of the advantages of participation. Also, by not having the group aid in implementation planning, you did not take advantage of its expertise.

Re-evaluate your last decision. Circle the #569 you just wrote in your flow diagram. Then move to the first uncircled step above this one in your flow diagram.

Decision Point 570

You ask Frank if he is feeling better. Taking your question as sarcasm, he says, "I'd feel a lot better if I worked for another supervisor!"

What now?

A.   Tell Frank that you consider his statement insubordination and you are going to write him up for it. (GO TO 606)

B.   Ask him what his problem is. (GO TO 549)

C.   Ask him if his problem has something to do with alcohol. (GO TO 523)

Decision Point 571

It is one month later. Bill responds well to the periodic meetings you and he set up. This closer monitoring and more frequent coaching begin to show in Bill's confidence and technical performance. Yet, other problems begin to appear. You notice that he still is hesitant to initiate contact with his other team members when he is having a problem. And when he does ask for help, team members often misunderstand them or perceive them as an annoying call for reassurance. What is particularly disturbing is that Bill has yet to be accepted as a real member of the team. The group frequently excludes him from team lunches, and one of the group is giving him some mild hazing.

How would you react to this?

A. Start going to lunch with him regularly. (GO TO 546)

B. Set up an informal meeting between Bill and a new recruit from another division who has been more successfully accepted as a member of his team. (GO TO 524)

C. Give Bill a candid, accurate assessment of the social strengths and weaknesses of the other members of his work team. Advise him of specific strategies that he might use to gain acceptance into the group. Monitor his social performance closely. (GO TO 490)

D. Talk privately to the other members of Bill's team and encourage each of them to serve as Bill's mentor. (GO TO 560)

E. Ask his team leader to allow Bill to be the spokesperson for the team in an upcoming meeting with division management (at which all department members will be present), so that he will have a better chance to earn his team's acceptance. (GO TO 603)

Decision Point 572

Now that your change is at a very sensitive stage, you do not want to risk bringing in an unknown quantity. Using a new intern will allow you to be honest to your pledge of not jeopardizing the security of your full-time people. However, it will take you a considerable amount of time to find, orient, and train anyone new for this position. There is a better way.

Re-evaluate your last decision. Circle the #572 you just wrote in your flow diagram. Then move to the first uncircled step above this one in your flow diagram.

Decision Point 573

You begin your meeting with Eugene by describing the process your group went through to arrive at the "flexible assembly" recommendation. Eugene surprises you by saying, "I don't know where you came up with the idea of flexible assembly. It sounds like it might work, but what I'm concerned with is that you implement a system that can get the job done. The way you have described it leads me to believe that Robin would really have a hard time with it, but you must know best."

Like so many harried executives, Eugene seems to have fallen victim to a very poor memory. He was the person who introduced you to the idea of flexible assembly in the first place. Clearly his initial enthusiasm for flexible assembly was not the result of thorough analysis.

With the green light from Eugene, how would you proceed?

A. Have your group develop procedures for implementing "flexible assembly." (GO TO 522)

B. Go back to Robin to probe more deeply into the reasons for his concern about flexible assembly. (GO TO 613)

Decision Point 574

You have asked Frank to negotiate some standard of attendance that you both can live with. Frank responds that working Mondays poses a real problem because of his wife's problems. He says, though, that if he can get the next couple of Mondays off, he thinks he can straighten out things with his family situation.

How would you respond?

A. Tell him that Monday attendance is essential and that he should do the best he can to turn his attendance around. (GO TO 481)

B. Persuade him that letting him have Mondays off would set a bad precedent for the other employees. (GO TO 602)

C. Tell him that you are willing to let him miss the next two Mondays if he makes up the time on Saturday when the other employees are working overtime. After that, you will not be able to tolerate further Monday absences without disciplinary action. (GO TO 610)

Bob Blair does not work out as Bill's mentor. He is entirely too busy to give Bill all the attention he deserves, and he sometimes grows impatient when Bill does not catch on quickly. Mentors must have the time and resources to perform in that role.

Bill continues to show an inability to set correct priorities to his work tasks. In addition, he is beginning to show signs of a loss of confidence again.

What would you do now?

A. Begin yourself to give Bill a detailed account of how to contend with the challenges and problems in his work. Agree to meet with him in three days to review his progress and advise him on new situations. (GO TO 534)

B. Talk to Bob Blair about sharing responsibility for breaking Bill in. (GO TO 550)

C. Remind Bill of his agreement that he would take initiative if he had questions or was having problems. Tell him that he will not succeed unless he begins to ask questions, tells Bob Blair of his problems, and begins to take control of his own situation. (GO TO 595)

D. Take time to remind others in your group that helping Bill adapt to his job is important. (GO TO 611)

It is two weeks after your speech. You have completed your public relations campaign announcing computerization through the media and via speeches to community groups. On each occasion you repeated the new motto for the LCLD, "Looking for Better Ways to Serve You Best."

Almost everyone reacts positively to this new motto except Ms. B. Miffed by your apparent effort to discredit her administration, she is cold to your computerization plan. This is not much of a problem except that she still has many friends in LCLD. Noteworthy among these is Mel Simmons, the head librarian at the Crystal Lake Branch. He becomes increasingly resistant to the *BIBLIOTEK* training. At one point, he even refuses send his aides to training sessions conducted by Sloan Kilgore at the District Office. His claim is that the scheduling of these sessions interferes with branch work schedules.

What action would you take?

A. Ask Mel Simmons for his cooperation with the computerization effort. (GO TO 600)

B. Tell Mel Simmons to do whatever it takes get his aides to complete the training so that his branch will be on schedule. Tell him that otherwise you will close the branch to patrons during the training. (GO TO 555)

Decision Point 577

You decide to begin implementing flexible assembly. Immediately you run into resistance. The members of your team are miffed about not being included in the process, and Larry Beeson tells you that he has had considerable experience with "flexible assembly" at another firm--experience that would have led Arion in another direction.

Re-evaluate your last decision. Circle the #577 you just wrote in your flow diagram. Then move to the first uncircled step above this one in your flow diagram.

Decision Point 578

You tell Frank that your boss is pressuring you for more work. Frank responds that you should make her understand that everyone in your group is doing the best he or she can. Now what would you say?

A. Explain the necessity of good attendance if production goals are to met and point out to him how much his attendance is adversely affecting production. Urge him to do better. (GO TO 481)

B. Ask him what difficulty he is having that keeps him from producing as much as he is capable of producing. (GO TO 563)

C. Tell Frank that his performance may be one of the reasons your boss is pressuring you. Indicate that if he doesn't improve his attendance, you will be forced to give him a written warning. (GO TO 541)

Surprisingly, this appeal really works, and two members of Bill's team begin coaching Bill, taking him under their wing. You are delighted to see that Bill is finally accepted into the group. Actually, assigning more than one mentor is not a good idea because it raises the potential for conflicting advice. Predictably, two weeks later, Bill and his team leader have a mild disagreement, and two of Bill's new mentors give him different advice on how to handle it. Unsure what to do, Bill comes to you.

What would you do now?

A. Give Bill a candid assessment of the social strengths and weaknesses of the other members of his work team and advise him of specific strategies he might use to solve his problem with his boss without upsetting either of his two mentors. (GO TO 530)

B. Talk to the two mentors independently and privately and see if you can mediate this problem for Bill. (GO TO 506)

Now is not the time to maintain flexibility. You want no one to question your commitment. It is important to be explicit about the schedule.

Re-evaluate your last decision. Circle the #580 you just wrote in your flow diagram. Then move to the first uncircled step above this one in your flow diagram.

What would you do at this meeting?

A. Lay out an implementation plan for flexible assembly. (GO TO 559)

B. Continue the discussion by having members explain why they support the "flexible assembly" approach. (GO TO 513)

C. Assign one member to develop and present an argument for flexible assembly and another member to play "devil's advocate" and present counter-arguments. Once those arguments are all out, lead a general discussion. (GO TO 601)

Decision Point 582

You have decided to establish an explicit plan for Frank to follow that will correct his attendance problem. As a result, Frank's attendance does improve. Unfortunately, however, after he slips and earns his second warning, the problem shifts. Frank never misses a Monday thereafter, but on two consecutive Mondays, his performance is far below acceptable levels. On the first Monday, he receives two "emergency phone calls" from a woman who identifies herself as his wife. This keeps him from his work for a total of 45 minutes after which he is listless and unproductive. On the second Monday, he leaves work at lunchtime and returns 30 minutes late complaining that he had serious family business to attend to. Your action apparently corrected one problem but created another.

Re-evaluate your last decision. Circle the #582 you just wrote in your flow diagram, and move back in your flow diagram to the first uncircled number above this step.

Decision Point 583

The progress of the *Solaris* project improves markedly, and Bill seems to have weathered his crisis of confidence. Although you have cut his responsibilities, he still shows signs of time mismanagement and a poor sense of priorities.

What would you do now?

A.   Agree to meet daily with Bill to coach him on how to handle the specific, day-to-day problems that come up in his work. (GO TO 496)

B.   Tell K. C. Wong that he is responsible for Bill's performance. Tell K. C. that you do not want him to sacrifice the objectives of the *Solaris* project, but that you think Bill deserves more of his time. (GO TO 564)

C.   Begin yourself to give Bill a detailed account of how to contend with the challenges and problems in his work. Agree to meet with him in three days to review his progress and advise him on new situations. (GO TO 571)

D.   Talk to K. C. Wong about sharing responsibility for breaking Bill in. (GO TO 567)

Decision Point 584

This accomplishment calls for fanfare not only to reinforce those who made a contribution, but also to dramatize progress to generate support for the total effort. Your approach lacks gusto. Re-evaluate your last decision. Circle the #584 you just wrote in your flow diagram. Then move to the first uncircled step above this one in your flow diagram.

Decision Point 585

Inviting Randy to join the group does not work well. At the meeting he begins by announcing that Arion's success will be due to "good engineering" and that moving the techs to production will make "good engineering" much harder. This attitude does not set well with your team members, and they respond defensively. The meeting continues with sniping between your group and Randy.

The next day you get a call from Gordon Garvin suggesting that the two of you get together with Eugene Marshall to see if this change is really necessary. Although Eugene had committed to clearing things with Gordon Garvin, bringing Randy into the group so soon forced Eugene to deal with Gordon under adverse circumstances. Also, having Randy join the group has not increased its progress; in fact, it has solidified positions.

Re-evaluate your last decision. Circle the #585 you just wrote in your flow diagram. Then move to the first uncircled step above this one in your flow diagram.

Decision Point 586

You figure that if Frank's problem is one of drinking, experts should handle it. When you tell Frank to report for counseling, he becomes angry at you and denies that he has a drinking problem. As Frank continues to talk, he becomes more emotional and more angry.

What would you do now?

A. Tell Frank that if he doesn't report for counseling, you will write him up for insubordination. (GO TO 533)

B. Say something like, "Frank, if it isn't alcohol, then what is it?" (GO TO 549)

531

C.   Say, "Okay, okay, you say it's not alcohol, but tell me honestly Frank, have you really been sick for the last three Mondays out of four, or is it something else?" (GO TO 537)

Decision Point 587

You decided to let Bob Blair handle this situation. Bob wants to tell Bill that Sam needs practice dealing with problems like this and that he should stay out of it next time. Bill disagrees strongly with Bob's position and storms out of his office muttering something about loyalty. Bill enters your office the next day still hot over the issue. You succeed in settling him down.

Clearly, Bob is not the person to do mentoring; he simply does not have the time or patience. What should you do now?

A.   Tell Bill how should have handled the situation with the client in light of Sam's fundamental weaknesses, Bob Blair's responsibilities, and the particular client involved. (GO TO 599)

B.   Inform him that Sam needs practice bailing himself out and that he should not get involved in Sam's development. (GO TO 460)

C.   Tell Bill that clients should be allowed to say whatever they want even if it is uncomplimentary, and that one important part of being a Venus employee is to be a flak-catcher. (GO TO 615)

Decision Point 588

You attend the meeting and take the opportunity to correct the false rumor that computerization will lead to the closing of the branch. Further, you assure them that computerization will actually enhance the viability of the Crystal Lake Branch. Once the branch is computerized every Crystal Lake patron will have access to the entire LCLD collection, and therefore better service. It is now six months since your announcement, and the Live Oak Branch computer system is now up and operational two weeks before the deadline. You now have to decide how to acknowledge this achievement.

A.   Send a memo to all employees congratulating the Live Oak staff for its achievement. (GO TO 584)

B.   Hold an open-house "celebration" at the Live Oak Branch so other employees can see the system in action. Publicly congratulate members of the branch. Arrange for press coverage of the event. (GO TO 529)

Decision Point 589

You decided to implement the "flexible assembly" plan. You spend five days diagraming the modified assembly lines, determining personnel assignments, and planning new equipment. At the end of that time you understand what steps need to be taken to implement the change. You realize that each member of your group has an important role to play if the process is to be successful. Marilyn will have to have much more flexible scheduling procedures. She will also have to shift from handling large quantities of relatively few parts to handling smaller quantities of a larger number of parts. Larry will have to reorganize his assembly lines, train his lead supervisors in the new process, and integrate most of the engineering techs into his group. Robin will absorb a number of the new techs and will also have to decide how to handle increased parts testing and more specialized warranty work. When you give the members their assignments, there is a bit of grumbling. You remind them that this project is important. Two weeks later, when you check back, little progress has been made, and the group seems to be generally resistant to your direction.

You are now faced with few options, none of which is very attractive. By implementing the change without involving your team, you have forced a top-down implementation pattern on a situation that called for delegation: (1) the change does not require immediate action; (2) the problem the change addresses is not commonly recognized; (3) knowledge relevant to the change is dispersed throughout the organization; and (4) your team was successful when you have offered it a voice in decisions in the past.

Re-evaluate your last decision. Circle the #589 you just wrote in your flow diagram. Then move to the first uncircled step above this one in your flow diagram.

Decision Point 590

You asked the employees who laughed to tell you what they saw. The people were embarrassed and appeared to be nervous. Finally one of them said: "We were just laughing at a joke Frank told at lunch. It didn't have anything to do with you." What would you do now?

A.   Call Frank over to a more private place and ask him what's on his mind. (GO TO 549)

B.   Warn Frank that he had better stick to work and forget about making smart comments. (GO TO 606)

Decision Point 591

You wait to verify the facts of the episode before taking action. Unfortunately Bill resigns the next morning minutes before you can talk to his team leader. Apparently a more immediate response was necessary.

Re-evaluate your last decision. Circle the #591 you just wrote, and move to the last uncircled step in your flow diagram.

Decision Point 592

Your answer is unresponsive to a latent issue that is likely to be the basis of the question--control. In general, administrative changes are more resisted than technical changes simply because they realign control and power relationships. As a change, computerization has an administrative component, so this question originates with a concern about a loss of power and control. Specifically, computerization often scares professionals because they fear that it will result in more restrictions to their autonomy and less influence in the organization.

Re-evaluate your last decision. Circle the #592 you just wrote in your flow diagram. Then move to the first uncircled step above this one in your flow diagram.

Decision Point 593

You call Eugene's office and set up a meeting for next Tuesday. At that meeting, which of the following would you do?

A.   Lay out the advantages and disadvantages of each of the three alternatives you have and, with Eugene, select an alternative to pursue. (GO TO 532)

B.   Accept "flexible assembly" as a fait accompli (i.e., accomplished fact) and get Eugene's okay to proceed with the implementation. (GO TO 577)

C.   Before the meeting give Randy Winslow a call before he leaves for England with the idea of informally "checking out" his opinions on the different alternatives. (GO TO 474)

534

D. Discuss with Eugene the major issues in the change process and be prepared to negotiate a series of cost, timetable, and political issues. (GO TO 518)

Decision Point 594

His previous supervisor is very informative. He says: "Frank Wilson? Why, I know Frank very well. He was one of my best workers. I was real sorry to see him take the transfer over to your shop. We got along real well. I think the only reason he took the transfer was that he and his wife got back together, and he needed the extra money. Attendance record? No, Frank never had attendance problems when he worked for me."

What would you do now?

A. Call Frank aside upon his return and have a talk with him. (GO TO 493)

B. Discuss the matter with your manager in order to get her advice and input in handling the situation. (GO TO 469)

C. Call the Human Resources Department to see what disciplinary options are open to you. (GO TO 457)

D. Call the Human Resources Department to see if there are other departments that need people with Frank's qualifications so you can transfer him there. (GO TO 514)

E. Talk to some of Frank's co-workers to see if they have any idea what might be causing Frank's absences. (GO TO 499)

F. Write Frank up for chronic absenteeism and leave a copy of the warning in an envelope on his desk for him to find when he comes in. (GO TO 487)

Decision Point 595

Bill continues to have difficulty on Bob Blair's team. Bob and the other team members are too busy to help him, and there are signs that they are growing irritated with his distracting questions. Through the grapevine, you learn that Bill has contacted a firm that had heavily recruited him. Bill is badly in need of mentoring, and your actions have yet to provide this for him.

What would you do now?

A.   Take time to remind others in your group that helping Bill adapt to his job is important. (GO TO 611)

B.   Agree to meet daily with Bill to coach him on how to handle the specific, day-to-day problems that come up in his work. (GO TO 511)

C.   Begin yourself to give Bill a detailed account of how to contend with the challenges and problems in his work. Agree to meet with him in three days to review his progress and advise him on new situations. (GO TO 534)

D.   Tell Bob Blair he is responsible for Bill's performance. Tell Bob that you do not want him to sacrifice the objectives of the *Dart* test system, but that you think Bill deserves more of his time. (GO TO 575)

Decision Point 596

Your speech goes well. In the question-and-answer session that follows, only one question emerges from the floor: "Does computerization mean that I will have to follow regulations on fines, returns, and maximum withdrawal levels that I have been waiving for some of my elderly patrons?" How would you respond?

A.   "Computerization means increased service, not more restrictive controls on professionals. All of us make judgments about the administration of rules on our patrons. While the computer will give the District Office a more thorough record, increased controls will occur only if practices are excessive." (GO TO 491)

B.   "The new system will better serve patrons like this. The computer will automatically inform them by mail of their overdue withdrawals. That should save you from having to make waiver decisions." (GO TO 539)

C.   "If the rules at LCLD are outdated, then we should have a look at them." (GO TO 592)

Decision Point 597

You have decided not to share the information about the importance of the change with your group. When you call your group together and describe plans for bringing the engineering techs into Production, none of your people displays any enthusiasm for the ideas you have presented. You know that if you were to give them a general assignment to work on, it is unlikely that much would be accomplished. However, you realize that if you were to spell out specific steps for each person to take in implementing the change, each person would comply and you could monitor and control the group's progress.

Faced with the group's lack of motivation, what would you do?

   A.   Spell out all you have heard including the importance of the change and the risks involved. (GO TO 504)

   B.   Provide members of your group with detailed instructions as to what they are to do to bring about the change in Production to implement "flexible assembly." (GO TO 589)

Decision Point 598

You have asked Frank to negotiate some standard of attendance that you both can live with. Frank responds that working Mondays poses a real problem for him right now, but if he can get the next couple of Mondays off, he thinks he can straighten out in a month or so.

How would you react to this?

   A.   Tell him that you are willing to let him miss the next two Mondays if he makes up the time on Saturday when the other employees are working overtime. After that, you will not be able to tolerate further Monday absences without disciplinary action. (GO TO 610)

   B.   Tell him that Monday attendance is essential and that he should do the best he can to turn his attendance habits around. (GO TO 481)

   C.   Persuade him that letting him have Mondays off would set a very bad precedent for the other employees. (GO TO 602)

Decision Point 599

Your candid assessment was exactly what Bill needed to progress through his present developmental stage. Bill needed information about how to fit in socially, and you provided that information.

It is now two months later, and Bill has become a highly valued member of your group. His technical, social, and political integration into the organization seems complete, and you have recommended that he receive the highest performance rating available to young recruits. His accomplishments, once only known to the members of the group, are increasingly becoming visible to division management. You are really proud of him.

Recently, however, Bill has been having difficulty putting his personal life in order. Since he and his wife live in the country, his two young children are enrolled in a one-room school. His wife has expressed concern that the school is not stimulating enough. In addition, Bill has reported having trouble with his commuting. It seems that he is occasionally unable to get to work on time because of icy roads.

In light of Bill's problem of integrating his private and professional life, what would you do?

A. Do nothing. You've gone far enough. Bill's personal life is up to him. (GO TO 607)

B. Encourage him to take initiative on this problem. Explore alternatives with him and advise him what to do. (GO TO 484)

C. Introduce Bill to a person in another division who, like Bill, lives in the country and has school-aged children. (GO TO 454)

Decision Point 600

Your approach does little to neutralize the resistance of Mel Simmons. His skepticism, fueled by Ms. B's ego involvement, persists in spite of your efforts, and it seriously interferes with your change program. You need to act swiftly and forcefully.

Re-evaluate your last decision. Circle the #600 you just wrote in your flow diagram. Then move to the first uncircled step above this one in your flow diagram.

Decision Point 601

On occasion it may be necessary to do things to help a group improve its decision making. Your group seemed to be supporting a solution no one agreed to. Your technique surfaced a broad set of issues and forced the group to reconsider its recommendation.

Your approach works well. You assign Marilyn to present the case for "flexible assembly" and Robin to present counter-arguments. The discussion that follows is quite lively, and a number of new ideas about the advantages and disadvantages of flexible assembly get voiced. The most positive support for flexible assembly comes from Larry. He argues that, over the long term, Arion will have to develop strong capabilities in custom production, and that flexible assembly is the technique that will disperse those skills throughout Production without diluting them.

Your team generally agrees with Larry's thinking. A number of concerns about flexible assembly come up as well. Robin expresses the strongest argument against it. He says that it won't work well because people will be confused about what they are supposed to do and that supervising mixed teams will be nearly impossible. As you press him, he is unable to come up with examples of what he means or real evidence to support his position. He finally says that he doesn't really think any change in the way things are done is necessary. You decide to poll the group. Although Marilyn and Larry are fairly supportive of flexible assembly, Robin is noncommittal but says that he will go along with whatever you decide. It is clear that the group has completed its original charge.

At this point what would you do?

A. Instruct the group to begin studying how to implement the flexible assembly approach. (GO TO 522)

B. Schedule another meeting. Arrange to meet with Robin privately in the mean-time. (GO TO 456)

Decision Point 602

You have told Frank that letting him have Mondays off would be a bad precedent for the other employees. He answers that he doesn't know what else he can suggest. What would you say now?

A. Tell him that Monday attendance is essential and that he should do the best he can to turn his attendance around. (GO TO 481)

B. Tell him that you want to help him, but you must protect the interests of the company as well. Offer to withhold a first warning until the next Monday he is absent, and promise you will have to give him a second warning the following Monday if he is absent again. Explain that this means that he can miss Mondays but only at the expense of getting closer and closer to being terminated.

At the same time, it fits his need to have more time to work out his personal problem. (GO TO 527)

C. Tell him that you are willing to let him miss the next two Mondays if he makes up the time on Saturday when the other employees are working overtime. After that, you will not be able to tolerate further Monday absences without disciplinary action. (GO TO 610)

Decision Point 603

Bill fumbles and mumbles his way through the presentation much to the chagrin of the entire team. Knowing his performance was weak but hoping for approval, he asks his colleagues for their assessment of his performance. They respond with little tact, and Bill resigns a week afterward.

Putting Bill in a situation that was beyond his capabilities is very risky. Therefore, re-evaluate your last decision. Circle the #603 you just wrote, and move to the last uncircled step in your flow diagram.

Decision Point 604

You decided to ask Linda to carry your message back to her people that there are no plans to close the Crystal Lake Branch. This settles things down for a while, but Linda reports to you that a lot of insecurities remain about the future of the branch.

You should really have gone out and clarified the situation in person. This would have had two main advantages. First, since the rumor was unfounded, visiting the branch would have allowed you to demonstrate your credibility. You could have told them the branch would not close and be proven correct over time. Second, appearing in person would have given you the chance to explain how computerization helps rather than hinders the longevity of the branch. As it was, you opened yourself up to communication distortion by sending your message through Linda. While she would not have meant to misquote you, this is too important an issue to risk the possibility of missed signals.

Re-evaluate your last decision. Circle the #604 you just wrote in your flow diagram. Then move to the first uncircled step above this one in your flow diagram.

The decision to involve your team was a good one. A delegation process makes sense because: (1) the change does not require immediate action, (2) the problem the change addresses is not commonly recognized throughout the organization, (3) knowledge relevant to the change is dispersed throughout the organization, and (4) your team has been successful when you have offered them a voice in past decisions.

Larry, Robin, and Marilyn are all experienced production people who believe in their abilities to "mass produce" almost any system. You schedule your meeting with them two days from now.

As you are preparing to go home for the day, you run into Tom Meyers, the Director of Marketing. You begin to chat about business in general, and Tom brings up the issue of customization. He tells you that his market research indicates that within two to three years foreign producers will dominate the standard PBX market on the basis of price (Arion's present niche). However, there will remain plenty of money to be made in custom systems since foreign competitors lack that capability.

In effect, Tom Meyers has echoed Eugene Marshall's point of view. Surely bringing custom production into your department is vital, but not terribly urgent. Unlike so many other things, it looks like you finally have enough lead time to approach this deliberately.

As you plan your meeting with Larry, Robin, and Marilyn, you are not sure what the agenda of the meeting should be. Specifically, you are not sure how much of your conversations with Eugene and Tom you want to relate to your team. Foreign competition is a natural anxiety producer, and the notion that existing markets could disappear is rather unnerving.

Which of the following would you do?

A. Do not relate the information you heard from Tom and Eugene in order to avoid raising their anxiety level. (GO TO 597)

B. Provide a sketchy outline of what you have heard from others. (GO TO 508)

C. Spell out all you have heard including the importance of the change and the risks involved. (GO TO 504)

Decision Point 606

You are telling Frank that he must respect your position as his supervisor. He tells you, "While it is obvious to me that you don't respect me, at least I have enough self-respect not to put up with your being on my case. I don't have to take that crap from my family, and I don't have to take it from you. I quit!" With that he walks out the door.

This situation has gone further than you thought it would. While you have "taken care" of Frank's attendance problem and maintained discipline in your work group, you have lost a skilled employee. This may cause difficulties, particularly if you are behind schedule. You will have to find a replacement and spend valuable time training that person. Furthermore, there is a chance that the new employee will cause you more difficulty than Frank did.

Under these circumstances, we want to offer you a second chance. GO TO 463, and you will learn Frank's problem and can start the interactive case over from that point.

Decision Point 607

Your frustration in dealing with Bill at this point is understandable. He is not as mature as his background promised. Certainly, you invested an incredible amount of time and effort in his development. Given all this work, it is a shame that you really want to give up on him.

Two months later, Bill's commuting difficulties multiply, and his attendance record worsens. This results in his project failing to meet important milestones, and now you are clearly going to have to take some action.

Bill will not become an effective employee until he learns to balance the demands at work and in the rest of his life. This challenge can be met through mentoring.

What would you do now?

A. Encourage Bill to take initiative on this problem. Explore alternatives with him and advise him what to do. (GO TO 484)

B. Introduce Bill to a person in another division who, like Bill, lives in the country and has school-aged children. (GO TO 454)

Decision Point 608

You decided to take time to try to find out the source of the rumor before taking any other action. This was incorrect. Rumor control during the implementation of change is a crucial activity. False rumors must be corrected immediately, no matter what the source. That way the accurate information will itself discredit the person who started the rumor.

Re-evaluate your last decision. Circle the #608 you just wrote in your flow diagram. Then move to the first uncircled step above this one in your flow diagram.

Decision Point 609

You decide to persuade Eugene that your team's recommendation makes a great deal of sense. The more you say, though, the more Eugene resists the idea. At one point he even criticizes your people as being prone to "superficial analysis." The discussion is not going well, to say the least. Your conversation is interrupted by a phone call. Sitting there in his large office and waiting for him to finish the call, you have to decide what you are going to do next.

A.   Defend your team's decision. Indicate that the idea of a "super-team" is only an interim move. Tell Eugene that your team's analysis was thorough. (GO TO 536)

B.   Ask Eugene what his specific concerns are with the idea so that you can return to discuss them with your team. (GO TO 468)

Decision Point 610

Frank responds well to the plan the two of you have worked out. He does miss the next two Mondays, but he makes up the work on the subsequent Saturdays, and as a bonus, he tells his colleagues that you have been more than fair with him. He even talks a fellow worker out of looking for a job with a competitor that pays more.

Congratulations! You did very well. You handled a difficult situation admirably. This completes the Problem Employee Interactive Case.

Decision Point 611

You have spoken to the others in your group about the importance of helping Bill. Unfortunately there is no noticeable change in Bill's attitude or performance. When no one is assigned as mentor, no one mentors. The only outcome of your action is that a group member advises Bill incorrectly on how to complete a technical task.

What would you do now?

A.   Coach Bill on how to be the member of a test engineering team. (GO TO 482)

B.   Agree to meet daily with Bill to coach him on how to handle the specific, day-to-day problems that come up in his work. (GO TO 511)

C.   Remind Bill of his agreement to take initiative if he had questions or was having problems. Tell him that he will not succeed unless he begins to take control of his own situation. (GO TO 595)

D.   Begin yourself to give Bill a detailed account of how to contend with the challenges and problems in his work. Agree to meet with him in three days to review his progress and advise him on new situations. (GO TO 534)

E.   Tell Bob Blair that he is responsible for Bill's performance. Tell Bob that you do not want him to sacrifice the objectives of the *Dart* test system, but that you think Bill deserves more of his time. (GO TO 575)

Decision Point 612

You take no definite action except to ask Linda Hemingway to keep you posted on developments. This might work in other circumstances, but here you should have investigated more deeply. You should consider the complaints as a signal that the branch people may resist more firmly unless you convince them otherwise. You may learn something if you look into the matter more thoroughly. There could be a basis in fact for their concerns that they are not stating directly. The best action is to see if there are concerns beyond their stated concerns. Otherwise, the resistance will probably snowball.

Re-evaluate your last decision. Circle the #612 you just wrote in your flow diagram. Then move to the first uncircled step above this one in your flow diagram.

Decision Point 613

Your conversation with Robin is not very fruitful. He continues to be vague about his feelings toward "flexible assembly." He tells you that he would prefer to gradually introduce it rather than be forced to deal both with the disruption it will cause and the problems the new work will pose for his group.

What would you do now?

A. Meet with your entire group and share this general problem. (GO TO 492)

B. Have your group develop procedures for implementing flexible assembly. (GO TO 526)

Decision Point 614

You asked Frank why Mondays pose such a problem for him. He says, "It just seems as though all my problems converge on that day."

What would you say now?

A. Tell him that you are willing to let him miss the next two Mondays if he makes up the time on Saturday when the other employees are working overtime. After that, you will not be able to tolerate further Monday absences without disciplinary action. (GO TO 610)

B. Tell him that Monday attendance is essential and that he should do the best he can to turn his attendance habits around. (GO TO 481)

C. Persuade him that letting him have Mondays off would set a very bad precedent for the other employees. (GO TO 602)

Decision Point 615

Your comment about being a "flak-catcher" has little effect. Bill apologizes for being so aggressive with the client and goes back to work. Two weeks later, you overhear Bill making disparaging remarks about several design engineers who "think they know more about control systems" than his project team. Later that day you hear that Bill engaged in verbal bantering in the company cafeteria with a design engineer. The bantering escalated into name calling and ended when Bill called a designer "a jerk who should design with a crayon." Fearing that this attitude may endanger the necessary work relationship between the team and the designers, you decide to intervene.

What would you say to Bill?

A. Tell him how he could have handled the situation in terms of the necessity of good relationships between the designers and his team, the responsibility to deal with such conflicts in a more diplomatic way, and the particular attributes of the design group involved. (GO TO 599)

B. Tell Bill that he should let his team leader deal with the designers for a while until things cool off. (GO TO 494)

C. Verify the story of the cafeteria incident with his team leader before calling Bill in. (As it is now 4:30 p.m., this will require a one day delay.) (GO TO 591)

Decision Point 616

At this point you need either to differentiate your philosophy from Ms. B's or to get her support for computerization. Re-evaluate your last decision. Circle the #616 you just wrote in your flow diagram. Then move to the first uncircled step above this one in your flow diagram.

Decision Point 617

You have decided to give your group the assignment that Eugene gave you. This is unwise. He gave you a very cryptic assignment in an informal encounter, and the assignment has far-reaching consequences for the entire company. Certainly you want to clarify what he is asking you to do and what problem or opportunity he is responding to before involving your group in this matter.

Re-evaluate your last decision. Circle the #617 you just wrote in your flow diagram. Then move to the first uncircled step above this one in your flow diagram.

It is now two days later. Frank has not returned to work yet. You tried to call him at home yesterday and got no answer. What would you do now?

A. Talk with some of Frank's co-workers to see if they have any idea what might be causing Frank's absences. (GO TO 499)

B. Check with Frank's previous supervisor to see what his past attendance record was like. (GO TO 594)

C. Discuss the matter with your manager in order to get her advice and input in handling the matter. (GO TO 469)

D. Call the Human Resources Department to see what disciplinary options are open to you. (GO TO 457)

E. Call the Human Resources Department to find out if there are any departments that need people with Frank's qualifications so you can transfer him. (GO TO 514)

F. Continue to wait for Frank to return so you can have a talk with him. (GO TO 493)

The situation with Bill continues to worsen. He botches a critical test given to him with inadequate instructions, and the other members of his team "jump all over him." Too embarrassed to tell you, Bill sulks for two days before signing his resignation letter. You now have to face the direct and indirect costs of finding a replacement for Bill.

Apparently, Bill needed more support and advice than K. C. had the time or willingness to provide. Since K. C. was not an effective mentor, re-evaluate your last decision. Circle the #619 you just wrote, and move to the last uncircled step in your flow diagram.

Decision Point 620

You plan to promise that no one will lose his or her job because of computerization. This is an unnecessarily broad commitment. You do not want to give unconditional guarantees like this one, or you will be in the position of severely losing credibility if you have to terminate a person for cause.

Re-evaluate your last decision. Circle the #620 you just wrote in your flow diagram. Then move to the first uncircled step above this one in your flow diagram.

Decision Point 621

You encourage the group members and remind them of the importance of the project. They agree to increase their effort. Four days later, you check with Robin. He tells you that no one seems to be getting anywhere in developing recommendations.

At this point what would you do?

  A. Have Randy Winslow (the head of the engineering technicians) join the group to stimulate things. (GO TO 585)

  B. Arrange to meet with your group at its next meeting. (GO TO 462)

Decision Point 622

Frank thanks you for the advice and agrees to call the family counselor. He is absent the following Monday, but on the next Tuesday, you learn that he has resigned his position with the company. Two weeks later, you get a call from Human Resources. Frank has filed a lawsuit on the grounds that the counselor to whom you referred him caused the breakup of his marriage. The judge agrees with the plaintiff and orders your company to pay $15,000 in punitive damages. The ruling hinged on the fact that you acted as an agent of the company in referring Frank to a counselor and thus such a referral constituted a condition of employment.

Even though you made the referral on the best of intentions, supervisors are best advised not to make specific referrals except to company counselors. Since you were not aware of this potential liability, re-evaluate your last decision. Circle the #622 you just wrote in your flow diagram. Then move to the first uncircled number above this one in your flow diagram.

Dart is an assignment that makes sense for a new employee like Bill. It is sufficiently technically challenging to offer a means to develop a sense of competence, an important concern among most new employees.

It is one month later, and from what you've heard, Bill is doing okay. The test team leader, Bob Blair, has said little except that Bill is performing much as he did when he was new with the company. Bill has completed several test analyses, but his rate of output is markedly slow. According to Blair, Bill does not manage his time well. He seems slow to get a sense of priorities. He spends a large amount of time on unimportant procedures, and then is entirely too superficial on a report intended for a client. The last time you talked to Blair, he apologized for not spending more time with Bill.

Yesterday you took the time to visit Bill in his cubicle. The following discussion took place:

You: (after pleasantries) How do you like working on the *Dart*?

Bill: Fine, just fine, I'm learning a lot.

You: Good! Have you found your thesis work helpful?

Bill: Well, yes. Sort of. Professor Babcock was sure off though. I guess he never had to meet a payroll.

You: That's pretty typical. But Bob Blair tells me that you are making a meaningful contribution.

Bill: He did? Wow! Well, I've tried.

You: Do you like working with Don (a *Dart* team member)?

Bill: Well, yes, I guess so. I don't see him much.

You: You don't? I thought you two would have been working hand-in-hand.

Bill: Well, he has helped me a couple of times, but I don't see him much. I did have a problem I thought he could help me with, but I guess I was hesitant to ask.

What would you do now?

A.   Take time to remind others in your group that helping Bill adapt to his job is important. (GO TO 611)

B.   Coach Bill on how to be the member of a test engineering team. (GO TO 482)

C.   Agree to meet daily with Bill to coach him on how to handle the specific, day-to-day problems that come up in his work. (GO TO 511)

D.   Remind Bill of his agreement to take initiative if he had questions or was having problems. Tell him he will not succeed unless he begins to ask questions, tell Bob Blair his problems, and begin to take control of his own situation. (GO TO 595)

E.   Begin yourself to give Bill a detailed account of how to contend with the challenges and problems of his work. Agree to meet with him in three days to review his progress and advise him on new situations. (GO TO 534)

F.   Tell Bob Blair he is responsible for Bill's performance. Tell Bob that you do not want him to sacrifice the objectives of the *Dart* test system, but that you think Bill deserves more of his time. (GO TO 575)

Decision Point 624

You plan to deal with feelings of insecurity about the change by acknowledging that LCLD is over-staffed, but you will deal with that through natural attrition. This honest, straightforward approach is perfect for a situation in which people are resisting change because of employment insecurity.

You now must decide what you will say in your speech about the specifics of the implementation plan. What would you do?

A.   Outline a specific timetable for the change specifying training objectives and implementation targets. Arrange time targets for early stages that are rather pessimistic to "guarantee" early perceived successes. (GO TO 503)

B.   Outline a specific timetable for the change specifying training objectives and implementation targets. Arrange time targets for all stages based on "most likely" outcomes. (GO TO 535)

C.   Stay clear of specifying a timetable so you can keep your options open. (GO TO 580)

You turn over the implementation of the change to your team. They work well together and come up with a solution that you had not even considered. The team devotes a great deal of time to working out the details of its plan, and you sense that the group is truly excited about it. When the group presents their plan to you, you suspect that there may be some difficulty in getting Eugene Marshall and Gordon Garvin to accept the recommendations. Your suspicions are correct. Eugene, on Gordon's advice, rejects the plan out-of-hand. Your group is very angry and is not likely now to be very helpful in further efforts at integrating the techs.

A delegation approach to change requires you to maintain involvement with the group. You need to be much more active in what the group comes up with. After all, you have a much better understanding of the organization than members of the group do. Re-evaluate your last decision. Circle the #625 you just wrote in your flow diagram. Then move to the first uncircled step above this one in your flow diagram.

Solaris is an assignment that makes sense for a new employee like Bill. It is sufficiently technically challenging to offer a means to develop a sense of competence, the initial concern among most new employees.

It is one month later, and from what you've heard, Bill is not working out as well as you expected. In fact, the whole *Solaris* team effort has failed to live up to your expectations. Originally enthusiastic about Bill, K. C. Wong has expressed grave reservations about whether Bill was really ready for this assignment. He even went as far as to suggest that you replace Bill with a more experienced person so the team can get back on track.

You review the technical reports. They confirm your suspicion that the *Solaris* system is so complex that the team should use tried-and-proven solutions rather than the novel approach that Wong was so excited about.

You call Bill into your office, and after an exchange of pleasantries, the following conversation takes place:

You: Bill, what's your assessment of the problems of the *Solaris* project?

Bill: I don't know. Everything we try just seems to blow up on us. The booster is really hairy and we can't seem to figure out a way to monitor thrust parameters.

551

You: And how do you feel about your contribution?

Bill: I've talked to K. C. about this, and I think I'm way over my head. I just wish I'd taken more course work in aeronautics, because some properties of this system put me in deep yoga.

You: What do you mean?

Bill: The other two guys really know their stuff, and they've been real nice in giving me tests to run that are easy, but I just don't think I'm making much more of a contribution than a technical assistant. And, you know, I don't even think I'm a good technical assistant. I'm botching even the simplest runs. It's not fair to them...

What would you do now?

A. Tell Bill that it's probably best to stick it out. Bolster his sagging confidence and suggest that he talk to someone in the *Solaris* design team about a good reference book in aeronautics. (GO TO 472)

B. Give Bill one of the other assignments you had originally considered for him, and replace him with another member. Bolster his sagging confidence by assuming responsibility for the misplacement. (GO TO 488)

C. Agree to meet daily with Bill to coach him on how to handle the specific, day-to-day problems that come up in his work. (GO TO 464)

D. Move another person from your department onto the *Solaris* project team to relieve some pressure on Bill. Talk to K. C. Wong about the importance of pacing Bill so he can regain his confidence, but not at the expense of meeting *Solaris* milestones. (GO TO 583)

E. Tell K. C. Wong that he is responsible for Bill's performance on the team. Tell K. C. that you do not want him to sacrifice the objectives of the *Solaris* system, but that you think Bill deserves more of his time. (GO TO 619)

Decision Point 627

Announcing a new philosophy at this point shows a lack of leadership. You are essentially contradicting yourself. Your credibility may not recover. Re-evaluate your last decision. Circle the #627 you just wrote in your flow diagram. Then move to the first uncircled step above this one in your flow diagram.

It is one month later, and Bill's work is good. For the last two years, you've wanted someone to organize the administrative part of your job, and Bill has done just that. You feel more prepared for upcoming budget negotiations than ever before. You have not always given him the most interesting tasks, but you are sure Bill has learned a great deal about how the engineering program works. He's also now familiar with the accounting system.

While Bill was willing at first, he has begun to balk at some of the tasks that you've assigned him recently. You attribute this to a friend he has made who introduced him to the concept of the half-life of his technical education. Bill's frustration with the assignment came up in a recent meeting.

You: When you're through with the budget, please update the PERT.

Bill: Another one?

You: Yup, Betty has got a lot of typing to do, and she doesn't have the time.

Bill: (eyes down) I hope there will be some engineering when I finish.

You: I know you do, Bill.

Bill: If I don't get started pretty soon, I'm afraid I'll lose my edge. Do you know that the half-life of my educational background is 18 months? As I figure it, my technical know-how has already decreased 9 percent! That scares me. I talked to K. C. Wong about helping him on the *Solaris* project, and we sure think I'd be able to lend a hand.

What would you do after Bill completes the PERT diagram update?

A. Give him *Assignment 1*. Junior Control Engineer, *Dart* Project. Join a team of four members to test a ballistics control system for a *Dart* missile. Bob Blair is the project manager. The *Dart* missile is like other systems developed previously, except that the new control system requires several standards never required before. Smythe's senior thesis in school was on ballistics control systems. Likelihood of Bill making a contribution to the team - Good. Value to Bill's development if he is personally successful - Fair. (GO TO 623)

B. Give him *Assignment 2*. Junior Control Engineer, *Solaris* Project. Join a team of three members to test the propulsion control system for a *Solaris* booster.

K. C. Wong heads the team. Wong is very enthusiastic about Bill joining the team. K. C. graduated from the same engineering school as Bill. The *Solaris* project will require a unique control system that has never been implemented before. The project is presently behind schedule because of the novelty of its design. It would offer a fantastic learning opportunity for any junior engineer. Likelihood of Bill making a contribution to the team - Fair. Value to Bill's development if he is personally successful - Very Good. (GO TO 626)

C. Give him *Assignment 4*. Junior Control Engineer, Systems Test Group and Member, *Micascope* Divisional Task Force. Join a task force of seven members conducting a manufacturing feasibility study of *Micascope*, a laser refracting targeting system. The task force is chaired by the assistant-to the divisional manager. This assignment would give Bill a chance to work with the most dynamic members of the division. The feasibility study proposed is controversial with some task force members committed to manufacturing and some dead set against it. The division manager is said to favor manufacturing, but he has agreed to "let the chips fall where they may." While he hand-picked the members of the task force from other departments, his confidence in you permitted him to ask you to appoint the department member of your choice. Since all of the other members of your group are busy with project work, Bill seems like a natural. Likelihood of Bill making a contribution to the team - Fair. Value to Bill's development if he is personally successful - Very Good. (GO TO 557)

D. Continue him as your administrative assistant, but find him administrative tasks with an engineering component. (GO TO 528)

INDEX

and motivation, 183-84

and training, 25

and vertical job loading, 23

Dependencies, 163

Diligence, in ethics, 208

Directive leadership, 124, 126-27

Discipline systems, 52, 53

Disclosure, in ethics, 208

Disinterestedness, in ethics, 208

Displacement, 12

Documentation, 61-63

  of final agreements, 148

  and problem employee, 53

Downward communication, 63-66

Due process, 203

Duties, positive, 202

Effort:

  and motivation, 7-8, 11-12

  and performance, 7, 11, 12-13

80/20 rule, 45

Emotion, in conflicts, 141, 145

Employees:

and conflicts, 135-48

and job design, 26-27

new, see New employee

problem, see Problem employee

rights of, 202-3

work habits of, 53-54

see also Subordinates

Employment contracts, 199-200

Equal treatment, 203

Escalation, 161

Esprit de corps, 79

Ethics, 199-214

  as emerging field, 199-200

  flow diagram, 211-12

  and hidden agenda, 205-6

  interactive case, 209, 213-14

  and justice, 200-204

  and manipulation, 204-8

  module reading, 199-210

  rights and duties in, 200, 201, 202-3, 206, 208

  standards for action, 200-204

563

NOTES

NOTES

NOTES

NOTES

NOTES

NOTES

NOTES

NOTES

NOTES

NOTES

NOTES

NOTES